Social Issues

Social Issues: Conflicting Opinions

Edited by
Nils I. Bateman
Lynchburg College

David M. Petersen
Georgia State University

Prentice Hall, Englewood Cliffs, New Jersey 07632

Library of Congress Cataloging-in-Publication Data

Social Issues : conflicting opinions / edited by Nils I. Bateman,
David M. Petersen.

p. cm.
ISBN 0-13-815994-7
1. United States—Social conditions—1980– 2. Social problems.
I. Bateman, Nils I. II. Petersen, David M.
HN65.S5715 1990 89-31389
306'.0973—dc19 CIP

Editorial/production supervision and
interior design: Mary Araneo
Cover design: Diane Saxe
Manufacturing buyer: Carol Bystrom

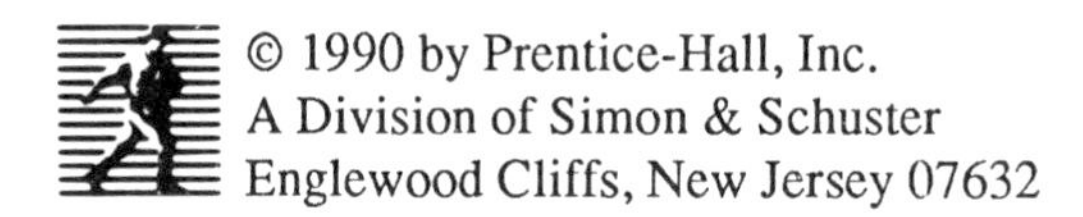

Printed in the United States of America

10 9 8 7 6 5 4 3 2 1

ISBN 0-13-815994-7

PRENTICE-HALL INTERNATIONAL (UK) LIMITED, *LONDON*
PRENTICE-HALL OF AUSTRALIA PTY. LIMITED, *SYDNEY*
PRENTICE-HALL CANADA INC., *TORONTO*
PRENTICE-HALL HISPANOAMERICANA, S.A., *MEXICO*
PRENTICE-HALL OF INDIA PRIVATE LIMITED, *NEW DELHI*
PRENTICE-HALL OF JAPAN, INC., *TOKYO*
SIMON & SCHUSTER ASIA PTE. LTD., *SINGAPORE*
EDITORA PRENTICE-HALL DO BRASIL, LTDA., *RIO DE JANEIRO*

Contents

Preface

This book is primarily a collection of previously published material dealing with social issues. The first set of issues concerns the basic nature of social behavior. Is social behavior genetically programmed, learned, or a combination of genetics and socialization? What are the effects of the mass media on learning and behavior? Would our youth and society be better off if we legalized drugs such as marijuana? Are gay teachers appropriate role models for students?

The second section takes up issues dealing with social inequality. Issues covered in this section concern the welfare system, affirmative action, aparthied, comparable worth (pay equity), and mandatory retirement.

The third section focuses on issues related to social institutions. How is the family affected by abortion and should abortion have greater legal restrictions? Is the "religious right" a threat to basic freedoms? Are professors biased politically toward the L word? Is the power of political action committees a corrupting influence of governmental processes?

The final section deals with social change. How should we deal with illegal immigration? What is the future of the women's movement? Is the environment headed for disaster or will technology solve our coming crises?

The criteria for selecting issues to be included in this book are based on our experiences teaching introductory sociology classes. During the last decade we have found that our students are increasingly less interested in social issues and problems presented in an abstract academic format. We have found greater responsiveness when students are forced to examine issues from a variety of perspectives. We have attempted to select issues that are of interest to the "typical" student and which can be related to the theory, methods, and content presented in most basic introductory sociology textbooks.

In selecting the articles to be included we looked for material that took a definite pro or con position on an issue. Each issue has at least one pro and one con selection. For example, on the drug issue we have one article arguing for legalization and another article arguing against legalization. A second criteria was that the material be on a level readily understood by a motivated student. As a result we have avoided the technically difficult literature in most of our professional journals.

The material selected includes writings by academics, industry researchers, journalists, politicians, and a variety of other people advocating particular positions on issues. The issues and articles have been arranged to approximate the general content of most introductory sociology textbooks.

Finally, we would like to thank the following reviewers for their input and suggestions: Donald Landon of Southwest Missouri State University, George F. Stine of Millersville University, and John F. Zipp of Washington University–St. Louis.

Social Issues

INTRODUCTION

Social Issues: Conflicting Opinions

In April 1960, one of the editors of this book, three other white students, and a number of black students were arrested in Tallahassee, Florida after a march and demonstration that originated at the all-black Florida A & M University campus. The march was in response to the arrest of black students from Florida A & M and white students from the all-white Florida State University who had been involved in a sit-in at the lunch counter of a local department store. The city police had broken up the march with tear gas and had arrested those who were "slow" to leave.

About a dozen students were crammed into a small holding cell. After fifteen or twenty minutes a member of the all-white police force appeared at the door of the cell. His only comment was, "I want a real good look at the four f...ing nigger lovers." In the next hour, another half-dozen policemen came to the door of the cell with interesting but unoriginal suggestions as to what they would do if they met the students on a dark street. The comments concerning the white female students were equally graphic and uninspired.

This was a period of time when the civil rights movement focused increased attention on the discriminatory racial practices of the country in general and the South in particular. Most of the South in 1960 was segregated by race. There were black schools and white schools. Restaurants, theaters, transportation, and most other public facilities were segregated. Public restrooms and even water fountains were segregated—blacks often did without or spent time and effort locating facilities for blacks only. Work places were generally segregated, including local, state, and federal agencies. Black people were rarely given the opportunity to apply for jobs that would allow them to interact as equals with whites. On southern military bases, almost all the black civilian workers were restricted to such low-level service jobs as janitors and maids.

Many conflicts arose out of the civil rights movement. Some staunch segregationists argued that the races should not interact on any basis that required equality. Private schools were opened to avoid integration in the educational system. The military and national guard were called in at various times to enforce court orders requiring integration or to quell the mobs that were aroused by the court orders. Other people were concerned about private property rights. They argued that any business, open to the public or private, had the absolute right to refuse service on any basis, including race, creed, religion, or gender. Aligned against the segregationists was a coalition of organizations and individuals, primarily black, but including some whites. This group argued for equality of opportunity and equal access to all public facilities.

Many of the issues of the civil rights movement have receded from public consciousness as society has changed. Few people now argue that public facilities should be segregated, although we do have *de facto* segregation in many areas. Blacks moving into white neighborhoods sometimes get harassed and driven out. The 1987 episode in Forsyth County, Georgia, reminds us that the basic question of equal rights has not been completely resolved. Forsyth County is basically an all-white county in northern Georgia. When a peaceful demonstration was planned to protest this form of segregation, the scene turned into a replica of the 1960s. The KKK turned up and a mob collected, shouting obscene threats at the demonstrators.

The above issues were in large part a reflection of the dynamics of the civil rights movement. Over time society has modified some conditions, and many forms of discrimination have become illegal. Other issues have arisen, such as busing to create integrated schools; affirmative action; and the right of private organizations, partially subsidized by tax breaks, to discriminate. Issues, particularly controversial ones involving the races, are frequently a product of social change and social movements.

Social change and related social movements that develop to promote change, to block change, or to move things back to a prior condition always seem to be present in complex societies. What becomes a social issue is in large part a reflection of the social context. Social conditions become issues or problems when there is a public perception of the condition as a problem. Issues may disappear because they have been fully or partially resolved or because the public no longer perceives them as issues. One of the purposes of social movements is to focus attention on conditions or issues believed to be in need of change.

Just as the civil rights movement has attempted to focus attention on minority issues, the women's movement has attempted to bring women's issues into public awareness. Issues concerned with discrimination against women have come and gone because they have either been resolved or perceived by the public as having been resolved. Many women's issues of course remain unresolved. Historically, the women's movement has been involved with a variety of issues including slavery, the right to vote, and labor laws dealing with work conditions.

Other issues arise from a combination of factors. The issue concerning violence on television and aggressive behavior is, for example, a reflection of research and academic interest but also clearly involves economic, ideological, and other factors as well. Sometimes significant people or groups can redefine a condition as an issue or problem. During the Reagan administration programs such as "Just Say No" contributed to an increased concern over illegal drugs, particularly marijuana and cocaine. Obviously, the tragic deaths of University of Maryland basketball player Len Bias and other athletes have also provided a strong impetus. From a sociological perspective, additional questions need to be asked. Has there been a change in drug use or has the impetus for the issue developed out of the political arena and from media hype? Are cocaine and marijuana more dangerous than alcohol and prescription drugs? Has the increased awareness and concern over the use of illegal drugs as a problem been produced by a change in the objective condition or is it a result of changes in the political and public climate?

In this book we hope to place contemporary social issues in a perspective that is conducive to this type of questioning in order to enlarge our understanding of the forces at work in society. The issues range across the sociological continuum from basic questions about human nature, to concerns about how religion is affecting society, to the future of the planet, if there is to be a future. The contributors include scholars, journalists, politicians, and people who have a vested interest in one or another of the issues. The material included is primarily from the nontechnical literature. It is a compilation of opinions based on values and ideology and of information based on a variety of data sources. The reader should be aware that even where there is an abundance of scientific studies, authorities, experts, and laypersons may still disagree on the interpretation of the evidence. There is frequently great difficulty in giving a precise answer to questions even when they appear to be empirical. We hope we have constructed a book that will motivate students to think critically about issues of the day and one that will encourage students to apply the sociological perspective.

This book presents material on sixteen social issues. Each issue has been formulated as a question. We have tried to select material that provides distinctive positions on each side of the issue. The issues are divided into four sections dealing with major areas in sociology. *Part I* deals with issues of human nature and socialization. *Socialization* is the process of acquiring the skills and knowledge that a society requires of a "normal" adult. How does society turn an infant into a functioning adult? This complex task is termed socialization.

Issue 1 deals with the age-old nature versus nurture debate. Is our social behavior determined by society through the socialization process or is it determined by biology. Daniel Freedman provides a sociobiological argument that male–female relations in general and male dominance in particular are genetic. The response is from Naomi Weisstein who uses studies of primates and data from cultural anthropology to counter the claim that dominance and subjugation are genetic.

Issue 2 takes up the subject of violence on television and aggressive behavior. Most of us believe that television affects children. Many are concerned with racial and sexual stereotyping. Others worry about shortened attention spans and children who don't read. The articles presented focus primarily on the question of whether or not violence on television increases aggressive behavior in the young. The American Broadcasting Company (ABC) Social Research Unit provides a critical evaluation of a National Institute of Mental Health (NIMH) report linking television to aggressive behavior. The response is a fairly sharp attack by the senior scientific advisors for the NIMH report.

Issue 3 deals with the legalization of marijuana. Is marijuana use associated with a variety of physical and behavioral problems among the young? Does it take away the motivation of our adolescents? Would legalization produce benefits such as tax revenues, or would it send an inappropriate message of escapism? These and other questions are debated by two American conservatives. Issue 4 takes up the question of whether or not gay teachers are appropriate role models. Peter Fisher argues that a teacher's sexual orientation is irrelevant, while Anita Bryant argues that gays are dangerous role models.

Part II deals with issues revolving around social inequality. *Social inequality* concerns the unequal distribution of things that are valued by a society, such as money, power, and prestige. How should a society divide its resources? Are some groups handicapped by social barriers in the competition for education, income, and jobs? These and other questions are covered in the five issues contained in Part II.

The first issue in this part, Issue 5, deals with the welfare system. Sar A. Levitan argues for a stronger federal role in welfare and that welfare is necessary and rational. Walter E. Williams, in response to Levitan, argues against government interference with market forces in general and specifically against income redistribution and the welfare system. Issue 6 is concerned with affirmative action. The U.S. Commission on Civil Rights provides a rationale for and a description of affirmative action programs. Harvey Mansfield provides a broad attack on affirmative action from the perspective of American values and the intrusion of government.

Issue 7 takes up the problem of apartheid and economic sanctions against South Africa by presenting the views of two U.S. Senators from opposing parties. While neither side favors apartheid, Democrats and Republicans differ in the severity of the sanctions they propose. The Democrats generally favor stronger sanctions, while the Republicans tend to favor milder sanctions.

Issue 8 takes up the question of comparable worth. Should we require employers to pay workers in such traditional female occupations as secretary, nurse, and librarian the same wage as is paid to workers in traditional male occupations with a similar value? Is it possible to establish similar value? If similar value can be established, should market forces still be the primary factor in determining salaries? Are market forces currently the primary factor in determining salaries? These and other questions are taken up in the articles covering this issue. Issue 9 takes up the question of mandatory retirement. Is mandatory retirement another form of age discrimination? Does the elimination of mandatory retirement generate problems such as reduced opportunity for the young? These questions and others are addressed by Claude Pepper who argues against mandatory retirement and Robert Thompson of the U.S. Chamber of Commerce who presents the case for mandatory retirement.

Part III deals with issues related to social institutions. *Social institutions* are the sets of role statuses and norms that focus on the basic needs of a society. The primary social institutions are generally considered to be family, religion, economics, politics, and education. Issue 10 concerns the family and legalized abortion. Kenneth Kantzer and Paul Fromer argue that public sentiment is developing to end legalized abortion and that abortion is disrupting the basic moral structure of society. Amanda Spake argues that in spite of impressions created by the media, the grass-roots sentiment is still pro-choice. Issue 11 deals with the religious right and its involvement in secular areas. Jerry Falwell gives his agenda for the future and discusses his plans for promoting morality in public life and for combating the legislation of immorality. Daniel McGuire argues that the new religious right is a fanatical movement at odds with the basic assumptions of American society.

Issue 12 delves into charges by Accuracy in Academia (AIA) that liberal professors slant their courses to the "left." Malcolm Lawrence, the former president of AIA, describes his organization and provides examples of how professors slant their classes. Jon Wiener counters that AIA is a paper tiger and that its attack has had the effect of mobilizing the political center to defend the academic freedom of faculty members. Issue 13 deals with the influence of political action committees (PACs). The rapid growth of PACs during recent years has generated a number of attempts to control their growth and power. The material for this issue was taken from a Senate debate over a bill that would limit the amount of money that candidates could receive from PACs.

Part IV deals with the general area of social change. By *social change,* we mean major modifications in cultural patterns and structure over time. Issue 14 deals with congressional attempts to control illegal immigration. Much of this debate revolves around sanctions against employers and the provision of legal status for resident illegal aliens. Issue 15 concerns the state of the women's movement. Betty Friedan provides her assessment of the current position of the movement and what can be done to rejuvenate it. Phyllis Schlafly counters with observations about feminism and contends that the movement is no longer viable. The final debate, Issue 16, provides two different views of the future of the world. The *Global 2000 Report to the President* provides a pessimistic view. The report argues that drastic policy changes are needed to forestall serious population and environmental problems. Julian Simon argues that the ingenuity of humans will resolve problems of population, natural resources, pollution, and so forth and that we will continue to prosper as a species.

ISSUE 1

Is Social Behavior a Reflection of Biological Factors?

Do biology and genetics play a significant role in human social behavior? This issue is explored from the perspective of sociobiology and focuses on behavioral differences between the sexes. *Sociobiology* is the systematic study of the biological basis of social behavior. Sociobiology owes its current popularity in large part to E. O. Wilson's two books, *Sociobiology: The New Synthesis* (1975) and *On Human Nature* (1978). Human sociobiology attempts to explain social behavior on the basis of genetics and biology. Some social behaviors are thought to have a genetic basis, but not all behaviors result in a gene's being perpetuated in the species. Those behaviors that increase the chances of survival of the organism increase the probability that the organism will produce offspring and therefore spread the gene within the population.

The sociobiologists thus assume that certain social behaviors such as aggression, altruism, and male-female relations have a genetic basis. These behaviors will be perpetuated if they increase the reproductive success of the individual or of close relatives who also carry the genes for the behavior. The sociobiologists argue that what really matters in evolution is the survival of genes rather than the survival of individuals. They thus agree that apparent altruistic behaviors, such as that of the worker bee sacrificing itself in defense of the hive, cannot be explained on the basis of individual survival but on the basis of kin selection. What matters in evolution is the survival of genes that are shared with relatives.

If an animal sacrifices itself to protect its offspring or other relatives, the individual's genes are sacrificed, but the genes of the kinship group are perpetuated. Does this account for the willingness of family members to donate kidneys and other organs to kin? How many cousins or siblings would it take before we would sacrifice our lives? One sibling's survival would be a genetic loss; two would be the break-even point; and three would be a genetic profit.

Some of the behavioral differences between the sexes are also assumed by sociobiologists to have a genetic basis. Since human females face a nine-month pregnancy and a number of years of child rearing, their best strategy is to find a male with good genes who will also help raise the children. Human males, on the other hand, do not have the same responsibilities attached to sexual behavior and pregnancy. Sociobiologists therefore argue that men will attempt to impregnate any females they can. Additionally, females are presumed to have a biological advantage in that they can be sure an offspring is actually theirs. Males simply have to take the word of the female. In order to perpetuate his genes, a male's best strategy is to have sex with as many women as possible. A female, due to the limitations of pregnancy and child care, should attach herself to a male who will provide for her during this period of dependency. Thus, the double standard of sexual behavior between males and females.

Sociobiologists also argue that male dominance is in part genetic. Men became larger and faster because of their roles as hunters and warriors. Women became submissive and dependent due to childbirth and child rearing. We have therefore developed sex-linked genes associated with aggression, dominance, and subordination. The view that women are biologically predisposed to dependence and subordination has a long history stretching from the Bible, to Aristotle, to Freud, to Desmond Morris.

The social and behavioral sciences have not generally accepted this view. The diversity of patterns in behavior and temperament across cultures has given rise to the belief that nurture or environment is the primary factor in social behavior. Differing conditions cause social structures to develop which fit those conditions. Margaret Mead's classic work, *Sex and Temperament* (1935), in spite of recent criticisms, illustrates the flexibility of roles and personality. In New Guinea, she found one people, the Arapesh, who felt that a gentle temperament was appropriate for both sexes. A second tribe, the Mundugamoor, held that an aggressive and suspicious temperament was appropriate for both men and women. The third tribe, the Tchambuli, regarded an aggressive dominant temperament appropriate for women and an artistic, dependent, and sensitive temperament right for men.

Thus Mead assumed there was not an innate link between sex and temperament.

The two sides presented here involve a sociobiologist arguing that there are genetic predispositions for male aggression and dominance and correspondingly for female passivity and dependence. The second writer argues that primate studies do not support male dominance and that female subordination is relatively recent in human history.

ISSUE 1 YES:

Men, Women, and the Status Hierarchy

Daniel Freedman

Having established that human males and females either are born with or soon exhibit behavioral tendencies that characterize them thereafter, let us pursue a second line of sociobiological evidence. This we can call the comparative approach. How close to primate social patterns do humans come? Particularly, how do we compare with regard to the development of dominance-submission relationships?

As I have said, it is obvious that boys are more prone than girls to temper outbursts by the end of the first year, although there are indications of this tendency even in the earliest days of life. By three years, where peers are available, boys are ready to run in groups and to play more aggressive games than do the less mobile girls. This pattern can be observed even in settings that overtly try to suppress aggressive behavior. I recall visiting a Hong Kong churchschool in which toy guns were forbidden and in which all parents espoused a religiously motivated antiwar position. Nevertheless, the three-year-old boys (not the girls) daily fashioned guns out of handkerchiefs, excitedly shooting at each other over the entire play period. We videotaped one such play period, and only a single girl can be seen (peripherally) participating in this activity.

It was a similar story in our visits to playgroups at the Sri Aurobindo Ashram in Pondicherry, South India, an experiment in cooperative living, where the aim is to rear "children of the future"—that is, children steeped in cooperation and nonsexist attitudes. Despite the fact that these sentiments were deeply felt by both parents and teachers, we found that the behavior and drawings of the Ashram boys and girls were differentiated in about the same ways as those of boys and girls in any other setting....

Probably as a result of basic temperamental differences, boys and girls, like monkey and baboon youngsters, tend to play with others of the same sex—from the first moment that such a choice is possible. Look at any sandbox or playground: two-year-old boys will be near boys and toddler girls will be near girls....By two and one-half years, the boys' groups have become more mobile; by four years, they are all over the playground, even as four-year-old girls tend to play in the sandbox. The boys clump into rather larger groups as well, and by six years they already have the looks of what we eventually call a gang. Even at six, girls gather in groups of rarely more than four playmates and often congregate in the sandbox, side by side, talking and "baking" pies....

What about other cultures? In 1971 I had the opportunity to travel around the world with a group of college juniors under a junior year abroad type of arrangement. We stayed about six weeks in each country, observing and videotaping four- to seven-year olds at play in school playgrounds, looking for boy–girl similarities and differences. We observed Japanese children in both Tokyo and Kyoto, Chinese in Hong Kong, Balinese in a small village in Bali, Australian Aboriginals in and around Darwin, and Ceylonese in Kandy; in India we worked at the aforementioned ashram in Pondicherry, as well as in several New Delhi schools including a school for the blind: we finished our trip in Kenya observing Kikuyu and Masai youngsters. We also managed to get drawings from these children to the translated instructions of "draw anything you wish." When we returned to the United States, I made similar observations and obtained drawings at Navajo and Hopi school settings in New Mexico and Arizona....

There were of course differences in each place, making each unique and memorable. But, in every single setting, including the school for the blind, boys tended to be with boys, girls with girls; boys tended to cover more space in their play and to engage in more rough physical contact. Boys were louder, more frenzied, more disorganized, and less neat; girls tended to play in smaller groups and to engage in less spread out, quieter, more orderly games. Girls tended also to stay closer and to be more obedient to the teacher and to rely more on adults to settle disputes than did boys (even as Draper...has found among !Kung Bushmen children). Boys had shorter attention spans and, if not playing a competitive game, they were far less content to stay with one activity for long periods of time; by contrast, we clocked girls swinging upside down from parallel bars for 20 minutes and more. These observations were made by both male and female observers, and in every place video or film samples were made that corroborate these generalizations.

Although boys were often rough, we also saw affection exhibited everywhere by both sexes. In all cultures, children of either sex can be seen holding hands or keeping their arms around one another. But cultures seem to push boys to greater extremes in this regard, some encouraging, others discouraging their affectionate display: in Bali this was exceedingly common behavior; in Chicago, relatively rare.

TABLE 1 Sex Differences in Free Drawings Over Nine Cultures: Comparative Percentages in the Five Most Consistently Differentiating Categories[a]

	Sex	American (Chicago)	Ceylonese (Kandy)	Aboriginal (Arnheim)	African (Kikuyu)	Indian (Delihi)	Balinese (Batuan)	Chinese (Hong Kong)	American Indian (Navajo)	Japanese (Kyoto)
Vehicles	M	15.0%	68.4%	48.6%	86.4%	33.8%	41.6%	17.0%	54.0%	33.3%
	F	0.0[b]	7.1[b]	3.5[b]	61.9[b]	11.6[b]	1.0[b]	6.0[b]	29.0[b]	12.12
Monsters	M	15.0	0.0	5.4	0.0	5.6	10.5	10.6	2.0	57.1
	F	3.1	0.0	0.0	0.0	12.5	0.0	4.0	0.0	12.5
Flowers	M	10.0	63.2	5.4	3.7	73.2	80.2	19.1	2.0	23.8
	F	21.9	78.6	31.0[b]	3.2	79.1	95.1[b]	54.0[b]	9.7	75.0[b]
Male figures	M	40.0	21.1	5.4	3.7	18.3	1.2	25.5	32.0	19.0
	F	3.12[b]	14.3	6.9	1.6	12.8	1.0	4.0[b]	22.6	0.0
Female figures	M	5.0	10.5	8.1	4.9	4.3	1.2	4.2	0.0	4.8
	F	65.6[b]	14.3	44.8[b]	3.2	33.7[b]	0.0	22.0[b]	9.7	93.8[b]
Number of subjects	M	20	19	37	81	71	86	47	50	21
	F	32	14	29	63	86	70	50	31	16

[a]Twelve categories were scored. Except for the Japanese children, aged three to six, all the children were five to seven years old.

[b]$p < .05$.

Boys everywhere were more interested in how our cameras and recording equipment worked than were the girls. Also, boys tended to ham it up when being filmed, whereas girls everywhere tended, initially, to coyness and embarrassment when the camera was on them. Eibl-Eibesfeldt...found the same differences in his extensive filming around the world.

With regard to inhibition of aggression, all the children seem to have developed choose-up games (for example, odd or even fingers in the United States, paper-stone-scissors in Japan) for the purpose of defining who shall first occupy a resource such as a slide. In this, however, there was considerable variation. For example, in Nigeria, among the rigidly age-graded Hausa, Jerry Barkow...reports that the older of any two children always goes first.

As for the drawings, boys everywhere were obviously more attracted to and intrigued by vehicles of transportation: trucks, airplanes, and rockets (and also horses among the Navajo). Even among the Kikuyu, where girls were rougher than any other girls in their play and where they, too, drew many moving vehicles, boys were even rougher and drew even more vehicles.

Flowers also provided some interesting comparisons. Whereas girls everywhere were more prone to draw flowers, *all* Balinese and most Ceylonese children had flowers in their drawings: Balinese boys, however, would intersperse airplanes and other vehicles among their flowers; Balinese girls never did so (Table 1)....

WHO'S THE TOUGHEST?

Certainly, it was our experience that children were everywhere far more alike than different. In fact, the sexes differ far more than do the cultures. Although Balinese boys may appear softer and gentler than, say, Kikuyu boys of Kenya, the contrast between boys and girls as just recounted was far more consistent than were such cross-cultural contrasts.

Now, a finding of immense importance: if one asks two four-year-old boys, "Which of you is toughest?", in 80% of such twosomes both children will answer, "Me!" As Berry Brazelton, the noted Harvard pediatrician, found when I asked this question of his four-year-old son and a friend, not only is the response given with gusto but the two boys may also feel compelled to demonstrate the truth of their answer. In this case the boys began pelting Berry and me with handy objects, and I had made the point better than I had wished. Yet I have never seen a pair of girls, or even a boy-girl pair, react with anything but embarrassed giggles or lack of interest when asked the same question.

Girls are just not as concerned about demonstrating superior toughness, nor are boys particularly interested in demonstrating that they are tougher than girls. Culture-specific? We have tried the "Who is tougher" question with four-year-old boys and girls in Zurich, Ethiopia, Nigeria, and among the Navajo, always with similar results....True, American boys are given much leeway for demonstrations of aggression, whereas Nigerian Hausa village boys are careful of such spontaneity and tend to act as if older equals tougher, but the greater male interest in the question is unmistakable.

By six years of age, a tremendous change occurs in the answers to this question. Boys now agree about 80% of the time on who is tougher and, more than that, the group as a whole is in agreement right down the line. A hierarchy has been formed, known to all, whose order is acknowledged by everyone. Such clear-cut hierarchies of toughness exist in every interacting group of children over six we have observed and are present in rudimentary form among four- and five-year olds. More often than not, teachers are completely unaware of toughness hierarchies, and in our experience they usually do not believe they exist until their students so inform them. Usually, the hierarchy is linear: boys at the top, girls at the bottom, with overlap in the middle.

It is an absorbing fact that within these groups everyone pays much attention to those high in the hierarchy and little to those at the bottom. Everyone can readily name the boys at the top and tend to agree more on their rank than on the lower ranking boys or girls. That is, there is simply greater accuracy in ranking the upper half of the hierarchy. As I mentioned in discussing subhuman primates, Michael Chance...has called this phenomenon "attention structure," inasmuch as a dominance-submission hierarchy may be ascertained by noting who pays attention to whom. Certainly, if the leadership is constantly reasserting its dominance with random attacks, as among the macaques, a potential victim had best keep his attention upward. But in humans something similar happens without physical attacks. Most of our attention, most of our talk and gossip, is directed to and about dominants in our lives. Among graduate students, for example, the favorite topics of gossip are the professors. Among the professors, it is the chairman or other perceived bigwigs in academia. One puts down those above him, complains about them, makes jokes about them, and tries to learn all about their personal foibles. In this way one can partially equalize the difference in status, but the net result is a lot of time spent on the topic of the head men and women.

The popularity of gossip columns involves the same principle. About whom do we read? The mighty, the rich, the beautiful, the acclaimed, and the powerful. And which of us can resist at least a glance at these personal tidbits, particularly when they take the hero or heroine down a notch or two. Like grade-school children, all of us simply pay more attention to and know more about those at the top....

We have tried to establish hierarchies other than toughness with our school children—who is smartest, the best athlete, the most handsome—and in each case we found that although there may be overall agreement on hierarchical positions the arrangement is kept in dynamic flux by the tendency for each child (especially boys) to think he or she is better than anyone else! We have called this practice *overrating* and in boys it is clearly a carry-over from the four-year-old male's feeling that he is the greatest. Each six-year-old boy (and, as we shall see, each male of any age) tends to rate himself several slots higher than the group has done. It is as if a male achieves a preeminent concept of his invincibility early in life and, thereafter, external circumstances must serve to modify this initial sense of limitlessness.

Consider the boyish charm of former heavyweight boxing champion Muhammad Ali. It consisted of his continual and often rhymed avowal, even as he undoubtedly maintained as a four-year old, that he is Number One, or the best in the West, and the coincident proof that, in fact, he probably was ("Liston is great, but he'll fall in eight"). Thus, Ali represented fulfillment of the four-year-old male's sense of omnipotence, living proof that it can really happen. Cocky and arrogant, he dared anyone to depose him.

As far as I can see, the male sense of omnipotence is part of an evolutionary heritage among hierarchically arranged species. It is the crux of what motivates the hierarchy, the psychological basis for male vying with male. Without overestimation of self, there can be no hierarchy, no challenge to the establishment. It is the basis for sibling rivalry, for father-son competition, for the Oedipus complex, and for the substantial psychological literature supporting the existence of that complex.

Primatology has in fact supplied a biological basis for father-son rivalry to replace Freud's literary one: if the male child, as a member of a hierarchical species, initially must have a sense of invincibility, a part of him will always consider all other males as less than himself. And only a father who has himself achieved some equilibrium around this issue can deal reasonably with his sometimes insulting and defiant youngster. Thus, few fathers achieve the level of empathy with sons that mothers do...because they are natural competitors. First sons, since they are next in line, generally are the toughest for a father to handle; the second son finds the first son the biggest challenge; and so on. Unfortunately, I know of no good statistical data to confirm these observations. Although unique family constellations would complicate the research, a statistical study in this area is feasible, and it would have the merit of combining into one paradigm the issues of father-son rivalry and male-male sibling rivalry.

If males exhibit an overblown sense of self-worth and competitiveness, does this not lead to greater disorganization in all-male groups? Here we come back to the Savin-Williams study. As we saw earlier, although there were more challenges within the male groups, the boys nevertheless arranged themselves almost immediately into followers and leaders. By contrast, the all-female groups often had the problem of identifying their leaders. Friends in the feminist movement have complained to me about the inability of fellow activists to make quick decisions and about their reluctance toward taking leadership roles. In Savin-Williams's cabins, alpha girls were, after all, more a source of advice than leadership. It is easy to see the adaptive value in war or big-game hunting of the rapid organizing of male participants into followers and leader, and so it is tempting to make the logical jump that Savin-Williams...did: have men evolved to behave in this way? Indeed, Tiger...has written an entire book on this theme, stressing the ongoing importance for males of affiliation within all-male groups.

What of those male hierarchies that started at six years of age? Is there much change over the years, and do more intellectual endeavors replace athletics as the major criteria of ranking? One might suspect that in an academically oriented high school such as the University of Chicago Laboratory School (populated largely by the children of professors) an academically oriented pecking order would take over. Not so! Glenn Weisfeld has studied high-school boys first observed at age six:...the hierarchy developed among them at that time, based largely on athletic ability, still holds at age fourteen....Alphas and betas are still near the top, and the omegas are still down where they were when the hierarchy formed originally. What will happen when these lads themselves become professionals and academics, as the majority will doubtless become? Will the peer experiences of the past eight years evaporate or are expectations set for life? My guess takes us somewhere in between, but the answers lie with further studies.

We have no comparable longitudinal data with girls, but one can anticipate that such a study would not yield the clear-cut results obtained with boys. Try as we might, we have never found a trait or any traits around which girls hierarchize themselves with the same emotional intensity that boys exhibit over toughness, athletic ability, or even good looks. Certainly, either a boy or a girl feels better having won a contest than having lost it, but most girls are apparently not as preoccupied with competition. Even Maccoby and Jacklin...,in their heroic attempt to dampen out sex differences agreed that the overall evidence indicates that boys are more aggressive and more attracted to its display. That is, boys are more involved both directly and vicariously in social competition, whether it be fighting, play, or comedy....(Maccoby and Jacklin's compendium on sex differences has been roundly criticized by Block....She rightfully points to a consistent trend in that book to turn away from demonstrated sex differences, insisting we just don't know when it is more justified to say we probably do know.)

As I have discussed elsewhere...,even when a male courts a woman it is with one eye on the status hierarchy. If he perceives himself as low, his confidence as a lover is commensurately low, and failure seems inevitable.

As for modern women, transmuted as they may be in the "male" direction of assertive competition, only a relative few seem to be playing the status game with the gusto and involvement of males. This is not to say that working women do not derive a sense of worth from their work. For one thing, as families become smaller, today's woman needs more and more to achieve a sense of self-worth via extrafamilial channels. More female status groups are developing, and more women are entering traditionally all-male hierarchies; some already occupy alpha positions in such mixed groups (for example, Meir and Gandhi in politics), and many more will do so in the future. This is probably the first time the world has witnessed such similarity in male and female goals, so that it is perhaps surprising that things are going as well as they are. However, before we welcome a millennium of sexual equality, let us consider some further facts.

WOMEN WITH MEN, WOMEN WITH WOMEN

It is time to discuss those dodgeball games again and to try to explain why a team of girls, although athletically superior to a team of boys, nevertheless collapsed and allowed the boys to win....When playing other girls, of course, these exceptionally fine athletes were competitive, coordinated, and in total control. It is as if there were two sets of personalities—one reserved for female-female competition, the other for male-female noncompetition. No complementary schism characterized the boys, who merely enjoyed winning for a change, although they tried harder when they realized the girls were giving way.

Following these studies, it was pointed out to the experimenter that dodgeball may be defined by both sexes as a boys' game. What would happen in a spelling bee in which activity girls are notoriously better? Cronin thereupon conducted a spelling bee using the same twelve-year olds, but a comparable collapse was not seen among the boys. Although consistently outspelled, boys, on average, exhibited excessive self-confidence, far more than warranted by their relative talents.

In general, women often find this male hubris baffling..., and it is by now a well-known fact that women's groups *must* exclude men if the average woman participant is to speak openly. The very presence of men, however silent they remain, is inhibiting, especially to younger women. It can be described as a sort of reflexive "insignificant little me" response. If anything, this attitude encourages male competitiveness, and, on the contrary, males in the absence of females appear less competitive....

On the other hand, our data show that girls aged six to eight in *all-girl* classes take "toughness" more seriously; furthermore, they are more prone than coed girls to overrate their own toughness. In fact, they did so at higher rates than did boys in mixed classrooms. These young girls were more outspoken than their coed counterparts, engaged in more vigorous gymnastics, and in general were more spontaneous....These effects are apparently not limited to younger girls: there are data that women of comparable backgrounds will develop rather different personality traits depending on whether they enter an all-women's or a coed college.

My own introduction to this phenomenon was through a boyhood friend who had left Chicago to take a job with IBM in Poughkeepsie, New York. There he encountered a type of woman he had never before known, the Vassar woman, and I still recall the awe with which he spoke of these independent, immodest, potent women. Mervin Freedman, reporting on a large and thorough study of Vassar alumnae who had attended between 1929 and the late 1950s, noted:

> The alumnae who were attending graduate or professional schools displayed a rather impressive picture of accomplishment. For the most part these students found the academic demands made upon them to be no greater than those to which they had been accustomed as undergraduates; in some cases the work was even a bit easier. Moreover, these women had learned that academic competition with men presented no great difficulty....

Similarly, the Carnegie Commission on Higher Education...asserts that an unusually high proportion of successful women come from the smaller women's colleges....Yet the trend is toward coeducation. Is this not ironic? For according to the evidence, coeducation increases inequality, despite the greater opportunity for specialization in large coed schools. Consider the famous women's college Smith, which briefly became a coed institution. They found, however, during an experimental period, the lesson we, too, have learned—the presence of males changed performance and attitudes toward the self in a way not conducive to the female's sense of independence. Smith has since returned to the all-female format. Sarah Lawrence is another example. Now torn in two by forces for and against coeducation, it cannot return to the all-female format for financial reasons, and its future as a major institution of learning is now in doubt....

We cannot have it both ways. If we want women oriented primarily toward childrearing and male supremacy, coed schools are perhaps best. If we want outspoken, independent women, all-female schools seem to be in order.

What do all-boy schools do for boys? In an experiment outside Washington, D.C. a formerly coed school was split into same-sex classrooms....The boys' rooms became noisier and noisier, until one teacher described the situation as resembling a boiler factory. The boys, however, were more spontaneous and less inhibited about questioning the teacher; moreover, they reported enjoying school much more. The girls in this experiment, like girls in other all-girl classes, found themselves less shy and more talkative in class; they also said they enjoyed school more.

Have we made a mistake in mixing the sexes and allowing them to inhibit one another? To answer this question, we have to ask ourselves a whole series of questions. For example, do we, as a society of both men and women, want more dominant women? The answer is not simple, and I would like to close by noting some of its complexities.

For one thing, if behavior at lower phyletic levels is a predictor, then dominant women will probably mean lowered birthrates. Indeed, psychiatric clinics are reporting increases in cases of male impotence, which case workers (intuitively) relate to the rise in women's independence. Here we must invoke the behavioral "law" Konrad Lorenz somewhat playfully called Beatrice's Law after his daughter-in-law, who first thought of it while watching fish. She found that as long as the female child was awed or even frightened by the male, copulation proceeded normally. But if the male for some reason was awed or fearful of the female, copulation would almost certainly not occur. Similar observations have since been made among other species, including the rhesus monkeys of Cayo Santiago.*

The human male is no exception. It is apparently imperative for the male to feel superior to the female—or at least unafraid—for continuously successful

*Such cases of impotence can probably be explained at the physiological level by sympathetic-parasympathetic nervous system interaction of the sort generally found in fearful animals....

copulations, and it may well be for this reason that males everywhere tend to demean women, belittle their accomplishments, and, in the vernacular (clearly laden with symbolism) "put them down." I have not heard of a culture in which the males do not engage in this chauvinistic sport, although cultures certainly vary with regard to women's rights. And, as I have already implied, women more often than not go along with this strategy, agreeing to hold in abeyance the anger that would appear to be inevitable. This is, then, the setting for those recurrent and familiar battles between men and women, for the female's sense that "he never listens to me" and for the male's sense that women are not to be taken seriously.

David Gutmann...has observed similar changes in males and females over the life span in five different cultures: the Navajo, Druze (Israel), Lowland and Highland Maya (Mexico), and a Kansas City middle-class population. In all these cultures, he found that in the early years of marriage women tended to abrogate their own egoism and instead to enhance their husband's self-esteem. Only as the parenting years were ending, again in all five cultures, did females tend to be outspoken and more assertive. Males tended to develop complementary changes, becoming more passive and giving with age; consequently, marriages tended to reach a new stability. On the other hand, those males who continued to insist on enhancing their own egos, Gutmann asserts, were those prone to heart attacks and other diseases usually associated with stress and early demise. Whereas Gutmann speaks of a "parental imperative" and gives these events a psychoanalytic interpretation, the pattern lends itself even better to an evolutionary explanation.

A young male's motor is fueled by a sense of omnipotence and ample supplies of testosterone; as a young adult, his ego soars, and the world is his oyster. Everything appears possible. The female, in the cause of childbearing, yields and caters to this frequently insufferable egotist, for only in this way can she be sure he will stay. As I have suggested, there appears to be something reflexive in young women that causes them to defer to men. Although not necessarily aware of her behavior, the marriageable female tends to massage the male ego so that he will care for her and her children and proceed up the golden ladder of success, however success is defined by the culture. But once the young are raised, when the parents are about 45 years of age, *relative* testosterone levels rise remarkably in females as levels fall in males....The time for female leadership has then arrived, and Gutmann indeed found just this turnabout in each of his five cultures.

My interim conclusion? For true equality of the sexes, we need a world of fifty-year olds and older. Because of the consequences of gametic competition, younger men and women are at existential odds. No matter the culture, the sexes simply have different ideal solutions for getting their gametes into the next generation, and it is for this reason, despite love and the "parental imperative," that they tend to see life in different ways.

ISSUE 1 NO:

Tired of Arguing about Biological Inferiority

Naomi Weisstein

Biology has always been used as a curse against women. From Darwin to Desmond Morris, from Freud to Robin Fox, from animal behaviorists who consider themselves open-minded but "realistic," to the sober professors of ethology, the message has rarely changed: men are biologically suited to their life of power, pleasure, and privilege, and women must accept subordination, sacrifice, and submission. It's in the genes. Go fight city hall.

Since the late 1960s, there's been an explosion of evidence showing the remarkable variety and adaptability of animal behavior. But even though we have more, not less, scientific evidence of female autonomy and power than we did 15 years ago, there's been little change in what most people *think* biology tells us.

The view of females as biological seconds still infests much of behavioral biology. Even the new kid on the Darwinian block, *socio*biology, attempts to scientize the old misogyny by positing specific sex-linked genes for such behavior as dominance and submission. Thus biology becomes not only destiny but personality as well.

Though this is the mainstream of contemporary biological thought, it is not, fortunately, the only stream in town. Divergent views have recently begun to question the astoundingly naive assumption that only males act and have begun to observe what females of different species actually do with their lives. The results for female primates—our closest relatives—are startling.

In the past 15 years, primatologists,* many of them women like Thelma Rowell, Jane Lancaster, Alison Jolly, Dian Fossey, Jane Goodall, and Biruté Galdikas, have found that female status in the primate world is often high, ranging from assertive to clearly dominant.

"By concentrating on prosimians [for instance, lemurs and indri], one can argue that female dominance is the primitive and basic condition, for among all the social lemurs ever studied, this is so," says anthropologist Sarah Blaffer Hrdy in her delightful and brilliant tour through female primate behavior, *The Woman That Never Evolved* (Harvard University Press).** Alison Jolly's *Lemur Behavior: A Madagascar Field Study* (University of Chicago Press) describes dominance in a prosimian. Females grab food from males, push them out of the way (to "displace them," they often don't even push—males just get up and leave if a female approaches), and hit them up-side the head when they get cranky. Not that males don't play "typical" aggressive games. They wave their tails at each other in "stink fights," establishing a threat hierarchy presumably by who smells the worst. The females couldn't care less. A female will "bound up to the dominant male (established by the stink wars), snatch a tamarind pod from his hand, cuffing him over the ear in the process." Similar female dominance is observed in other more advanced species—from squirrel monkeys in South and Central America (New World monkeys, still fairly primitive) to the talapoin in Africa (an Old World monkey, not very primitive).

Perhaps more interesting than out-and-out female dominance is the peaceable kingdom of the monogamous primates who share child-rearing. Marmoset fathers carry their offspring except when suckling. A siamang father carries his offspring after the first year of their lives. Defense is also usually shared. One of the more fascinating aspects of monogamous primate life is the duetting, or combined territorial calls of the harmonious pair. In the early morning in the forests of Malaysia, a female gibbon will begin her hour's long great call with her mate supplying back-up vocals. As distinct from more hierarchical species, fights among mates are rarely observed (although pairs are intensely territorial and do attack invaders). Rather, monogamous primates seem to spend a great deal of time just digging each other, grooming, hugging, and huddling together. Interestingly, sex is relatively infrequent, a corrective to the widespread caveman theory—argued, for instance, by Donald Johanson and Maitland Edey in *Lucy* (Simon & Schuster)—that human females abandoned estrus cycles and developed continuous sexual receptivity in order to keep the male monogamous and faithful.

*The study of primates has fired much scholarly activity. Those scholars quoted here are from such disciplines as zoology, biology, and anthropology.

**I have relied on Hrdy's gathering of primary sources for many of the observations made here. Hrdy's interpretations, however, solidly within sociobiology, differ markedly from my own. Hrdy believes human males will almost inevitably dominate because they are larger and stronger and because she reads the female primate record as one of competition, rather than cooperation to resist male tyranny. She holds these views despite her own detailed account of how culture, not biology, has suppressed what she considers the "natural" assertiveness and aggressive sexuality of females, and despite her own evidence showing a good deal of primate female cooperation, if not heroism, and the great variation in primate female status even among species where the body size is at least as great as it is in humans (including the equal, monogamous DeBrazza's and simakobu monkeys).

Monogamy is not infrequent in primates, from some prosimians (for example, indri) all the way up to the lesser apes, gibbons, and siamangs. Many species are downright romantic. Titi monkey mates will sit for hours pressed close together, their tails entwined; male marmosets will patiently feed their mates (as will 14 species of New World monkeys).

Even among the "classics," the hierarchal species of Old World monkeys like baboons and macaques, the picture has changed. While every male member of a troop of Amboseli baboons outranks every female member, each has a specific social position that depends on the rank of the *mother*. Knowing the rank of the mother, claims Glenn Hausfater (as quoted in Hrdy), allows you to predict much of an Amboseli baboon's daily life: its diet, the amount of spare time spent foraging and resting, even the average number of parasite ova emitted in a stool (an indication of the quality of the food it gets)—as well as its ability to displace other animals, and the amount of time it will be groomed, deferred to, or harassed—all indications of "dominance." With Japanese macaques, the social organization revolves around grandmothers, mothers, daughters, and sisters. The highest-ranking or "alpha" male outranks the highest ranking female in terms of specific behaviors like displacing others, or taking their food, but his power requires acceptance from influential females.

The emerging picture, then, for females in the primate world, is almost diametrically opposed to what is commonly believed. Female primate behavior is tough, assertive, and socially central. But—here is where interpretation comes in—the variations described are *between* species, and it is possible that each species inherits its specific social behavior. If so, humans, by extension, could be argued to have inherited a rare and virulent form of male dominance. What is more interesting, therefore, is to go back over the data and examine the variations *within* species or between closely related ones. Here, variations in social behavior will most likely be environmental, not genetic.

Among a group of Japanese macaques (Arashiyama west) imported to Texas, the original "alpha" female was deposed by a middle-ranking female and her female relations, reported Harold Gouzoules in *Primates.* A new dominance hierarchy was established and the former alpha and her kin were lowered in rank. Similarly, peasant revolt was reported for a troop of savanna baboons, where the once dominant females were pushed to the bottom of the hierarchy. Parallel rebellions have been observed in a variety of other baboon and macaque species.

These are important data. The overthrow of lineages in hierarchical Old World monkeys upsets the sociobiological belief that dominance or other specific behavioral traits are fixed by the genes. What really seems to be inherited is a lot of political acumen plus the specific social structure of rank. When, through politics, this structure is overturned, behavior turns with it. These data indicate that what's in the genes is not a *specific* social behavior like dominance, but a *general* social understanding: an ability to figure out when to strut your stuff, when to rebel, and when to lie low. (Upsets in rank also suggest that among monkeys, submission is not gladly borne. That's a very different message from the idea that an animal is "naturally" submissive, as some sociobiologists want us to believe.)

The rise and fall of lineages within a generation means that dominance *per se* is not inherited. So do the facts of sexual selection, which turn out to be more complex than previously believed. For instance, a stock-in-trade of comic-book biology is the most tyrannical male winning out in the mating season, thereby reproducing his own shady character and eventually making it a species-wide trait. But observations show that among such species as chimps, females often neglect the most dominant male (as established in threat or fight hierarchies) in favor of the more sociable and less disruptive males. Since rape is virtually unknown among nonhuman primates (subadult orangutans appear to be the one exception), this means the most dominant male doesn't necessarily get the breeding advantage.

Dominance would thus appear to be neither a fixed trait (that is, one always expressed because it is "inherited") nor one assured through the process of sexual selection. But this conclusion applies to individual animals. How about whole sexes? Here, too, there is some reason to believe that dominance can depend just as much on the environment as on the genes. Perhaps the most impressive example of a turnabout in male behavior is in a species of monogamous langur on the Mentawei islands off the coast of Sumatra. All other known langurs are polygamous, highly aggressive, and male dominant (although here, too, as with other Old World monkeys, dominant males are transient and females form the coherent social nucleus of the troop). Life for most langurs is hell. Females fight each other; males kill each other. By contrast, however, the Mentawei island langurs appear to exhibit the harmonious relations of monogamous pair bonds.

What has happened? Since they are genetically so close to their warring cousins, something in the environment of these langurs has radically altered their behavior. The speculation is that human hunting pressure drove the Mentawei island langurs into the protection of monogamy. But what is more important than *why* they got there is *that* they got there. If nearly the same genes produce male tyrants in one environment and gentle companions in another, then genes alone don't determine these specific behaviors in primates. What behaviors will be expressed may depend, in much larger part than previously thought, on what primates are faced with, *not* what they're born with.

The evidence is piling up. Females are generally assertive and central to many primate social organizations. Relations between sexes can change radically with changes in the environment. All these observations should figure critically in the contemporary view of male and female "nature"; and yet, they usually don't. The data come in, but much contemporary evolutionary theory doesn't change. Why?

It is important to understand how profoundly, pervasively, and totally, bias can affect something as purportedly "scientific" as biology. You need much more than evidence to bring down as cherished a notion as male dominion. Whenever privilege is at stake, theories justifying privilege will linger on well after the evidence has overturned them.

It isn't necessarily a conscious conspiracy. Rather, the new data are not acknowledged, or they are treated as trivial, or appropriate implications from them are overlooked. The data don't act to influence the theories, and so the theories remain the same.

This is nowhere more comically evident than in the strangely Victorian accounts of the evolution of human female sexuality. The human female orgasm, according to Donald Symons's 1979 book, *The Evolution of Human Sexuality* (Oxford), is a "byproduct of selection for male orgasm." (And Symons's work was hailed by zoologist E.O. Wilson as "the most thorough and persuasive account of human sexual behavior thus far that incorporates a professional understanding of sociobiology.") Symons claims that women have orgasms as a service to men, not because orgasms would be independently pleasurable and useful to women. Furthermore, orgasms are not assumed to be a part of our evolutionary history and thus found in lower primates as well. As David Barash also writes in *Sociobiology and Behavior* (Elsevier), "The female orgasm seems to be unique to humans."

Since females don't ejaculate, orgasm *is* harder to document in them. But since the late 1960s (well before the Symons and Barash works were published), females in a number of species—rhesus monkeys, stumptail macaques (Suzanne Chevalier-Skolnikoff has provided a wealth of data here), Japanese macaques, orangutans, chimps, baboons—have been observed during sexual activity doing something that really could be nothing else. At a certain point they clutch their partners (frequently, other females), freeze, then pant, moan, open their mouths in a particular way, and make involuntary spasmodic body gestures. Maybe they're faking it? Actual physiological measurements in laboratory studies performed by Frances Burton show that rhesus monkeys go through at least three similar stages of the four that Masters and Johnson describe for women.

I would suggest that difficulty in establishing orgasm among lower female primates has nothing to do with the evidence and everything to do with the androcentric bias that can't imagine why females of any species would develop orgasmic capability independent of males. Sexuality still means male-defined sexuality. (After all, it wasn't until Masters and Johnson's pioneering studies of sexuality in the human female that we ourselves went beyond the male-defined notions. It is hardly surprising that behavioral biology hasn't got there yet.*)

*Sociobiologists recently presented as late-breaking news the dreary fable that women's faithfulness and men's philandering arise from their conflicting evolutionary histories. The July, 1982, issue of *Science Digest*, for instance, explains that a woman needed a good male provider to ensure the survival of her young, while a male tried to make as many young as possible so that at least one or two would survive. But in nonhuman primates we find no behavior like this. In monogamous species neither sex strays. In nonmonogamous multimale troops the females mate with as many males as possible. Male chimps stand in line and wait their turn as female chimps in estrus choose consort after consort. Female Barbary macaques are even more extreme in estrus, mating with as many as 11 different males in a day. Hrdy has proposed that saturation mating is optimum female strategy because then every male thinks he is a father and has reason to see his young survive. This strategy could work as well in human societies if they had not handled the problem of uncertain paternity by imposing Draconian restrictions on women's sexuality. The brutality of such measures alone would alert a less male-biased scholarship to the possibility that culture is protesting too much, suppressing what may be a strong female disposition towards many mates.

Perhaps the most telling example of bias concerns the famous juvenile female, Imo, a Japanese macaque living with her troop at Koshima Islet. Scientists provisioned the troop there with sweet potatoes. Imo discovered that washing sweet potatoes got the sand off. Her discovery quickly spread among the other juniors in the troop, who then taught their mothers, who in turn, taught their infants. Adult males never learned it. Next, scientists flung grains of wheat in the sand to see what the troop would do. Rather than laboriously picking the wheat out of the sand grain by grain, Imo discovered how to separate the wheat from the sand in one operation. Again this spread from Imo's peers to mothers and infants, and, again, adult males never learned it. The fact that these Japanese macaques had a rudimentary culture has been widely heralded. But what are we to make of the *way* culture spread in this troop?

If Imo had been male, we would never have heard the end of the "inventive" capacities of primate males, and since generalization spreads like prairie fire when the right sex is involved, no doubt their role in the evolution of tool use and—why not?—language as well. But the urge to grand theory withers when females are the primary actors, and when the task relates to food—at least food without killing. Imo has been described as "precocious" and left at that. (Precocious, indeed! How would you get the sand out of wheat?*)

The lesson of Imo's fate is important. Bias is as much a matter of what is put into theory as what is observed in the first place.

So what does primate biology imply—apart from bias—about our human possibilities? When we look at all the data, and try to interpret them without androcentric bias, what do we have?

"Primates live in pairs, harems, unisex bands, multimale troops, as solitaries, as flexible communities that group and split, and as small subunits which attach to and disengage from very large associations: Females can be dominant, subordinate, equal, or not interested. Virtually every known social system except polyandry (one female, several males) is represented," writes Blaffer Hrdy. That means we belong to an order remarkable for its flexibility, its capacity to adapt to changing environments, needs, and ideas. Except for one species of baboon around the horn of Africa, females are not subordinate in the primate world to anything like the degree intimated by mainstream behavioral biology. Indeed if we derive the meaning of the word "natural" from lower primates, we must conclude that human female subjugation is anything but natural. It is an abomination on nature.

This *does* leave us with a problem, however. If biology tells us that female subjugation is unnatural, how did we get into the patriarchal mess we're in?

Enter Man the Hunter. It has been argued that humans evolved in especially murderous, male-dominant ways because of the exigencies of our particular prehistory. "We are uniquely human even in the noblest [sic] sense because for untold millions of years, we alone killed for a living," writes Robert Ardrey in his 1976 apologia for male privilege, *The Hunting Hypothesis* (Atheneum). But, popular as

*Imo took the wheat to the water where the wheat floated and the sand sank.

this view is, it is as wrong as the biological view of male domination. Humans started out small, uncoordinated, with crude tools and a rudimentary language. "A more vulnerable state for a hominid, fresh from the boondocks, in competition with the full paid-up carnivores of the grasslands is hard to imagine" writes John Napier in criticizing Ardrey's statement. "There is absolutely no evidence," said Richard Leakey in a recent television interview, "that we became human through hunting." "Up until very recent times," he explained, "there's no record at all of human aggression. If you can't find [it] in the prehistoric record, why claim it's there?"

In fact, it's more likely that it was Woman the Gatherer who led the procession down the evolutionary pike. The stone tools found with fossil evidence from some 2 million years ago are small and crude. The most damage these could have done would have been to chop roots into small tough salads, and the evidence overwhelmingly points to gritty roots and tubers as our primary diet for the millions of years we ranged over the dry and inhospitable African savannas. Females would have been under most pressure to gather these roots and tubers because they had to provide not only for themselves but for their young. Anthropologist Nancy Tanner, in her book *On Becoming Human* (Cambridge University Press), argued that mothers and young, learning and gathering in a social environment of growing cognitive and communicative proficiency, were the central actors in our evolution. (Suggestive of Imo's talents, chimp females use food-gathering tools with greater frequency than males—as is also described by William McGrew in *The Great Apes.*) According to Tanner (and to Adrienne Zihlman in a recent article in *Signs*), socializing, communicating females took us into the present.

It is now thought likely that the subjugation of women did not start until some 12,000 years ago when hunting and gathering were replaced with domesticated plants and animals. Current hunter-gatherer societies (for example, the !Kung and the Mbuti) give us some idea of how we may have lived in much of our human history; and in these societies, women are most fully equal to men and often supply the major portion of food. But as anthropologist Eleanor Leacock has shown in *Myths of Male Dominance* (Monthly Review Press), even where women aren't the main foodgetters (for instance, in the hunting-fishing-and-trapping Montagnais-Naskapi of the Labrador Peninsula), equality between the sexes still prevails. Indeed, Leacock has argued that equality persisted well into early horticulture, and anthropologist Connie Sutton dates the subjugation of women to the development of the state.

Wherever women's troubles started, hunter-gatherers are of utmost importance to our understanding of our genetic legacy. They tell us that male dominance is not in our genes: It is not something we inherited in becoming human, along with the big brain and the small canines. It emerged afterward. It is a specific *cultural legacy.*

But culture carries with it a capacity to change it, and this is the really awesome part of our evolutionary story. Male dominance is one kind of cultural legacy. The vision of a just and equal society is another. What biology has bequeathed to us in those millions of years of gathering on the plains is the capacity to choose between specific cultures, to evaluate our lives, to intervene in our own fate. Biology has provided us with the ability to explore our possibilities, to change what is in the present and try something we would like better for the future. Our biological legacy is the ability to choose how we would like to live.

Rather than a curse against women, biology is a promise to us. Biology shows us that the subjugation of women is anything but natural and fixed. It seems to be a late human invention not likely to have been in the transitional ape-human populations, nor evident in what may well have been the social organization of human society for much of the time that we have been human.

Even without our capacities to create and change specific cultures, biology tells us that we belong to an order stunningly flexible in its social arrangements and capable of great change within species. With this cultural capacity, possibilities expand. Biology tells us that there is nothing genetic stopping us from having full sexual and social expression.

Biology tells us, finally, to get to work.

ISSUE 2

Does Violence on Television Produce Aggressive Behavior?

The influence of television on behavior has been widely debated. Certainly our children spend a great deal of time watching television—some as much as seven or eight hours a day. What is the effect on children (or adults) who watch television two hours a day, or four, or six, or eight?

Television programming has been called a "vast wasteland." Concerns over the content of television programs include the extent to which it perpetuates sexual stereotypes. On TV, women who do work are usually employed in traditional female occupations. For those portrayed as homemakers, the high point of their day is the discovery that their detergent works. Another concern is the sexual content of programs. What message is being conveyed when sex is so often portrayed as recreational, exploitative, and casual?

This issue addresses the question of violence on television and whether or not it is related to aggressive behaviors. There are disagreements about what constitutes violence. In the articles that follow, you will find that some measures of violence on TV include cartoons, natural calamities, and the news. Other measures would restrict violence (aggression) to human behavior that has the intent of doing harm. Whatever the measure, any regular viewer of network television will probably see a variety of murders, assaults, and rapes.

Many, if not most, social and behavioral scientists believe that aggressive responses can be learned through observational learning or social modeling—that is, children learn aggression in much the same way they learn other behaviors: by watching parents, peers, and others. There have been a number of laboratory studies that have demonstrated that children will imitate at least for a short time aggressive behavior they have observed themselves or seen on film.* In the first type of study, there are two basic conditions: (1) the adult plays quietly with a set of toys in a room with the child observing; and (2) the adult plays aggressively by hitting, kicking, pounding, or yelling. The adult then leaves, and the child is frustrated in some way. Children who watch aggressive adult role models are consistently more aggressive in their play than those who watch unaggressive role models.

In the second type of laboratory study, subjects watch brief film clips of aggressive behavior, such as a boxing sequence. Generally those viewing the violent film clip will, when given the opportunity, shock a confederate more often than a control group that viewed a nonviolent film.

There are those who argue that anger can actually be reduced by expressing aggression. This idea comes from the Freudian concept of *catharsis.* The basic idea is that committing aggressive acts will drain off aggressive feelings and that participating in aggressive acts through observation (i.e., watching TV) can also reduce aggression. This involves the common-sense notion of "blowing off steam" or "getting it out of your system." There are studies suggesting that this method of reducing anger can be effective particularly when the aggressor can strike directly at the person who is provoking the aggressive feelings. In general, studies of television and aggression have not supported this position.

The articles presented here are based on a 1972 National Institute of Mental Health (NIMH) report on television and social behavior and an NIMH follow-up report *Television and Behavior: Ten Years of Scientific Progress and Implications for the Eighties* issued in 1982. The original 1972 report came to the cautious conclusion that there was some indication of a causal relationship between viewing violence on television and aggressive behavior for some children (those predisposed to be aggressive) in some environmental contexts. The 1972 report has been criticized concerning the make-up of the committee that produced the final summary. The television industry was given positions on the committee and had veto power over other members of the committee. Many people had difficulty believing that the television industry representatives were truly impartial. If violence

*For further information and available studies, see a general social psychology textbook such as, Kay Deaux and Lawrence Wrightsman, *Social Psychology in the 80s,* 4th ed., Brooks/Cole, 1984, Ch. 8.

attracts viewers, the industry has a vested interest in providing violence. The 1982 report is more critical of TV and its effects on children.

In the first article, two researchers from the American Broadcasting Company (ABC) examine the major conclusions of the 1982 NIMH report. They conclude that there is no proof of a causal relationship between television violence and aggressive behavior, that there is no consensus among researchers that television violence leads to aggression, and that the effects of television on attitudes is ambiguous. The second article by senior NIMH scientific advisors is a systematic refutation of the assertions in the ABC article.

ISSUE 2 NO:

Researching Television Violence

Alan Wurtzel and Guy Lometti

The subject of television violence and its impact on viewers is a complex question for which there are no simple answers. After more than thirty years of scientific investigation, the issue of television violence remains open to debate. Although the body of literature on television and violence continues to expand, results have been largely inconclusive, and there are still few definitive answers.

Recently, the National Institute of Mental Health (NIMH) released a report entitled *Television and Behavior: Ten Years of Scientific Progress and Implications for the Eighties*. Among many of its findings was the conclusion that a causal relationship exists between television violence and aggressive behavior. However, a careful examination of the research which was used to support the NIMH position indicates that the evidence does not warrant such a conclusion. ABC feels, therefore, a responsibility to place the NIMH report—and other research regarding television's effects—into perspective.

This research perspective on television and violence was written to provide broader insight and understanding of the primary issues involving research on television and violence. The information is presented in a straightforward manner so that we can reach beyond the scientific and academic community and communicate with the general public. Included is a summary of ABC broadcast standards and practices policies and procedures which are the guidelines employed by the network to ensure that when violence is depicted in entertainment programming it is handled responsibly.

SCIENCE VS. VALUES

The issue of television violence can be addressed on two different levels: as an objective *scientific* question and as a subjective *values* issue. In dealing with subjective values, divergent opinions and viewpoints are unavoidable because conclusions are based upon reasoning which is both rational and emotional. Despite the ability to develop strong positions on either side of an issue, there is no definitive way to prove that any one position is absolutely and unequivocally correct. By contrast, scientific study requires rigor, objectivity, and the adherence to a predetermined set of rules and procedures. Conclusions must be based solely on empirical evidence and must be judged by analyzing the assumptions which underlie the study and the methods which are employed in the research.

The NIMH conclusions are based entirely upon scientific evidence. Therefore, they must withstand the rigor of scientific analysis and review. Our careful examination of the research indicates that the conclusions which the NIMH reaches are unsubstantiated when subjected to scientific analysis.

In May of 1982, the National Institute of Mental Health released the first of a two-volume report entitled *Television and Behavior.* The first volume is essentially a summary report detailing the advisory panel's conclusions on a broad range of research topics relating to television and its effects. The publication of this research summary stimulated controversy and debate despite the fact that Volume 2, which contains all relevant technical information and background reports, was not released until the following October.

During the five-month interim between the publication of Volumes 1 and 2, the national press reported and reviewed the findings of the NIMH panel—focusing in particular upon the conclusions which addressed the issue of television and violence. Without the benefit of any supporting research material it was impossible to evaluate the NIMH position on this subject. With the release of the technical volume, however, it is now possible to assess their conclusions.

BACKGROUND OF THE NIMH REPORT

The 1982 NIMH report, *Television and Behavior,* is a follow-up to the 1972 *Surgeon General's Report on Television and Violence,* a study which was initiated after a series of congressional hearings on the impact of television violence on behavior. This government inquiry resulted in one of the most ambitious social science undertakings in recent history. Over $1 million was allocated to sponsor original research directly addressing the relationship between viewing television violence and subsequent behavioral violence. The result of this elaborate investigation, documented in the surgeon general's report, was inconclusive with no direct causal relationship established between television and violent behavior.

Ten years after the publication of the surgeon general's report a follow-up review was initiated. This update was conducted under the auspices of the NIMH by establishing a seven-member advisory board; of the seven participants, four had contributed to the surgeon general's original study. The NIMH Advisory Board commissioned researchers to review and evaluate all of the research to date concerning television and behavior. Included in the review was some of the same research which had been sponsored by the surgeon general in 1972. Despite the impression that the 1982 NIMH report contains new research, in fact, only one new violence study is actually reported.

The NIMH report, *Television and Behavior*, is essentially a review of existing research which has already appeared in the literature and which has been previously assessed and evaluated. Thus, the NIMH is *not* a new addition to social science literature; it is simply a reiteration of information which has already been made available. Nevertheless, the NIMH Advisory Panel arrived at four major conclusions concerning the relationship between television violence and aggressive behavior and social attitudes:

- NIMH conclusion no. 1: the research findings support the conclusion of a causal relationship between television violence and aggressive behavior.
  ABC response: the research does not support the conclusion of a causal relationship.
- NIMH conclusion no. 2: there is a clear consensus among most researchers that television violence leads to aggressive behavior.
  ABC response: there exists a significant debate within the research community over the relationship between television violence and aggressive behavior.
- NIMH conclusion no. 3: despite slight variations over the past decade, the amount of violence on television has remained at consistently high levels.
  ABC response: there has been a decrease in the overall amount of violence in recent years.
- NIMH conclusion no. 4: television has been shown to cultivate television-influenced attitudes among viewers. Heavy viewers are more likely to be more fearful and less trusting of other people than are light viewers as a result of their exposure to television.
  ABC response: the research does not support the conclusion that television significantly cultivates viewer attitudes and perceptions of social reality.

Following are detailed analyses and evaluations of each of the four NIMH conclusions.

In the technical report chapter on television and violence, the author cites and evaluates 14 studies which lead him to the conclusion that "overwhelming evidence" exists to establish a positive relationship between viewing television violence and subsequent violent behavior. Despite the NIMH panel's assertion that some 2500 studies were conducted on the subject of television and behavior, only 14 are used to substantiate the claim of direct cause and effect. Before we analyze these studies in detail, we must discuss three key aspects regarding all television violence research: (1) the definition and measurement of violence and aggression; (2) the use of correlation to imply causation; and (3) the use of "convergence theory" to reach a conclusion.

Central to the issue of the impact of television viewing on violent behavior is the very definition of the term violence. When we talk about the need for a definition, we must consider two separate issues: (1) the definition of violent actions or depictions within television programs, and (2) the definition and measurement of violence and/or aggressive behavior.

The problems involved with arriving at a definition of violence are many because violence is not always obvious and clearcut. The circumstances under which an action occurs, the acceptability of the action by a culture's norms and mores, and the use of an action as self-protection are all examples which can radically alter whether or not an action is considered violent.

Nevertheless, we can arrive at a useful practical definition from Krattenmaker and Powe: "Violence is the purposeful, antisocial infliction of pain for personal gain or gratification that is intended to harm the victim and is accomplished in spite of societal sanctions against it." Obvious as this definition might be, there are a number of researchers who would strongly disagree. Some, for example would insist upon calling any action in which pain is inflicted, even in self-defense, violent. Others would want to expand the definition to include unintentional violence such as accidents, slapstick comedy, or even acts of nature like a hurricane or tornado.

Scientists have been arguing over definition for years and we will not resolve the disagreement here. The point, however, is that the way in which violence is defined will play a large part in determining the amount of violence which is found in program content. So it is important to keep in mind the specific definition of violence employed in any particular study. It is also important to recognize that when different studies use different definitions of violence, we can not compare their findings.

Controversy over the definition of violent content is only one aspect of the debate. (It should be noted that there is no universally acknowledged definition of the terms "violent" and "aggressive" as they are applied to behavior. Since most researchers use the terms interchangeably, we will consider them synonymous.) Of equal importance—and equally controversial—is the way in which scientists attempt to *measure* violent or aggressive behavior. In order to address the question of television's impact on behavior, we must first be able to define, identify, and measure violent behavior. Otherwise how can we know that there has been any effect at all?

The crucial question, of course, is whether or not exposure to television violence causes its occurrence in real life. The concern which everyone has is over *real* violence: the purposeful, antisocial infliction of pain which is intended to harm a victim or destroy property. Of course, it is simply impossible to observe this kind of behavior in research subjects on a systematic basis. Consequently, researchers have substituted other measures which can be observed and analyzed. But these measures are not violent behaviors as we commonly define the term. For example, research studies have measured violence with paper and pencil tests; by asking children to rate their classmates as to who is most aggressive during play; by observing children playing in a schoolyard; and during laboratory experiments by requesting a subject to ostensibly inflict electric shocks on others.

We might assume that the violence which the studies refer to is antisocial, harmful violence but in reality it is not. The research does not address the crucial question with which we are all concerned: "Does exposure to television violence cause people to commit actual violence?" As two critics of the current violence research, Krattenmaker and Powe, have stated, "The social science research to date simply has not left this question unanswered; it has left it unasked."

CORRELATION TO IMPLY CAUSATION

The NIMH report concludes that a cause-effect relationship between television viewing and aggressive behavior has been clearly established. This assumption is based on a variety of studies which utilize "correlational" techniques. Few research techniques create as much confusion and are subject to as much misinterpretation as correlation. A correlation is simply a statistical measure of the interrelationship or association between two different variables. The problem with a correlation is that while it can tell us the degree to which two things are related, it can not tell us which came first nor whether one caused the other. In fact, it is often the case that despite a high correlation between two things, the association is actually being caused by a third condition which affects the other two.

For example, consider the fact that there is a high correlation between sales of bathing suits and sales of ice cream. Thus, it would appear that the sale of bathing suits and the sale of ice cream are related since as one goes up, so does the other. However, we can never say that bathing suit sales "causes" ice cream consumption to rise, nor can we say that the increase in ice cream sales "causes" people to buy more bathing suits. It is more than likely that neither really has much to do with the other despite the fact that they are highly correlated. Rather, it is because both bathing suit sales and ice cream sales are affected by a third condition: hot weather during the summer months. It is this external third condition which actually causes both the sale of bathing suits and the sale of ice cream to rise.

The point is, correlation can never tell us anything about causation. Thus, when we talk about correlation between television viewing and aggressive behavior, all we are really saying is that there seems to be some relationship between the two. And when a causal relationship does exist (determined by other methods) a correlation does not necessarily indicate which of the two variables is the cause and which is the effect.

A correlation between viewing television violence and aggressive behavior could be produced by any of the following: (1) viewing violence leads to aggression; (2) aggressive tendencies lead to viewing violence; (3) both viewing violence and aggressive behavior are the products of a third condition or set of conditions such as age, sex, income, or family socioeconomic level. In those correlational field studies which do control for these third factors, the extremely small levels of association between television and behavior virtually disappear. This indicates that the "relationship" between television viewing and subsequent behavior is more likely the result of a variety of external conditions which have absolutely nothing to do with television itself. Some of these third variables include the level of aggressivity among peers, parental behavior (aggressivity, anger, etc.), parent-child interaction (ways children are punished, nurtured, etc.), demographic factors, and intelligence.

Another important point to remember about correlation is the strength of the association and the amount of behavior which it can "explain." Correlations of 1.0 are "perfect" in that they indicate that there is a direct relationship between two variables. A correlation of zero indicates absolutely no relationship. Correlations which run from zero to .20 indicate very weak relationships; those which run from .20 to .60 indicate moderate relationships; and those running from .60 to 1.0 indicate strong relationships. Virtually every study cited by the NIMH report found correlations of less than .20 in associating television viewing with behavior. This weak correlation combined with the inability of correlation to determine causality indicates that the NIMH's conclusion is unwarranted.

USE OF CONVERGENCE THEORY

The NIMH report acknowledges that no single study conclusively links viewing television with violent behavior. However, the advisory panel insists that because there is a "convergence" of scientific evidence their conclusion is justified. In social science, convergence—the analysis of many different studies which point in the same basic direction—is sometimes used when no definitive evidence can be found to clearly support a position. The problem, however, is that the use of convergence can perpetuate unintended biases, flaws, or illogical assumptions which may exist within even a large body of research literature. It was the application of the convergence approach which led to the widespread belief among the scientific community of the time that the world was flat and that the sun revolved around the earth. By relying on a similar approach and by refusing to challenge basic assumptions, a variety of scientists made the same mistake despite the fact that convergence theory would suggest that they were all correct.

NIMH STUDIES

The NIMH technical chapter on violence and aggression in Volume 2 cites fourteen studies which the author suggests proves a positive relationship between television and violence and which the NIMH report relies upon to reach its conclusion of a cause-effect relationship. Of these fourteen studies, half were conducted in foreign countries with cultures, norms, and programming much different than those found in the United States. Approximately one-third of the studies were unpublished and consequently were never subjected to scientific peer review and evaluation. Two studies were not even cited as research investigations but were reported as "personal communication" between the researcher and the NIMH author. The lack of scientific documentation in a number of cited studies makes a thorough analysis and evaluation of the work impossible. Further, a number of significant studies which the author uses to substantiate his case for causality were, in fact, either written by the author himself or by his colleagues.

Despite the assertion of a distinct cause-effect relationship between television and aggression, only four field experiments (which contain the only type of research methods that can support such a causal claim) were reviewed. Of the four, one found no relationship between television viewing and aggressive behavior; one found no long-term effects; one found no differences in the level of aggressive behavior between viewers and nonviewers; the one which did find an effect used delinquent Belgian adolescents who were exposed to unedited theatrical motion pictures and not television programming. Further, elements in the design of the latter study preclude a valid causal interpretation.

The remaining studies are not able to adequately address the question of causality. In these field surveys, the relationship between television and aggression was quite small. Few, if any, statistical controls were employed to take into account third variables which could affect the relationship. However, when statistical controls were used, the relationship between television and aggression was reduced to insignificance. For example, in one study, the results showed a small, positive relationship between television and aggressive behavior. Further analysis revealed that this relationship was spurious once third variables such as sex and grades in school were taken into account. The TV and aggression relationship was reduced to zero. The technical report chapter only cites the first part of this analysis, however, and it fails to mention that the relationship between television and aggression was not established in subsequent analyses.

There are two other studies cited by the NIMH which merit a brief mention. The first was conducted by Belson and investigated the relationship between television and aggressive behavior among adolescent boys in London. Although the NIMH report states that Belson found a relationship between television and aggression, in fact, the relationship was not straightforward. Those boys who viewed a great deal of television and those who viewed little television tended to behave *less* aggressively than did moderate viewers. This finding—not reported by the NIMH—runs counter to the report's conclusion that there is a positive and direct relationship between the amount of television viewed and subsequent aggressive behavior.

The only new research report on television and violence in the NIMH report is a study by Milavsky et al. conducted by NBC. The study was conducted in two United States cities over a three-year period and employed a number of highly sophisticated research techniques designed to eliminate many of the technical criticisms which have invalidated previous research efforts. The NBC findings do not support the NIMH conclusion of a causal relationship between television and aggressive behavior. Although the study appears in its own chapter in the NIMH report, it is not discussed in the chapter on violence which the advisory panel relied on in drawing its conclusion.

In sum, a review of the studies and their findings strongly indicates that the NIMH Advisory Panel's conclusion of a causal relationship between television and violence is ill-founded and unsupported by any of the research data which [are] currently available.

The NIMH panel arrives at this conclusion based upon two points: first, that a majority of academic researchers believe that a causal relationship exists between television and aggressive behavior; and second, that the sheer number of scientific studies in the literature supports the contention as opposed to the number of studies which do not.

OPINION OF RESEARCHERS

In fact, there is no consensus among researchers regarding the relationship between television and aggression, and a spirited debate continues within the scientific community. In a recent study by Bybee, 486 academic researchers were asked their professional opinion of the influence of television on aggressive behavior. Only 1 percent reported that television was "the cause" of aggressive behavior. Further, the majority did not feel that television was an important contributory cause of aggressive behavior. Clearly this is not a consensus.

While it is true that there are more studies published in the literature which have found some effect between television viewing and aggressive behavior, this says more about the academic research process and the criteria employed for publication in scientific journals than it does about the television violence issue. It is an acknowledged fact that research studies that report an effect are far more likely to be accepted for publication than those studies which do not find an effect. Since editors naturally prefer to report results, publication policies can result in a distortion of the scientific evidence which actually exists. In the academic research field, where an individual's professional standing is based largely on published work, there is a real incentive for researchers to produce studies that do demonstrate an effect.

The research literature on television and violence has been reviewed and evaluated by other academic scientists than those who participated in the NIMH study. Although many have concluded that the research evidence does not support the conclusion that television violence causes aggressive behavior, their work was ignored by the NIMH panel.

The only way to address the question of how much violence is on television is to systematically analyze a representative sample of television programming by conducting a "content analysis." To accurately identify content trends; these analyses must be performed over a period of years. Only two such content analyses were included in the NIMH report. Of these two analyses only one—by Dr. George Gerbner and his colleagues at the University of Pennsylvania—is used by the NIMH to support its view that violent content has remained at a consistently high level.

Since 1967, Gerbner and his associates have produced the yearly Violence Profile—an analysis of the violent content of network television programming—research that has been supported by NIMH funding. An additional conflict is the fact that Dr. Gerbner is a member of the NIMH Advisory Panel which is responsible for the report and for its conclusions.

The other major content analysis study included in the NIMH report is conducted annually by the CBS Office of Social Research. The CBS study and the Gerbner study utilize radically different definitions of violence and consequently arrive at very different conclusions. While Gerbner maintains that violence is at a consistently high level, the CBS data indicate that the level of violence has decreased over the past decade. Since the NIMH relies so heavily upon the work of Dr. Gerbner and his colleagues, we will first analyze their content analysis and then compare it with the CBS study.

GERBNER CONTENT ANALYSES

The Gerbner content analyses have generated a great deal of controversy within the research community, including Newcomb, Coffin and Tuchman, and Blank. Criticisms focus on three major issues: (1) the definition of violence which Gerbner uses; (2) the index which Gerbner constructs and uses to report the amounts of violence in programming; and (3) the sample which is analyzed and used to generalize to a full-year season.

The way in which violence in program content is defined is crucial because more than anything else, it affects the study's findings and conclusions. Earlier we discussed the difficulty in arriving at a commonly agreed upon definition of violence. Gerbner defines violence as: "The overt expression of physical force against self or other, compelling action against one's will on pain of being hurt or killed, or actually hurting or killing." What makes the Gerbner definition unique is that this definition is applied not only to serious and realistic depictions of violence but is expanded to *include* comedy and slapstick, accidents, and acts of nature such as floods, earthquakes, and hurricanes. By employing such a definition, the Gerbner analyses arrive at violence figures which distort the amount of realistic violence actually on television. For example, in a number of Gerbner content studies, over one-third of all the violence counted did *not* result from human action but was caused by accidents or acts of nature. Without an understanding of the violence definition, we would incorrectly attribute far more violence to programming than actually exists.

Gerbner uses a Violence Index to measure the amount of violence on network television. A number of researchers have concluded that the Violence Index is an arbitrary and idiosyncratic measure which does not accurately reflect program content. Rather than simply count the number of violent incidents per program, Gerbner combines various numerical scores, some of which are weighted to reflect his own theories and controversial assumptions. For example, the Violence Index arbitrarily *doubles* the "rate of violent episodes per program," *doubles* the "rate of violent episodes per hour of programs," and combines together percentages with straightforward numerical sums. In response to this overwhelming criticism of the index, Gerbner replies, "The rates are doubled in order to raise their relatively low numerical values to the importance that the concepts...deserve."

By adding together the research equivalent of "apples and oranges," the index provides a biased and inaccurate picture of television content. As one noted researcher, B.M. Owen, commented, "One is always free to add apples and oranges if one wishes, but it isn't at all clear what the result means, and some people may take it seriously."

Gerbner and his colleagues utilize a one-week sample of prime-time network programming to generalize about the entire yearly television season. The use of one week's worth of programming to represent the total content of a fifty-two-week season is clearly inadequate.

CBS CONTENT ANALYSIS

The CBS study uses a thirteen-week sample of prime-time network programming to represent a full year, clearly a more adequate, representative sample than Gerbner's. CBS also employs a more reasonable definition of violence: "The use of physical force against persons or animals, or the articulated, explicit threat of physical force to compel particular behavior on the part of a person." This definition attempts to analyze only realistic violence and consequently excludes from the analysis accidents, acts of nature, and comedy or slapstick.

The CBS findings have shown a measured downward trend in the amount of violent program content among the three networks from 1973 through 1981, the last year for which data are available. Although the CBS study offers a much different picture of violent content than does the Gerbner study, the NIMH report dismisses [its] findings without comment.

Only the Gerbner and CBS studies measure television content over a long enough period of time to permit any sort of trends to be identified and measured. The NIMH report does mention a number of one-time content analysis studies but they are of little value in addressing the primary question. For example, one study cited by the NIMH utilized the capsule program descriptions in *TV Guide* as the method of analyzing the violence that appeared in programming.

The cultivation theory suggests that viewers absorb a unique and biased "social reality" from watching television. According to the theory, which has been put forth by Dr. George Gerbner, television presents a distorted reflection of the world which does not accurately represent what exists in real life. Consequently, people who watch television will perceive the world from a "television perspective" and not as it really is. Although the NIMH Advisory Panel indicates that the case for this cultivation theory has been clearly established, Hawkins and Pingree, the authors of the technical report chapter reach a different conclusion. They state, "the evidence concerning the causal direction of television's impact on social reality is not sufficient for strong conclusions."

As in the case of the content issue, the NIMH relies almost exclusively on the research of Dr. Gerbner and his associates to substantiate their claim that the cultivation theory is true. Although a number of other researchers have conducted work in this area, over half of all the studies reviewed by the NIMH were either conducted by Gerbner himself or by his associates. Thus, his methods and conclusions are clearly central to the issue of cultivation.

A number of independent researchers have been strongly critical of the cultivation hypothesis and of the research that supports it. Their criticisms address three key issues: (1) the use of correlation to imply causation; (2) the methods by which attitudes are measured; and (3) the application of certain research techniques in attempting to answer the research question.

The cultivation hypothesis states that television viewing causes distorted social attitudes and perceptions. Although the cultivation research utilizes correlational techniques, the theory's proponents interpret the findings to suggest causality. As we have demonstrated earlier, correlation can not indicate cause and effect. Further, in every cultivation study reported by the NIMH report, the correlation between television viewing and an individual's attitudes are extremely small, when they are found at all. In most cases, only 3 percent of a person's social attitudes are related to television viewing. In other words, 97 percent of a person's attitudes and perceptions are related to factors *other* than exposure to television.

What is especially significant is that television's minuscule relationship to social perceptions decreases even further when we consider such important external conditions as the individual's age, sex, race, and place of residence. Once these variables are taken into account, the cultivation effect of television on social attitudes and behaviors is virtually nonexistent.

The second area of criticism regarding cultivation research concerns the way in which viewer's attitudes and perceptions are measured. Individuals are asked a series of questions: one possible answer being the "TV answer," which the researchers say reflects how the world is shown on television, and the other response, a "real world" answer, which the researchers say reflects how the world really is. For example, a respondent might be asked to estimate how likely they are to be a victim of crime. Overestimating their chances of victimization is considered the "TV answer" since the researchers believe that exposure to violence on television cultivates fear and mistrust. Critics of the cultivation theory suggest the questions that are asked are highly selective, and items which do not support the cultivation theory are simply omitted. In addition, the "TV answer" is often arbitrarily determined by the researchers. Further, it has been found that on occasion, of the two responses from which an individual must choose, *both* were incorrect. Thus, the respondent is placed in the situation of having to select an answer when the only alternatives available are both wrong.

RESEARCH TECHNIQUES

One of the major criticisms of the cultivation theory involves the various procedures that are used to investigate the hypothesis. A number of researchers have attempted to replicate the findings of Gerbner and his colleagues and were unable to find the effects which were predicted by the cultivation theory.

Other researchers have been highly critical of specific methods. For example, a number of studies used a sliding baseline in segmenting individuals into the crucial "heavy" and "light" viewing categories which, according to the theory, determines how they will perceive the world. Instead of establishing a strict definition of "heavy" and "light" viewers, these categories are frequently determined by the idiosyncrasies of each sample. Further, although the categories are not consistent from study to study, findings are compared as though they were identical. For example, in one study school children who watched three hours of television were classified as "heavy" viewers; in another, children who watched three hours were classified as "light" viewers.

Another point of criticism is that cultivation researchers group together viewers who fall into differing categories. When these groups are analyzed separately, the findings do not support the cultivation theory. For example, cultivation researchers group "nonviewers" who do not watch television with "light" viewers who watch less than average. When nonviewers are analyzed independently of light viewers, their fear and mistrust scores are actually *higher* than light viewers. Similarly, "extremely heavy viewers" are grouped with "heavy viewers." When extremely heavy viewers—who view eight or more hours of television daily—are analyzed independently, they are found to be *less* fearful and mistrusting than heavy viewers. In both of these instances, when unlike groups were analyzed separately, the findings were in direct opposition to what the cultivation theory predicts.

Overall, when the cultivation theory is examined closely, it is found to be far less compelling than the NIMH report indicates. Consequently, there is no justification for the strong conclusions which the advisory panel reached.

Conflict is a legitimate aspect of literature and drama yet we also recognize the sensitivity and care we must exercise when considering its use. ABC Television has established policies and procedures which enable us to handle violence and other controversial themes responsibly and tastefully. We make every effort to maintain the integrity of the story line, but we do not accept the gratuitous use of violence nor do we tolerate stories that glorify violence or suggest that violence is without consequences to those who use it. The care and concern with which we approach violence is indicated by the various procedures and resources which we utilize in the evaluation of dramatic material and is outlined as follows.

BROADCAST STANDARDS AND PRACTICES

All entertainment series and specials are produced under the scrutiny of the Broadcast Standards and Practices Department (BSAP). Each program script is carefully reviewed by Broadcast Standards and Practices Department editors, and every violent action within the script is carefully evaluated. Each violent action must have a thematic justification, and the depiction should portray only the minimum necessary to maintain the integrity of the story line. Gratuitous or excessive violence is eliminated, and unique and detailed depictions of violent actions which might be copied or emulated are either modified or eliminated. In addition to reviewing all scripts, every program is screened and approved in a rough-cut and final form by the Broadcast Standards and Practices Department editing staff before the program is considered acceptable for broadcast on ABC.

One of the tools which the BSAP editors use in evaluating program content is the Incident Classification and Analysis Form (ICAF) system. The ICAF was developed by the BSAP Department in conjunction with social scientists from the ABC Social Research Unit. The ICAF enables every editor to systematically categorize, quantify, and weigh every violent incident within a program and provides editors with a qualitative and quantitative measure of a given program's violent content.

The ICAF system is especially useful because it not only counts incidents of violence but differentiates the severity of the violence and considers the overall context within which the violence is portrayed. The ICAF system enables the BSAP editor to identify those elements within a program that may be excessive and gratuitous and is an important aspect in the overall evaluation of program content.

The ICAF system is continuously monitored and reviewed by the ABC Social Research Unit. This procedure maintains its high levels of reliability and validity and ensures that the ICAF remains a sensitive and accurate instrument for the identification and categorization of violent program content. Used in conjunction with the editor's professional judgment, the ICAF is a highly effective tool for maintaining ABC's standards of acceptability and appropriateness.

ABC SOCIAL RESEARCH UNIT

The Social Research Unit is a part of the ABC Marketing and Research Services Department. One of its functions is to provide support services to the Broadcast Standards and Practices Department. In addition to the administration of the ICAF System, the Social Research Unit provides BSAP with relevant research information to ensure that all policies and guidelines reflect the most current data available.

Contemporary social science research is reviewed on a continuing basis and plays an important role in maintaining appropriate standards for the portrayal of violence in programming. In addition to reviewing research which appears in the scientific literature, the Social Research Unit conducts a number of proprietary studies which are designed to assess the impact of our programming on viewers and to survey audience attitudes toward depictions of sensitive program material.

Another related activity of the Social Research Unit is to conduct workshops and seminars for the broadcast standards editing staff. Training workshops are an important element in professional growth and are held on a regular basis. This service ensures that established policy guidelines are consistently and accurately applied to the evaluation of all ABC programming. At a typical training workshop, representatives from the Social Research Unit, as well as outside expert consultants, discuss and evaluate editing policies and procedures. The case study approach is frequently used and has proven to be an excellent method in increasing and refining the abilities of the broadcast standards editors. In addition, ICAF procedures are regularly reviewed to retain the high reliability levels of the coding and to refine and improve the overall ICAF system.

The goal of these workshops and seminars is to increase the capability of the BSAP editors by improving their editing skills and by broadening their perspective and understanding of the viewing audience.

At the very beginning of this article we indicated the complexity of the television violence issue. Our review of the scientific literature demonstrates how true that statement is. Research is clearly a valuable means by which we can understand more about the medium of television and its social impact. But research is only useful after we have assessed each study's strengths and weaknesses and placed it in its proper perspective. Our analysis of the research which the NIMH has used to substantiate their conclusions regarding television and violence indicates that there are more unanswered questions than there are definitively settled issues.

At the same time we recognize our responsibility to ensure that when violence is presented in the context of a dramatic program, there exists a legitimate and thematic justification for its inclusion. Further, it is our practice to limit the portrayal of violence to that which is reasonably related to plot development and character delineation. The excessive depiction of violence is rarely necessary and gratuitous portrayals are considered inappropriate for the television medium.

We believe that ABC's policies and procedures have proven to be an excellent method of exercising our responsibility. We will continue to demonstrate care and concern in the future by providing our viewers with programming which meets the highest standards of appropriateness and social responsibility.

This article is reprinted by permission from the American Broadcasting Companies' *A Research Perspective on Television and Violence*. The ABC publication contains bibliographic references for all studies discussed in this article.

ISSUE 2 YES:

Defending the Indefensible

Steven H. Chaffee, George Gerbner, Beatrix A. Hamburg, Chester M. Pierce, Eli A. Rubinstein, Alberta E. Siegel, and Jerome L. Singer

The National Institute of Mental Health (NIMH) project for which we were senior scientific advisers resulted in the publication of *Television and Behavior: Ten Years of Scientific Progress and Implications for the Eighties*. The two volume report was prepared as an update to a 1972 report to the surgeon general. The new NIMH report has recently come under public attack by some members of the television industry. The substance of that criticism, which we believe to be unfounded, calls for an informed response.

This article is specifically intended as an open reply to a statement written by Alan Wurtzel and Guy Lometti for the American Broadcasting Companies, Inc., the text of which precedes us in this issue of Transaction/Society. The ABC statement purports to be a rigorous and objective refutation of the NIMH report; however, it is neither rigorous nor objective. It is a shallow attempt, ostensibly for public consumption, to focus on only one portion of the NIMH review, rehash industry attacks on independent research of the past ten years, ignore or distort both the evidence presented in the NIMH report and the consensus of the field, and present conclusions that obscure the issue and deceive the readers. It would be no exaggeration to compare this attempt by the television industry to the stubborn public position taken by the tobacco industry on the scientific evidence about smoking and health.

A telling indictment of the ABC position is inherent in findings on the effects of television that are ignored in their statement. Research has long since gone beyond the issue of violence. The summary (Volume 1) of the NIMH report devotes only 9 out of 91 pages to that topic. Similarly, only 72 out of 362 pages of technical reports in Volume 2 deal with violence and aggression. Some other topics include: health-promoting possibilities; effects on cognitive and emotional functioning; effects on imagination, creativity, and prosocial behavior; and effects on education and learning. These are all parts of a related body of data that only confirms the obvious conclusion: television is an influential teacher of children and adults. Ironically, the networks have pursued and used the concept of positive programming in defense of some of their children's productions. The research on positive effects is no better or worse than that on violence and aggression. Yet the industry, by some convenient logic, accepts the former and disputes the latter.

What is especially distressing about ABC's effort to discredit a carefully developed assessment of research is that it only serves to confuse and deter the considerable opportunity for constructive change. It is now more than a decade since the original surgeon general's report. In testimony before Senator Pastore in March 1972, all three network presidents acknowledged, with some qualification, the findings on televised violence and pledged to improve television for children. (The most forthright and responsive statement was made by Elton Rule, president of ABC.) Surely the creativity, talent, and considerable resources of the television industry could have been put to better use than the renewed campaign of obfuscation and evasion after ten years of significant scientific progress. Instead of a positive response to that evidence, quality programming for children on commercial television has become increasingly rare.

The ABC argument is scientifically indefensible. By the very manner in which it was constructed, it is only the latest example of unwarranted resistance to the clear policy implications of overwhelming scientific evidence. The renewed attempt to evade, undermine, and discredit the work of hundreds of scientists summarized in the NIMH volumes and to shape the course of public discussion by selective attention and misrepresentation, is unworthy of an industry that professes—and is licensed—to serve the public interest.

The ABC response reads like a slick brief for the defense replete with carefully worded misinterpretations, omission of large bodies of relevant evidence, and sheer misstatements of facts. It begins by calling into question the entire body of research reviewed in the NIMH report as "simply a reiteration of information which has already been made available." ABC sees this as a fatal flaw, despite the fact that the foreword to the NIMH report and most of the press coverage made clear that the report was not based on new research but was a comprehensive and integrative review of existing research. The ABC interpretation suggests that once published, research findings quickly go stale and lose their validity or relevance. On the contrary, findings accumulate with later studies, testing, confirming, and extending those published earlier.

What is especially lacking in rigor or objectivity is the premise by ABC that research on violence stands in isolation from the larger body of research reviewed by the NIMH report. Perhaps the most telling confirmatory evidence on the effects of televised violence is that it is now only one part of a massive body of research.

A pattern of effects has emerged from all this evidence. It would be anomalous if the findings on violence and aggression did not fit into this larger pattern.

Ignoring that crucial issue, ABC isolates four specific conclusions from what is actually a minor part of the NIMH report. We address only some of the many violations of the principles to which the ABC statement claims to be dedicated. We begin by discussing the ABC summary of and response to each of the four NIMH conclusions that are addressed. First, to the conclusion, "The research findings support the conclusion of a causal relationship between television violence and aggressive behavior"; ABC responds, "The research does not support the conclusion of a causal relationship."

The attribution of causality is a complex way of defining relationships, even in the physical sciences. The question is not how irrefutable the causal conclusion may be, especially in the social sciences, but can it be invoked at all. In 1972, the Surgeon General's Scientific Advisory Committee, of which two distinguished members were full-time scientists for NBC and CBS respectively, and of which three other members had been part-time consultants to the industry, came to the unanimous conclusion that there is "some preliminary indication of a causal relationship, but a good deal of research remains to be done before one can have confidence in these conclusions." The update provided much additional research to add confidence to the conclusions.

Most research in the field has concerned itself with the linkage between "televised violence" and "aggressive behavior." Rarely have scientists attempted to observe, let alone induce, "violent behavior." The ABC statement uses a subterfuge in equating aggressive behavior with violent behavior and then asking if televised violence causes violent behavior. While few studies, for obvious reasons, can legitimately explore that connection, one notable instance does exist. The study by Belson did find such a causal connection between televised violence and actual antisocial behavior. Despite the fact that the study was funded by CBS, when it was independently published in book form, it was dismissed by the industry as merely "correlational." That charge is now leveled by ABC against the NIMH report's conclusions.

Although even the stimulation of harmful tendencies in millions of children is of no small consequence, ABC obfuscates the issue. It states baldly that "the point is, correlation can never tell us anything about causation." Even theoretically, let alone in a practical way, this is not true. Correlation is a necessary but not sufficient condition in a causal relationship. To argue that a study is "correlational," as the industry did with the Belson study, is not legitimately to dismiss its significance. If there had been no correlation, the question of causation would have been settled long ago. Study after study by independent investigators found significant correlations.

Wurtzel and Lometti develop something called "convergence theory" to argue that scientists can be led to accept any "widespread belief" on which many different studies seem to converge. If there is any substance to that curious criticism, it must be in the basic assumption behind the operation of the television industry itself. Ten billion dollars annually are expended on the "widespread belief" that advertising induces people to buy products. There is no more definitive causal relationship between advertising on television and subsequent buying behavior than there is between televised violence and later aggressive behavior.

No researcher cited by NIMH argues that television violence is the only or even necessarily the main factor in aggression. The conclusion on which there is a significant "convergence" is that it is a contributing factor. Having set up a strawman relationship between causation, correlation, and convergence, ABC argues that only a handful of studies support the NIMH conclusions.

The ABC statement begins: "The NIMH technical chapter on violence and aggression in Volume 2 cites fourteen studies which the author suggests proves a positive relationship between television and violence and which the NIMH report relies upon to reach its conclusion of a cause-effect relationship." The chapter referred to is a comprehensive review not just of fourteen studies but of the larger penumbra of research on televised violence which further illuminates this body of findings. Ninety-five publications are referenced in this chapter, most of which support the major argument.

Wurtzel and Lometti point out that this chapter does not discuss a study by NBC researcher Milavsky, one that dismissed television's effect on aggression as negligible, "although the NBC study appears in its own chapter in the NIMH report." Precisely because another chapter was devoted to the NBC study would it have been superfluous to incorporate its findings in the chapter under discussion. It was NIMH and our committee that invited the NBC researchers and requested the inclusion of the NBC study as a separate chapter of Volume 2. What ABC implies was an omission is the result of a conscientious effort on the part of NIMH and our committee to include all relevant research. The conclusions of the NBC study were carefully considered in the final evaluation and summary published in Volume 1.

ABC has not refuted the NIMH conclusion of a causal relationship between television violence and aggression and has misstated both the convergence and weight of evidence bearing on the issue. To the second summarized conclusion, "There is a clear consensus among most researchers that television violence leads to aggressive behavior"; ABC responds, "There exists a significant debate within the research community over the relationship between television and aggressive behavior."

ABC found one (unpublished) study, by Bybee et al., that it could construe as suggesting there is no consensus among academic researchers. ABC misrepresented that study. The sample polled was not all "academic researchers," as ABC states but members of professional societies in speech and journalism, an unknown proportion of which are researchers. More importantly, researchers in the field of television include many social scientists who were absent from the sample.

Even more deceptive is ABC's interpretation of the results of that survey. The issue is not whether television is *the* cause of aggression. No responsible researcher makes that claim. All complex behavior has many causes. What the research results showed is that television is a significant contributor to such behavior. On that point, the Bybee study cited by ABC actually showed a clear consensus. About two-thirds of those polled agreed that television increased children's aggressive behavior. Had more scientists from other fields been included, that consensus would probably have been even higher. The authors of the Bybee study are themselves distressed at ABC's misrepresentation of their findings.

Attempting to neutralize the findings in the great preponderance of published studies, ABC claims that studies that find an effect are more likely to be published than studies with no findings. That seeming anomaly would have disappeared if ABC had correctly stated that well-designed studies, with clearly developed hypotheses, and careful statistical analyses, leading to scientifically defensible conclusions, are more likely to be published in reputable scientific journals than poor studies with inconclusive results. It is insulting to the research community to state as ABC does—baldly and without qualifications—that "since editors naturally prefer to report results, publication policies can result in a distortion of the scientific evidence which actually exists." In that sentence, the ABC statement attempts to discredit the entire formal process of scientific publication.

ABC cites seven references to claim that many academic scientists have concluded that the research evidence does not support the causal linkage. That list of seven all but exhausts the list of "many." ABC has not refuted the NIMH conclusion that there is a clear consensus among research scientists on this issue. To the third summarized conclusion, "Despite slight variations over the past decade, the amount of violence on television has remained at consistently high levels"; ABC responds, "There has been a decrease in the overall amount of violence in recent years." ABC's contention about a decrease in the overall amount of violence is based on an in-house CBS report and is not supported by independent studies. It also does not necessarily contradict the NIMH conclusion.

Singled out for special attention by ABC is an extensive and long-standing research project called Cultural Indicators, conducted at the University of Pennsylvania's Annenberg School of Communications since the late 1960s. The project began as a study for the National Commission on the Causes and Prevention of Violence (the "Eisenhower Commission") and continued under various foundation and medical auspices to investigate many aspects of television content and viewer conception of social reality.

Ignoring its proper name, broad scope, many publications and assessment by NIMH and others, ABC reaches back six years to claim that "the Gerbner content analyses have generated a great deal of controversy within the research community." Of the authors cited as being responsible for the "controversy," Coffin, Tuchman, and Blank were network employees and Newcomb a humanistic scholar whose dialogue with the Cultural Indicators team was as supportive as critical of the effort. All complex research relevant to social policy does and should be debated. ABC conceals the actual debate from the readers of its statement; it does not mention the rebuttals published in the same journals—and usually in the very same issues—as the works cited. The ABC authors repeat perennial network objections as if they had never been addressed and dealt with both in the literature and in the NIMH report. At least three chapters of Volume 2 of the NIMH report provide critical overviews and assessments of all aspects of the content analyses ABC insists are "controversial." One of these, an overview of measures of violence in television content, compares several measures including those of Cultural Indicators and the CBS study. It finds "no detectable trend" and observes: "Regardless of measure, changes that within the scope of 2 or 3 years would appear to constitute an upward or downward shift become, in the long run, oscillations." That and other similar reviews of the research evidence by independent scholars led NIMH and our committee to conclude that despite variations over the years, violence on television "remained at consistently high levels."

The ABC statement supports its contention of a decrease in the amount of violence by reference to a CBS study not subject to peer review or other scientific scrutiny and not regularly published. It was introduced into the 1981 congressional hearings on "Social/Behavioral Effects of Violence on Television" as the industry's attempt to counter evidence presented by researchers at the hearing. An examination of the 1981 hearing record shows that CBS succeeded in "reducing" the amount of violence reported by excluding a significant (and unreported) amount of violent representations. The violence monitoring effort announced by ABC itself with much fanfare a few years ago did not seem to yield results suitable for its own statement.

ABC argues, "the CBS study and the Gerbner study utilize radically different definitions of violence and consequently arrive at very different conclusions." The CBS study definition of violence, not cited by ABC, is: "The use of physical force against persons or animals or the articulated, explicit threat of physical force to compel particular behavior on the part of a person." Wurtzel and Lometti state that "Gerbner defines violence as: 'The overt expression of physical force against self or other, compelling action against one's will on pain of being hurt or killed, or actually hurting or killing.' " The two definitions are in practice virtually identical. ABC argues, "What makes the Gerbner definition unique is that this definition is applied not only to serious and realistic depictions of violence, but is expanded to include comedy and slapstick, accidents and acts of nature such as floods, earthquakes, and hurricanes." Both definitions include the use of physical force in any context. The difference is not in definition, as ABC claims; it is in what CBS chose not to include in its report.

The counts CBS excluded from its report were those it claimed, without evidence, to be "harmless" acts of "accidental" and "humorous" violence. The evidence reviewed by NIMH indicates that violence in any context may teach powerful lessons and can be harmful in its effects. Even with such manipulation, the CBS study was only able to reduce its violence score from 138 incidents a week in 1972–73 to 105 a week in 1980–81. That is still more violence in one week of prime-time watching alone than most people experience otherwise in a lifetime. It can hardly be seen as contradicting the NIMH finding that "violence on television remained at consistently high levels."

How much of all that mayhem is "accidental" and "humorous" violence that the networks claim is "harmless"? Here again, ABC is wide of the mark. They claim that "in a number of Gerbner studies, over one-third of all the violence counted did *not* result from human action but was caused by accidents or acts of nature." (Emphasis in the original.) ABC deals with prime-time programs alone. The source of ABC's observation on "human action" is the original report to the surgeon general, *Television and Social Behavior, Volume 1, Media Content and Control.* Those figures refer not to prime time but to the combined results of prime-time and weekend daytime children's (mostly cartoon) programs. In cartoons, humanized animals rather than humans, strictly defined, commit most violence. Therefore, the "over one-third of all the violence counted" was not "caused by accidents or acts of nature" but mostly by cartoon "animals" committing anthropomorphic mayhem. ABC uses cartoon violence only to obfuscate the facts, not to express concern over the most violent and exploitative part of programming, what the trade calls the "kid-vid ghetto." A careful look at table 67 in the original report would have revealed that when only regular programs (rather than cartoons) are considered, as in prime time, nine out of ten acts of violence are perpetrated by human agents. Table 69 in the same series also shows that of these acts of hurting and killing people only one-fifth appear in a "light" or "humorous" context, with consequences that, according to available evidence, cannot be blithely dismissed.

Where does that muddle leave those real "acts of nature such as floods, earthquakes, and hurricanes" that according to ABC "distort" the amount of violence reported? In light of the facts they also shrink into insignificance. An analysis of Cultural Indicators data for fifteen sample periods since 1969 shows a grand total of only thirteen fictional "acts of nature" hurting and killing. The viewer bombarded with violence every hour of prime time has to watch an average of three and a half weeks to encounter one act of "accidental" violence. The social pattern of such victimization (i.e., what types of characters tend to get hurt or killed "accidentally") may be far from inconsequential. The rarity of the occurrence makes the ABC claim groundless. The argument that an "expanded" definition "distorts" even one set of violence figures used in the NIMH report is both deceptive and trivial.

One of the oldest claims of network publicists, renewed here despite ample clarification through the years, is that the Violence Index "is an arbitrary and idiosyncratic measure which does not accurately reflect program content." ABC maintains that rather than counting the number of violent incidents per program, "Gerbner combines various numerical scores, some of which are weighted to reflect his own theoretical and controversial assumptions." This ignores responses published since 1972 and the annual publication of the Violence Index in which the "simple count of the number of violent incidents per program" is separately tabulated for the convenience of those who prefer that simple measure to also considering the pervasiveness of violence in all programming and lethal vs. nonlethal consequences. An extensive review of tests in Volume 2 of the NIMH report found that the Violence Index "meets the critical statistical and empirical requirements of an index: unidimensionality and internal homogeneity."

ABC's quibble with the sample employed in the Violence Index is similarly misdirected. Without citing any support, the ABC authors state that "the use of one week's worth of programming to represent the total content of a fifty-two-week season is clearly inadequate." As explained many times, and reviewed in at least two technical chapters of the NIMH Report, but ignored by ABC, experiments with up to seven weeks of programming have not produced notably different results. The NIMH review concluded:

> These studies thus indicate that while a larger sample might increase precision, given the operational definitions and multidimensional measures that are sensitive to a variety of significant aspects of television violence, the 1-week sample yields stable results with high cost efficiency.

The consistency of violence and other measures of fictional demography and power from year to year would be hard to explain with a sample that is inadequate to the task for which it was designed.

The extensive research evidence supporting the definition of violence and its measurement in samples of television content has not been examined by ABC; it has been ignored. The ABC claims appear to be designed for the uninitiated, repeating contentions network publicists have been propagating for over a decade. The ABC statement did not refute the NIMH conclusion that violence on television remains at consistently high levels. To the fourth summarized conclusion, "Television has been shown to cultivate television-influenced attitudes among viewers. Heavy viewers are more likely to be more fearful and less trusting of other people than are light viewers as a result of their exposure to television"; ABC responds, "The research does not support the conclusion that television significantly cultivates viewer attitudes and perceptions of social reality."

ABC challenges the extensive body of research findings on television's cultivation of viewer attitudes and conceptions of reality. The ABC statement claims that even though the NIMH report accepted many of the findings of the cultivation analysis, "the authors of the technical report chapter reach a different conclusion." Those authors stated, "The evidence concerning the causal direction of television's impact on social reality is not sufficient for strong conclusions." The technical report chapter by Hawkins and Pingree supports the cultivation theory and confirms findings cited by NIMH. "Causal direction" is not an issue in cultivation theory which holds that the pervasive and repetitive patterns of television cultivate, rather than only create, attitudes and perceptions. After the passage cited by ABC, Hawkins and Pingree observe that "the relationship between viewing and social reality may be reciprocal." In their view of many studies, including their own, Hawkins and Pingree conclude:

> Is there a relationship between television viewing and social reality? Most studies show evidence for a link, regardless of the kind of social reality studied. These studies cover

> a diverse range of areas including prevalence of violence, family structures, interpersonal mistrust, fear of victimization, traditional sex roles, family values, images of older people, attitudes about doctors, and concern about racial problems.... Relationships between viewing and demographic measures of social reality closely linked to television content appear to hold despite controls.

Another example of the criticisms cited by ABC is the assertion that cultivation researchers group nonviewers with light viewers. When nonviewers are analyzed independently, ABC states "their fear and mistrust scores are actually *higher* than light viewers." Similarly, it is said that extremely heavy viewers are grouped with heavy viewers, but when extremely heavy viewers are analyzed independently, "they are found to be *less* fearful and mistrusting than heavy viewers." The facts were reported in an article in the same journal from which ABC selected its information, but they were omitted from the ABC statement. Nonviewers and "extremely heavy viewers" are very small and atypical groups (about 5 percent of the population each). Their deviant responses are trivial in size and not significant statistically. The inclusion of these deviant groups means that the NIMH conclusions about cultivation are underestimated; when they are excluded, the resulting patterns are even stronger for the remaining 90 percent of the population.

A series of additional repetitions of criticisms already dealt with in the research literature and reviewed in the NIMH report further strains the credibility of the ABC "critique." Clearly its authors are aware of the scholarly exchanges that have taken place; they seem not to have missed a single negative comment, no matter how far-fetched. Yet they seem to be oblivious to the more numerous extensions and confirmations of findings by independent scholars in the United States and abroad.

The ABC statement deceives the reader not familiar with the research literature. It is thus the ABC statement and not the NIMH report that distorts, in its general design as well as its details, the evidence on television and violence that it purports to place in perspective.

ISSUE 3

Should Marijuana Be Legalized?

Drugs have been used since ancient times. Opium use dates back to the Greeks, and references to marijuana appear in early Persian and Hindu writings. When the Spanish arrived in the New World, the Incas were chewing coca leaves, and peyote was being consumed in the American Southwest. Opiates have also had a long history in Western society, particularly in the form of patent medicines. By the end of the eighteenth century, patent medicines containing opium and extracts from the coca plant were widely available in the United States. Coca-Cola started as a patent medicine but was changed into a soft drink containing an ingredient coming from coca. It was indeed "The real thing."

The Harrison Act in 1914 was the first serious attempt by the U.S. government to control drugs. The act permanently altered the nature of drug use in the country by requiring people who dealt in opium and cocaine to register with the federal government, pay taxes, and keep records. The law was not specifically aimed at the large number of drug users but was designed to enable the government to gain control over the distribution system for the drugs.

The Harrison Act also allowed physicians to prescribe drugs such as opium. Subsequent court decisions, however, eliminated the physician's right to provide drugs to addicts for maintenance purposes and eliminated their right to prescribe narcotics to any addict, even if part of a treatment program. Thus, addiction was removed from the control of physicians and became a criminal matter. There is, of course, still controversy over drug maintenance programs. Many argue that we should supply addicts with a daily dosage of drugs, as many European societies do and as some U.S. localities have done with methadone for heroin addicts.

Marijuana appeared in American society in much the same way as did opium and cocaine. It was an ingredient in many patent medicines but was not used as widely as the opiates because of its insolubility. In the early part of the twentieth century, the use of marijuana by blacks in the South and Mexican-Americans in the Southwest became more widespread. A number of factors, including the use of marijuana by minority groups, the political climate that led to the creation of the Harrison Act, and the constitutional amendment banning alcohol use, caused states to start passing antimarijuana laws in the 1930s.

At that time, Harry Anslinger was the commissioner of the Federal Bureau of Narcotics. Anslinger led a crusade against marijuana by using a variety of scare techniques. There is disagreement over his motives. Some think he was simply a right-wing conservative who truly believed that marijuana was a dire threat to American society; others believe that he was overly ambitious and used the issue to elevate himself and the bureau to national prominence. As a result of Anslinger's campaign, the Marijuana Tax Act of 1937 was passed, classifying marijuana as a narcotic and placing it under the same controls as opium and cocaine.

Marijuana was used by a fairly small part of the population until the 1960s when usage took a quantum leap and the user population began to shift. Increasingly, marijuana was being used by middle-class, white students. The severe penalties for marijuana possession came under fire as children of judges, physicians, politicians, and professors were sentenced. Many states began to reduce penalties, and some, such as Oregon in 1973, moved toward decriminalization.

The failure of government attempts to deal effectively with illegal drugs has again raised the issue of decriminalization or legalization of many of these drugs. The cover story of the May 30, 1988 issue of *Time Magazine* was, "Should Drugs Be Made Legal?" Both conservatives and liberals are now asking for a public debate of the issue.

The following articles were written by two conservatives, who argue the case for and against legalization of marijuana.

ISSUE 3 NO:

Marijuana Should Not Be Legalized

Richard Vigilante

December 1972 was a milestone in the campaign to relax American marijuana laws. Up to that time the political side of the conservative movement had been arrayed in more or less solid opposition to any easing of the laws. But in its issue of December 8, 1972, *National Review* ran an article by conservative youth leader Richard Cowan that argued forcefully for legalization. The editor-in-chief endorsed Cowan's position, at least up to the limit of decriminalizing possession for personal use, and the two senior editors, with some reservations, agreed.

Numbers of conservative intellectuals had long argued that an individual's use of marijuana or other drugs should not be regulated by the state. But from about 1972 on conservative thinkers and political leaders began to adopt the mainstream political position—that legalization was an empirical question, not a philosophical one. The question had to do with the effects of the drug, and not, as in the case of heroin, with the rights of man.

Mr. Cowan argued, as I think he was correct to do, from an empirical standpoint. He advanced nine propositions that he asserted had been "established by responsible scientific inquiry," which, if accepted, would convince any reasonable person that marijuana ought to be at least decriminalized. The import of these propositions was that marijuana used in moderation is harmless, and that its use was so widespread that the state could only do harm by trying to restrict it.

Cowan's article had a tremendous impact. Representatives of the National Association for the Reform of Marijuana Laws (NORML) still speak lovingly of

National Review. Because of this, and because much more evidence about the effects of marijuana is available now than was available in 1972, I think it is worthwhile to review Cowan's article against the current evidence.

The first thing to be said about any attempt to judge whether marijuana is dangerous enough to be legally restricted is that the available evidence can either confuse the issue or illuminate it depending on our own attitudes.

A great number of scientific studies have been done on marijuana since 1972. But for the most part these provide tantalizing but uncoordinated fragments of evidence. Much of the work has been done by independent researchers, many of whom have a crusading attitude toward the drug. Crusaders for different sides distrust each other and almost invariably attack the procedures used by researchers on the other side.

As a result the argument over marijuana, like a number of other current political arguments that revolve around the subtle interaction of psychology and hard science, has degenerated into random volleys of hard scientific fact, with each side having quite enough facts to prove its case except that the opposing side has as many and can prove the opposite. It is like current arguments in economics, in which everyone is armed with scores of statistics that no one believes, but still almost no public commentator is willing to shift the ground of the argument away from the facts and toward more subjective discussions of human nature, where the resolution really lies. Intelligent discussion of the marijuana laws has fallen victim to our fear of the subjective.

To avoid getting caught up in the nearly inevitable arguments over the quality of evidence, almost every assertion of fact in this article is drawn from U.S. Government sources, specifically the National Institute on Drug Abuse. References are given in the exceptional case. I do this not because the government is an inherently trustworthy source, but because NIDA has a history of being very even-handed in its approach to marijuana. In the Sixties and early Seventies, when there was little evidence to back up the fears of marijuana foes, NIDA said as much. In fact, Robert Dupont, NIDA director in the mid-Seventies, supported decriminalization and was widely quoted as saying that marijuana was no more dangerous than alcohol.

More recently, as the evidence has multiplied, NIDA reports have become much more cautionary, though NIDA still refuses to endorse the more extravagant claims of marijuana foes. Those extravagant claims aside, the current evidence indicates that marijuana is more dangerous than Cowan's article indicated. Dupont, by the way, while no longer at NIDA, now opposes decriminalization and predicts that the results of widespread marijuana use will prove to be "horrendous."

Below, a review of Cowan's nine propositions:

1. Marijuana is non-addictive—I use the word technically. It has always been a favorite claim of marijuana supporters that it is not "really" addictive because it doesn't cause withdrawal symptoms. Marijuana is supposedly "only" psychologically addictive. The distinction, with its suggestion that an addiction rooted in the psyche is not serious, has always been foolish. The mistake arises, I think, out of a desire to restrict the argument to "hard" evidence. Psychological addiction seems subjective and "soft."

In any event there is now very strong evidence that marijuana is "technically," to concede Mr. Cowan's usage, addictive, though in fairly subtle ways. NIDA says that "tolerance to cannabis—i.e., diminished response to a given repeated drug dose—is now well established." The old street myth of reverse tolerance—that the effects of the drug grow stronger with repeated use—has been conclusively disproved.

Where you find tolerance, dependence is usually not far behind. NIDA notes that under experimental conditions involving higher doses of marijuana than typically used in the United States, withdrawal symptoms including irritability, restlessness, decreased appetite, sleep disturbance, sweating, tremors, nausea, vomiting, and diarrhea have been observed. Some of the same symptoms were observed in another study in which patients chose their own doses of the drug.

None of this suggests that marijuana can cause the hideous withdrawal symptoms associated with heroin and other dramatically addictive drugs. What it does suggest is that very subtle withdrawal symptoms, perhaps too subtle for the user to associate consciously with the drug, may reinforce a psychological habituation. All habituation is prompted by reward and punishment, pain and pleasure. Marijuana directly stimulates the pleasure centers of the brain. (Alcohol does not.) This would be one of the main causes of any psychological addiction. The subtly unpleasant effects of abstaining after continual heavy use may add to the group of pleasure-pain alternatives that promote habituation to marijuana.

But the real point is that it is the habitual use of a mind-altering drug that is disastrous, rather than any particular basis for the habituation. And the process of becoming an habitual user is far more complex than the marijuana boosters, with their talk of technical addiction, suggest. Gabriel Nahas, a professor of anesthesiology at Columbia, has been eloquent on this point: "The desire for instant gratification is a profound psychological reinforcer. Physical dependence does not develop with central-nervous-system stimulants such as cocaine, which is known to create...one of the most enslaving types of drug dependence. Addiction to a drug is not a function of the ability to produce withdrawal symptoms. Drug dependence results basically from the reproducible interaction between an individual and a pleasure-inducing biologically active molecule. The common denominator of all drug dependence is the psychological reinforcement resulting from reward associated with past [use of the drug] and the subsequent increasing desire for repeated reinforcement."

So much for theory. Are there marijuana addicts? Well, there are American schoolchildren, hundreds of thousands of them, who smoke five or ten joints every day of their lives and devote a very considerable portion of their time and energy to ensuring that they will have a steady supply. If that is not addiction, it will do until the real thing comes along.

2. The use of marijuana does not in itself lead to the use of heroin. A meaningless statement then and now. What "in itself" would lead to the use of heroin? Cowan is like Hume, who couldn't see the causal mechanism when one billiard ball struck another and propelled it across the table. What did he expect to see?

Marijuana is cheap and readily available. It introduces the user to the pleasures of procuring instant gratification from chemicals. It is usually not so strong or disorienting as to frighten the first-time user away from repeated use. In the punishment-reward balance so important to habituation, it beats alcohol hands down—direct stimulation of the pleasure centers, no sickness or noticeable hangovers. It is the ideal beginning to a life of drug abuse, notwithstanding that most occasional users will never so much as see heroin in real life.

Phoenix House is America's largest residential program for the treatment of drug abuse. Of the 15,000 people treated there between 1968 and 1980, nearly all smoked marijuana. Which proves nothing. Except that the longest journey begins with a single step.

3. No one has ever died from an overdose of marijuana. As far as I know, this is true. It does not, as we shall see below, mean that marijuana has not been an agent in many deaths.

4. Marijuana used in moderation *causes no identified physical or mental problems for individuals who are otherwise healthy.* I will deal with mental-health effects, including brain damage, at a later point.

There is no doubt that smoking marijuana has very severe effects on the lungs. The most well-confirmed effects are those other than cancer—inflammation of the lungs, difficulty in breathing, chronic bronchitis, emphysema. Partly because marijuana smoke is so harsh and partly because marijuana smokers typically inhale deeply and retain the smoke for as long as they are able, a single joint may have an effect on the lungs as serious as that of 16 tobacco cigarettes. A U.S. Army study observed emphysema in 18-year-old marijuana smokers, whereas tobacco smokers usually do not develop such conditions until they have smoked for between ten and twenty years.

It has been established that marijuana smoke can produce pre-cancerous conditions in human lung tissue. Marijuana smoke contains larger amounts of cancer-causing hydrocarbons than does tobacco smoke. Cannabis residuals, the equivalent of cigarette "tar," have been shown to be tumor-producing when applied to animals in experiments. There is no firm epidemiological evidence linking marijuana with cancer. It would take twenty years or so to establish such a link. But laboratory evidence suggests that such a link will eventually be found.

Marijuana use increases the heartbeat and can produce angina pectoris in heart-impaired adults after exercise. The effect is more serious than that caused by tobacco smoke. No one with any sort of heart ailment should use marijuana.

There has been a good deal of speculation that marijuana reduces the body's immune response, particularly the formation of white blood cells, thus making the smoker more susceptible to disease. So far the evidence for such an effect in human beings is weak and contradictory. But animal tests have consistently indicated a definite reduction in the immune response.

THC (tetrahydrocannabinol), the most important active ingredient in marijuana, can cross the placental barrier between mother and unborn child. The THC concentrates in the child's fatty tissues, including the brain. THC is definitely carried in mother's milk. There is some disputed evidence that marijuana produces a higher rate of miscarriages and stillbirths in monkeys. Because of the risks to the unborn child, evidence of birth defects is difficult to obtain. But fetal tissue is extremely sensitive to foreign chemicals. Experience has shown that many substances which are safe for adults are teratogenic (capable of producing birth defects). Even NORML agrees that pregnant or nursing women should avoid marijuana.

There is some evidence that heavy marijuana use reduces both male and female fertility. Granted, there are few studies in this area that do not have some defect. One famous study showed a decrease in the level of testosterone (the primary male hormone) in heavy users. But the study has been challenged because of the failure to use adequate control groups and because the testosterone levels, while low, stayed within normal ranges. Still NORML, a hostile witness, summarizes research in this area by saying, "The heavy use of marijuana for long periods of time can temporarily reduce the production of sperm and testosterone."

Another study, showing that female users had an abnormally high rate of defective menstrual cycles, has also been criticized because of defects in the selection of the control group. The most well-documented studies in this area are ones showing abnormalities in the count, mobility, and structure of the sperm of male users. This evidence is strong and backed up by animal studies. There is no proof that the effect persists after use is discontinued.

In short, Cowan's assertion that there are no adverse health effects from marijuana use would be irreponsible if repeated today. But the health effects we have been discussing are also produced by lots of substances conservatives would not want banned by the FDA.

5. Marijuana does not induce criminal behavior or sexual aberration. In fact, it tends in most users to inhibit violence. Again I will aggregate discussion of mental-health effects in one section below. Here I will note that there have been persistent reports from clinical psychologists of impotence in chronic users, though such case histories cannot be considered to be as authoritative as a formal study of the subject. Also, the assertion that "in most users it tends to inhibit violence" is in itself an admission of the powerful effects of the drug. Indeed it should be obvious that marijuana would not be used if it did not have a powerful effect on the brain. But there has been so much rhetoric about marijuana's being a "harmless recreational drug" that the obvious is often overlooked.

6. Marijuana in moderate use *has little effect on the driving ability of experienced users of it—the contrast with the socially equivalent alcohol consumption is to the disadvantage of alcohol.* According to NIDA, "a driver under marijuana's influence is not as likely to lose control of the car" as a driver under the influence of alcohol. But driving- and flight-simulator performance-test results and actual driving behavior "all tend to show significant performance and perceptual deficits" as a result of being high. Marijuana smokers have been found to be over-represented in fatal highway accidents as compared to non-users of the same sex and age group.

The most interesting tests are those which show that experienced pilots who predicted that marijuana would not affect their performance and noticed no deterioration in their performance after using it actually performed markedly less well under the influence of one joint. The danger here is that both driving and flying performance decrements persist even after the feeling of subjective intoxication is gone. The user doesn't have to feel high to be a worse driver. Moreover THC lingers in the body long after the equivalent amount of alcohol has been flushed away.

7. Long-term abuse (gross overuse) should be assumed to be harmful, but in fact there is as yet no conclusive evidence to that effect. In no way a scientific statement. What does Mr. Cowan mean by "long-term abuse (gross overuse)" if he doesn't think that "long-term abuse (gross overuse)" is harmful? It has been a consistent tactic of the marijuana advocates to obscure the common-sense objections to the use of the drug with pseudo-scientific appeals to the legal standard of reasonable doubt. This may be a necessary consequence of having to argue for the drug's legality by proving its harmlessness.

There is a science-fiction tale set at a future time when all drug addiction has been eliminated—or rather, replaced. The new addiction is to direct electrical stimulation of the pleasure centers of the brain. There are no side effects, physical addiction, withdrawal agonies, or any other health effects whatsoever. All the addict gets is what he wants in its most pure, uncorrupted form. But he spends his whole life getting it. Which brings us to the real objection to marijuana use.

8. The moderate use of marijuana does not lead to changes in social behavior or to a loss of motivation. It may correspond with an observable change in people's lives but it is not the cause of that change.

9. Twenty-five million people use or have used marijuana. Marijuana is readily available today to anyone of minimum ingenuity who looks for it. A few facts:

Nearly fifty million Americans have now tried marijuana, but it is among young people that its use is growing most rapidly. The overwhelming majority of chronic users are under age twenty-five.

According to 1980 figures, 10 percent of high-school seniors were daily users averaging 3.25 joints a day. (The 10 percent figure may be slightly lower today.) Other recent figures showed approximately 15 percent of 14- to 15-year-olds as current though not daily users. Similar sets of statistics show a consistent picture—marijuana use is much more prevalent among young people today than in the early Seventies.

The marijuana smoked in the U.S. today is usually imported and has a far higher THC content than the domestic marijuana usually smoked here in the Sixties. It may be as much as ten or twenty times as potent.

As mentioned earlier, THC lingers in the body: 30 to 50 per cent of the THC may remain a week after the marijuana is smoked. Someone who smokes even once or twice a week is never entirely free of it. A daily user may always be either under the influence of the drug (though he will not always feel high) or withdrawing from it.

As was pointed out in a recent paper from the Heritage Foundation, the first professionals to challenge seriously the late-Sixties consensus that marijuana was harmless were clinical psychiatrists, usually associated with school or college health programs. These clinicians, who come into daily contact with chronic marijuana users, have described the psychological effects of the drug in remarkably consistent terms. Louis J. West of the Department of Psychiatry at the University of Oklahoma Medical Center observed numbers of students who were suffering the effects of chronic use as typically described by school psychiatrists. He describes the symptoms of chronic use as "diminished drive, lessened ambition, decreased motivation, apathy, shortened attention span, distractibility, poor judgment, impaired communication skills, less effectiveness, magical thinking, derealization, depersonalization, diminished capacity to carry out complex plans or prepare realistically for the future, a peculiar fragmentation in the flow of thought, habit deterioration, and progressive loss of insight." He concluded, "There is a clinical impression of organicity to this syndrome that I simply cannot explain away."

Other symptoms include short-term memory loss, decrease in logical skills and speaking in non-sequiturs, follow-the-leader behavior, and tendencies to paranoia. This last often focuses on the use of the drug itself. A chronic user will often become angry at the suggestion that the drug is having a harmful effect on him. Vigorous denials of addiction are common among users who have smoked continuously for three or four years and are very unwilling to stop.

The psychological effects of the drug are particularly dangerous for children and adolescents. Dr. Nahas again: "Chemical stimulation of the pleasure centers endangers the adolescent's chance to develop his own natural resources for joy and emotional stability. Fooled by the effects of a drug, he is unable to judge either the extent or the consequences of his 'habit.' " A NIDA spokesman on younger users: "Their lives seem to narrow in focus, as they become more preoccupied with the rituals of drug use and with drug-using friends. The youngster may frequently be fatigued, depressed, and moody. S/he may have a tendency toward paranoia....Mood-altering drugs provide a quick and simple escape from the stresses that are a normal part of growing up. A youngster who continually blots out pain, boredom, or frustration never learns to cope with them....Being stoned is a self-absorbing, self-limiting, anti-social experience." Again this is common sense.

It is an obvious disaster for a young person at that critical time of figuring out the world to be continually exposed to delusional thinking.

Early on in the marijuana debate, the symptoms we have been discussing were lumped together and identified by marijuana foes as the "amotivational syndrome," by which they meant a specific mental-health effect with its physiological basis in THC's interaction with the brain. In the words of Kolansky and Moore, two Philadelphia psychiatrists who pioneered this area, it is "a *specific* and *separate* clinical syndrome....a toxic reaction in the central nervous system due to regular use of marijuana and hashish." Marijuana advocates have vigorously denied the existence of any such specific syndrome. Whether these symptoms are part of a specific syndrome based on toxic reaction to THC or whether they are simply the accumulated effects of continually putting the brain out to pasture is not an unimportant question. But neither answer is reassuring.

One indication of a specific syndrome based in physiological damage rather than subjective reactions would be persistence of the symptoms. A number of clinicians have reported lasting deficiencies in intellectual functioning among former chronic smokers. There is also experimental evidence from several sources for changes in brain-cell structure as a result of exposure to marijuana.

Robert Heath, Chairman of the Department of Psychiatry and Neurology at Tulane University Medical School, has detected permanent changes in the deep brain areas of rhesus monkeys that smoked daily for six months. The deep brain areas are thought to affect the emotions, behavior, and pleasure reactions. Heath's technique is controversial, and, like most studies in the field, his has been criticized. Among other problems, his technique is too dangerous to use on human beings, and the effects he describes cannot be detected by safer methods. But Heath has answered the most important criticisms, and his work seems to stand up.

Specific syndrome or no, all these elements—the persistence of THC in the body, its direct stimulation of the pleasure centers, its other pleasant delusional effects, mild withdrawal symptoms, paranoia about criticism of marijuana use, etc.—are potential building-blocks of a self-perpetuating chronic use of the drug. And however much the advocates of marijuana deny its mental-health effects, the drug culture itself confirms them. Chronic users are "potheads"—and everyone knows what *they* are like. Potheads can't remember anything, they care about little other than getting stoned, they do badly at school or at work. They are clannish and paranoid. They are—drug addicts, at least temporarily; "burnouts," useless, boring, empty-headed, irrational, stupid, and not fit to function as responsible adults, especially in a democracy. Although potheads are not typical of pot smokers generally, anyone under the age of 35 can testify, on the basis of personal experience, to the truth of the above description.

The very occasional use of marijuana is probably no more harmful than many other (quite legal) activities. Still, if the evidence available today about the dangers of frequent use had been available 15 years ago, the argument that marijuana should be legal because it is harmless would never have gotten off the ground. Moreover, the special dangers for young users and the prospect of 10 to 15 percent of the adolescent population being too doped up to mature normally or get an education certainly justify, in theory, state intervention.

On the other hand, use by an adult and sale by adults to adults are not such serious matters as to justify arrest or even lesser legal penalties. (Chronic use by adults is quite a serious matter, but it isn't practical to forbid only chronic use.) Nor is there evidence that stricter laws against marijuana would be effective. Use among children has gone up since decriminalization has become common. But there is not enough evidence to link the events. Certainly marijuana use was widespread even when it was more illegal than it is today. As for forbidding use by children and legalizing it for adults, that hasn't worked very well for alcohol or tobacco.

Which leaves conservatives where? With a situation they may find unpalatable but should not find surprising. Marijuana was freely available in the United States for most of our history. It was rarely used. Now it is being used in large amounts. That is cause for alarm but there is probably no political solution, or at least no direct one. We can speculate about public policies that may indirectly encourage drug use, but there is no particular reason to believe that the government can mount a "program" to solve the marijuana problem. Like any number of current tendencies toward stupid, superficial, mind-blanking hedonism, it may continue unabated. The reasons why a very large percentage of the people in a society should all of a sudden decide they want to spend lots of time in a dream world are, after all, mysterious. In the meantime, we can do our bit for clear thinking by reminding people that it is the dream world itself, not any side effects of entering it, that is the real enemy.

ISSUE 3 YES:

Marijuana Should Be Legalized

Richard C. Cowan

Mr. Vigilante uses the "marijuana isn't harmless as everyone thought" strawman that has served the supporters of marijuana prohibition remarkably well for ten years. By characterizing the opponents of marijuana prohibition as "marijuana boosters" or "advocates," he ignores what I called my "thesis," which is that the *laws against marijuana are more harmful than it is, and in fact make it more harmful than it would be if it were legal.*

I was and am in favor of the legalization of marijuana, but not because I thought in 1972 or think now that it is "harmless." Nothing is harmless to everyone or at every dosage level. Neither I nor the National Organization for the Reform of Marijuana Laws (NORML) claims that marijuana is harmless, nor have we *ever* based our arguments for "decriminalization" or legalization on that premise.

Why, then, did I begin the article with nine assertions of fact about marijuana? Well, it is necessary to remember the temper of the times. Back in 1972, most conservatives believed that one puff on a joint made you an addict first of pot and finally of the *inevitable heroin,* and then, if you didn't commit suicide, or get killed in a car wreck, or die of some hideous brain disease, you became a Democrat. This, after all, was what we were told by the "narcotics" bureaucracy, our recognized experts.

The fact is that the "narcotics" bureaucrats had been making a variety of wild claims about the perils of pot for decades, making it virtually impossible to do research on the subject. Today, since they can no longer block all research on the drug, the narcocrats simply sponsor ideologically reliable researchers who can be counted on to produce politically useful results. And conservatives generally swallow it whole, because they do not apply to marijuana the same high intellectual standards with which they analyze other subjects, nor do they apply the same standards to the laws against it that they apply to other laws.

I am unwilling to concede that the National Institute on Drug Abuse is an unbiased source, but would recommend the February 1982 report of the National Academy of Sciences/Institute of Medicine, *Marijuana and Health.* It is certainly not "pro-pot," but it is pro-science. And it does not support any of Mr. Vigilante's more extreme claims. Of even greater interest is the National Research Council report of June 21, 1982, which was promptly suppressed by the narcocracy because it questions the efficacy of marijuana prohibition and advocates complete decriminalization and the consideration of legalization, while specifically stating that "marijuana is not harmless."

Now on to Mr. Vigilante's specifics—his responses to my original points.

1. Is marijuana addictive? Of course marijuana is "habit-forming," or, if one must sound sinister, "psychologically addictive." Almost everything pleasant is habit-forming. Television, for example.

Mr. Vigilante is correct in saying it is now established that marijuana tolerance does develop. However, there is some evidence that tolerance develops much more rapidly for pure THC, the principal psychoactive ingredient, than for the weed itself. This is a major problem in the attempt to use THC as a substitute for marijuana in either research or therapy.

In practice, an experienced smoker does not require massive doses to get high, and tolerance does not always lead to dependence. Indeed, there are many poisons and allergens to which people may develop "tolerance," but certainly not dependence. By the time I finish this I may even develop a tolerance for Mr. Vigilante.

What the highly politicized Dr. Nahas seems to be saying is that addiction comes from the carrot of pleasure rather than from the stick of withdrawal. This may be polemically necessary, since marijuana withdrawal is at worst a small stick, but it is also a redefinition of addiction that is certainly not widely accepted—nor is the existence of a "pleasure center" in the brain.

The 1982 NAS report mentioned above says: "Cannabis dependence does not mean the same thing as cannabis addiction. Dependence means only that a withdrawal syndrome can occur when drug-taking is stopped. Addiction implies compulsive behavior to acquire the drug." In fact almost any activity, e.g., handwashing, can become the object of compulsive behavior, but, as even Mr. Vigilante acknowledges, in terms of "addiction" marijuana doesn't compare with heroin, or the barbiturates, which was my point in 1972. Incidentally, it also does not compare with either alcohol or tobacco.

2. I have never played billiards with Hume, but I have no difficulty with cause and effect. Post pot ergo propter pot may be the longest-running classifiable logical fallacy in contemporary political folklore. Of course most heroin addicts had previously used marijuana. The logically relevant question is how many pot smokers become heroin addicts and why.

Back in 1972 the narcocrats told us that "marijuana leads to heroin" because after a while the marijuana "addict" can't get high enough on mere marijuana, so he goes on to the hard stuff. I know at least one judge who used this as an excuse to send pot smokers to prison. Why not, since they were all going to be heroin addicts anyway?

What is interesting here is Mr. Vigilante's line of reasoning. "[Marijuana] introduces the user to the pleasures of procuring instant gratification from chemicals." Nonsense. What about aspirin, for fast, fast, fast relief? Or Speedy Alka Seltzer? Or the rush for the morning's first cigarette? Or nasal sprays? Or alcohol?

"[Marijuana] is usually not so strong or disorienting as to frighten the first-time user away from repeated use." In fact, many first-time users do not even get high. Many find it unpleasant. After all, marijuana is, as Mr. Vigilante says, "cheap and readily available," and the law is demonstrably not an effective deterrent, but most people still do not smoke. Pot "beats alcohol hands down," but there are four times as many drinkers as pot smokers. Obviously, most first-time users of alcohol are not deterred from continued use.

The NAS report says, "The use of marijuana follows that of alcohol and tobacco. It is preceded by acceptance of a cluster of beliefs and values that often reflect disavowal of many standards upheld by adults." The behavioral deterioration commonly associated with drug abuse often *precedes* the drug abuse, but of course is aggravated by it.

So why do we say that a life of drug abuse begins with marijuana and not alcohol? Because that is where we arbitrarily draw the line that makes both marijuana and heroin illegal. The law creates the only real connection: both are on Schedule One of the Controlled Substances Act. That is another story, but I do detect certain elements of cause and effect. Hume must have been a very bad pool player.

3. The fact that no one has ever died from a marijuana overdose was perhaps more important in 1972 than today, but it does indicate the low toxicity of the drug. Thousands of people die every year from overdoses of aspirin, Darvon, alcohol, and of course tranquilizers, as well as heroin and cocaine. As for marijuana's being an "agent" in many deaths, perhaps, but Mr. Vigilante never gets around to introducing any hard evidence.

4. Marijuana used in moderation *causes no identifiable physical or mental problems for individuals who are otherwise healthy.* At the risk of appearing "irresponsible," I think that this is still generally true, with the important qualification that some individuals may be sensitive to substances in doses that are innocuous to most. Some people should abstain from even the smallest doses of any psychoactive drug.

Now on to the lungs. Obviously any kind of smoke will at some level have an adverse effect on the respiratory system. However, Mr. Vigilante's statement that "there is no doubt that smoking marijuana has very severe effects on the lungs" simply is not true for any level of usage that could be considered moderate, including daily use.

His statement that a single joint may have an effect on the lungs as serious as that of 16 tobacco cigarettes is a distortion of a study by Donald Tashkin of UCLA. Tashkin was referring to one effect—impeding air flow—not to overall lung damage. None of his subjects had any serious respiratory problems. Moreover, Tashkin said, "we are not suggesting that smoking marijuana...will necessarily produce symptomatic or disabling respiratory impairment." Mr. Vigilante needs to learn that the narcocracy is not above quoting authorities out of context, even reversing the implications of their research.

It is true that marijuana smoke contains 25 percent more "cancer-causing hydrocarbons than does tobacco smoke," but this difference is not significant given that all but the heaviest marijuana smokers consume far less smoke than even moderate tobacco smokers. Of course, if one drew the incorrect inference that one joint equaled 16 cigarettes instead of one and a quarter...

Incidentally, the respiratory risk associated with smoking marijuana might be significantly reduced by using a water-pipe. However, the latest triumph of the War on Drugs, in Texas and several other states, is the outlawing of water-pipes because they are drug paraphernalia!

5. Again I must refer to the context of 1972, when "sexual aberration" meant rape, not impotence. This was a part of the Reefer Madness type of propaganda. For many years it was claimed that marijuana caused criminal insanity, with extremely violent and brutal crimes.

Mr. Vigilante says: "The assertion 'that in most users it tends to inhibit violence' is in itself an admission of the powerful effects of the drug." That seems to be reading a lot into a little. All that this means is that people who are smoking are usually less rowdy than people who are drinking.

Mr. Vigilante says: "It should be obvious that marijuana would not be used if it did not have a powerful effect on the brain." Well, what is it supposed to affect? The feet? As to its being "powerful," the effect is dose-related. Small doses have a small effect, and large doses have more.

6. Here our differences would be quibbling.

7. Mr. Vigilante says: "It has been a consistent tactic of the marijuana advocates to obscure the common-sense objections to the use of the drug with pseudo-scientific appeals to the legal standard of reasonable doubt. This may be a necessary consequence of having to argue for the drug's legality by proving its harmlessness." What this tells me is that Mr. Vigilante seems never to have read—or at least understood—anything by anyone favoring legalization. Once again, our premise is *not* that marijuana is harmless.

8. This point, more than any of the others, illuminates the context of 1972, the "late hippie" period. The social turmoil of the period from, say, 1964 to 1974 was extraordinary, and marijuana was often blamed for what people saw. Well, as Mr. Vigilante observes, marijuana is more prevalent than ever, but Ronald Reagan now occupies the White House and the campuses are covered with alligator shirts.

The people who started smoking in college in the Sixties as "revolutionaries" are now "establishment" executives and professionals, and many of them still smoke, although generally without the knowledge of their senior partners. There is a great deal more smoke than kinky sex in the closets of America.

I cannot let pass without comment his list of other symptoms of chronic use: "short-term memory loss, decrease in logical skills and speaking in non-sequiturs, follow-the-leader behavior, and tendencies to paranoia." This would also be an excellent description of conservatives *discussing* marijuana. They forget that the government tells them something different about pot every few years, and never ask what happened to the old horror stories.

Speaking of "paranoia," I am reminded of what Henry Kissinger said about a well-known non–pot-smoker: "Even paranoiacs have real enemies." Several million of these "paranoid" potheads have been arrested and even kept in prison for long periods of time. Mr. Vigilante cites paranoia about criticism of marijuana use as a symptom of chronic users. Since this criticism is used as an excuse for putting chronic users in jail, is it really paranoia?

Now, if I may, I would like to explain what I consider to be the principal dangers of marijuana for children and adults.

First, for children there may be greater physical dangers than for adults. For example, around the time of puberty any disturbance in hormone levels could have serious consequences. Some studies have indicated that moderately heavy smoking can reduce testosterone levels temporarily to a low/normal level. This would be of little importance to *most* adults, but for *some* children it might have permanent consequences, which, given the different rates of maturation, might not be immediately apparent. This is not to say that one joint and Junior is a permanent soprano, or Susie will grow a beard. Whatever the risk may be it is dose-related. The more the child smokes, the greater the risk.

Obviously, with heavy smoking there might be some immediately apparent, and probably reversible, respiratory problems, but generally speaking, I would be more concerned about the development of the child's mental processes. A person under the influence of marijuana can still think and deal with the real world. However, marijuana does alter consciousness in such a way as to encourage nonlinear thought. If a person has a good understanding of the real world, if he is mature, experienced, educated, and skilled at linear thought, this state may not be dangerous. In fact it may be useful. It offers the possibility of new perspectives—which should subsequently be analyzed when not stoned.

Being stoned may also reduce the critical faculties, in the sense that one is apt to be more enthusiastic about things than when "straight." Since much humor is based on incongruity, things may seem very funny, especially to the inexperienced user.

It should be obvious that while there is nothing terribly sinister about all of this, it could pose serious problems for children, for the immature of all ages, and for people who just do not think very well. The effect is again dose-related. The more one smokes, the greater the effect. The longer one stays stoned, the less frequently one can align oneself with the linear real world.

Smoking, as Mr. Vigilante says, is also used to escape the pain of the real world, especially the problems of growing up. Children certainly need to learn to deal with life's problems without sedation, and being stoned may very well make things worse. Still, as a teacher of troubled children said to me once, "If I had all of their problems I might get stoned, too." It is often rightly observed that drug abuse causes problems in the schools, but the degree to which problems in the schools cause drug abuse is seldom appreciated. However, it is easier to blame drugs than to confront the more basic problems.

Frankly, I am confused by Mr. Vigilante's conclusions. First, he says that if we knew then what he thinks he knows now, the argument that marijuana "should be legal because it is harmless would never have gotten off the ground." Then he says, "On the other hand, use by an adult and sale by adults to adults are not such serious matters as to justify arrest or even lesser legal penalties." In other words, it's "harmless" enough to be legal?

He correctly observes that it would not be practical to outlaw only "chronic" use. "Nor is there evidence that stricter laws against marijuana would be effective." Texas presents remarkable evidence of the failure of very harsh laws to deter. As he says, "marijuana use was widespread even when it was more illegal than it is today." Indeed this was the period of most rapid growth.

If we were to take the resources wasted on keeping marijuana from adults and redirect them toward keeping it from children, legalization might even reduce the availability of pot in the schools.

Mr. Vigilante arrives at no specific conclusion, so I will now try to explain what I think the conservative position on marijuana and the laws should be, and why.

The reasons why marijuana should be legalized, with conservative leadership, are fairly simple and straightforward. And they have nothing to do with marijuana's being "harmless."

Conservatives generally understand, as liberals often do not, that laws can have an effect opposite to that which is intended. Price controls can aggravate inflation. Busing for racial balance has caused more segregation. Legislated equality creates greater inequality. Similarly, because of its prohibition, marijuana—the most popular illicit drug by far—is thrown into the same distribution channels and cultural milieu as other, much more dangerous substances. The finite resources devoted to suppressing marijuana are hence not available for the suppression of these more dangerous substances, or for just keeping all drugs away from children, who are supposedly our primary concern. (Although, in fact, marijuana use by children seems to have reached the saturation point and started declining—in spite of, rather than because of, prohibition.) Contraband marijuana will always be of uncertain potency and purity, especially by the time it reaches children, the least sophisticated buyers.

At the same time, the profits from the marijuana traffic are an important contribution to the underworld. The enforcement of the marijuana laws is a substantial burden on the criminal-justice system and a major source of police corruption. A large number of people have been drawn into an illegal industry, and more than twenty million people regularly do business with them. This must undermine their respect for the law in general.

Meanwhile, marijuana is more easily acquired by a 16-year-old who should not use it than by a sixty-year-old cancer or glaucoma patient who needs it. Marijuana is not perfect in its therapeutic applications, but for many people it is the only thing that will stave off blindness, agony, even death. Nothing so clearly demonstrates the limited vision of some anti-marijuana crusaders than the legal and bureaucratic interference with its medical use. There are specific legislative remedies for this problem, but they are opposed by the supporters of prohibition for ideological reasons. Conservatives should, at the very least, endorse the use of marijuana for medical reasons, instead of attacking it as "the back door to legalization."

In general, the politicization of drug research undermines the credibility of valid drug information. In the short run, untrue but frightening reports about the dire effects of pot may result in reduced consumption. In the long run, these reports will be seen to be false, and users will, in reaction, disbelieve even the reports that are true. Even worse, warnings about the effects of other drugs also lose credibility, with most unfortunate consequences. Statements such as "marijuana is the most dangerous drug" are not just harmless hyperbole—they necessarily imply that angel dust, speed, and heroin are "safer."

Some supporters of marijuana prohibition argue that the legalization of sale or cultivation, or even the decriminalization of simple possession, will convey the message, especially to children, that marijuana is "harmless." These people, carried away by their own polemics, have thus attributed a meaning to changing the marijuana laws that in the contemporary American context is unique, with legality implying both safety and sanctity, not only for adults but also *especially for children.*

The first thing to understand is that while questioning the validity of reports on the dangers of marijuana does not imply that marijuana is "harmless," it must raise questions about the veracity of the anti-marijuana crusaders at some level.

Consider the implications of what I am saying, if I am correct. The narcotics police are an enormous, corrupt international bureaucracy with billion-dollar budgets, and multibillion-dollar graft opportunities. They have lied to us for fifty years about the effects of marijuana and now fund a coterie of researchers who provide them with "scientific" support. Some of these people are fanatics who distort the legitimate research of others for propaganda purposes.

I realize that this is much more extreme than saying that marijuana is harmless, which, again, it is not. If I am right, then the anti-marijuana propaganda campaign is a cancerous tissue of lies undermining law enforcement, aggravating the drug problem, depriving the sick of needed help, and suckering in well-intentioned conservatives like Mr. Vigilante, and countless frightened parents.

I conclude my response to Mr. Vigilante with a challenge to all the supporters of marijuana prohibition for a full-scale debate of the real issues involved here. First, of course, is what are the real effects, and dangers, of marijuana? But also, what are the lies that have been and are being told about it, and why are they being told? Also we must discuss the overall drug problem, including alcoholism. And last but not least, we must discuss the effects of prohibition on law enforcement, the corruption of the narcotics police, and the intrinsically immoral methods that are routinely, and necessarily, used to enforce the laws.

ISSUE 4

Are Gay Teachers Dangerous Role Models?

Attitudes toward homosexuality have changed through the ages. In preliterate societies, exclusive homosexual relationships seem to have been uncommon. Studies, however, have indicated that a majority of these societies at least tolerated homosexual relationships, usually between mature males and boys. Homosexual relations between men were considered a high form of emotional expression during the classical Greek era* and were also an accepted pattern of behavior in ancient Rome. The ancient Hebrews, on the other hand, seem to have been almost homophobic. Following in the Hebrew tradition, a number of early Christian writers condemned homosexuality. Paul, in the First Letter to the Corinthians, wrote that males who "abused themselves" with other males would not inherit the kingdom of God.

From the middle ages to modern times, Western society has been generally negative about homosexuality. In the past, many Europeans were put to death for homosexual acts. British law mandated the death penalty for anal intercourse until 1861. U.S. laws have also been fairly harsh in dealing with homosexuality. These laws typically make various acts illegal, but not homosexuality. Thus, one could be an admitted homosexual but not

*For additional information see, Vern L. Bullough, *Sexual Variance in Society and History*. Chicago: University of Chicago Press, 1976.

break the law unless one of the forbidden acts occurred. Frequently, such acts are not specified but fall under catch-all terms such as *crime against nature* or *unnatural act.*

The enforcement of these and other laws relating to sexual acts depends to a great degree on time and place. One locality will ignore the laws while another will attempt vigorous enforcement. During the early 1960s, the state of Florida formed a legislative committee modeled after Joe McCarthy's Un-American Activities Committee. The Florida committee searched the state for communists and came up empty-handed. In what many people believe was an attempt to legitimize itself, the committee changed its focus to homosexuality. Most estimates put the percentage of the adult male population who are exclusively homosexuals at 2 to 4 percent. Therefore, an investigative unit will nearly always be able to find homosexuals in any sizeable population of males. The committee was named after a former Florida governor and legislator named Johns and became popularly known as the "Johns" committee. The primary technique used by the investigators was to hang around public "johns" peeping through holes in the stalls. A number of faculty members at various educational institutions were forced out of their jobs as a result of such public restroom investigations. Selective enforcement of sex laws and discrimination against those in such vulnerable populations who vary from the sexual norms continues.

Since the 1950s, there have been a number of states and localities that have modified their laws against homosexual acts and in a number of instances created laws protecting the rights of homosexuals. These changes have come about in part because of a changing social climate which made people more tolerant of diverse life styles and less likely to discriminate against people who fall into a minority status. Additionally, gay activist groups have exerted political pressure in some areas as their numbers have grown. There is, however, a fear that remains for many gays concerning the consequences of "coming out." There are a number of localities that still discriminate against gays, particularly those who are teachers.

Anita Bryant was best known as a singer and spokeswoman for the Florida Citrus Commission until the late 1970s. At that point, she and her husband got involved in an attempt to overturn a Dade County, Florida, ordinance that banned discrimination against gays in housing and employment. In the bitter battle that followed, Bryant raised the issue of gay teachers and the Biblical injunction against sodomy. As a result of the Dade County fight, Bryant and her husband formed a fundamentalist organization, Protect Our Children, which was to spearhead a nationwide campaign. Since that time, the organization has folded. In the debate that follows, Bryant argues that gays are dangerous role models who may influence the sexual orientation of the young. She also delves into child pornography and suggests that children are under greater sexual threat from gay teachers. Peter Fisher counters the argument that gays are inappropriate role models and argues that children face equal or greater sexual threat from heterosexual male teachers.

ISSUE 4 YES:

Homosexual Teachers: Are They Dangerous Role Models?

Anita Bryant

"Most gay people as they grow up—in their church, school and home—are not aware of any gay adult, so they have no model. Most homosexuals think they are the only ones in the world, that they are absolutely isolated and, therefore, they grow up with all sorts of feelings of self-doubt and even self-hatred. It would be so important that there be some gay teachers in the schools who could serve as models for that one in ten children who is gay."

That is the statement made by Father John J. McNeill, a Jesuit priest who was introduced on "The Phil Donahue Show" as "the moral theologian, one of the founders of the New York chapter of 'Dignity,' an organization of Catholic homosexuals, and presently a student at the Institute of Religion and Health in New York." Phil brought him on the show to present "the other side of the theological viewpoint," since Father McNeill is also the author of a very controversial book, *The Church and the Homosexual.*

After Father McNeill made the statement quoted above, Phil Donahue quickly stated, "That is the sticky point, for if those teachers are going to be models, those people who are on the other side of this spectrum are going to come right back at you and say, 'We got you now because you are admitting that these people can be role models, so why are they also not going to be role models for heterosexuals who are going to admire them and then think they are wonderful and say why don't we try it?' "

Father McNeill's answer was, "We have had heterosexual role models for that one out of every ten homosexual children for centuries and it never changed them. Sexuality is given and is unchangeable, and as they grow up they become aware of what their sexuality is. If homosexuals, they need a role model of how to live out a good life as a homosexual."

My primary concern was voiced as a mother, not as an entertainer. Known homosexual schoolteachers and their possible role-model impact tore at my heart in a way I could not ignore. Two things in particular troubled me. First, public approval of admitted homosexual teachers could encourage more homosexuality by inducing pupils into looking upon it as an acceptable life-style. And second, a particularly deviant-minded teacher could sexually molest children. These were possibilities I was unwilling to risk. Added to these concerns was my deep-rooted biblical orientation which condemns the act of homosexuality. For me not to have stood up in protest would have been something my conscience could not tolerate. I had that right as a mother, a citizen, a voter, and a tax-paying resident of Dade County.

The homosexual community rhetoric made it appear that I had unfounded fears. But there are men of science who do agree with my views. Dr. Herbert Hendin, Director of Psychosocial Studies at the Center for Policy Research in New York, reminds us that society has a stake in heterosexuality and the family, as well as a responsibility to insure that homosexuals who are performing their jobs are not harassed or fired for their sexual lives. He does emphasize, however, that this does not mean that we have to approve of militant homosexuals' demands to teach children that homosexuality is an acceptable alternate life-style or to teach homosexual sex-education classes in public schools on a par with heterosexual sex-education classes. Doctor Hendin wrote this in 1975 for the New York *Times*.

Doctor Shirley Van Ferney, who counsels troubled adolescents and is a member of the psychiatric staff at New Jersey's Medical Center in Princeton, advises parents to fight the militant homosexuals' demands. She warns:

> Homosexuality should be put back in the closet where it belongs... the gay rights movement sweeping the U.S. is a threat to the nation's children.
>
> *Constant media coverage of the gays has made their life-style appear to be commonplace and acceptable rather than unusual and deviant....* This is particularly disturbing to those who are concerned that their children could easily be misled into thinking that homosexuality is an attractive kind of life-style to adopt.
>
> *Parents are absolutely correct to be fearful of the effects all of this is having on their kids....*
>
> Homosexuals are so active on high-school and college campuses that there is hardly a child in America who has not been exposed to their influence.
>
> You have a right to raise decent children in a decent society. *But that right will be taken away from you unless you make yourself heard.* If parents capitulate to the homosexual influences which surround them, society as we know it will be destroyed.

New York psychiatrist Charles Socarides says homosexuality flies in the face of the one fact we know, which is that male and female are programmed to mate with the opposite sex. This is the story of two and a half billion years of civilization, and any society that hopes to survive will have to recognize this. He further declares:

> There's no doubt in my mind that if homosexuality is further normalized and raised to a level of complete social acceptability, *there will be a tremendous rise in the incidence of homosexuality*.
>
> It would have dire effects for society.
>
> Homosexuality militates against the family, drives the sexes in opposite directions and neglects the child's growth and sexual identity.

Doctor Samuel Silverman, associate professor of psychiatry at Harvard Medical School, urged parents to "protest vigorously if any of their children's teachers are professed homosexuals." He said what others of us have been saying all along—it's admirable to be tolerant and sensitive to people's civil rights, but what the militant homosexuals are seeking *cannot be classified as legitimate civil rights*—and "a homosexual teacher who flaunts his sexual aberrations publicly is as dangerous to children as one of the religious cultists." This psychiatrist underscores what those of us who stood in protest feel so strongly—the militant "gays" are not fighting for their own civil rights but are, in actuality, *attempting to win converts to their way of life*.

The National Observer explored the subject of whether or not homosexual teachers are dangerous role models and described California's current superintendent, Wilson Riles, as being "one of the few school administrators who will discuss the issue on the record. He acknowledges gay rights under the law, but draws the line at advocacy." Riles explains: "When you have a teacher who becomes an advocate of his or her own sexual behavior, this goes beyond why that person was hired....It then becomes an exhibitionist situation. It's really not our job to try and justify any kind of sexual behavior."

Another Californian who backed our stand was U.S. Senator S.I. Hayakawa who believes it's all right for employers to refuse hiring homosexuals because of sexual preference. "Civil rights doesn't entitle a person to a job and never has. I would be very, very hesitant to allow homosexuals in the teaching profession," the seventy-year-old former educator added. He said he would have voted with us to repeal the Dade County ordinance.

In all the exchanges of words there was one thing frequently overlooked—children have rights, too. In describing the boldness of the libertines, one editor expressed the belief that it is perhaps not coincidental that as the more liberal life-styles come into the open, divorce rates soar, leaving the debris of human tragedy behind to suffer. The debris? Our children. His column reported:

> A Grand Jury in Florida indicted the headmaster and a group of homosexual teachers for recruiting and sexually abusing students in a private school. This goes a long way toward proving homosexuals DO recruit and DO prefer their partners young. Thus we believe Miss Bryant's group, "Save Our Children," is aptly named.

My files are daily increasing in size as material reaches me confirming that children are being lured into homosexual activity in schools by homosexual teachers.

It was Gables Youth Resource Officer Tony Raimondo and Officer Steve Spooner along with John Sorenson who took special interest in our Miami situation and brought many such cases to our attention.

> A lot of regular people have the general attitude of "live-and-let-live" about homosexuality. People generally presume that in the homosexual world, it's a case of a couple of guys living together and not bothering anybody.
>
> That simply is not the case.
>
> A couple of guys might live together for a while, but eventually one of them is going to get tired of it and go out looking for new kicks. He will go looking for a boy; he will start occupying bus station rest rooms or whatever, or will become a Boy Scout or Cub Scout leader.
>
> We've found them in the Big Brother programs, among the staffs of youth centers, in the Foster Home program.
>
> I will say that no community, in Dade County or anywhere in the country, is unaffected.

Actually, enough material has been gathered for a complete book on the subject of child pornography and sexual exploitation of children. The Washington *Star* (April 11, 1977) reports that children have become commodities and are bought, sold and traded for the financial gain of involved adults. This newspaper states that child porn peddlers are aided in their efforts by such groups as the American Civil Liberties Union (ACLU), which believes censorship of such material violates the First Amendment protecting free speech. The horror described by a Los Angeles police officer when he saw a photo of a man about thirty and an eight-year-old boy performing sex, was akin to what I felt upon opening the mail in our home in the early days of the Miami battle.

> "What put me to work," said Lloyd Martin (head of a special six-officer unit with the L.A. Police Department that deals with sexual exploitation of children) "was one picture....The look on that boy's face...No amount of words can describe it. It wasn't fear. It was more a look of 'somebody help me.'..."
>
> In order for pornography to survive, there must be a new product. They'll do anything to make that almighty buck.
>
> Authorities say that perhaps 70 percent of the child porn market now involves young boys—"chickens" in the vernacular—and adult male homosexuals. A vast and well-organized network caters to the "chicken" trade with books, movies and boy prostitutes....
>
> Equally depressing is the ultimate effect of this activity on the children themselves. Those studying the problem feel the children will suffer lasting harmful effects and...will probably grow up and become sexual abusers themselves.
>
> Said Dr. Vincent Fontana, a child sex abuse expert at New York's Foundling Hospital: "There is a great deal of psychological scarring of these kids, and God only knows where they will end up...."

Morrie Ryskind, writing in the Los Angeles *Herald-Examiner*, pokes fun in a sad sort of way at the local jet set for whom homosexuality is considered "in." He speaks of one such individual who lauded a TV film on the subject as a "towering achievement of sensitivity." Ryskind's reaction was that it was "a sleazy tale. Towering achievement, my foot. This was a wretched bore." Ryskind reported that the general manager of the TV station said he had no qualms about showing the film at 8:00 P.M. when children could view it, because he felt it would provide "greater understanding and acceptance of homosexuals by all ages." Ryskind continued, "Now I can respect the quiet gays—but not the flaunters. I resent the attempt to make it appear to impressionable youngsters that the gay life is equal to or perhaps superior to the norm...." He calls their efforts "phoney semantics," and ended his column by saying, "...one vote for Anita Bryant."

The Chicago *Tribune* presented a series of four exhaustive articles dealing with the subject of child pornography and ran headlines on one front page, SICKNESS FOR SALE. Among other shocking things they labeled what was happening to children as "emotional and spiritual murder."

> A nationwide homosexual ring with headquarters in Chicago has been trafficking in young boys....The ring is masterminded by...a convicted sodomist....His closest associate is a convicted murderer and thief.

The report included the story of Gerald S. Richards, one of the midwest's leading child pornographers, and described him as "a flesh profiteer who fed off the young, who filmed, processed and sold child pornography film, who sold the sexual services of his young male models....For all anyone knew, he was a schoolteacher."

More than ten years ago the Miami *Herald* sounded a serious warning entitled "Morals Squad Takes Homo Issue to Parents" (April 12, 1966). Two detectives of the Dade County Sheriff's Department were lecturing at junior high-school assemblies and PTA meetings, warning even then of the widespread recruitment of juveniles into homosexuality. "Innocent youngsters and apathetic parents are a dangerous combination," the detectives said. "One of the major recruitment systems operates within the schools."

Miami citizens did not respond. I pray to God this will not happen elsewhere across our land and that what I have told you in this book, and in this chapter particularly, will rouse you from your apathy.

Homosexual teachers: Are they dangerous role models? What could be more convincing than what you have just been reading? I quote William A. Rusher, respected journalist, who writes:

> A teacher of young children...plays an important part in shaping their attitude toward many things. Without even intending to do so, teachers convey to their classes, in a thousand subtle ways, their concept of what is "desirable" and what is "undesirable," what is "wise" and what is, or may be "unwise." Rightly or wrongly, many generally tolerant parents, who have no particular objection to their children being taught by homosexuals who do not reveal their sexual orientation, are concerned at having them taught by self-proclaimed homosexuals.

> ...today's self-proclaimed homosexuals tend to be defensively aggressive on the subject. The crux of the matter is whether, at any age when a child's ultimate sexual orientation may still be undetermined, there should be placed over it—in authority, in loco parentis, and implicitly as a model of conduct—a teacher who insists upon publicly affirming his or her own homosexuality and treating it as simply "one valid alternate life-style."

ISSUE 4 NO:

What Does a Gay Teacher Teach Your Child?

Peter Fisher

One Saturday several weeks ago Marc stormed into our apartment in a rage after spending the afternoon with some gay friends petitioning for the Clingan-Burden bill.

It had been a successful afternoon: Marc and the others had collected more than seven hundred signatures in support of the bill. Most of these had come from straight people, who were surprisingly sympathetic about the need for employment protection for gays. Public attitudes seemed to be changing: a year ago when we had first tried petitioning in public we had encountered a good deal of hostility and mockery.

Marc had enjoyed the afternoon, but as he rode home on the subway he began to dwell on one incident that had only mildly irritated him earlier in the day. By the time he reached home he was furious. He had spent fifteen minutes trying to convince one homosexual to sign in support of legislation that would have extended civil rights protection to him.

The fellow had identified himself as gay, listened to an explanation of the petition, and then said that he couldn't sign it. Most homosexuals enjoyed molesting children. Most gay people did not deserve to have their right to work protected, especially not if they were teachers.

Marc pointed out that he taught young children and had never had the slightest urge to molest any of them. He asked the fellow whether he had had any gay teachers when he was in school. Yes, there were several he thought had probably been gay. Had they molested him? No. Or anyone else? No. Did he know of any child who had been molested by a homosexual? No. Did any of the homosexuals he had ever known take a sexual interest in children? No.

Why did he think, then, that homosexuals were child molesters? No reason, but *everybody* knew they were. He walked off without signing.

Some homosexuals have the most bizarre notions of what all gay people—except themselves—are like. The anti-Semitic Jew. The Negro who doesn't like blacks. Now the homosexual who can't stand gay people.

Outside of the gay world it is not surprising to encounter the myth that homosexuals are child molesters. Many straight people believe it.

I have never known anybody who claimed to have been molested by a homosexual during childhood. I have never known a homosexual who expressed the slightest interest in molesting children. I know that children do get molested by somebody from time to time, because there are criminal statistics to prove it. I do know that many people assume that it is homosexuals who are responsible for the majority of these cases, because many straight people have told me so.

Who really wants to have sex with a child?

CHILDREN

Children have certain basic sexual rights. Among these are the right not to be involuntarily exposed to the sexual activities of others and the right not to be forced or coerced into engaging in sexual acts against their will.

We recognize how stimulating sexual activity can be, regardless of whether or not one is personally involved in it: sex in public is forbidden because it forces others to become involved without their consent, if only as witnesses. In the case of children, this principle is considered particularly important because children are believed to be especially impressionable.

Protection from involuntary sexual involvement is not restricted to cases involving the use of force. Threats, bribery, and the misuse of a position of authority are also considered to be forms of coercion. For this reason, it is considered improper for an employer to have sexual relations with an employee or a teacher to have sexual relations with a student. In both cases, the person in the subordinate position may feel compelled by extenuating circumstances to play along when he or she would not otherwise choose to do so.

The principle of free choice in sexual matters poses some problems with regard to children. Consent is the most basic principle of sexual morality, but below a certain age children are not considered competent to make a decision when sex is involved. Fear or misplaced respect may lead them to permit inappropriate sexual liberties. Ignorance may lead them to consent to things they would never agree to do if they knew the consequences. When does a child become competent to make decisions about his or her own sex life?

A wide variety of laws has been passed to protect the sexual rights of the young. During the years between adolescence and marriage, for example, nearly all heterosexual acts are technically illegal, under statutes concerning fornication, juvenile delinquency, indecent behavior, and acts corrupting the morals of a minor.

One problem is that it is difficult to say when childhood ends. Although we do not grant full adult status to young men and women in our society until they reach the age of eighteen or twenty-one, many other societies consider puberty the beginning of adulthood and encourage marriage during the mid-teens.

In our society, there seems to be a belief that until a certain age children are not ready for sex and know next to nothing about it. Kinsey and his associates found, however, that sexual activity, even prior to puberty, was common—70 percent of the men and 50 percent of the women interviewed—although adults tended to forget many of their early experiences. Adolescents recalled many more early sexual experiences, so the researchers suggested that their findings represent a bare minimum of childhood sexual activity.

Most of this sexual activity is kept secret from parents, for even at this early age the message has been clearly received: sex is taboo.

The young are certainly capable of sex long before the legal age of consent and many seek it out frequently without any apparent harm. Nevertheless, our laws forbid them to engage in sexual relations until they are well into sexual maturity, and often past the peak of their sexual desire. Presumably this is justified on the basis that they are not yet psychologically mature or that their moral training is incomplete.

In many other societies, young people marry, raise families, and adopt full adult responsibility in their mid-teens, so Western ideas about psychological maturity can well be questioned.

Regardless of the laws, it seems reasonable to follow the Indiana Institute for Sex Research in calling young men and women sixteen and over "adults," young people between twelve and sixteen "minors," and reserving the term "children" for those under twelve who are unlikely to have reached puberty.

There is some question as to whether the existing laws actually protect or infringe on the sexual rights of young people. Should a sixteen-year-old boy be subject to arrest for sleeping with a fifteen-year-old girl? Should a twenty-one-year-old "man" be subject to imprisonment for having sex with a consenting "boy" twenty years old? Does the government have the right to regulate sex in whatever way it chooses?

Some people will agree that adults have the right to engage in any sort of sexual relations that does not infringe upon the rights of others. Clearly such a right would be violated by the majority of legislation in this country regulating sexual activity, even for married individuals.

Although most of the sexual activity that goes on during childhood involves children of approximately the same ages, instances of "child molestation" do occur. In the vast majority of cases, the adult involved is male.

A quarter of the women Kinsey interviewed said that sexual advances had been made toward them by adult men before they entered adolescence. Most often these advances involved exhibition of the male genitals, fondling, masturbation, and the like—actual coitus was rare. Twenty percent of the cases were incestuous.

In a recent study of child molestation by the American Humane Association it was found that there were ten to twelve times as many cases of heterosexual molestation as homosexual molestation. Female homosexual molestation was so rare as to be insignificant. The men who molested children were found to be known to the child or parents in 75 percent of the cases. In 60 percent of the cases the child was coerced by the direct use of force or the threat of bodily harm.

In studying sex crimes, homosexual molestation involved coercion so seldom that the investigators at the Indiana Institute for Sex Research eliminated the category of "homosexual aggression" from their list of sex offenses, while finding it quite necessary to retain the category of "heterosexual aggression." Their data also indicated that heterosexual offenders tended to pick younger children than homosexual offenders picked.

What kind of man molests a child? The largest category of offenders was labeled "pedophiles," although the researchers pointed out that this did not always indicate a sexual preference for children, but simply that many of these people considered children acceptable sex partners.

Another category of child molesters was labeled "socio-sexually underdeveloped." These were individuals, usually with a puritanical upbringing, who preferred adults as sexual partners but were unsuccessful in establishing adult relationships due to fear, guilt, or ineptitude. They seemed to be continuing a pattern of preadolescent sexual behavior with children because they could not find other sex partners and had failed to mature psychologically themselves.

Amoral delinquents—sociopaths—represented another type of offender. These individuals seemed to feel no moral restraints with regard to sex: it made little difference to them whether their sex partner was an adult or a child, female, male, or even animal.

A large number of those engaging in sexual relations with children were found to be mentally defective. Alcohol was often involved in cases of molestation—especially where violence was employed—but use of other drugs seemed to have little or no role in sex crimes.

According to the Institute for Sex Research, the younger the victim, the less strongly the molester was oriented toward homosexuality. Of those arrested for homosexual molestation of children, 75 percent had had sexual intercourse with women prior to their offense and about half were married at the time of the offense. Furthermore, those who had engaged in homosexual molestation of children had often engaged in heterosexual molestation of children.

These findings imply that a sexual interest in children—pedophilia—is not rigidly divided along lines of sexual orientation: those who like children tend to be interested in both sexes. It must be remembered that "homosexual" molestation means that the two individuals involved were of the same sex, not necessarily that either or both of them were homosexuals.

Of those convicted of homosexual molestation, half were judged to be pedophiles, a tenth mentally defective, and a tenth drunk. the rest of the cases were attributed to amoral delinquency, situational factors, and the like.

Violence was almost never a factor in "homosexual" offenses, and most of the time it appeared that the "victim" was not unwilling. Naturally, many of those accused of sex crimes claim that their victims sought out the experiences or encouraged them. Only where these claims coincided with the prison record of the facts of the case did the sex researchers accept these claims as true—it is not unlikely that some "innocent" convicts were excluded for this reason. In 70 percent of the cases involving children, both the convicts and the records agreed that the boy was either receptive or encouraging. This was found to be true in more than 80 percent of the cases involving minors and 90 percent of the cases involving adults, age sixteen and over.

These findings are not particularly surprising. Homosexual activity is awfully common, and the strong male sex drive during adolescence—when heterosexual activities are often restricted—helps to explain why many boys are not averse to homosexual experiences with older men.

From this study of homosexual child molestation a pattern emerges. Interest in children is comparatively rare and usually appears to be a form of pedophilia in which *both* heterosexual and homosexual interests are common. In cases where the homosexual orientation is stronger, the preferred sex object is sometimes an adolescent, but more often a young adult sixteen or over. In many cases where minors are involved, situational factors are important—the adult in question has been unable to find a more desirable partner close to his age and has had a costly lapse in judgment. In other cases, psychological immaturity or a strict sexual upbringing has made adult relations impossible, and the individual appears to be continuing an earlier pattern of adolescent homosexual activity which he found less threatening.

It should not be denied that the facts do indicate that a small minority of the male homosexual population does prefer boys in their mid-teens or early adult years as sexual partners. How concerned should we be about this?

Some people will be concerned and outraged no matter what. While they may consider a heterosexual experience with a sixteen-year-old girl an indication of poor judgment and irresponsibility, a homosexual experience with a sixteen-year-old boy indicates the most monstrous depravity. These attitudes reflect our cultural biases. If the law and public opinion were based on the fact that a young man is biologically an adult at this age, there would be less justification for concern.

There may well be a basic biological tendency, which is suppressed in our society, for homosexual relationships to form between older and younger males. Although this pattern appears in other mammals and in other societies past and present, it is surprisingly uncommon in our own. In ancient Greece, a young man was expected to take an adolescent boy for his lover and provide him with a moral education and training in athletic and military skills.

In the gay world of America, homosexual relationships between adolescent boys and adults are quite uncommon—a good deal less common than comparable heterosexual relationships. Adult homosexual relationships tend to form between individuals of roughly the same age, as is the case for homosexual relationships in earlier years. But this may be a matter of social conditioning, convenience, and shared interests. A fair percentage of young homosexuals find older men especially attractive, and some of the most stable relationships are found between individuals who are several years apart in age.

When I began to look outside of my circle of high school friends for homosexual relationships, I found myself much more attracted to men a good deal older than I was. When I began to frequent the bars I usually entered relationships with men in their twenties or early thirties, because they were the ones I preferred. I did not have a relationship with a man younger than myself until I was twenty-five.

There are a number of psychological factors which make some gay men prefer partners who are younger or older than themselves. For the young homosexual, an older man is more sexually experienced, stable, and less likely to be promiscuous. For the older homosexual, a young man may be more affectionate, more easily aroused, and less likely to compare his partner's sexual performance with that of others. To some extent, elements of a father-son relationship may also enter the picture: the older homosexual may be more protective and provide emotional support for his younger companion.

Although few adult homosexuals will risk involvement with an underage boy, there are some places where adolescents who are interested in homosexual relations can be found. Many hustlers and most runaways are still in their teens and often have a basically homosexual orientation. Some young boys frequent the tea rooms in search of older sex partners. In some public parks there are particular areas where young boys who wish to be picked up will congregate.

If a young man does not actively seek out sex with an older homosexual, he is unlikely to ever be approached. Two thirds of the cases of "homosexual molestation" which were studied involved older friends or family acquaintances, not the lurking strangers of our myths. Nor are those who become involved with adolescents usually "dirty old men." The average age is about thirty—an age that I, at least, found appealing when I was an adolescent. For many adolescent gays, involvement with older homosexuals often seems less risky than involvement with their peers; fewer tales are likely to be told.

Actually, it is not so surprising that adolescent boys have a tendency to become involved with older men. Although we seldom recognize the fact, such relationships are institutionalized in our society. Think of the comic books, adventure movies, and TV programs directed at adolescent boys. So many heroes have younger sidekicks, so many boys have older buddies: Batman and Robin, Superman and Jimmy Olsen, Buck Rogers and Buddy—the list could go on and on, and most of the super he-men have curiously platonic relationships with adult women.

The issue of sexual relations with children is likely to draw increasing attention as reforms in sex legislation are considered. The important role of alcohol, rather than other drugs, and the influence of a puritanical rather than "permissive" or simply informative sex education, provide food for thought. The time may come when the age of consent for both homosexual and heterosexual relations may be made more realistic. At present, however, heterosexuals constitute a far greater "threat" to children and adolescents than homosexuals do.

GAY TEACHERS

Teaching is one of the professions in which the highest percentage of homosexuals is to be found—more than twice the incidence of homosexuality in the population at large in some cities.

Homosexuals are just as likely as heterosexuals to like children and to want to help them grow and learn, yet homosexuals are much less likely to have children of their own. For gays who want to work with children, teaching is a reasonable solution.

In spite of the generally low salaries, teaching is a profession held in high esteem. For gays of either sex who realize that society considers a homosexual orientation inferior, teaching may provide a source of the self-esteem and social recognition that may be important for happiness.

Denied the opportunity to live their lives as they choose with any degree of safety, many gay people restrict their sex life and compensate for it by a greater devotion to learning. Most gays do not become actively involved in the gay world until they have finished high school or college, and they often end up spending nights studying rather than dating or searching for a marital partner. It is not surprising, then, that they are often drawn to academic life. Gay teachers sometimes bring more knowledge to the classroom simply because they have devoted more time to acquiring it.

We have a long tradition of acceptance of unmarried teachers. Until recent years, only unmarried persons were considered suitable as teachers in many parts of the country. Teaching is one of those few professions which provide a certain guarantee against suspicion of homosexuality.

Because an unmarried teacher is assumed to be devoting his or her life to children, some of the onus for not marrying and raising a family is removed. The teacher was not attractive enough to find a husband or wife, it is said, or was simply unfortunate in never meeting the right person. Even though he may have no children of his own the educator is held in high regard for contributing to the well-being of the coming generation.

Lacking children of his own, the homosexual may take comfort from the idea that if he passes on the knowledge that he has acquired, to the children he teaches, he survives in them in a sense. Only in this way does he gain any sort of personal immortality.

Often it is the unmarried, childless teacher who is best able to relate to his students because he has no other, conflicting demands upon his attention or interest. He does not carry anger at his own children over into the classroom. He is better able to compartmentalize his life. Off work, he has no need to concern himself with children; on the job, he is better able to give them his full attention.

How many of us look back with special fondness to an "old maid" teacher who played an especially important role in shaping our intellectual development, or to a dedicated, unmarried man who inspired us because of his devotion to his field of study? How many ever stop to wonder whether these teachers were homosexual?

To the homosexual, for whom family life and friendship in a heterosexual society can be sparse, the school may provide a surrogate family and social circle which receives all the devotion and loyalty that others would direct elsewhere. The teaching staff works together, shares confidences, and will often join as a team to help a problem child make a more satisfactory adjustment. Some homosexuals find the companionship in teaching that they have been unable to find elsewhere and respond by investing their love in their work.

Should a teacher be discovered to be homosexual, he will very likely lose his job. A heterosexual may lead a wild sex life outside of working hours, may be unfaithful in marriage or break other sexual taboos, but his private sexual life is seldom considered to have any bearing on his ability or right to teach. Heterosexuals, by and large, have a right to their own private sex life—homosexuals do not.

Because of the danger of being discovered, some homosexual teachers severely limit their private lives, avoiding homosexual contacts, and in the process, miss the opportunity to meet someone with whom to share a fulfilling relationship. While not completely curtailing their sex lives, others feel they must take special pains to cover their tracks, traveling to other cities in search of sex or love, and living in constant fear of discovery and loss of job and pension. The homosexual has little security in the school system, regardless of how fine a teacher he may be or how discreet his private sex life. In most places, a whisper can wreck a career.

A gay teacher—or a straight one—may be accused of homosexuality, even when he has never given any indication of it in school. All it takes is one student who dislikes him sufficiently to start the rumors flying. Time and again teachers have been dismissed on the basis of charges that they have made homosexual advances to students, although there is no proof that they have done so. These cases seldom come to court where the charges might be put to the test. The school board doesn't want to tie its hands with legal technicalities and the victim seldom wants further publicity.

An accusation of homosexuality is usually considered sufficient grounds to subject a teacher to an investigation of his private life that he has been careful to keep secret. Such investigations, often handled through private detective agencies, are sometimes initiated for other reasons—political differences between the teacher in question and the school board, for example. If homosexuality is discovered, it provides a handy excuse to sack a good teacher for spurious reasons.

Gay teachers in New York have faced a new problem in recent years with respect to the issue of community control over local schools. Teachers who are of different race or ethnic background from the majority of the community may be charged with homosexuality in order to provide grounds for replacing them. In several school districts this became such a recurring problem that the United Federation of Teachers was finally forced to protect the rights of homosexual teachers.

Although it is now difficult in New York City to get a teacher fired on the ground that his private life involves homosexuality, gay teachers still face discrimination. The City Board of Examiners, which controls the licensing of teachers, conducts investigations into the backgrounds and private lives of teaching applicants and considers "homosexual tendencies" to disqualify anyone from teaching. In its generosity, the board will make a few exceptions: if a prospective teacher will agree to undergo compulsory "aversion therapy" in order to be "changed" into a heterosexual, the board will consider hiring him—if the therapy is "successful."

But can a child ever really be safe with a homosexual teacher, even one who has been "cured"?

As a matter of fact, a child is a good deal safer with a homosexual teacher than with a heterosexual teacher. In the last forty years of the New York City school system, for example, only one case of homosexual molestation has been brought to court, while many heterosexual teachers have been officially charged with improper sexual involvement with their pupils.

Are children safe with heterosexual teachers?

PROPAGANDA

What would happen if discrimination against homosexual teachers were made illegal? Many straight people fear that homosexuals would proselytize among their students.

Some say that if a child identified with a homosexual teacher he would turn out to be homosexual himself. Others believe that gay teachers would argue in favor of homosexuality at the first opportunity, trying to convince their students that it was glamorous, something worth experiencing no matter what the risks.

It is said that if we were to actually permit homosexual "perverts" to lead their lives freely and openly, increasing numbers of people would decide to become homosexual and the human race would eventually die out. It is perplexing that homosexuality can be portrayed as so grossly unnatural and yet so infinitely appealing in the same breath. Perhaps those who rely on this argument find homosexuality more attractive than they would like to admit.

The argument that to permit is to condone or encourage is a specious one. The law allows individuals to adopt the religion and political philosophy of their choice, but this is seldom interpreted as promoting any particular religion or political affiliation. Homosexuality is not an ideology or a creed in the first place—it is not something that can effectively be taught or preached.

The whole suspicion that to permit homosexuality would be to encourage it probably rests with unconscious recognition of the way in which heterosexuality—permitted—is promoted in every conceivable way. Homosexuals are often accused of flaunting their sexuality, of forcing it upon others, and of making it the most important fact of their lives. These accusations would seem far more just if directed at heterosexuals.

Heterosexual propaganda begins in the school from the very start. All the primers have nice little girls and boys, but you don't find close, affectionate relationships that might be interpreted as homosexual. If you encountered anybody who by the furthest stretch of the imagination might have been homosexual, it was probably in the form of a warning against taking candy from strangers. There are no gay couples in reading texts—all adults are heterosexual, and most are married.

In later school years, as students encounter literature written by homosexuals, or history concerning individuals who were homosexual, this aspect, is completely obscured.

How many people knew Walt Whitman was gay when they first encountered his poems in high school? Explicitly homosexual passages—"Many a soldier's kiss dwells on these bearded lips..."—might occasionally have been treated as metaphorical rather than literal, but questionable poems were more commonly omitted from collections of poetry. Who found out that Tchaikovsky was gay in music appreciation or heard about Michelangelo's sexual orientation in fine arts?

The whole concept of "platonic" love had to be invented in our society—not in Plato's—to explain why that kindly old fellow Socrates took such an interest in beautiful young men. Do you remember going over the Socratic dialogues in school and having it tediously explained to you why they didn't mean what they seemed to mean? Any indication of homosexuality and especially of the beauty of homosexual love is carefully excised from all the material young students receive. Lovers are presented as friends, if at all. Sex in general is shrouded in romanticism, and homosexual sex is nonexistent.

History is written from a strictly heterosexual viewpoint. Achilles and Patroclus were the best of friends. Alexander loved his horse, Bucephalus, rather than Hephaestion. Caesar's *wife* was beyond suspicion, but who knew that "the 'mistress' of every man in Rome" was not? Frederick the Great was said to use men as tools and to show little sign of human warmth: who knew that his father had executed his lover before his eyes? Dag Hammarskjöld is remembered as a man of peace, but not as a homosexual statesman. By default, every single important figure in the arts or in history was apparently heterosexual.

In high school, any student who is suspected of having homosexual tendencies is likely to be sent for "guidance" or compelled to undergo psychiatric treatment. In some parts of the country students believed to be homosexual can be expelled and forced to continue their education in trade schools—if they still wish further education, that is. Apparently the risk that these young people might contaminate those around them is deemed sufficient justification for suspending any and all of their rights. Apparently those already enrolled in trade schools are not considered important enough to merit such "protection."

In those forward-looking schools where sex-education courses are available, few take even a neutral stance on the subject of homosexuality. On the contrary, homosexuality is usually presented along with venereal disease as a dangerous sickness to be avoided at all costs by walking the sexual straight and narrow. Most parents shudder at the possibility that a homosexual might teach a course in sex education.

In spite of the deluge of heterosexual propaganda, in spite of the cruel treatment of young people who are found out to have homosexual interests, homosexuality continues to appear at the same rate in each new generation. If this much propaganda cannot sway a young person from a homosexual orientation, it seems highly unlikely that even an equivalent amount of gay propaganda could convert a basically heterosexual youth. Sexual orientation is not a matter of persuasion—it runs far deeper than that.

Do homosexual teachers proselytize at all? The opportunities to do so are certainly limited.

In most parts of the country, any teacher who lets it be known that he is gay, much less advocates a homosexual life-style for his students, will lose his job, regardless of his teaching qualifications. Although it is expected that straight teachers make their heterosexuality perfectly obvious and encourage it in their students, it is intolerable for a homosexual teacher even to be known to be gay. Rather than proselytize, the gay teacher must make every effort to conceal his homosexuality.

In many towns and cities the gay teacher must hide his homosexuality simply to protect himself against his students. Harassment of teachers who are suspected of being homosexual is not uncommon—some parents condone or encourage such attacks. In some circles, beating up "queers" is a proof of manhood, evidence that a teen-age gang, for example, is held together by the youthful *machismo* of its members, rather than "latent" homosexual feelings for one another.

What constitutes propaganda? Many people assume that a homosexual would be unfit to teach a course in sex education because he would proselytize for homosexuality. It seems absurd to imagine that any gay teacher would be foolish enough to actually do so. But if he were to present the various current opinions about homosexuality, ranging from sin to sickness to acceptability, he would be accused of propagandizing, while the straight teacher who presented only the most medieval view of homosexuality would be viewed as perfectly fair. For a known homosexual to even appear to be living a happy life would strike some people as propaganda: everyone knows homosexuals are wretchedly unhappy. A straight teacher cannot risk presenting a balanced view of homosexuality today—it is much less likely that a gay teacher would be allowed to.

It should be clear that a gay teacher is in no position to proselytize, and if he were and wished to he wouldn't succeed. Unfortunately, in some instances it would be highly advantageous if a gay teacher *were* free to be open about his homosexuality.

Speaking from my own experience and that of many gay friends, high school can be hell for a young homosexual. Young men or women who are first becoming aware that they are homosexual are placed under an enormous emotional strain. Why are they different from everyone else? Why do people hate homosexuals so much? How can they hide the truth from family, friends, and school authorities?

How many high school students are troubled by inner conflicts over homosexuality which they dare not express to anyone? How many "inexplicable" youthful suicides can be traced to the isolation and fear imposed on young homosexuals? Just as a student who is a member of any other minority group can benefit from the opportunity to talk to a teacher who shares his minority status, the chance for gay students to talk about their problems with a gay teacher would be of enormous value. Members of other minority groups can at least turn to family and friends; the young homosexual cannot.

What would a gay teacher say to a gay student who approached him with problems in coming to grips with his homosexuality? Hopefully, he would point out both the positive and negative sides of the issue. The student should feel no shame or guilt: homosexual love is as valid and valuable as any other form of love. On the other hand, he should not think that the gay life will be a bed of roses, given the antihomosexual biases and discriminatory practices in America.

A gay teacher might point out, where others would not, that there is no need to decide that one is either strictly homosexual or strictly heterosexual. Openness to both heterosexual and homosexual experiences should be encouraged, for it will lead to greater freedom and happiness in the long run. The student should be reassured that he need not devote himself to a constant struggle to deny his homosexual interests, nor should he feel obliged to identify himself for once and for all as a homosexual as many young people mistakenly do. Sex should be placed in its proper context as a positive form of self-expression and self-exploration, rather than any sort of rigid commitment.

Many people argue that even if a gay teacher makes no deliberate attempt to proselytize, the very fact of his homosexuality will have a profound influence on his students. Others insist that a male homosexual cannot provide an adequate masculine image with which his male students can identify, and that a female homosexual provides a poor model for femininity.

The schools already have a disproportionate number of homosexual teachers, yet there has been no increase in homosexuality in our society. Gender and role identifications are likely to solidify in the earliest stages of childhood, and by the time a child reaches school age he or she is unlikely to undergo any significant changes in these areas.

Some people say that gay teachers are a bad moral influence on their students aside from their homosexuality. Their lives are different: they do not marry, they have sexual relations with many different people, they do not share society's values. The same attitude is not taken with regard to unmarried heterosexuals, of course, no matter how promiscuous the lives they lead. Actually, gay people tend to have the same basic values as nonhomosexuals. They were brought up in the straight world and heterosexual "morality" has been deeply ingrained in them, often to their detriment.

Gay teachers are sometimes better prepared to deal with problems of sexual identity and behavior in their students than straight teachers. Living in a heterosexual world, most homosexuals have acquired a sensitivity to the nuances of heterosexual behavior as well as having a natural familiarity with homosexuality. The straight teacher, on the other hand, is usually completely unprepared to deal with any indications of homosexuality in his students.

In a teaching program in a state hospital, for example, one teacher felt he could best help a schizophrenic adolescent boy in his care by encouraging him to form an extremely dependent relationship with him. Soon the boy became seductive toward him, displaying and seeking more and more open expressions of affection—some of them frankly sexual. His heterosexual teacher panicked, not because of the seduction itself, but because of the response to it he found in himself. Ashamed of his reactions and fearing that he was developing homosexual tendencies, he tried to keep the whole matter a secret and strongly rejected the boy, causing him a great deal of emotional damage. When the matter finally came to light, the professional staff pointed out that had the teacher been less terrified of homosexuality he could have saved the boy a painful regression.

When one of the emotionally disturbed children under Marc's care showed a similar pattern of behavior, on the other hand, Marc was able to deal with it perfectly comfortably. Well aware of the difference between the expression of affection and the expression of sexuality, he did not confuse his pupils with mixed signals and was able to read their behavior as signs of their needs, not his. He was able to express the affection they needed without feeling that his masculinity was threatened.

One boy who was particularly affectionate began to become more and more so until he bordered on being seductive. Finally one day he told Marc that he wanted to kiss him on the lips. "There's nothing wrong with kissing people," Marc said, "but it's not appropriate for children to kiss their teachers on the lips." The boy was able to accept this as a statement of fact, rather than a rejection, and his seductive behavior soon faded away.

The cherished belief that gay teachers are some sort of ravening sexual monsters seems strange when an examination of the statistics concerning incidents of child molestation shows that the overwhelming majority of cases involve *heterosexual* seduction or assault. Actually, there are many more cases of heterosexual assault of teachers by students than the reverse.

The only thing that "proselytizing" of the heterosexual or homosexual variety is likely to influence is the tolerance with which developing youngsters view those who differ from them. Here we can see that the barrage of heterosexual propaganda has had far-reaching effects: homosexuals are generally despised and treated as objects of derision rather than human beings.

An open acceptance of diversity would provide us all with greater freedom, not usher in new totalitarian sexual attitudes to replace those encouraged today.

ISSUE 5

Does Our Welfare System Work?

The first attempts on a national level to provide help for those in need followed the hardships and difficulties of the Depression. The Social Security Act of 1935 provided a basic income for those in the population who had retired from their jobs. Unemployment insurance was provided for those temporarily unemployed, and there was assistance for widows, single mothers with dependent children, and the disabled who had little or no means of support.

After the Depression, however, poor people were virtually ignored by the rest of society. They were rediscovered with the publication of *The Other America* by Michael Harrington in 1962. A number of programs in the 1960s attempted to reduce poverty rates. Many of the programs focused on socializing the young, teaching basic skills, and job training. The success of these programs is a matter of debate. In any case, the Vietnam conflict diverted the nation's attention and resources.

The actual number of people below the poverty line depends on the measuring stick. Most of us probably think people are poor when they are unable to afford the basic necessities of life: food, clothing, shelter, and health care. But what are the standards even for such necessities? What kind of food? What kind of shelter? In a society that is dependent on the electronic media for information, are you poor if you can't afford a television set? What about a new car, an old car, or any car? Various organizations and agencies have developed minimum budgets for families of differing size in different locations. The Social Security Administration estimated that it would require $11,611 for an urban family of four to meet basic costs in 1987. The U.S. Bureau of the Census, using a similar measure, estimates the number of people with incomes under the poverty line in 1987 at 32.5 million people, up from a low of 23,000,000 in 1973.

Contrary to public opinion, the majority of the people below the poverty line are white. Blacks and other minority groups generally have higher poverty rates, but they constitute a smaller proportion of the population. Although Social Security and other benefits have helped, the elderly are still overrepresented among the poor. Female-headed households with dependent children are the fastest growing group falling below the poverty line.

The ramifications of being poor are widespread and pervasive. Poor people evidence higher illness, accident, and death rates which helps to explain why the United States lags behind other industrial nations on most health measures. Our medical system does not provide adequate health care for the poor, relative to other industrial societies.

What are the causes of poverty? Some argue that the poor suffer from genetic deficiencies, such as low intelligence. If this is the answer, what does it say about Americans in general? People who migrate from one country to another are generally from the "lower orders" of the society they are leaving—not all, but a disproportionate number. We are a nation of immigrants. If intelligence is hereditary and our poverty stricken immigrants were low in intelligence, what does it say about modern Americans? Are Americans intellectually inferior? Sociologists tend to interpret poverty as a reflection of socialization and other societal factors. Children learn the poverty-related values and attitudes that keep them out of the mainstream of society from their parents. Limited opportunities, prejudice and discrimination, inadequate educational institutions, and a variety of other social factors are thought to be among the causes of poverty.

Not everyone falling below the poverty line is on welfare. The working poor comprise a significant portion of our population. People employed at minimum-wage jobs, currently earning $3.35 per hour, make less than $7,000 per year from which deductions are made for Social Security, insurance when available, and in many cases federal and state taxes. Those at the bottom of our occupational hierarchy face a dilemma: Frequently they are better off on welfare than they are working.

The current welfare system has been accused of creating family instability by making it difficult to receive welfare when there is an adult male in the household, thus forcing fathers to desert their families and of generating a self-perpetuating cycle of poverty through illegitimacy. It is probably the system of payments to welfare mothers for their dependent children that is most responsible for the current outcry about welfare. The

Aid to Families with Dependent Children (AFDC) program faces various charges from welfare opponents. Some argue that AFDC makes it too comfortable and easy for recipients and that many women deliberately have children out of wedlock to avoid working. As a result, they argue, the stigma on illegitimacy has been reduced, and female-headed households on welfare have dramatically increased. The 1965 Moynihan Report, which contended that the growing number of female-headed families on welfare was keeping blacks from achieving equality, is receiving new respect from many observers. However, studies have failed to establish that welfare encourages illegitimacy.

Under the Reagan administration, there has been a systematic attack on welfare programs in general and AFDC in particular. More stringent eligibility requirements have slightly reduced the number of recipients, and benefit increases have lagged behind inflation, effectively reducing AFDC payments. A number of states are now experimenting with programs that require AFDC recipients to earn their benefits through work or education. The hope is to return the recipients to the workforce.

In the following debate, Sar Levitan argues that our system of welfare has provided a successful safety net that protects diverse elements of American society, including the middle and upper class, from the vagaries of the economic system. Walter Williams responds to Levitan with the argument that income redistribution is negative and that market forces should dominate.

ISSUE 5 YES:

The Evolving Welfare System

Sar A. Levitan

Half a century has elapsed since the United States embarked on the development of its welfare system. Driven by the devastating impacts of the Great Depression, the architects of the New Deal designed a structure that would provide a measure of economic security to all Americans. In doing so, they followed in the footsteps of other industrialized nations.

Broadly defined, the American welfare system as it evolved over the years is the product of a sustained drive for greater economic security by all income groups; it is not merely a vehicle for providing assistance to the poor. Through social insurance programs, tax expenditures, and human capital investments, government aid reaches far into the ranks of middle- and upper-income America. Federal social welfare policies not only seek to prevent extreme deprivation among the most disadvantaged, but also attempt to cushion the impact of economic misfortune and uncertainty on more advantaged and affluent members of society. The resulting safety net has been remarkably successful in shielding diverse segments of the population from the full brunt of the vagaries and hardships implicit in a free market economy.

Despite these achievements the system has failed to gain universal acceptance. In recent years, attacks on the welfare system have grown more strident and shrill. Critics have sought to link rising incidences of crime, drug abuse, divorce, and other social ills with federal social welfare interventions. Some have even claimed that the welfare system is the direct cause of an alleged unraveling of the American social fabric and moral fiber.

As a result of these assaults, the terms *welfare, mess,* and *crisis* have become virtually inseparable in contemporary public discourse. Criticisms of the welfare system have emanated from diverse sources. Liberals have found fault with the absence of federal standards for a comprehensive system of income support and constraints on the more aggressive use of government powers to improve the quality of life. Conservatives contend that the welfare system has grown too large and unwieldy, frequently undermining the very objectives that it is designed to achieve. Under attack from all sides, the image of the welfare system as irrational, unmanageable, and in need of immediate and wholesale reform has come to dominate popular wisdom in the mid-1980s.

The notion of a welfare crisis is enhanced by tendencies to define the American welfare system narrowly as providing cash and in-kind assistance only to the poor. Without a perceived stake in the system, the middle class majority responds quickly to suggestions that welfare is a mess—too costly, mismanaged, unfair, and in many cases undeserved. When the welfare system is defined more realistically to include the host of entitlements and protections against economic insecurity available to the nonpoor, perceptions of crisis and prescriptions for sweeping retrenchment lose much of their appeal.

A balanced and objective analysis would reveal that reports of a welfare crisis are greatly exaggerated. Removed from the distortions of budget battles and political ideologies, the record of federal social welfare interventions suggests that the system is a rational and necessary response to emerging societal needs and has functioned relatively well under the pressures of competing interests and conflicting demands.

PURSUING ECONOMIC SECURITY

Viewed in the context of societal goals first articulated half a century ago, the welfare system has nearly achieved its fundamental objectives. Most of the destitute have been assured at least a meager stipend to meet basic needs, and the percentage of Americans living in poverty declined dramatically during the three decades following World War II. Social security and medicare have removed the greatest threats to solvency in old age. Workers forced into idleness have gained temporary support through unemployment compensation programs, and disabled workers are protected by insurance which provides medical care and basic income. Tax expenditures and federally sponsored financial institutions have enabled unprecedented numbers to purchase their own homes. Favorable tax policies have spurred the growth of private health insurance and government regulations have guaranteed employees that their private pensions would be available upon retirement. Substantial public investments in education, training, and employment have enabled millions to enter or remain in the mainstream of the United States economy, thereby reaffirming the promise of opportunity that lies at the heart of American society.

The role of the welfare system in enhancing economic security across diverse income groups is clearly reflected in its historical development. The cornerstone of the system, the Social Security Act of 1935, was crafted in response to the great uncertainties and hardships imposed by the great Depression and was designed primarily to insure a basic income during the so-called golden years or when forced idleness strikes. Unemployment and old age insurance provided the bulk of protection against deprivation, while means-tested assistance to the poor was restricted to small numbers of widows and single mothers with dependent children, the aged, and the blind. Subsequent expansions of the social security system—including aid to dependent orphans in the waning days of the New Deal era, support for the disabled under Eisenhower, federally financed health insurance under Johnson, and improved retirement and disability benefits under Nixon, Ford, and Carter—further increased the use of public funds to minimize economic insecurity without regard to personal income.

Contrary to today's view of the welfare system as synonymous with aid to the poor, public attention did not focus on the plight of the impoverished until the late 1950s, more than two decades after creation of the social security system. Following World War II social policy was preoccupied with helping veterans adjust to civilian life by subsidizing their training and education. The help was offered to all veterans without regard to their economic status. In the 1950s, amid optimism that rapid economic growth during the postwar period could bring prosperity to the least advantaged, federal policy also focused on economic development efforts within depressed areas rather than on direct assistance to those in need.

The persistence of poverty despite rising affluence during the 1960s prompted expansion of cash support under the Aid to Families with Dependent Children (AFDC) program for the nonaged poor. This included liberalization of eligibility requirements and enhanced benefits that rose more rapidly than average earnings. The federal government also accepted responsibility for expanded direct aid to impoverished aged, blind, and disabled persons through the establishment of the Supplemental Security Income (SSI) program in 1972. Substantial additional help for the needy, including the working poor, was authorized with the creation of the food stamp program in 1972 and its expansion during the recession in 1974. The working poor were also helped by wider coverage of the minimum wage and unemployment insurance laws during the Carter administration.

In-kind assistance has also been offered to low-income Americans when necessary to compensate for market inadequacies, and to insure that public funds would be devoted to the fulfillment of basic human needs. Low-income housing programs were initiated when it became evident that income support alone would not serve as a short-term remedy for an inadequate private housing stock. Health care coverage under medicaid represented further acknowledgment that cash stipends could not guarantee access to essential services in an efficient manner when individual needs are not directly related to income. In some cases it was easier to persuade Congress to provide in-kind help rather than cash assistance. For example, food stamps gained political support both as a response to the cry of hunger and malnutrition as well as a boost to the United States farm economy.

Because assistance to the poor is commonly viewed as unearned, it attracts the greatest political attention and controversy. Yet means-tested aid constitutes only a sixth of the total transfer payments provided through the broader welfare system and less than a tenth of total federal outlays go to the poor. The federal share of the AFDC budget, commonly associated with welfare, accounts for only about 2 percent of federal income transfers, and total outlays for the program (including state and local contributions) represent 0.5 percent of personal incomes in the United States. An analysis of in-kind benefits within the welfare system would yield similar results with large portions of aid (including indirect subsidies) for housing, health care, and other supportive services directed to the nonpoor.

As a matter of policy as well as politics, the American welfare system has never identified income maintenance as an appropriate long-term response to economic misfortune and deprivation. The initiatives of the Great Society were founded upon the premise that only a two-pronged assault on poverty could lead to greater economic security for the poor: income support to meet immediate basic needs coupled with attempts to expand economic opportunities and to change institutions in order to promote long-term self-sufficiency. Guided by this philosophy, the Great Society sought to stimulate public investments in education and training, seeking to open doors to permanent employment for the disadvantaged. During the late 1960s and 1970s, federal support for educational programs (ranging from primary and secondary schools to vocational and postsecondary education) and job training initiatives increased substantially. All segments of American society shared in the fruits of these investments, although they have not been sufficient to provide alternatives to long-term dependency for a minority of the nation's poor.

The development of diverse tax and sectoral policies not commonly associated with the welfare system further illustrates the extent to which federal social welfare policies have reduced economic insecurity for all income groups, rather than more narrowly aiding the poor. Tax exemptions and expenditures are now designed to enhance personal economic security in areas ranging from home ownership to employee benefit programs and individual retirement accounts. A wide array of credit programs, supplemented by price supports for many agricultural commodities, also attempt to promote economic stability by aiding financially troubled businesses. Disaster assistance routinely offers some measure of protection against natural calamities, while trade adjustment assistance and import restrictions have been employed to minimize economic disruptions associated with international trade. Certainly these federal interventions differ in important respects from the social investments and transfer programs typically linked with the welfare system. The point here is simply that a wide range of federal initiatives are part of a quest for economic security and well-being of all Americans, and this push for security, more than any narrower effort to help the poor, defines and sustains the modern welfare system.

The broad layer of additional security provided by the welfare system and related federal initiatives has contributed to greater economic stability since World War II, even though periodic recessions persist. The American public's resistance to major retrenchments attests to the broad support for these reforms and virtually guarantees that an extensive welfare system serving as a buffer against economic uncertainty is here to stay. Indeed, some measure of protection against economic misfortune and aid to the poor are rational and necessary responses to rising societal affluence. Just as private insurance to reduce financial risk becomes more affordable and attractive as personal income increases, government policies to spread or socialize the risks of a free market system become more prudent and popular with growing national wealth. The potential for humanitarian aid to relieve deprivation and for longer-term investments to help the disadvantaged become contributing members of society also increases with rising national income. In the absence of federal interventions through the welfare system, the gap between rich and poor would tend to widen in an advanced economy, generating unacceptable income disparities and straining the fabric of an open, free, and democratic society.

Even in the conservative political climate of the late 1970s and 1980s, the welfare system has continued to respond to changing concepts of need and economic security amid rising affluence. For example, in 1979 Congress enacted financial support for residential heating costs in response to rising energy prices. Subsidies for telephone service in the wake of the AT&T divestiture have also gained growing acceptance as part of our definition of basic needs for low-income Americans. A parallel extension of the welfare system's scope has occurred in the realm of income security for the nonpoor with the adoption of new tax expenditures for individual retirement accounts. These changes are clear reminders that the welfare system is still evolving, responding to changing economic and social conditions while also reflecting the higher expectations and aspirations of an increasingly wealthy nation.

LESSONS OF THE PAST

What of the alleged failures of the modern welfare system? Federal interventions in the complex realm of social policy have brought their share of frustrations and excesses. Yet the more important issues are the extent to which social welfare policies and programs have been revised to reflect the lessons of the past, and the standards by which progress in the welfare system is measured. A balanced and reasonable assessment suggests that we have learned from our mistakes—some inevitable, others the result of overly ambitious efforts—during two decades of frequently bold innovation, and that past gains have been generally encouraging in light of the ambitious and competing goals set out for the modern welfare system.

The designers of the emerging welfare system, from the New Deal to the founding of the Great Society, tended to underestimate the deep-seated problems associated with poverty. The authors of the Social Security Act in 1935 assumed that needs-tested public assistance would wither away as younger workers became fully covered by social insurance—an expectation that was shattered by changing demographics and steadily expanding welfare rolls and benefits during the postwar period. Similarly, a central premise of President Johnson's War on Poverty was that investments in education and training, civil rights protections, and community organizations representing the have-nots could dramatically lift this generation's poor out of deprivation and ensure their children a decent life. Cycles of poverty and dependency have proved considerably more intractable. It became increasingly clear that there are no easy answers or quick solutions to discrimination, economic deprivation, and other social ills. As some of the experiments turned out to be counterproductive as well as politically divisive, the ensuing disillusionment sorely taxed the nation's will to sustain the welfare system in pursuit of steady but incremental gains.

Because many social problems have proved more pervasive and persistent than originally believed, the welfare system has been forced to rely upon more varied and costly strategies for their long-term amelioration. Such comprehensive, long-term approaches frequently involved offering preferential treatment to targeted groups at the cost of legitimate aspirations of the more fortunate. It has proven extremely difficult politically to defend these actions. Social programs requiring high initial investments and yielding delayed or cumulative benefits have often been abandoned, being victims of public resentment and insufficient commitments of funds over too brief a period of time. Every solution to deep-seated social ills has created new problems. Even when government interventions have achieved their intended results, the process of change in some instances has generated unwanted side effects and posed new problems for policymakers. One clear lesson provided by the experience of the past two decades is that the search for remedies to complex social problems is inherently difficult, particularly when the process involves helping the have-nots to compete effectively with those who have made it. In a democratic society, those who have gained privileged status generally have the clout to abort such changes.

The experience of recent decades suggests that the federal government must proceed on several fronts simultaneously if it is to be successful in efforts to alleviate poverty. For example, unless suitable employment and economic development programs are also initiated, the training of low-income workers is unlikely to have a significant impact on overall poverty levels or welfare caseloads when provided amid high unemployment or in declining economic regions. In contrast, although income transfers address the immediate needs of the poor, they do not result in lasting improvements in earning capacity and self-sufficiency unless complemented by public efforts to enhance the skills of recipients and to alter the institutions that trap them in poverty. The interdependence of these antipoverty strategies can create the appearance of failure when individual initiatives are viewed in isolation, particularly when concomitant interventions necessary for their success are not undertaken. At the same time, the benefits of comprehensive approaches are cumulative and can far exceed the potential of isolated efforts.

One of the clearest lessons arising out of America's experience with the modern welfare system is that poverty cannot be eliminated solely through reliance upon income transfers. Income maintenance is an essential component of any antipoverty effort, but a strategy relying upon transfers alone can neither enhance self-sufficiency nor avoid conflicts in labor markets.

In a society in which wages for millions of workers are too low to lift them out of poverty, the provision of adequate cash assistance to the nonworking poor—if unaccompanied by incentives to supplement assistance with earnings—inevitably raises serious questions of equity and generates strong political opposition among taxpayers. Income transfers large enough to lift low-income households above the poverty threshold, if not tied to work effort, would trigger large drops in labor force participation or force massive public expenditures to the nonpoor in order to preserve acceptable work incentives. The political and economic realities have contributed to the demise of successive guaranteed income schemes during the past two decades and demonstrate the need for federal strategies that assist both the working and dependent poor.

The rhetoric of the Great Society and subsequent initiatives often placed heavy emphasis on the expansion of economic opportunity for the less fortunate. This promise has never been fulfilled through a sustained and adequate commitment of societal resources. Many of the dilemmas posed by the modern welfare system—perverse incentives discouraging work by welfare recipients, neglect of the needs of the working poor, high levels of youth and minority unemployment, and burgeoning costs of universal entitlements—arises from an inadequate emphasis on the extension of economic opportunity in current policies. Beyond fundamental guarantees of equal access and civil rights, the welfare system's attempts to broaden opportunity have relied upon relatively small and frequently sporadic investments in job training, public employment, compensatory education, and meaningful work incentives. These initiatives, despite yielding promising results, have fallen far short of their necessary role as equal partners with income maintenance in advancing the goals of the welfare system. To help the millions of the unskilled and deficiently educated, it is necessary to recognize that work and welfare go together as an appropriate public policy.

The difficulties associated with the expansion of economic opportunity through the welfare system are substantial, ranging from the technical and economic to the cultural and political. The heavy reliance upon transfer programs in recent years reflects the fact that assurances of income security tend to be less threatening to established interests; they are easier to adopt than broader efforts to open avenues to self-support and economic advancement. Nevertheless, if the nation is to avoid the debilitating effects of its emphasis on income maintenance, there is no alternative to reviving the promise of opportunity in America. When the nation discards today's prevailing negativism it should turn to this urgent task of broadening access to opportunities for work and self-advancement for all Americans.

WE CAN DO BETTER

Recognizing that the welfare system is here to stay and that it will continue to evolve, difficult questions and challenges for the future remain. Much concern is presently focused on the perceived inability of American society to afford the broad range of commitments to economic security already enacted at the federal level. The clamor to rein in public expenditures has profound implications for the political base and stability of the welfare system, generating lasting tensions between universal and means-tested provision of benefits. Most importantly, the appropriate roles of federal, state, and local governments as well as the private sector in the modern welfare system have been seriously questioned in recent years. The establishment of a new consensus is required regarding the legitimacy and optimal scope of federal efforts to bolster the economic security of all Americans.

The affordability of the welfare system is, except in the extreme, essentially a normative judgment reflecting society's willingness to forego some measure of personal consumption and alternative public outlays in exchange for greater collective security. In some cases, the exchange of current income for future economic or national security is relatively direct—social insurance programs requiring prior contributions or investments in defense supported by higher taxes—while in other instances the decision to sacrifice personal income represents a hedge against unforeseen misfortunes or hardships, an awareness that "there but for the grace of God, go I"—disaster relief, food stamps, and medicaid. For the most targeted means-tested initiatives, public expenditures are humanitarian attempts to relieve deprivation; they are enlightened acknowledgments of the broader societal benefits associated with reductions in poverty. All these societal choices are predicated on an awareness of societal affluence, on the belief that the nation can afford to defer a portion of today's consumption for tomorrow's economic or national security.

Without question, the potential for reasoned assessments of society's capacity to support social investments and protections has been diminished in recent years by the fiscal policies of the Reagan administration. By combining rapid increases in defense spending and deep reductions in the federal tax base, President Reagan has intentionally created budget conditions in which social welfare expenditures appear unaffordable. Both historical and international comparisons suggest that, with the adoption of responsible fiscal policies, the American welfare system has not exceeded the bounds of affordability. With the exception of Japan, the United States has devoted a smaller proportion of its gross national product to social programs than any other advanced industrialized nation.

The Reagan fiscal policy has failed to address the crucial legitimate issue regarding the future affordability of the welfare system. It concerns the optimal social investment or protection against economic uncertainty through entitlements and tax expenditures for the nonpoor while still fulfilling our societal responsibilities to those in need. The rise of federal social welfare expenditures during the 1970s was primarily the result of dramatic increases in the cost of nonmeans-tested entitlements such as social security and medicare. Between 1970 and 1984, means-tested programs accounted for one-seventh of the $337 billion rise in total transfer payments. Coupled with open-ended subsidies for middle- and upper-income groups through credit and tax policies ranging from student assistance to interest and retirement savings deductions, the principle of universal eligibility in many social welfare programs has clearly strained resources available for other components of the welfare system.

Burgeoning universal entitlements are gradually becoming a focus of potential spending cuts in the continuing budget difficulties precipitated by the Reagan administration. The current debate is hardly conducive to a thoughtful restructuring of the broader welfare system, framed as it is by the artificial pressures of misguided fiscal policies. Yet in some perverse fashion the problem of massive federal deficits may provide the political will for a much-needed reexamination of the balance between help for the needy and subsidies to the more fortunate in the welfare system. By curtailing expenditures for lower-priority initiatives aiding the nonpoor, the Reagan budget reductions of the mid-1980s may create opportunities for the emergence of a more efficient and effective welfare system in the years ahead.

The conflict between goals of targeting and universality within the welfare system can never be fully resolved. Without question, universal provision of cash assistance and social services engenders broad public acceptance and a strong base of political support, as illustrated by the evolution of social security, medicare, and veteran and college loan programs. Yet the extension of federal aid without regard to income necessarily expands vastly the costs of government interventions, and dilutes their effectiveness in helping those most in need. On the other hand, as Wilbur Cohen has often remarked, programs that are narrowly targeted to serve poor people inevitably become poor programs. The challenge is to strike a balance between the goals of targeting and universality that give every American a stake in the welfare system while still allocating the requisite resources for those who need them most, and to do this with due regard to the dignity of recipients.

The Reagan administration's rhetorical crusade to focus federal aid on those with greatest need has not been unfounded. Despite the difficulty of judging the appropriate balance between targeting and universality, a strong case could be made by 1980 that too large a share of scarce federal resources were being diverted into benefits for the nonneedy. Unfortunately, the administration's response to this imbalance has proven to be narrow, inequitable, and devoid of vision. Eligibility for programs aiding the poor has been restricted to the most needy as a means of slashing federal outlays. No broader effort to shift resources from universal entitlements or subsidies for the affluent to means-tested programs serving low-income Americans has been undertaken. Only this year, with opportunities for significant budget savings from means-tested programs seemingly exhausted, has President Reagan challenged the flow of aid to middle- and upper-income households through the broader welfare system.

The Reagan administration has similarly clouded the perennial debate over the appropriate sharing of social responsibilities among federal, state, and local governments as well as the private sector. The Reagan program, under the banner of New Federalism, has aggressively sought to shift responsibility for the administration and financing of social welfare initiatives to the states. The Reagan administration has also relied heavily upon the conviction that social welfare efforts, whenever feasible, should be left to private voluntary efforts. This perspective, founded on ideology rather than empirical evidence, has been useful in buttressing attempts to reduce federal expenditures but precludes a balanced and reasoned assessment of appropriate public and private roles in the modern welfare system.

Taking the principle of subsidiarity (i.e., the belief that the federal government should not undertake functions that can be performed by a lower level of government or private groups) to the extreme, opponents of federal intervention seek to obscure the reasons much of the responsibility for the welfare system has fallen upon the federal government. Contrary to idealized notions of community responsibility, state and local governments in prior decades consistently failed to marshal the will and the resources to alleviate poverty and expand economic opportunity for the most disadvantaged. By definition, the poorest states and localities faced the most severe problems while having the least capacity to redress them. Competition among states and localities also has discouraged responses to pressing social needs prior to federal intervention, as these smaller jurisdictions have attempted to attract new businesses and industries by holding down tax rates and public expenditures. Because the federal government relies upon more equitable financing structures and a broader revenue base than state or local jurisdictions, its capacity to support large-scale income maintenance and human resource programs is far greater. For all these reasons, any effective welfare system must include a central federal role in setting national priorities, providing direction for equitable policies and program development, and generating the resources necessary to meet social welfare goals.

These principles are not inconsistent with the belief that decentralized program administration can be an appropriate response to regional diversity and bureaucratic inefficiency. In some realms, community decision making and program administration are crucial to the effectiveness of the welfare system, ensuring that interventions are tailored to local needs. Strategies for assistance which are well suited for conditions in the South Bronx may have little relevance to the problems of the disadvantaged in rural Appalachia. The existing structure of federal programs in education, employment and training, economic development, and a host of other areas already reflects this need for local control over the specific form and substance of social welfare initiatives.

Given the unwillingness or inability of state and local governments to marshal adequate resources for the amelioration of social problems, the hope advanced by President Reagan that the private sector can fill the breach created by federal retrenchments appears even less credible. The nation's voluntary agencies and associations have not proven able to compensate for losses in federal aid through greater reliance upon private philanthropy. As a detailed Urban Institute study of some 6,900 nonprofit organizations across the nation has documented, private social welfare agencies have fallen far short in their attempts to fill gaps left by domestic budget cuts. The business community is neither equipped nor inclined to accept responsibility for the wide array of problems confronting the nation's disadvantaged. Even in areas in which the private sector presumably has a direct and immediate interest, such as occupational training under the Job Training Partnership Act, the evidence shows that industry molds social programs to serve its own profitability goals—ensuring quick and efficient placements to minimize training costs to fill job vacancies, investing little to develop skills among those most in need. The broader public interest cannot be either adequately protected or promoted through a reliance on private-sector initiatives alone.

The need for a strong federal role in the welfare system is clear, and yet public understanding of this federal responsibility has been undermined by the virulent antigovernment ideology of the New Right and nourished by President Reagan. The most pressing question for the future of the welfare system may rest upon the nation's ability to regain confidence in government responsibility for the welfare of the citizenry and belief in the legitimacy of collective action to meet societal needs. If America's political leadership continues to denigrate the federal government as a vehicle for advancing the common good, further progress in strengthening and improving the welfare system (as well as in other legitimate and proper realms of governmental responsibility, ranging from protection of the environment to safety in the workplace) will remain stymied. Through a clearer understanding of past experience, the nation can rekindle its faith in the ability of the welfare system to provide not only income for the poor but also greater opportunity and equity for all Americans. In this era of retrenchment, no challenge is more important than refreshing our memory of past accomplishments and refocusing our vision for the years ahead.

ISSUE 5 NO:

Work, Wealth, and Welfare

Walter E. Williams

The preceding statement by Sar A. Levitan is an example of the failure to acknowledge a few absolutes in this world: (1) the government cannot give everyone the privileges of a monopoly; (2) government allocation of resources is a zero-sum game, and a game biased in favor of the skilled, the educated, and the wealthy; (3) to every benefit there is a cost; and (4) we cannot make cats bark and dogs meow. The primary theme of "The Evolving Welfare System" is income redistribution. Accordingly, the reasons we should have income redistribution are to "prevent extreme deprivation" and "cushion the impact of economic misfortune and uncertainty on more advantaged and affluent members of society."

In the federal budget year 1981 the amount of official transfers was enough to give $12,000 to every person at the bottom 10 percent of the income distribution or $6,000 to every person at the bottom 20 percent. According to Gordon Tullock in *Economics of Income Redistribution,* that translates into $48,000 or $24,000 for a family of four if all transfer payments were given to the poor. In 1981 actual payments in cash and food stamps to an average family of four in the Aid to Families with Dependent Children program totaled only $6,500. The poor receive nowhere near the total amount of government transfer payments. That is clear evidence that concern for the poor is only a tiny fraction of the real motivation for income redistribution in the United States. As Tullock insightfully points out, "The major motive for government income transfer in the modern world, and in fact throughout history, is simply that the recipients of the money would like to get it, and they have the political power,...to implement their desires." The bulk of transfer programs are not means-tested, and the primary beneficiaries of transfer programs are persons with both significant political influence and pretransfer incomes above the poverty level. These facts are good evidence that selfish goals and envy are the prime motivating factors behind the demand for government programs for income redistribution. The primary beneficiaries of the welfare state are not poor, uneducated people but better off, better educated people. A small but indicative sample of transfer recipients who are by no means poor are: well-to-do elderly who receive medicare, huge agribusinesses and other businesses, college students, professors, and Amtrak passengers.

According to Levitan, the growth of the welfare system was in part a response to "the persistence of poverty despite rising affluence during the 1960s." While such a statement captures the popular sentiment, it is factually wrong. United States poverty was in a steep decline during the period. In 1950 poverty characterized 30 percent of the population; by 1964 that figure had fallen to 18 percent. The decline occurred at a time when annual expenditures on poverty never exceeded $6 billion. From 1964 to 1968, the years associated with President Johnson and the beginning of the Great Society programs, poverty fell 5 more percentage points to 13 percent. The facts about poverty, which contradict conventional wisdom, are: (1) prior to the Great Society programs, poverty was not persisting—it was in steep decline; and (2) the reduction in poverty over the period cannot be attributed to massive social expenditures. The data show the opposite pattern: poverty expenditures are higher now but the poverty rate (nearly 14 percent) is higher than anytime since 1967.

In addition to feeding the myth that the Great Society program was responsible for major poverty reduction, Levitan offers us another: "The working poor were also helped by wider coverage of the minimum wage and unemployment insurance laws during the Carter administration." The minimum wage, far from helping the poor as a class, discriminates against the employment of the poorest. Those with the least skills are required by law to be paid a wage greater than their productive capacity. Few employers will hire a worker for $3.35 an hour when that worker's output is only $2.00 an hour.

The minimum wage law is a seller's collusion that has the characteristic of any other collusion. For example, when the Big Three automakers and the United Automobile Workers lobby for a minimum price on foreign cars, through the mechanism of a tariff, they are not motivated by a desire to raise import car prices so Japanese people will be better off. They seek to raise the price of their competitor's product as a means to achieving the prices of a monopoly for their domestic product. Using minimum prices to reduce foreign competition allows American automakers to charge higher prices, earn higher profits, and pay autoworkers higher wages. This is a principle that underlies all collusions and does not change just because the discussion switches from autos to labor services.

Levitan is one of the few holdouts on the unemployment effects of the minimum wage. In almost any field, we can discover the areas upon which a wide professional consensus exists by examining what the elementary college textbooks have to say about the matter. If we randomly pick up any economics textbook including a discussion of the minimum wage, we will find a broad consensus among economists that minimum wages cause higher unemployment for the least skilled workers.

Our relatively generous unemployment insurance laws have an effect easily anticipated by an economist. Since 1948 the average duration of unemployment has increased by four weeks. It has done so because with unemployment payments as high as $250 a week some people search more leisurely for employment, are less diligent in keeping a job, and choose more seasonal employment. None of these actions enhance the value of an employee in his own eyes or those of the employer.

One truth is discovered by Levitan, but he applies it in a painfully naive way: "Every solution to deep-seated social ills has created new problems." Levitan's solution: "The experience of recent decades suggests that the federal government must proceed on several fronts simultaneously if it is to be successful in efforts to alleviate poverty." This solution is tantamount to asking the government to make dogs meow and cats bark, something inherently impossible. An ironclad law of reality is that government cannot establish a special advantage for one citizen without simultaneously establishing a special disadvantage for another. Government allocation is a zero-sum game.

Levitan supports labor laws such as the minimum wage and the Davis-Bacon Act, which requires that some workers be paid the "prevailing" wage. These laws benefit some workers, namely those who keep their jobs despite higher wages. People disadvantaged by these collusive agreements are nonunion and low-skilled workers. The most tragic feature of the plight of the disadvantaged may be misidentification. Typical explanations for disastrously high levels of unemployment among teenagers range from no jobs being available to racial discrimination. No one bothers to ask why were there plenty of jobs available for teenagers at one period while there are fewer now, and what has been the role of labor laws in their disappearance? Theaters used to have several ushers; teenagers used to bag and deliver groceries, polish and clean cars at new-car showrooms, deliver mail during the Christmas holidays, and perform many other tasks now either not done or done by machinery or adults.

Occupational and business licensing laws confer advantages and higher incomes on some people. This comes at the expense of others who are forced to accept lower-paying alternatives. Some cities have restrictive licensing ordinances or outright prohibitions on street vending. These laws enhance the monopolylike power of established merchants, but they cut off the bottom rungs of a traditional economic ladder for the poor. Taxi licensing laws, requiring up to $65,000 per vehicle in New York, protect the income of incumbent taxi owners, but they deny entry to the fledgling entrant who has the skills and equipment to be a good owner-operator but not the money for a license. There are several thousand licensing jurisdictions in the United States that rig the economic game in favor of the more advantaged.

Coupled with numerous artificial market barriers are public schools that destroy the career chances of inner-city children on a daily basis. Many public schools confer diplomas certifying the attainment of a twelfth-grade education, and often the holder is functionally illiterate or can barely read and perform computations mastered by sixth graders elsewhere. Contrary to the self-serving admonishments of the educational establishment, more educational finance is not necessarily the answer. A restructuring of educational delivery is a large part of the answer. Teachers, principals, and administrators get paid whether children can read and write or not. Sadly enough, students get elementary, junior high, and high school diplomas whether they can read and write or not. There is little effective accountability and incentive in many ghetto schools. Accountability and incentive can be introduced by giving effective power to parents. Like middle-class ones, poor parents ought to be able to opt to take their children out of schools that perform unsatisfactorily. Greater parental satisfaction and student achievement are seen in non-public schools in ghetto areas such as the Black Muslim schools, Catholic schools, and emerging independent schools. These all operate on budgets much smaller than those of public schools; yet they do a better job of educating. A voucher system or a tuition tax system could introduce sorely needed competition. Educational vouchers would give parents a greater measure of control since they could effectively fire a school by taking their voucher to another school. Such competition would force public schools to do a better job.

A basic flaw in Levitan's argument is the failure to realize that if youngsters are denied education, how meaningful can it be to call for "broadening access to opportunities for work and self-advancement"? Career handicaps produced by poor education are often erroneously interpreted as racial discrimination. How can we be sure if it is racial discrimination or poor qualifications that account for unemployment, underemployment, and underachievement for many blacks?

Most of the problems cited by Levitan are the direct result of government power creating a special privilege for one American at the expense of another. Occupational and business licensing laws, minimum wage laws, and monopolylike power conferred on labor unions do just that. The welfare system, which has played a major role in the destruction of families, is another part of the problem. In the welfare culture, income is something that is not earned, but a matter of "entitlement." More money is not the result of traditional values such as hard work, sacrifice, and discipline. In the welfare state, more money is the result of complaints, whining, protest, and hustling. The values appropriate for success in the welfare system have little or no value in the marketplace.

Aside from questions concerning the efficacy of the welfare state in reaching its stated objectives, there is the question of morality. The moral question is understood when we recognize that government has no resources of its own. There is no Santa Claus or Tooth Fairy to give congressmen the resources to finance the welfare state called for by Levitan and others. This forces us to realize that the only way Congress can give one American a dollar is to first, through intimidation, threats, and coercion, confiscate it from another American. We must ask whether in a free society there is a moral case for forcibly taking that which is the property of one person to give to another to whom it does not belong. In private transactions, such an act is correctly deemed to be theft. So the question is whether something clearly immoral when done privately becomes moral when done collectively under the color of the law.

Beyond this question is one of politics and our long-run relationship to our fellow human beings. Government allocation of resources heightens the potential for human conflict while market allocation tends toward reduction. Government allocation of resources represents a zero-sum game while market allocation is a positive-sum game. When one person is made better off through government allocation, another person is made worse off. Voluntary market transactions make both parties—buyer and seller—better off.

The traditional coalitions necessary for competition in the political arena are the ones that have divided and caused conflict among people for ages: including racial, regional, and religious coalitions. Civility is one of the rarest and most fragile qualities of our existence; the fight for group turf has rendered civil nations uncivil. To continue support and growth of the welfare state as envisioned by Levitan and many others is to court social disaster. What is more, it is an unnecessary risk. There is no evidence whatsoever that the welfare state can account for the development of the United States, and all its people, as the richest and the freest in history. There is significant evidence that the welfare state leads to economic stagnation, decline, and conflict not only in the United States but in other nations as well.

ISSUE 6

Is Affirmative Action Reverse Discrimination?

Affirmative action is defined by the U.S. Commission on Civil Rights as active efforts that take race, sex, and national origin into account for the purpose of remedying discrimination (see the Commission's 1981 report, *Affirmative Action in the 1980's: Dismantling the Process of Discrimination*). Discrimination is behavior that limits the rights, opportunities, or privileges of a group or category of people. It is often associated with prejudice, a negative attitude toward a group or category of people.

The U.S. Commission on Civil Rights report gives some examples of discriminatory practices engaged in by persons who do not believe they are prejudiced:

- Personnel officers whose stereotyped beliefs about women and minorities justify hiring them for low-level and low-paying jobs exclusively, regardless of their potential, experience, or qualifications for higher-level jobs.
- Hiring officials, historically white males, who rely on "word of mouth" recruiting among their friends and colleagues, so that only their friends and protégés of the same race and sex learn of the potential job openings.
- Employers who hire women for their sexual attractiveness or potential sexual availability rather than for their competence and employers who engage in sexual harassment of their female employees.
- Teachers who interpret linguistic and cultural differences as indications of low potential or lack of academic interest on the part of minority students.

- Guidance counselors and teachers whose low expectations lead them to advise female and minority students to avoid "hard" courses, such as mathematics and science, and to take courses that do not prepare them for higher-paying jobs.
- Real estate agents who show fewer homes to minority buyers and steer them to minority or mixed neighborhoods because they believe white residents would oppose the presence of minority neighbors.
- Families who assume that property values inevitably decrease when minorities move in and therefore move out of their neighborhoods if minorities do move in.
- Parole officials who assume minority offenders are more dangerous or more unreliable than white offenders and consequently deny parole more frequently to minorities than to whites convicted of equally serious crimes.

The Commission Report also discusses various types of organizational discrimination. Seniority rules, for example, when applied to jobs historically restricted to white males make minorities and females more subject to layoff—"last hired, first fired" and less eligible for advancement. Other practices include standardized tests geared to middle-class norms that have little to do with job performance and preferences shown by professional schools to admit children of wealthy and influential alumni, nearly all of whom are white.

In its attempt to remove the historic and current discrimination toward minorities and women, the federal government has moved away from the "color blind" methods emerging from the civil rights laws of the 1960s. When necessary, sex, race, or national origin may be taken into account in order to remedy illegal discrimination. Critics of affirmative action argue that the imposition of "quotas" discriminates against white males and allows unqualified applicants to fill positions.

The Bakke case is frequently cited in discussions of affirmative action, including both of the articles that follow. Bakke was a white male who applied for admission to the medical school at the University of California at Davis in 1973 and again in 1974. After he was refused admission, Bakke discovered that the medical school had a special admission program that set aside 16 of the 100 admission slots for minority students. Bakke's undergraduate grade-point average (GPA) and his scores on the science and general knowledge tests were higher than those of the minority students who were admitted. Bakke argued that if all of the 100 admissions were open to competition he would have been admitted. The case was carried to the U.S. Supreme Court which ruled that the medical school had violated Bakke's rights by establishing a fixed quota for minority students. The Court added that while a school could not use fixed quotas, it was constitutional for a school to adopt admission policies that used race as one of the factors in admission.

Additional information that was not widely discussed was that Bakke's GPA and test scores were also higher than those of the 84 nonminority students who were admitted under the competitive admissions policy (*Washington Post,* Oct 2, 1978, A12). The admission policy in general seems to have been subjective. The Dean of the medical school could select five of the 100 candidates, and these five were usually "well-connected." The general counsel of the University of California acknowledged that a system of preferential admissions favoring well-connected applicants may have existed at Davis. According to Dr. Toni Johnson-Chavis, a black graduate of the medical school who had a 3.5 GPA at Stanford, "This is grossly unfair. The people who were let in for special reasons were rich, white people who had poorer grades than Bakke." (*Washington Post,* Oct 2, 1978, p. A12)

What can or should be done to remedy the traditional patterns of discrimination in the United States? Is "reverse discrimination" as simple as it seems? If a business or governmental agency has few or no minorities in a large workforce, is it a strong indication that minorities are discriminated against if they constitute 40 percent of the population of available workers.

If white males dominate in positions of power, how do we guard against the perpetuation of this system via the "old boy" network? How do we guard against preferential treatment for the children of the "well-connected"? Consider these questions as you read the following discussions of the pros and cons of affirmative action.

ISSUE 6 YES:

The Underhandedness of Affirmative Action

Harvey C. Mansfield, Jr.

Affirmative action is settling down in our constitutional polity like a determined guest seeking to establish squatter's rights. Though the issue is far from settled, controversy has subsided. The Supreme Court has pronounced indecisively on several occasions and in several voices. The Democratic Party, trying to exist on a faded and confused memory of itself, has lost its early enthusiasm for affirmative action, but remains "committed" to it in the routine sense of that word—stuck with it. And the Reagan Administration, elected in a spirit hostile to affirmative action, has found it necessary, or merely convenient, to tolerate it, even to truckle to it.

Former Interior Secretary James Watt's fatal remark about a coal-leasing board he himself had appointed ("a black, a woman, two Jews, and a cripple") helped to bring the Administration's attitude to public attention. Secretary Watt should have been ashamed of himself, and perhaps under his boastful cynicism he was. But, in the usual manner of shame, he seemed to put the blame on others, on the groups clamoring for such treatment. To supporters of affirmative action, this was "insensitive" and insulting. Secretary Watt should have appointed the same people, minus the Jews, but without saying why. He should have known that to state the true purpose of his appointments was to render them useless for that purpose. He should have known that affirmative action works only when it is concealed and lied about. He should have known that, because everyone knows it; the concealment and the lies are all the more necessary because everyone knows the truth.

Affirmative action is obviously a way of helping people who are considered insufficiently capable of helping themselves. But just as obviously, this fact cannot be admitted. Or, if it is admitted in general—as when Justice Marshall said in the *Bakke* case that "meaningful equality remains a distant dream for the Negro"—it must be denied in all particular cases. The reason for wanting to help people is that we hold them to be equal in some sense, hence deserving of equal treatment, but if we help them, we imply that they are unequal in some sense, hence undeserving of equal treatment. Government and management must therefore give help through affirmative action while denying that they give it, indeed *by* denying that they give it, in order not to hurt the pride of the beneficiaries. Their pride, and America's recognition of their pride, is not beside the point: It is the point.

Affirmative action *is* a question of pride, more than has been realized on either side of the debate. So far, most of the argument has been about its justice. Proponents say that because of past injustices, blacks, women, and others on a lengthening list deserve to get a break—partly for revenge, and partly because their suffering has left them unprepared to take advantage of the opportunities that it is admitted they now have. Opponents have replied that past injustice will not be remedied by new injustice of a similar kind, in which people are treated as representatives of groups rather than as individuals. The justice of affirmative action is affirmed by a majority of intellectuals and denied by a majority of the American people. In such a contest, I have no doubt where my sympathies lie. But the injustice or wrongness of affirmative action does not reach the depth of its evil.

The problem of affirmative action appears less grave than it is because its proponents present it as a matter of mere justice: They merely ask us to live by the principles we profess. They pass over the means to get us to live by our principles, and opponents of affirmative action have been content, for the most part, to dispute them over principles rather than means. But the underhandedness of affirmative action is what is worst in it. Even if justice were secured by such means, the result would not be compatible with the dignity or pride of free citizens. Such means, moreover, whether or not declared unconstitutional by the Supreme Court, are a threat to constitutional government, which is concerned as much with means as with ends—and the threat is all the greater for not being widely understood.

To understand that threat, let us return to the necessity that affirmative action conceal the help it renders its beneficiaries. As a policy, it cannot claim success, because to announce an "affirmative-action appointment" as such is to insult the recipient by implying that he would not have got it on merit. It is a peculiar policy indeed where the administrator cannot admit he has done nothing, since this is hardly "action," yet cannot boast of doing something, lest his actions insult the beneficiary. Since the beneficiaries—the blacks, women, and others protected by affirmative action—cannot admit that they are incapable and undeserving, the only remaining solution, it seems, is to accuse the American people, or what is left of it after the protected groups have been subtracted, of discriminating against their fellow citizens on grounds of race, sex, or national origin. The unprotected must admit their guilt so that the protected do not have to admit their incapacity.

But the unprotected include many white males who favor affirmative action; they cannot be guilty of racism and sexism. White males who oppose affirmative action must be the guilty ones, responsible for all the ills that affirmative action seeks to correct. Not that those guilty white males *do* anything discriminatory; any overt action to discriminate would be illegal without affirmative action. Rather, it is their bad attitudes. Those white males glare balefully at the protected groups, wounding and disabling them with negative vibrations and looking out for any chance to do them in by wishing them ill.

This ludicrous picture of America, according to which opportunities for blacks and women have multiplied while racism and sexism have continued to run rampant, is what supporters and beneficiaries of affirmative action are required to believe. If opportunities were not open, we could not know that affirmative action beyond opening opportunities was needed; but since affirmative action is needed, the same Americans who opened them must secretly desire to close them. At a time when no American can publicly defend segregation, the most powerful Americans are supposed to desire it and to have succeeded in imposing it. Accusing one's fellow citizens of racism and sexism has become so routine, to be sure, that the seriousness of the charge has been forgotten. But to make a serious charge lightly is so far from an excuse as to be an aggravation. To accuse a group of "institutional racism" reveals a frivolous attitude in the accuser that is worse than the casual malice of which he complains.

None of this is meant to deny that prejudice exists in America. In one way prejudice is much greater than we know: Since we live in a democracy, prejudice exists not only against those held inferior but also against people we suspect of superiority. But affirmative action, under the guise of opposing racism and sexism, inflates those attitudes by imputing them to other citizens as the sole cause of remaining inequalities. Although affirmative action claims to be a temporary policy, it has a vested interest in the continuation of prejudice. "Progress" in race and gender relations is made doubtful because each advance occurs not by the gradual disappearance of prejudice but with a triumph over it. The beneficiaries are encouraged to think that they got jobs or promotions not on merit but as punitive compensation, like the recovery of stolen goods from thieves. This may be cause for satisfaction in the beneficiaries, but it cannot be the occasion for pride. The unprotected Americans—the "guilty" ones—are not ashamed; they are humiliated. They are not asked to live up to their ideals; they are forced to do so because it is assumed that they have not done so and will not do so on their own. This is a recipe for resentment.

To combat the prejudice it inflates, affirmative action has two modes, which Nathan Glazer has distinguished as hard (quotas) and soft (pressure without quotas). These are two modes of the same policy rather than two policies. Affirmative action with quotas will often be opposed because it is too blatant, although the policy as such is by no means so honest that its proponents will admit that merit is no longer the first consideration. Instead, they try to redefine merit: It no longer means the best, or the best available; it is made to mean acceptable, or beyond a certain minimum. Sometimes "merit" is defined as what society needs, and society's needs are more big shots who are blacks and women; ergo, promoting them is promoting merit. They serve as "role models," and the role they model is that of being patronized by white males.

Still, despite these evasions, quotas are too blatant. They have been tagged as "reverse discrimination," not to say racism and sexism. Affirmative action therefore retreats to less obvious methods that, it is hoped, will save face for both employer and employed. For example, in my "place of employment"—Harvard University—affirmative action is said to amount to no more than an earnest attempt to "identify and consider" the protected candidates. Similarly, according to Justice Powell's majority opinion in the *Bakke* case, universities may "consider race" for admissions but may not "use" it explicitly.

But this soft mode does not persist either. After time has passed, noses are counted, and if too many are found to be of the wrong color or sex, the order comes down to quit stalling, to find one now, lest quotas be imposed. This order comes down but does not go out. Soft and hard modes of affirmative action agree in their lack of candor; they vary only in the degree of pressure, as push differs from shove.

To manage its two modes, to coordinate the uses of insinuation and threat, affirmative action has its very own bureaucracy. Affirmative-action officers are to be found in the employ of almost every large company and university. They are paid by the employer but they do not work for him. They work toward the achievement of affirmative action, no matter what that does to their employer, because their job is to see that their employer abides by federal regulations. Their job is not like that of a lawyer, who might advise his employer on how to stay within the law while keeping his best interests in view; nor is it like that of a policeman, who enforces the law impartially and is paid by the government. Like everything else about affirmative action, its officers are in between. Their job is neither to advise nor to enforce, but to exert pressure.

It goes without saying that affirmative-action officers must be members of protected groups. No white male could be trusted to have the necessary impartiality for that position, not even if he were a proponent of affirmative action. He might wish to do his best, but some tincture of bias would surely inhibit him in the pursuit of justice. Besides, an unsuitable affirmative-action officer could not provide the necessary support and reassurance to the blacks and women who are his protégés. They might get the wrong idea that white males are not prejudiced against them.

All the bluster against discrimination conceals the fact that the civil-rights movement has lost its high idealism and has descended to a mundane concern for jobs and honors. The result is demeaning, but worldly ambition can keep its aura of heroism if it can be said to struggle against racism and sexism. That struggle not only justifies appointments not based on merit but also dignifies the self-interest of those who accept them. In reality, prejudice is now at a low point in our history. Most affirmative-action programs do their best to kick in an open door at which personnel officers, suppressing their supposedly wicked hatred for the blacks and women they have bent every effort to enlist, stand ready with effusive greetings and all-consuming grins. Where hostility is met, it is more often resentment at affirmative action than prejudice against the protected groups as such. And when it is hard to find a job, as it frequently is, the reason is usually not prejudice but the scarcity of jobs. Tokenism, in fact, is an understandable, even a reasonable defense against routine accusations of discrimination. One insincerity creates another—and deserves another.

As befits its underhanded nature, affirmative action has an underhanded history. Although it is now a centerpiece of government policy, affirmative action never made its way through the legislative process with public notice and debate. As is well known, Hubert Humphrey and other managers of the Civil Rights Act of 1964 expressly denied that quotas or preferential treatment were required by Title VII of that act, and they put that denial into the language of Title VII. "Affirmative action" began as an undefined, apparently innocuous, phrase in an executive order with no direct reference to any duly passed law, and it just grew, with the eager cooperation and inventiveness of the courts. Even now it has no fixed meaning, and, as I have said, its proponents find it convenient to avoid fixing one, adopting hard or soft meanings depending on whether affirmative action is on the attack or the defensive.

While the meaning of affirmative action was being arbitrarily expanded, its protection was arbitrarily extended. Whereas the Civil Rights Act of 1964 represented a national consensus, the culmination of a grand struggle by and for blacks, other groups have since taken advantage of the consensus on blacks to include themselves among the formerly oppressed and the currently bewildered. The women's movement, in particular, has taken a free ride on the injustices done to blacks. It provides no forthright argument that a society in which women stay at home is inferior to one in which they take paid jobs outside the home. Instead, the movement concentrates on "raising consciousness," which consists of showing women and men how they have always assumed women should be as they always have been. But slaves who can gain freedom merely by raising consciousness were never slaves. Men have in fact meekly surrendered, or eagerly offered, their privileges—only to be told that this is not enough. Men are still guilty, guilty, a thousand times guilty of sexism. Thus, affirmative action is both expiation of male guilt and a newfangled gallantry that many women deign to accept—they do not wish to push revolution too far. Women recognize that moderation is the way to have the best of both worlds. Let us hope they do not get the contrary: failing to keep the traditional courtesies they continue sexistically to prize while failing to gain, or savor when gained, an equal or greater-than-equal share (why not play to win?) of the top honors of this world. At the moment it is hard to think why they should not expect the worst of both worlds.

With such a dubious history, affirmative action has not been presented by its proponents as the fundamental change that it is. President Johnson spoke of the need for "equality of result" as something beyond "equality of opportunity," but the new equality was to be the result of living up to established principles. It was not a challenge to equality of opportunity but an improvement needed, it was said, because people do not have equal opportunities if they cannot take advantage of them equally because of a disadvantaged background.

"Background" is the key to the innovation made by affirmative action. One's background is the sum of one's nature, including both individual and human nature, and nurture, including both individual upbringing and the habits inherited from the history of a group. Equality of opportunity presupposes that nature is more powerful than nurture, that we have a fixed human nature, enabling an individual to overcome an upbringing of poverty and a history of deprivation. All the individual needs is an opportunity; his nature permits him to make a "fresh start."

Thomas Jefferson went so far as to conceive of a natural aristocracy to be elicited in the American republic through tests of merit. This reliance on nature has seemed too confining to more recent liberal reformers, many of them influenced by Marxism. They have concentrated on its limitations, particularly its self-interest, the selfishness of the old Adam. They have attacked the notion of a fixed human nature as reflecting a belief in original sin, which is bad because it is conservatism. Yet certain historically minded conservatives, with an exaggerated devotion to tradition, have joined these liberals in attacking the notion of a fixed human nature.

For both of these parties, history has proved to be a trap. The conservatives now have to admit that Communist revolution has an increasing share of contemporary history; so if man is history, our history is carrying us into revolution. The liberals, while meaning to extend reform by denying the limitations set by human nature, have in effect limited reform by calling into question our capacity to take advantage of it. Most liberals seem not to appreciate fully that affirmative action does not add to previous reform but criticizes it, and that the reform being criticized is liberal reform. They are used to thinking of progress in reform, by which one reform, inadequate or incomplete by itself, suggests anothei. With the advent of affirmative action, however, previous reform is declared ineffectual, not merely inadequate, and progress itself becomes dubious.

Those who favor affirmative action do not profess that they are abandoning equal opportunity; on the contrary, they promise to make opportunities really equal for the first time. They say that the natural endowments of the disadvantaged cannot overcome their histories right now, but at some time in the future, when those disadvantaged histories have been overcome by affirmative action, merit can once again be our standard and quotas be discarded. Affirmative action is thus professedly not an abandonment but a temporary postponement of equal opportunity. To say otherwise would be to admit that races and genders are permanently unequal.

But how long will it take to equalize the histories of blacks and women? At Harvard, the official policy is to continue affirmative action "until we have demonstrated to our own collective satisfaction that hiring decisions are absolutely color-blind and sex-neutral." *Absolutely* is a word not often heard at Harvard, where many people commonly say they do not believe in "absolutes." But the extremism of this absolute, which is necessary to the idea of affirmative action, has to be savored to be appreciated. It is not enough for us to decide, as best we can, on the basis of merit; each of us must be blind to his own color, neutral as to his sex. None of us can be trusted to decide on merit until each of us has repressed in himself any qualities that might possibly cause him not to decide on merit.

How is this marvelous repression to be achieved? Well, precisely by feeding the pride of race and sex in blacks and women and guilt of the same in white males. One state of mind—being absolutely color-blind and sex-neutral—is to be achieved by practicing its contrary. This is what is meant when we are asked to live up to our principles, to "close the gap between reality and ideals" (as the Harvard policy puts it). Since the goal is absolute, the policy adopted to get there will take a very long time to succeed, if it can ever succeed. And since the means used by the policy contradict the goals, even progress is unlikely. Affirmative action begins with the assertion that despite civil-rights legislation, prejudice continues and has got worse; then it concludes that despite the strength of prejudice, prejudice can and ought to be abolished; and last, it decides that abolition of prejudice can be accomplished by inflating it.

Some might think that the cure for the underhandedness of affirmative action is "open government," a policy of keeping nothing secret from the people. Not in the least! Open government was the means selected by the late, lamentable Carter Administration "to make government as good as the American people." It is also the operative ideal of the media, and it has a respectable source in the political philosophy of Kant. Open government, it is said, will make government more moral by making it more visible. This is just what affirmative action claims to do when it attempts to bring to light the informal truth behind a formal commitment to equal opportunity. It is no accident that affirmative action was most emphatically affirmed in the Administration that was devoted to open government.

Under affirmative action the same thing happens as under open government generally. A visible action that is at first taken as a *sign* of morality becomes a morality *itself.* A visible affirmative action taken to overcome racism, such as appointing a black to office, instead of being understood as a sign that racism is gone, is mistaken for a blow at racism. Attention is thus shifted from motive to result ("equality of result"), and it is wrongly concluded that we can destroy racism by appointing blacks—only the result matters, not the means. What begins as an attempt to infuse our public and private lives with morality ends as indifference to the means so long as the end is achieved; it ends as indifference to morality. The gap between reality and our ideals is not closed; it is merely papered over—with bureaucratic forms, in which empty accusations are answered by insincere protestations. The perfect example of this immoral moralism is the "consent decree"—an oxymoron if there ever was one—describing the treatment of a defendant who does not admit he is guilty but agrees under compulsion to act as if he were.

It would go too far to say that, in the matter of affirmative action, government by consent decree is replacing government by consent. But we have perhaps plumbed the depth of the harm done by affirmative action when we understand how it negates the principle of government by consent. The right to consent to government is often presented as a matter of justice, and rightly, because it is justice to count each person as one. But the right to consent is also a matter of dignity, because each person must *count* for something in order to be counted as one. It is the right to be treated as a person worthy of being taken seriously, as a rational creature capable of choice, who deserves to be persuaded and not taken for granted.

One cannot presume, therefore, how the right to consent will be exercised. One cannot suppose, for example, that blacks, because they are blacks, must want this and not want that. Of course, it is not always practicable to take a vote. It may be defensible to presume tacit consent in a situation from which one draws benefits, but consent that is presumed because of one's social and economic characteristics is an outrage. Whereas the first presumption declares what you have apparently consented to, leaving intact your right to withdraw consent, the second says what you *would* consent to, thus making actual consent unnecessary and bothersome. It is hardly surprising, and not reprehensible, that blacks should vote for blacks, but for them to do so automatically is no merit and deserves no praise. For the government to presume, as a matter of law, that blacks will do so is no mere prediction of how they will vote but an unthinking usurpation of their right of consent.

In the recent extension of the Voting Rights Act (1982), Congress flirted with the idea of affirmative-action consent that would have given protected groups the representation it presumed they would and should vote for. According to this bright idea, the government should no longer confine itself to guaranteeing the right to vote, but should now look to see how that right is exercised, in case voting by one method or another should deprive a minority of its fair share of representation, *as calculated without reference to elections.* This was an attempt at mandated racist voting, and it was narrowly and only partially defeated.

It is not enough to describe our problem as a gap between reality and our ideals. Such a description overlooks the right to consent, which is the key to all our other rights. Our problem is in one way greater than a gap between reality and our ideals, and in another way more honorable. It is a gap within our ideals, a gap arising from the right of consent and reflecting the reality that free men are not free of prejudice.

Since this is so, and is likely to remain so, do we want to conclude that freedom should be withheld until all prejudice has been abolished? That is the totalitarian way—which says, in contradiction of itself, that men are worthy of freedom but not of gaining it on their own. But then, if we avoid this contradiction and allow that people should have "freedom now," and not have to wait until government has declared them worthy of it, we must respect their right of consent. We must respect that right even in those who are prejudiced (and of course in those we merely disagree with). To do so is not merely a practical necessity—as if we were merely recognizing the gap between reality and our ideals—but a moral imperative derived from our central ideal, the right of consent.

Living together in freedom requires more than justice, for after justice has been exacted, people are not always in a mood to live together. To put ourselves in the right mood for free society we must recognize the dignity of other citizens. We must treat them, to repeat, as worthy of being persuaded. This morality of consent requires us to consent, for the sake of our morality, to a gap between reality and our ideals. It also provides a necessary check on our moralism, when we try to rush into reform too confident that those who are opposed are merely prejudiced. Moralism gives morality a bad name and makes free citizens angry and impatient with one another.

Properly understood, the right to consent neither prevents us from resorting to compulsion when necessary nor disables us from attempting reform when desirable. In this proper understanding, consent has its forms and procedures whose observance makes it necessary to persuade one's fellow citizens. Consent must be registered in legal elections to offices in bodies established by law so that it is clear who are the winners and losers. The point is to leave the majority capable of action after the minority has been heard. A person's right to consent is not violated when he has been outvoted, and his dignity has not been denied when he has been outargued. The forms and procedures of a free government give definition to the dignity of free citizens. It knows when it can act, and we know when we have been consulted.

All these forms and procedures, together with the spirit in which they are practiced, have been called constitutionalism. They ensure respect for the means by which the right of consent is exercised, and thereby they secure respect for the right of consent. They *constitute* a free society; without such forms a society might be tempted to believe that freedom is doing as one pleases, or doing what one thinks is required by justice.

Affirmative action has no regard for the forms and procedures that serve as protection of the right of consent. It has no patience with them when they seem to get in the way of justice, and no compunction about multiplying them when they are thought to advance justice. Any old procedure may be altered, any new procedure may be added; all that matters is the result. Thus, our government becomes ever more intrusive even as it increasingly shirks the task of persuasion.

Those who agree with some, or most, or all of what I have said against affirmative action may still think that something needs to be done, and I believe they are right. In the first place, the case of blacks should be separated from those of all the rest. They are the only ones who were brought to America against their will and then enslaved. True, they were later freed; but still they were held down as second-class citizens. How can they be made into first-class citizens? But is it not evident that this question should be re-phrased as, How can they make themselves into first-class citizens? To which the immediate answer must be, Not by affirmative action: not by receiving justice from others so much as by claiming their own places in the name of pride.

Blacks should look more at what they contribute to America, less at what they want from it. Their wants make them dependent and force them to accentuate the negative, so that they humiliate themselves in the very act of demanding their due. They should consider what they have done in America and whether this is worthy of being continued. They should transform their predilections into conscious deliberation, and consider what they can and should do with their lives, given their choices and the range of opportunities America provides.

To claim 11 percent of every activity on the principle of affirmative action is to say that blacks make no contribution of their own and that America would have lost nothing distinctive if it had sent all its freed slaves back to Africa. But blacks have one sure contribution to make, a valuable addition to their other valuable contributions to our culture. They have been the victims of democratic injustice and have seen freedom from underneath, and in consequence they know what most other Americans can hardly imagine, that democratic majorities can do terrible wrong. This is valuable information for a free people.

In considering what they can do, and want to do, the primary responsibility should be on blacks themselves. The policy I suggest is as far from "benign neglect" as from intrusive interference. It is that blacks should be asked to affirm their own actions.

ISSUE 6 NO:

The Remedy: Affirmative Action

U.S. Commission on Civil Rights

The introduction to this statement defined affirmative action to mean active efforts that take race, sex, and national origin into account for the purpose of remedying discrimination. It distinguished affirmative action plans, which use a wide range of antidiscrimination measures that may or may not take race, sex, and national origin into account, from the specific measures commonly occurring within such plans that implicitly or explicitly use race, sex, and national origin as criteria in decisionmaking.

The first part of this statement described discrimination as a process that perpetuates itself through the interaction of attitudes and actions of individuals and organizations. These beliefs and behaviors shape and are shaped by general social structures, such as education, employment, housing, and government. These elements together form processes that produce marked economic, political, and social inequalities between white males and the rest of the population. These inequalities, in turn, feed into the process that produced them by reinforcing discriminatory attitudes and actions.

The existence of this process makes truly neutral decisionmaking virtually impossible. The conduct of employers, guidance counselors, bankers, and others ... is but one example of how decisions that seem to be neutral, and may even be motivated by good intentions, may nonetheless result in unequal opportunities for minorities and women. These "neutral" acts become part of a cyclical process that starts from, is evidenced by, and ends in continuing unequal results based on race, sex, and national origin.

The second part of this statement then explained that civil rights law in some cases requires and in other cases permits a full range of remedial measures that take race, sex, and national origin into account. Civil rights law facilitates rather than obstructs those affirmative efforts needed to dismantle discriminatory processes.

The final part of this statement applies its problem-remedy approach to some of the major concerns voiced by opponents and proponents of affirmative action. This approach presents a format for productive discussion of these concerns. Its aim is to help distinguish the proper use of affirmative action plans and measures that take race, sex, and national origin into account from their abuse.

SELF-ANALYSIS, STATISTICS, AND AFFIRMATIVE ACTION PLANS

The starting point for affirmative action plans within the problem-remedy approach is a detailed examination of the ways in which the organization currently operates to perpetuate discriminatory processes. Treatment follows, not precedes, diagnosis.

Such an analysis identifies, as precisely as possible, the individuals, policies, practices, and procedures that work to support discrimination. Without that thorough investigation, an affirmative action plan risks bearing no relationship to the causes of discrimination and can become merely a rhetorical endorsement of equal opportunity that compiles aimless statistics and patronizes minorities and women. Such plans frequently prove counterproductive by arousing hostility in those otherwise sympathetic toward corrective efforts. But when based on a rigorous analysis identifying the activities that promote discrimination, affirmative action plans are comprehensive and systematic programs that use the tools of administration to dismantle discriminatory processes.

This examination is likely to be more accurate when performed by persons with an intimate knowledge of the organization and complete access to necessary information. Voluntary self-analysis, therefore, is the preferred means for uncovering discrimination.

In recent years, statistical procedures interpreting data based on race, sex, and national origin have been the dominant means for detecting the existence of discrimination. Their use is premised on the idea that the absence of minorities and women from the economic, political, and social institutions of this country is an indicator that discrimination may exist. A useful and increasingly refined method for self-analysis, such procedures have also been subject to misunderstanding.

One such misunderstanding confuses statistical underrepresentation of minorities and women with discrimination itself. Such data are the best available warning signals that discriminatory processes may be operating. Statistics showing a disproportionately small number of minorities and women in given positions or areas strongly suggest that a discriminatory process is at work. But such *quantitative* manifestations of discrimination raise questions rather than settle them. They call for further investigation into the *qualitative* actions and attitudes that produce the statistical profile.

Another misunderstanding of statistics has led to the rigid demand for statistically equal representation of all groups without regard to the presence or possible absence of discriminatory processes. Many people frequently leap from the misconception that unequal representation *always* means that discrimination has occurred to the correspondingly overstated position that equal representation is *always* required so that discrimination may be eliminated. This position reduces the use of statistics in affirmative action plans (in the form of numerical targets or "goals") to a "numbers game" that makes manipulation of data the primary element of the plan. It changes the objectives of affirmative action plans from dismantling discriminatory processes to assuring that various groups receive specified percentages of resources and opportunities. Such misunderstandings of statistics not only short circuit the critical task of self-analysis, but also imply the need for a remedy without identifying the discriminatory problem.

Once the activities that promote discrimination are identified, the task is then to put into effect measures that work against these discriminatory processes. As the first part of this statement has shown, discriminatory attitudes and actions can form patterns that reinforce discrimination. In such situations, sporadic or isolated measures that implicitly or explicitly use race, sex, and national origin as criteria in decisionmaking may make for some change but are unlikely to be successful in the long run. An affirmative action *plan*—a systematic organizational effort that comprehensively responds to the discriminatory problems identified by the analysis of the organization's operations—is required. That plan will set realistic objectives for dismantling discriminatory processes as they occur within the organization. It will include, as methods for achieving these objectives, antidiscrimination measures, some of which will, and others which will not, take account of race, sex, and national origin.

The basic elements of an affirmative action plan include:

- The organization's written commitment to providing equal opportunity;
- Dissemination of this policy statement within the organization and to the surrounding community;
- Assignment to senior officials of adequate authority and resources to implement the affirmative action plan;
- Identification of areas of underutilization of minorities and women and analysis of the discriminatory barriers embedded in organizational decisionmaking;
- Specific measures designed to overcome the causes of underutilization and remove discriminatory barriers;
- Monitoring systems to evaluate progress and to hold officials accountable for progress or the lack thereof; and
- Promotion of organizational and community support for the objectives of the plan by consolidating advances as they are achieved.

In the employment context, the design and implementation of affirmative action plans involve unions as well as employers. Unions have the authority to insist that employers bargain in good faith over the terms and conditions of employment (such as wages, promotion procedures, training, transfers, and seniority) that affirmative action plans can affect. If unions exercise this collective-bargaining power to press for or acquiesce in discriminatory provisions, or to block nondiscriminatory ones, they may be liable to injured employees. To encourage unions to use their power actively to oppose discrimination and to support affirmative action, the Equal Employment Opportunity Commission has adopted a policy resolution on collective bargaining. That resolution commits EEOC to take into consideration, when deciding who to sue for discriminatory employment practices, the good-faith efforts of unions and employers to eliminate discrimination through collective bargaining.

Unions have the right to request and obtain from employers information on hiring, promotions, and job classification arrayed by race, sex, and national origin. Union members have intimate, firsthand knowledge of plant practices. Unions, thus, are in an ideal position to help develop and implement affirmative action plans that will root out all manifestations of discrimination. Lacking employer cooperation, unions can use their considerable financial resources and legal expertise to inform employees of their legal rights and assist them in bringing legal actions.

GOALS, QUOTAS, AND "PREFERENTIAL TREATMENT"

As a Nation, we are committed to making our differences in skin color, gender, and ancestry sources of strength and beneficial diversity, not grounds for oppression or mindless uniformity. Consequently, agreement on the need to identify discrimination based on race, sex, and national origin and to eliminate it through an affirmative action plan is frequently, and often easily, reached. Few fair-minded persons argue with the objective of increasing the participation of minorities and women in those areas from which they historically have been excluded. Heated controversy occurs, however, over particular methods employed in affirmative action plans to achieve this common objective. The focal point of the controversy is usually those particular measures within affirmative action plans that explicitly take race, sex, and national origin into account in numerical terms. Those measures are popularly referred to as "goals," "quotas," or "preferential treatment."

These terms have dominated the debate over affirmative action, often obscuring issues rather than clarifying them. Many discussions fail to make the necessary distinctions, explained in the introduction to this statement, among affirmative action *plans*, the *measures* they implement that may use race, sex, and national origin as positive criteria in decisionmaking, and numerical *goals* that help assess the effectiveness of the plan's measures. The problem-remedy approach, the Commission believes, can help reorient this debate. It makes clear that the discrimination that exists within an organization forms the basis for the antidiscrimination measures that are implemented through an affirmative action plan. The problem-remedy approach stresses the nature and extent of discrimination and what measures will work best to eliminate such discrimination, not what word to use to describe those measures.

The civil rights community has labored hard to define the points at which measures that take account of race, sex, and national origin within affirmative action plans are essential or become objectionable. There is widespread acceptance of such measures as undertaking recruiting efforts, establishing special training programs, and reviewing selection procedures. On the other hand, firing whites or men to hire minorities or women, and choosing unqualified people simply to increase participation by minorities and women, are universally condemned practices. With respect to measures that do not fall neatly on either end of this spectrum, however, distinctions are far more difficult to draw. These distinctions are not made easier by calling acceptable measures "goals" and objectionable ones "quotas."

For example, as part of an affirmative action plan, an employer could use any one or all of the following: extensive recruiting of *qualified* minorities and women; revising selection procedures so as not to exclude *qualified* minorities and women; considering race, sex, and national origin as one of a number of positive factors in choosing among *qualified* applicants; specifying that among *qualified* applicants a certain ratio or percentage of minorities and women to white males will be selected. Similar measures taking race, sex, and national origin into account could be undertaken by colleges and universities in their admissions programs.

These actions could all be taken to reach designated numerical objectives or goals set by an affirmative action plan. Although the establishment of goals, and timetables to meet them, provides for accountability by setting benchmarks for success, their presence or absence does not aid in choosing which measures to use to achieve the objective of equal opportunity. The critical question is, Which measures taking race, sex, and national origin into account should be used in which situations to reach the designated goals? The answer to this question, the Commission believes, is best found by analyzing the nature and extent of the discrimination confronting the organization.

Obviously, some selection procedures, such as those ordered by the courts that among qualified applicants choose a specific percentage of minorities and women to white males, have characteristics of a quota. But attaching this label to measures that explicitly use race, sex, and national origin as criteria in decision-making does not render them illegal. The preceding section of this statement explained that the lower courts have repeatedly ordered percentage and ratio selection techniques to remedy proven discrimination. In *Weber* and *Fullilove*, the Supreme Court of the United States approved of measures that cannot easily evade the description of quotas. In *Bakke*, four of nine Justices approved a medical school's "set-aside" program, arguing that any system that uses race, sex, or national origin as a factor in selection procedures is constitutionally no different from such a quota system. A fifth Justice indicated that such a program would be legal under circumstances not present in that case. Rigorous opposition to all quotas, therefore, does not aid in distinguishing when to use, or not use, these kinds of legally acceptable, and sometimes required, affirmative remedies.

A debate that hinges on whether a particular measure is a goal or a quota is unproductive, legally and as a matter of policy. It confuses the means for assessing progress under an affirmative action plan (goals) with the measures (quotas) that some, but not all, plans use to reach these goals. It loses sight of the problem of discrimination by arguing over what to label remedial measures. Whichever measures taking race, sex, and national origin into account may be included within affirmative action plans—from recruiting to openly stated percentage selection procedures, with or without specific numerical targets—depends, as a matter of law and policy, on the factual circumstances confronting the organization undertaking the affirmative action plan. The problem-remedy approach urges using the nature and extent of discrimination as the primary basis for deciding among possible remedies. The measure that most effectively remedies the identified discriminatory problem should be chosen.

By broadening the present field of competition for opportunities, affirmative action plans, like all antidiscrimination measures, function to decrease the privileges and prospects for success that some white males previously, and almost automatically, enjoyed. For example, a graduate school with a virtually all-white, male student body that extensively recruits minorities or women is likely to fill openings that otherwise would have gone to white men with minorities or women. A bank with its base in the white community that invests new energies and funds in minority housing and business markets necessarily has less available capital to channel to whites. A police force that has excluded minorities or women in the past and substitutes new promotion criteria for seniority will promote some recently hired minorities or women over more senior white male police officers.

Such affirmative efforts are easier to implement when new resources are available. Additional openings, increased investment funds, and more jobs add to everyone's opportunities, and no one—neither white men nor minorities and women—has any better claim to these new resources than anyone else. Whether new resources become available, remain constant, or even diminish, however, decisions must be made. Frequently, the basic choice confronting organizations is between present activities that through discriminatory processes prefer white men and affirmative action plans that consciously work to eliminate such discrimination.

The problem-remedy framework does *not* suggest that the purpose of affirmative action plans is to "prefer" certain groups over others. When discrimination is a current that carries along all but those who struggle against it, there can be no true "color blindness" or "neutrality." In such contexts, all antidiscrimination measures, whether or not they take race, sex, or national origin into account, will help some individuals and hinder others. To criticize such efforts on the ground that they constitute "preferential treatment" inaccurately implies unfairness by ignoring the need to dismantle processes that currently allocate opportunities discriminatorily.

Measures that take race, sex, and national origin into account intervene in a status quo that systematically disfavors minorities and women in order to provide them with increased opportunities. Experience has shown that in many circumstances such opportunities will not result without conscious efforts related to race, sex, and national origin. Although it is appropriate to debate which kinds of "preferential treatment" to use under what circumstances, the touchstone of the decision should be how the process of discrimination manifests itself and which remedial measures promise to be the most effective in dismantling it.

What distinguishes such "preferential treatment" attributable to affirmative action plans from quotas used in the past is the fact that the lessened opportunities for white males are incidental, temporary, and not generated by prejudice against those who are excluded. The purpose of affirmative action plans is to eliminate, not perpetuate, practices stemming from ideas of racial, gender, and ethnic inferiority or superiority. Moreover, affirmative action plans occur in situations in which white males as a group already hold powerful positions. Federal law, Federal policy, and this Commission reject affirmative action when used, as were quotas in the past, to stigmatize and set a ceiling on the aspirations of entire groups of people.

Support for affirmative action to dismantle the process of discrimination does not mean insensitivity to the interests of white males. To the greatest extent possible, the costs of affirmative action should be borne by the decisionmakers who are responsible for discrimination, not by those who played no role in that process. In fashioning remedial relief for minorities and women, the courts have tried to avoid penalizing white male workers who were not responsible for the challenged discrimination. For example, rather than displace white male employees who were hired or promoted through discriminatory personnel actions, courts have directed that the victims of the discrimination be compensated at the rate they would have earned had they been selected, until such time as they can move into the position in question without displacing the incumbent. The Supreme Court has noted the availability of this "front pay" remedy as one way of "shifting to the employer the burden of the past discrimination."

In addition, the law prohibits "*unnecessarily* trammeling" the interests of white males, thereby protecting the existing status of white males (as distinguished from their expectations based on past practices) from arbitrary affirmative action plans. Thus, there may be situations where minorities and women do not obtain the positions they might otherwise hold, because doing so would require displacing whites from their present jobs. On the other hand, certain situations may require disappointing the expectations of some individual white males.

This balance between the national interest in eliminating discrimination against minorities and women and the interests of individual white men is especially difficult when employers lay off workers. Historically, the groups hit first and hardest by recessions and depressions have been minorities and women. They were the last hired and the first fired. Today, employment provisions that call for layoffs on the basis of seniority can have the same result. Minorities and women will tend to have the lowest seniority and be laid off first and recalled last in companies that excluded them in the past. To break this historical cycle and prevent recently integrated work forces from returning to their prior segregated status, this Commission has recommended, and at least one court has approved, a proportional layoff procedure. Under this system, separate seniority lists for minorities, women, and white males are drawn up solely for layoff purposes, and employees are laid off from each list according to their percentages in the employer's work force. There are other methods that would preserve the opportunities created by affirmative action plans with less impact on white male workers, such as work sharing, inverse seniority systems, and various public policy changes in unemployment compensation. If none of these or similar alternatives are pursued, the use of standard "last hired, first fired" procedures will mean that opportunities laboriously created in the 1970s may be destroyed during hard times in the 1980s.

In the short run, some white men will undoubtedly feel, and some may in fact be, deprived of certain opportunities as a result of affirmative action plans. Our civil rights laws, however, are a statement that such imagined or real deprivations cannot be allowed to block efforts to dismantle the process of discrimination.

Although affirmative action plans may adversely affect particular white men as *individuals,* they do not unfairly burden white men *as a group.* For example, Alan Bakke may have been denied admission to medical school because of an affirmative action program, but nearly three-quarters of those admitted were white. Affirmative action plans reduce the share of white men as a group to what it would roughly be had there been no discrimination against minorities and women. In this sense, an affirmative action plan simply removes the unfair advantages that white males as a class enjoy due to past discrimination. Emphasis on the expectations of individual white men under the status quo downplays their position as a group and the discrimination experienced by minorities and women. Such emphasis also overlooks the fact that affirmative action plans often produce changes in our institutions that are beneficial to everyone, including white males. In eliminating the arbitrariness of some qualification standards, affirmative action plans can permit previously excluded white men to compete with minorities and women for jobs once closed to them all. Court-ordered desegregation of school systems—which can be considered affirmative action plans for school systems—has revealed shortcomings in the education of all students and has led to improvements. Employers have used the self-analysis required by affirmative action plans as a management tool for uncovering and changing general organizational deficiencies.

OTHER CONCERNS

Serious civil rights enforcement efforts by the executive branch of the Federal Government have only been made during the last decade. These efforts have been as controversial as the civil rights laws themselves. Those subject to regulation and those whom the regulations are designed to protect have both voiced criticism and concern about Federal enforcement procedures. In the area of employment, for example, employers complain that Federal agencies administering equal employment opportunity laws and regulations impose burdensome, duplicative, and inconsistent requirements; fail to provide technical assistance; and hire enforcement officials who are often uncooperative, hostile, and unaware of the problems of employers. Community representatives find Federal agencies ineffective in achieving compliance, inadequate in informing citizens clearly and precisely how to avail themselves of the protection of the laws, and lacking adequate staff and resources. The serious problems marring the Federal civil rights enforcement effort are matters of great concern. This statement aims to clarify the conceptual framework that guides these sometimes haphazard enforcement activities. By sharpening necessary distinctions, this statement seeks to eliminate needless friction and misunderstanding among those involved, and, consequently, improve Federal civil rights enforcement efforts.

Perhaps the most serious charge against affirmative action is that it substitutes numerical equality for traditional criteria of merit in both employment and university admissions. Neither the Nation's laws nor this Commission calls for the lowering of valid standards. Affirmative action plans often require, however, the examination and sometimes the discarding of standards that, although traditionally believed to measure qualifications, in fact are not demonstrably related to successful performance as an employee or a student. Whether conscious or unconscious, overt or subtle, intentional or unintentional, the use of such standards may deny opportunities to minorities or women, as well as others, for reasons unrelated to real merit.

It is sometimes mistakenly believed that civil rights law requires the selection of lesser qualified minorities and women over white men. The Supreme Court of the United States has held that Title VII of the Civil Rights Act of 1964 does not require that minorities and women receive "preferential treatment," only that they not be victimized by illegal discrimination. Thus, if two applicants, one a minority or woman and the other a white man are, in fact, equally qualified for an available position, there is no general legal requirement that the employer *must* select the minority or woman. Employment decisions based upon an evaluation of true merit are permissible even when they have an adverse impact on minorities and women. However, just as standards unrelated to job performance cannot be used to exclude minorities and women, restrictive criteria not applied to white men cannot be imposed on minorities or women. Under the Federal contractor compliance program, for example, an employer cannot now require that minority and women applicants possess qualifications that were not previously required of incumbent white men. Nevertheless, less qualified persons need not be selected over persons who are, in fact, more qualified for a specific job.

Civil rights law does not prohibit all arbitrary selection procedures. Unless the intent is to discriminate, arbitrary selection standards (those that do not measure necessary skills) are unlawful only if they build on past discrimination against minorities and women or the discriminatory acts of others. In *Griggs*, for example, the North Carolina employer required as conditions of employment as a "coal handler" that job applicants pass written tests and have a high school diploma. As a result of segregated and inferior public education, relatively few blacks could meet these qualifications. The Court struck down the job requirements because they bore no relationship to job performance *and* they operated to exclude blacks victimized by *de jure* school segregation.

A more difficult issue arises when standards that accurately measure necessary skills disqualify more minorities and women than white men. Because of the pervasive and cumulative effects of discriminatory processes, few minorities and women may possess the experience or skills that certain positions demand. These valid standards, just like invalid ones, reinforce the economic, social, and political disadvantages caused by the discriminatory acts of others. In such situations, civil rights law does not require the selection of unqualified minorities and women. It does, however, encourage organizations and institutions to restructure jobs and develop new standards that are equally related to successful performance but do not disproportionately exclude minorities and women, or to develop training programs that give minorities and women opportunities denied them by other sectors of our society. Affirmative action, therefore, while leading to the dismantling of the process of discrimination, need not and should not endanger valid standards of merit.

Another major distortion of the concept of affirmative action results from the faulty implementation of affirmative action plans. University officials, for example, have inaccurately informed white male candidates, rejected for academic positions on the basis of their own qualifications, that their rejection was due to affirmative action requirements that had forced the university to select less qualified minorities or women. Minorities have been urged to accept promotions to positions for which they lack the necessary skills, in which they then fail, and they are then blamed for their failure. Minority or female "tokens" have been placed in situations where they face open hostility or lack of basic support, and the resulting isolation causes them to quit, which the employer then uses as a basis for not hiring more minorities and women.

Affirmative action plans, regardless of how well they are implemented, are viewed by some as perpetuating the belief of minority and female inferiority. These critics contend that measures that take race, sex, and national origin into account, no matter how benign their purpose, "stigmatize" minorities and women in ways similar to previous invidious labels of inferiority, unfitness, and helplessness. According to its critics, affirmative action casts doubt on the legitimacy of the achievements of women and minorities by implying that these accomplishments were not earned by hard work and on the basis of merit.

These alleged "stigmas," however, do not result from the concept of affirmative action itself. They predate the concept. They are caused by the prejudiced attitudes and offensive stereotypes our history of discrimination has produced. Arguments that affirmative action plans stigmatize minorities and women necessarily accept rather than contest existing discriminatory beliefs. Affirmative action plans, by disrupting the status quo that currently perpetuates stigmatizing attitudes, place minorities and women in competition with white men who before often had competed only among themselves. These plans jeopardize the relative advantages white men hold as a group because of their prior insulation from competition with minorities and women. Changes caused by affirmative action plans are more easily rationalized in accordance with existing prejudices portraying minorities and women as inferior and unqualified than with the nondiscriminatory attitudes the plans encourage.

Both critics and proponents of affirmative action acknowledge the difficulty of changing prejudiced attitudes. The arguments that affirmative action plans stigmatize minorities and women, however, use this difficulty to oppose affirmative action plans: There should be no affirmative action plans because their efforts to change discriminatory beliefs may exacerbate them. Such arguments only deserve attention when accompanied by concrete alternatives that overcome discrimination better than affirmative action plans. The Commission knows of no workable alternatives. Because of our understanding of the nature and extent of race, sex, and national origin discrimination, we are convinced that strict colorblind and gender-neutral approaches are foredoomed to failure.

Inept design and execution of affirmative action plans, of course, can "stigmatize" minorities and women. Affirmative action plans can feed perceptions of minority and female inferiority, for example, when they select unqualified or token minorities who are destined to fail, when they simply are statistical schemes for keeping litigators out of corporate treasuries, and when they do not restrain supervisors from acting on racist or sexist stereotypes. Faulty implementation of some plans, however, is no basis for labeling all affirmative action plans as stigmatizing.

Affirmative action plans have been subject to abuse. If undertaken with little or no understanding of the nature of the problem they are designed to remedy, affirmative action plans can lead at best to mechanical compliance in a continuing climate of animosity among racial and ethnic groups and between men and women, and at worst to subversion of the plan itself.

"GROUP ENTITLEMENTS"

Race, sex, and national origin statistics in affirmative action plans do not mean, as some have alleged, that certain "protected groups" are entitled to have their members represented in every area of society in a ratio proportional to their presence in society. As this statement has repeated, numerical data showing results by race, sex, and national origin are quantitative warning signals that discrimination may exist. While highlighting the effects of actions, they cannot explain the qualitative acts, much less their motivation, that cause those effects. The Commission shares the frustration of Supreme Court Justice Thurgood Marshall, who set out similar distinctions in a dissenting opinion in a recent voting rights case:

> The plurality's response is that my approach amounts to nothing less than a constitutional requirement of proportional representation for groups. That assertion amounts to nothing more than a red herring: I explicitly reject the notion that the Constitution contains any such requirement.... [T]he distinction between a requirement of proportional representation and the discriminatory-effect test I espouse is by no means a difficult one, and it is hard for me to understand why the plurality insists on ignoring it.

We reject the allegation that numerical aspects of affirmative action plans inevitably must work as a system of group entitlement that ignores individual abilities in order to apportion resources and opportunities like pieces of pie.

Individuals are discriminated against because they belong to groups, not because of their individual attributes. Consequently, the remedy for discrimination must respond to these "group wrongs." The issue is how. This statement has argued that when group wrongs pervade the social, political, economic, and ideological landscape, they become self-sustaining processes that only a special set of antidiscrimination techniques—affirmative action—can effectively dismantle. Such group wrongs simply overwhelm remedies that do not take group designations into account. Affirmative action is necessary, therefore, when two conditions exist: when members of identifiable groups are experiencing discrimination because of their group membership *and* the nature and extent of such discrimination pose barriers to equal opportunity that have evolved into self-sustaining processes.

These are rational, factually ascertainable conditions, not arbitrary value judgments or unthinking entitlements to statistically measured group rights based on statistically measured group wrongs. The first condition exists when evidence shows that discrimination is occurring. The second condition is more difficult to determine, but it is still a factual matter. We suggest that discrimination has become a self-sustaining process requiring affirmative action plans to remedy it when the following four characteristics are present:

1. *A history of discrimination* has occurred against persons because of their membership in a group in the geographical and societal area in question;
2. *Prejudice* is evident in widespread attitudes and actions that currently disadvantage persons because of their group membership;
3. *Conditions of inequality* exist as indicated by statistical data in numerous areas of society for group members when compared to white men; and
4. *Antidiscrimination measures* that do not take race, sex, and national origin into account have proven ineffective in eliminating discriminatory barriers confronting group members.

These four categories of evidence focus on the time, depth, breadth, and/or intransigence of discrimination. Their presence demands that concern about discrimination extend beyond the more palpable forms of personal prejudice to those individual, organizational, and structural practices and policies that, although superficially neutral, will perpetuate discriminatory processes.

The Federal Government, based on its experience in enforcing civil rights laws and administering Federal programs, collects and requires that others collect data on the following groups: American Indians, Alaskan Natives, Asian or Pacific Islanders, blacks, and Hispanics. It is the Commission's belief that a systematic review of the individual, organizational, and structural attitudes and actions that members of these groups encounter would show that they generally experience discrimination as manifested in the four categories set forth above.

The conclusion that affirmative action is required to overcome the discrimination experienced by persons in certain groups does not in any way suggest that the kinds of discrimination suffered by others—particularly members of Euro-ethnic groups—is more tolerable than that suffered by the groups noted above. The Commission firmly believes that active antidiscrimination efforts are needed to eliminate all forms of discrimination. The problem-remedy approach insists only that the remedy be tailored to the problem, not that the only remedy for discrimination is affirmative action to benefit certain groups.

Arguments against affirmative action have been raised under the banner of "reverse discrimination." To be sure, there have been incidents of arbitrary action against white men because of their race or sex. But the charge of "reverse discrimination," in essence, equates efforts to dismantle the process of discrimination with that process itself. Such an equation is profoundly and fundamentally incorrect.

Affirmative action plans are not attempts to establish a system of superiority for minorities and women, as our historic and ongoing discriminatory processes too often have done for white men. Nor are measures that take race, sex, and national origin into account designed to stigmatize white men, as do the abusive stereotypes of minorities and women that stem from past discrimination and persist in the present. Affirmative action plans end when nondiscriminatory processes replace discriminatory ones. Without affirmative intervention, discriminatory processes may never end.

Properly designed and administered affirmative action plans can create a climate of equality that supports all efforts to break down the structural, organizational, and personal barriers that perpetuate injustice. They can be comprehensive plans that combat all manifestations of the complex process of discrimination. In such a climate, differences among racial and ethnic groups and between men and women become simply differences, not badges that connote domination or subordination, superiority or inferiority.

From U.S. Commission on Civil Rights, *Affirmative Action in the 1980's: Dismantling the Process of Discrimination,* Washington, D.C., 1981.

ISSUE 7

Should the United States Impose Economic Sanctions against South Africa?

The Republic of South Africa is unique in its system of race relations. Most, if not all, modern nations discriminate on the basis of race, religion, or ethnicity, but no other nation has discrimination so built into its norms and laws. This pattern is in large part a reflection of the history of European settlement and exploitation. Whites—English and Afrikaners of Dutch descent—make up about one-sixth of the population, and they virtually control the wealth and power in the country.

The first European settlement of South Africa was established by the Dutch in the seventeenth century. Miscegenation involving white males and native females produced descendants of mixed ancestry who were referred to as *coloureds.* As a result of the Napoleonic wars, the British took control of the country in 1795. The British imported indentured servants from India who generally stayed in South Africa after their period of indenture, creating another group within the population. The largest group by far is the native black African population, frequently referred to as Bantu, represented by a variety of tribes with varying languages, customs, and traditions.

During the period of British control, attempts were made to correct inequalities in the social system. Slavery was abolished thirty years earlier than in the United States, and blacks, despite numerous restrictions, had the right to vote. The attempts to liberalize the system were, however, in conflict with the desire to maintain white control. "Pass" laws requiring identification and passes for entry into white areas were used to control the movement and location of the blacks.

In 1948, South Africa was granted its independence from England, and the National Party dominated by the Afrikaners came to power. In order to continue white supremacy, the policy of *apartheid* (an Afrikaner word meaning separateness) was developed. At the root of apartheid is the system of racial classification. The system goes far beyond black and white. Coloureds and Indians are divided into subgroups, and blacks are divided into various tribal units. The classification is primarily by ancestry and exhibits many of the same problems that existed in the American South where people were legally categorized as black or white on the basis of their ancestors.

Such a classification system determines, to a large extent, the opportunities available to an individual. In the apartheid system, as in the American South prior to the civil rights movement, there are separate facilities (restrooms, beaches, etc.), separate churches, and separate occupations for blacks, as well as social norms that require black deference. Blacks have no real political power, and they are generally required to live in black townships when they work in white areas. The South African government has created tribal homelands. The homelands are not the original territories of the tribes and tribal members are required to reside in the homeland. Black Africans constitute about 70 percent of the population and have been given about 13 percent of the land.*

Support for apartheid is not the issue in terms of U.S. policy toward South Africa. The question is what steps, if any, should be taken to bring pressure on the South African government to change its system. The approach of the Reagan administration has been one of "constructive engagement," a continuing discussion between the governments and private sectors of the two countries designed to move South Africa away from its racial system. Opponents of the president's policy have favored more direct pressure in the form of trade and economic sanctions. Supporters of the president's policy argue that economic sanctions will create more problems than they cure.

In the following debate, U.S. Senator Lowell Weicker presents arguments that American ideals of justice require us to express our intolerance of oppression and injustice by applying economic sanctions against South Africa. U.S. Senator Jeremiah Denton counters with the argument that the political and economic damage to South Africa would enhance Soviet objectives to the disadvantage of United States strategic and economic interests.

*For a general discussion and history of apartheid see Richard T. Schafer, *Racial and Ethnic Groups*, 2nd ed. (Boston: Little, Brown, 1984); and Steven Anzovin, ed., *South Africa: Apartheid and Divestiture*. (H.W. Wilson Co., 1987.)

In October 1986, both houses of Congress voted decisively to override President Reagan's veto of an economic sanctions bill. The bill bans new investments by Americans in South Africa; prohibits the importing of South African commodities such as steel, iron, uranium, and coal, and suspends South African Airway's landing privileges in the United States.

ISSUE 7 YES:

The United States Should Impose Sanctions

Lowell Weicker

Mr. President, this indeed is a moment for truth insofar as the attitudes of the United States of America toward the practice of apartheid. When I first came to the U.S. Senate, in 1970, everybody recognized that apartheid was wrong, but everyone said it would go away—let nature take its course; certainly something so evil and so bad will not continue. Give to the South African Government the time to be rid of this cancer.

So for the 16 years I have been in the Senate nothing was done, as much by this Senator as anybody else. But the cancer did not go away. It has spread. It is worse today than it was in 1970.

For those who believe that this is a matter of recent note and that any action on the matter of sanctions is precipitous, this is only excusing ourselves and fooling ourselves. We owe this assertion of moral responsibility to a bipartisan combination of forces now in Congress. Finally, both Democrat and Republican, House and Senate, wish to have the United States of America speak clearly on the greatest wrong of our times.

I especially want to thank my colleague from Massachusetts, Senator Kennedy, who has been down this lonely road for the past several years. We have worked together on many efforts, and the amendment which I submit at this time is submitted on behalf of myself and the distinguished Senator from Massachusetts.

Above all, I want to thank someone who is not even in this Chamber nor a part of the official political process of the United States, and that is Randall Robinson, a man who organized the demonstrations in front of the South African Embassy here in Washington, DC, and who, with just a handful, when this was no issue at all, protested this policy of evil, and in his words and statements contrasted it to the great ideals of this Nation.

If this measure is passed and if sanctions become law, the person most responsible for that is Randall Robinson and those of his circle who, day after day after day, kept this matter before the American people, when the American people did not care at all.

So, if anyone thinks that citizen participation is not important, it was not a Congressman, a Senator, or a President who brought the matter of South Africa to the attention of the American people. It was a citizen—in this instance, Randall Robinson.

In any event, both on and off this floor, many people have worked many hours and many days to fashion legislation. It is more than a simple statement of ideals. It is a product of the common concerns of this body that I assume will become the law of the land.

In saying that, Mr. President, I do not want to ignore the important symbolism that this legislation lays before the world.

It shows to our own Nation that the constitutional process can respond with a combination of outrage and precision when deciding how we will do business—or not do business—with enemies of humanity and decency around the world.

It shows to our allies that the world's strongest democracy can lead the way in pursuit of peaceful change in a climate of South African violence. And it shows to the people of South Africa that the United States and the world will not stand silent as Pretoria intensifies its brutality.

Even as we condemn the Government of South Africa, this Nation and others concerned about the deteriorating situation has not turned its back on conciliation. This Nation now and in the future stands ready to resume normal economic relations with South Africa if that Nation chooses to recognize political reality. And that reality, Mr. President, is an explosive situation that can only be extinguished by negotiation leading to a truly multiracial representative government.

The most comprehensive report on this situation is also among the most recent. Representatives of the British Commonwealth, after 6 difficult months of consultations and discussions with individuals in South Africa and the region, reached a disturbing conclusion.

Their report states:

> After more than 18 months of persistent unrest, upheaval, and killings unprecedented in the country's history, the Government believes that it can contain the situation indefinitely by use of force.... Put in the most simple way, the blacks have had enough of apartheid.... The strength of black convictions is now matched by a readiness to die for those convictions. They will, therefore, sustain their struggle, whatever the cost.

Mr. President, I know the responses proposed in this body and the House of Representatives and elsewhere are varied. Many of us have in these past months offered very different responses than the ones the Senate has before it today. No matter what our differences, what our emphasis, most in this body have come together to reject only one response. And that is the one that has fashioned for the United States our so far indelible association with apartheid across southern Africa. That response is the policy of noninvolvement crafted by successive administrations in this country. Any response that relies solely on a combination of diplomatic maneuvering the antiapartheid rhetoric is, to the suffering, a copout.

The call for economic sanctions is not a call to disengage from South Africa. It is a call to alliance with the majority of that country and a progression of U.S. policy from talk to action.

I know that this action has been and will continue to be condemned in some quarters as simply moral posturing. For my part, Mr. President, I plead guilty. I consider it vital that this Nation adopt a posture of morality that for all time will place the United States on the side of democratic opportunity in South Africa.

I know also Mr. President, that economic measures against South Africa are expected by some to meet an especially severe test of national purpose. To these critics, sanctions are wrong because the pain will likely extend beyond the government in Pretoria right to the people. It is an argument we have not heard from these same critics with regard to Nicaragua, or Cuba, or Libya, or the Soviet Union, or any of a score of other nations where economic relations are limited by political considerations.

Again, Mr. President, these critics are correct. As I and many others have said before, it is time we agree to that point and move on. The continued reliance on this argument as an excuse to do nothing is an outrage and an embarrassment to this Nation. Bishop Desmond Tutu writes last June 16 in the *New York Times:*

> I would be more impressed with those who made no bones about the reason they remain in South Africa and said, honestly, "We are concerned for our profits," instead of the baloney that the businesses are there for our benefit. We don't want you there. Please do us a favor: Get out and come back when we have a democratic and just South Africa.

We will hear in this debate, Mr. President, that Bishop Tutu and other foes of apartheid are not representative of the majority of South Africans. Because there are polls that show black respondents in South Africa to be divided on the question of sanctions as a tactic against apartheid, you will be told that advocates of sanctions are out of touch with the population.

And certainly there is no unanimity in the antiapartheid community anywhere in the world—not in the British Commonwealth, not in the U.S. Congress, indeed, not in South Africa itself. One prominent voice against sanctions is Chief Gatsha Buthelezi, the political and tribal leader of the Zulus. His also is a consistent voice against apartheid, against the hated homelands policy that seeks to isolate blacks on 13 percent of South African land, and against the continued detention of Nelson Mandela.

If it is this voice, the voice of Chief Buthelezi that the administration and other sanctions critics wish to hear, then where is the response to the despicable "group areas act" that sustains the homelands policy? Where is the response to his call for an unconditional release of Nelson Mandela? Where is the response to an end to apartheid? This is also the rhetoric of Chief Buthelezi.

I submit, Mr. President, that there is no response. I submit that the specter of Chief Buthelezi and others who seek an alternative to sanctions have been and will be raised only as a convenient excuse for continued inaction.

And I hope I'm wrong, Mr. President. I hope there is a response that could find economic relations with South Africa to be a positive force for change. It is not sanctions we seek, but political change.

Fortunately for the Zulus, Chief Buthelezi and his political party Inkatha were strong enough to reject so-called independence when Pretoria demanded it years ago. For the Ndebele Tribe, whose leadership made the same decision only this week, the road to rejecting the loss of their South African citizenship has run with blood. In Kwandebele, 100 people have died in 7 months of fighting over the issue of so-called independence. To Kwandebele, this form of independence would have caused every man, woman, and child in this 1,000 square-mile area to lose even their meager rights as South Africans.

Many of the South Africans of this and other so-called homelands must by law separate from their families for months at a time simply to earn enough money to live. If their families seek to follow them, they must live in cardboard and tin shacks on the outskirts of white areas where they face the police-backed violence of vigilantes, the murderous and random reign of "comrades," the bulldozing of their communities, the hunger and the disease and the overwhelming poverty.

With an estimated 10,000 religious, civic, and labor leaders in jail, there are few voices left to raise in defense, even in the limited venue offered by apartheid. Increasingly, reports are heard of torture and mutilation by the police.

In April, the Lawyers' Committee for Human Rights issued a detailed report of South African police and army abuse aimed specifically at black children. Using South African Government figures, the group reported that 209 children under 16 were killed in political violence from January 1985 through mid-February 1986. More than 2,000 children were detained without charge under the state of emergency from July to March, a full 25 percent of all those detained.

Here is how the *Los Angeles Times* reported the committee study:

> Even more shocking to the monitoring group, however, was the pattern of frequent and widespread torture of children as young as 10 and 11 by the police. More than 30 cases are cited in the report of children who were beaten, whipped, abused sexually, deprived for days of sleep and food and tortured with electric shocks.
>
> For instance, Joseph, 14, whose last name was withheld in the report for his protection, says he was arrested while playing soccer and held for 9 days at an army camp. He said soldiers had burned him with cigarette lighters, cut him with broken bottles and shocked him repeatedly with electric current. His hands were twisted and blackened

> from the shocks, the report said, and his body badly scarred from the burns and cuts inflicted on him.
> "A white soldier took my right arm and bent it behind my back," the report quotes Joseph as saying as he recalled the start of his interrogation at the camp. "He then took out a lighter, and he held it beneath the wrist of my right hand...I could smell my flesh burning."
> Later, the soldiers used electric current to shock him, Joseph said. A wire would be tied around his right hand, water was poured on him and he was given electric shocks.
> "Each time my body would convulse with the shocks," he recounted. "It ripped out my thumbnail and took a chunk of flesh out of my thumb."

That story is repeated countless times every day in the South Africa that up to now we claim as our ally and friend.

We cannot reach our hands into South Africa and wrench solution out of dissolution. What we can accomplish is the levying of a certain price on the continuation of intransigence in South Africa. The benefits of trade, airline travel and access to American banking and investment remain a tangible sign of U.S. acceptance of Pretoria's policy. South Africa is a nation where whites comprise 15 percent of the population yet control nearly 60 percent of the disposable personal income. Meanwhile, the disparities of South African life go almost unnoticed in the white community.

Richard Manning, the Johannesburg bureau chief for *Newsweek* magazine recently expelled from South Africa writes July 7 and I quote:

> Most whites care little about how substandard nutrition and health care hamper the growth of black children. Most know little of the miserable black school system or of the shabby living conditions in the townships and homelands. Most are ignorant of the atmosphere of repression—armored police vans and daily arrests on every block—that turns young blacks against the white authorities and anyone who supports them.

This ignorance carries a very great price for the whites of South Africa. It is sustained in large measure by the absence of economic pressure by the free world. By refusing to carry the economic and political battle into the white community, the United States isolates that community from the rest of South Africa.

This veil of acceptance of the white community is setting the stage for even more tragic consequences. Every major black leader and organization in South Africa continues to call for nonracial and democratic solutions for the nation. Both tenets of the future will require a large measure of white participation and that participation must be encouraged, beginning now in the form of a white opposition to apartheid. This is an essential role of economic sanctions; the raising of a new era of white consciousness about apartheid.

We can only hope that direct Western action against apartheid serves to moderate the vicious polarization taking place in South Africa. This week in *Newsweek* magazine, Canadian Prime Minister Brian Mulroney was asked in an interview if he believed time is running out. His answer speaks directly to us as Americans. He said, and I quote:

> I don't know what's going to happen, but you can be absolutely certain that when the history of this day is written, what is going to count is that they achieved freedom and what countries assisted in that process. We can't forget the long sweep of history. I spent a weekend watching the United States celebrate Miss Liberty. Someday the people of South Africa are going to be organizing such a celebration. They will remember who helped them.

We remembered that the French helped us, just that one act, to sustain many difficult times over the years. Now is the time to stand up and be counted.

We can only hope that the current debate over sanctions is not too little too late. Last January, in a meeting with civic leaders in my State capital in Hartford, Bishop Tutu said one of his greatest concerns as a man of moderation, as a man of peace, as a man of God, was that if he were a young man in South Africa, he would no longer be listening to Bishop Tutu. That should be our greatest concern as well.

Mr. President, I want to be hopeful, but I must also be realistic about this Nation's policy up to now. By its fruitless trafficking with white oppression, this policy of inaction and rhetoric has become the greatest pro-Communist force existent in Black Africa. That is the truth that this Nation will pay for many times over in the decades ahead unless we exhaust ourselves traveling a road of peaceful change to justice on behalf of all South Africans.

No schoolchild in this Nation is unaware of the circumstances that invite communism, that have communism proliferate. It is disease. It is homelessness. It is ignorance. It is oppression. And all of these are there in full measure and more in South Africa, aided and abetted by the United States of America.

I said so in an interview several weeks back, and I repeat today that the greatest pro-Communist force existent in Africa today is the policy of constructive engagement.

If those are harsh words, they are true and there is going to be a price to be paid for that down the road.

Now, Mr. President, to the amendment before us I first want to commend the committee for devising its bill and its solutions to the problem. That committee bill is a long way from the present policy of constructive engagement, a long way, and it stands as a great credit to the Foreign Relations Committee and the Senators who participated in the writing and the passage of that bill.

And it certainly is a long way from the beginning of the debate on this subject several years ago and protests in front of the South African Embassy in Washington.

I have attempted in this amendment to tighten up in a series of small measures the provisions of that bill. I have worked hard and long, I might add, with the distinguished Senator from Indiana, as well as the Senator from Massachusetts. And this amendment embodies the following provisions:

First, it redefines South Africa to include Namibia in the sanctions.

Namibia, which borders on South Africa, is occupied by South Africa in violation of international law. The United Nations Security Council, with U.S. support, has called upon all countries to refrain from dealing with South Africa insofar as Namibia is concerned. The State Department is on record discouraging United

States investment in Namibia. The South Africa-established Government there has rescinded some aspects of apartheid, but segregation permeates housing, education, health care, transportation, and employment.

Second, this amendment then redefines South Africa to include Namibia in the sanctions. Also, it expands landing rights ban to include United States flights to South Africa.

This is a recommendation of the eminent persons group and one of the sanctions that will be applied by the Commonwealth without Britain. There are currently no flights from the United States to South Africa, but this is considered an important symbolic sanction. Because the committee language terminates a treaty relating to air travel between the United States and South Africa, no flights would be allowed between the two countries once this amendment is adopted. Any flight originating in South Africa must first land in a third country if the destination is the United States. The reverse would also be true under this amendment. The language in here also, I might add, includes the words "controlled by," thus preventing South Africans from leasing aircraft or having their aircraft leased for purposes of direct flight to the United States. Again, the reverse is true from the United States to South Africa.

Third, terminate dual taxation agreements with South Africa.

This amendment would terminate treaty entitled "convention between the Government of the United States of America and the Government of the Union of South Africa for the avoidance of double taxation and for establishing rules of reciprocal administrative assistance with respect to taxes of income."

The treaty currently prohibits double taxation of income of South African and United States nationals.

The treaty is an underpinning of tax relations between the United States and approximately 37 nations of the world. It is a statement of international cooperation that upholds a belief that economic activity carries with it a political benefit that should be encouraged rather than stifled by tax policy.

There is a separate component of U.S. tax policy that provides U.S. nationals a tax credit for taxes paid in other nations. This is a separate matter. The foreign tax credit is an effort to provide a measure of fairness in the U.S. tax code. The treaty with South Africa, on the other hand, is a recognition of the benefits of economic activity in South Africa and it flies in the face of this legislation.

Fourth, prohibit United States Government contracts and procurement with South Africa and assistance to trade and tourism.

Procurement United States Government entities would be prohibited from entering into contracts with any South African entity, except to maintain the normal operation of diplomatic and consular facilities.

This prevents the United States on an official basis from extending economic relations with South Africa beyond the absolutely essential.

Assistance to trade United States funds would be prohibited from aiding investment in or providing subsidy to trade with South Africa.

This would prevent diplomatic efforts to facilitate American involvement in the South African economy. It would not affect consular efforts to facilitate U.S. exports.

Promotion of tourism This would bar United States efforts to encourage tourist travel to South Africa. South Africa has campaigned internationally to attract visitors and artists to its resorts.

None of these provisions will cause a substantive change in United States relations with South Africa. They are, however, an important symbol of U.S. determination to distance itself from apartheid. The resumption of normal diplomatic and trade efforts by our representatives in South Africa can resume when Pretoria takes the necessary steps to insure political rights for the majority.

Fifth, bar South Africa from receipt of United States munitions and commodities that have the potential for both civilian and military use.

The project committee bill makes no mention of arms exports from the United States. Sale or export of these items to South Africa is prohibited by a 1977 United Nations arms embargo and in large measure by the United States own export controls.

The amendment would prohibit the sale or export to South Africa of items on the United States munitions list that are also subject to the United Nations arms embargo. Remaining items on the list may be exported if the President determines the export is solely for commercial purposes and not exported for use by the armed forces, police, or other security forces of South Africa or any other military purpose.

In addition, the President must submit to Congress every 6 months a report describing any license issued for export of munitions list items to South Africa...

Our task out here, very simply, is to obtain not 51 votes, but 67 or more. What we want is not a vote on South Africa but a law on South Africa, and there is a big difference in that. We are not unaware of the fact that we could well be facing a Presidential veto. Indeed, that has already been hinted at by the President.

So what is necessary in whatever clears this floor is that it have at least 67 votes; it needs to be, in order to become the law of the United States. There is much that we all want to vote on, but whatever our final conclusion, let us have it understood that it can marshal at least 67 votes when that test comes.

Last, Mr. President, I ask unanimous consent that a letter to the editor appearing in today's *Washington Post*, written by Malcom Fraser, the former Prime Minister of Australia, who is the cochairman of the Commonwealth Eminent Persons Group, be printed in the RECORD.

There being no objection, the letter was ordered to be printed in the RECORD, as follows:

What President Reagan Said About the ANC (By Malcolm Fraser)

I am sure my co-chairman, Gen. Olesegun Obasanjo of the Commonwealth Eminent Persons Group on South Africa, would want to join me in correcting the impression given by President Reagan's speech Tuesday night in Chicago.

Mr. Reagan said, among other things, the one South African group supporting sanctions was the African National Congress. He also said the ANC was dominated by communism.

In fact, the current leadership of that group is largely moderate, nationalist and pragmatic. After many decades of nonviolence as a policy, it was forced to respond to the violence of apartheid by violence of its own. It did that against a background of denial of political and legal rights to blacks. This view of the ANC is supported by Prof. Lodge of Witwatersrand University, who is an accepted authority on the ANC from South Africa itself.

The ANC is not the only black group supporting sanctions. The United Democratic Front and all its many affiliated groups across South Africa support sanctions. The trade union groups COSATU and CUSA support sanctions. Most prominent church leaders, such as Bishop Desmond Tutu and the Rev. Alan Boesak, support sanctions. Alan Boesak's origins were in the Dutch Reform Church. The leading Catholic hierarchy also supports sanctions. These groups all support sanctions as the only means by which the West can offer effective support to the legitimate cause of blacks.

Everyone knows sanctions would hurt blacks. But blacks are hurting every day. Many are dying daily as a result of attacks by the security forces. They also know that continued and increasing guerrilla warfare will hurt both blacks and whites. Most of all, the use of effective sanctions offers the only opportunity of averting that course.

The blacks in South Africa are seeking to exercise those same rights that President Reagan asserts for the contras in Nicaragua, where, incidentally, I support the president's policies.

The president has argued, as does British Prime Minister Margaret Thatcher, that sanctions should be avoided because they would hurt blacks. Even so, there are some sanctions, such as the denial of air links and the freezing of overseas bank accounts, that virtually inconvenience whites alone.

If the United States and Britain do not provide substantial support for the cause of blacks rights in the form of sanctions, the blacks will conclude, as our group indicated in its report, that they are on their own as far as the West is concerned. The black leadership would then make decisions leading to total guerrilla warfare in response to the violence of apartheid.

Because of numbers, the blacks would win such a contest. It may take up to eight or 10 years after great loss of life. The government arising from such a conflict would be pro-Soviet and anti-West. It would nationalize the totality of Western economic and commercial interest. That will be the consequence of maintaining present policies in the United States and Britain. In such circumstances, Western strategic and commercial interests would both be destroyed.

On the contrary, a government composed of current black leaders would be largely pragmatic and would want the economic system to continue. This is recognized by many members of both sides of Congress, and I hope current proposed legislation receives substantial support.

It is tragic that the two most powerful and effective leaders in the Western world, President Reagan and Prime Minister Thatcher, stand very much alone in not recognizing these factors.

What we are confronted with today is really not much different than that which confronted the United States in the late 1930's, vis-a-vis Nazi Germany. We chose to wait and we chose not to act. Were it not for a few courageous allies, a good portion of the Western World today might be under the heels of Adoph Hitler and/or his successors.

The laws of Nazi Germany vis-a-vis the Jews are identical to the laws of South Africa vis-a-vis black South Africa.

We said back in the 1930's that this is a matter far across the ocean and it will not impact on us. And we waited and we watched and we paid the price. We cannot wait and watch this inhumanity any longer.

If not this administration or this generation of voters, then future administrations and future generations of voters will have to pay the price. And the price to be paid will not be some political price on the floor of the U.S. Senate or in the elections. It will be the same price that we had to pay in 1940. It will be a price to be paid in blood.

This is the time to say no. This is the time to make the choice. This is the time for the United States of America to stand side by side with black South Africa and state the very ideals, once again, that this Nation was founded on and under which it exists. For humanity to be demeaned in the fashion that it is demeaned and trampled and murdered in South Africa is to demean this Nation and what it is that we stand for.

And the longer we wait, the little bit less we are in terms of our own value.

I hope this amendment will pass. I hope the legislation will pass the U.S. Senate, would then in conference be approved by the House and Senate and be signed by the President of the United States. That once again will reassert the moral leadership of this Nation, and most importantly, will have used our strength on behalf of those who do not have any, will have given opportunity to those who have none, will give life to those who daily lose theirs. These are the objectives. These are the worthy objectives of a Nation as great as ours.

From: *Congressional Record,* August 14, 1986 S11629–32.

ISSUE 7 NO:

The United States Should Not Impose Sanctions

Jeremiah Denton

Mr. President, I beseech my colleagues to agree with me that each side needs to listen to the other—listen carefully, because the issue of economic sanctions against South Africa will have major effects not only on people in South Africa but also on people elsewhere and on the interests of the United States and other Nations. Never before have the words "deliberative body" been more needful of real application to the mood and method which should be applied to the Senate's disposing of this issue. Let us deliberate on facts, on opinions and on likely consequences of proposed U.S. actions.

I would like to join the others who have congratulated the chairman of the Foreign Relations Committee for fashioning a useful proposal, now much amended, which some regard as not going far enough on sanctions, and others, including the administration, think goes too far.

The administration distributed a statement of administration policy an hour or so ago in which they state their strong opposition to enactment of S. 2701 because the actions it calls for would impede rather than advance the goal of promoting further change in South Africa.

This Senator has views on the bill itself but, more important than the ultimate specific features of the bill this body finally fashions, the bill needs to be considered in a larger context.

The South African issue will not go away and our further actions respecting the issue depend on the context in which most of us come to view the issue. I wish to try to contribute to some declarative indication of the definition of that context. In my view, Mr. President, the real context of these deliberations revolves around the question of the usefulness of the imposition of more and more sanctions, especially economic sanctions. It revolves not only around what further sanctions the United States should now impose on South Africa but with what conditions, for what reasons, and with what criteria those sanctions should be imposed.

As to reasons, this Senator agrees it is necessary, necessary not only for the United States to have humane domestic policies herself, but it is useful for us to consider encouraging or motivating other countries to act humanely in their domestic policy.

I suggest similar motives should exist regarding foreign policies of our own and of other nations notwithstanding our unanimous desire to effect the elimination of apartheid, at least in passing, one must note that the United States possesses neither the right nor the power to impose forthwith its own standards on other sovereign nations. But we can and sometimes should try to affect those nations. Indeed, frequently we have tried. Our success has been mixed. We have done so in the case of the Shah of Iran, for example, moving him to the left during the terms of several of our Presidents. Our experience was not entirely successful. Hopefully we will learn from the clumsiness and tragedy of having moved that ruler further left than his right wing would tolerate, then effectively abandoning him and his people to a much worse fate that the one we tried to correct. So we should move with caution. Our own historical record with the American Indian, the blacks of America is not exemplary so we should also move with humility.

To assess the degree of humaneness of domestic policies of our own or other nations, permit me to suggest that it would be helpful to consider the definition of a term I shall coin: "Political equilibrium."

Let us define perfect political equilibrium as a condition in which all of a nation's citizens consider their own political system as perfect just. I doubt if any nation exists in that condition of perfect equilibrium by that definition. But I acknowledge that there is a wide spectrum of relativity in equilibria among nations as defined.

I acknowledge that the political condition of South Africa definitely exists in a state of relatively severe disequilibrium. In the interest of not losing sight of proportion, at least in passing, we should note that the political conditions of a number of other states exist in at least a similar kind of disequilibrium. I would cite Poland, the Soviet Union, Nicaragua, Cuba, Ethiopia, Afghanistan, and others.

I would acknowledge nonetheless that the political condition in South Africa is in a state of disequilibrium that exceeds that of any so-called free nation in the world and as I said, I would agree that the United States might usefully consider sanctions intended to help move it toward equilibrium.

In the interest of proportion and honesty, I would add that the foreign policy of other nations should also be the subject of judgment on our part, and we should decide whether the United States should invoke sanctions respecting the humaneness of their foreign policies.

I would cite as examples for careful examination the foreign policies of the U.S.S.R., Cuba, Libya, Nicaragua, the so-called Government of Afghanistan, and others as perhaps decidedly more in need of further sanctions than South Africa.

The issue of sanctions against South Africa thus includes a number of subordinate questions. For example, should not sanctions against that nation be considered more in the continuum of events in the geographical and historical context and the political realities of South Africa rather than in comparison with simply our own present domestic standards and policies? If that consideration is properly made, then we could conclude whether a given set of sanctions would tend to improve the lot of those intended to be improved.

What effects are possible, probable, or certain on the political economic, or military interests of the United States, particularly vital, life or death, interests. Do such effects exist? This Senator believes so. What are the effects of a given set of proposed sanctions on the same kinds of interest of other states?

I believe, Mr. President, that only by a deliberative consideration, a lengthy consideration, an objective consideration, of those questions and others which I shall hear from my colleagues can we hope to proceed toward a useful, not to mention fair or sensible conclusion.

I have made these preliminary remarks not because I think everyone who has spoken has been without proper context but because from what I have heard from some Senators I truly believe that the mood and method in which we have been dealing with the question of sanctions have not been deliberative nor objective, nor full of a desire to learn what must be known as to effects before acting.

I truly believe that as we continue to deal with this issue, we are becoming prone, by inference in this bill, to committing not only a great injustice and folly but also to committing a mortal self-inflicted wound.

This process impends because rather than ask themselves the many questions mentioned above, perhaps too many of us may be populistically and simplistically dealing from purely domestic politically based motivations. I hope not. Having said all that, I know I have much to learn, as do others. I remain receptive to hearing all of what is said by those who propound these sanctions, by those who would amend these sanctions, and by those who would negate these sanctions.

I hope my colleagues will listen as attentively as I have listened and as I shall listen to what they say.

As to the bill itself, although possibly not extreme in itself, I am concerned that the Lugar sanctions bill caters to attitudes, aims, and assumptions that, if nourished, will grow into a vicious self-perpetuating cycle, a cycle requiring the imposition each year of tougher sanctions because one of the underlying assumptions seems to be that the more the violence the more the need for sanctions. This assumption ignores which parties are promoting violence and ignores the fact that those who are promoting it will be encouraged to promote more violence to get more sanctions.

This sanction cycle will be counterproductive to our objectives in South Africa, the achievement of a nonracial multiparty democracy in South Africa; will lead to the further impoverishment of South Africa, will have as yet unexamined consequences for our own domestic economy that will translate into lost jobs and decreased competitiveness for American industries.

Mr. President, let me be more specific about the path of folly which I see likely to develop unless some dangerous assumptions and criteria are abandoned. We must abandon illusions. We must deal with the following facts:

First, truly punitive economic sanctions will hurt economically—even to the point of starvation—those whom we want most to help. That point has two subpoints: economic growth will slow or stop, and, second, black South Africans themselves oppose sanctions and disinvestment.

So economically they will suffer and right now—spiritually, intellectually—they oppose sanctions and disinvestment.

Second, sanctions will hurt black South Africans politically and will, with high probability, leave them far worse off than they are now.

Third, punitive sanctions can hurt the U.S. economy and force some Americans out of work; ultimately our own economy, if this cycle continues far enough, can be destroyed. There is sufficient risk of that for us to consider the matter.

Fourth, sanctions will hurt the United States strategically, and if the cycle continues far enough can hurt it vitally in the strategic sense.

Fifth and last, sanctions can and will accelerate the accomplishment of global Soviet objectives, especially and most immediately on the continent of Africa.

I will deal with each of those five points individually. First, truly punitive economic sanctions will truly hurt economically—even to the point of starvation—those whom we want most to help. There is an old African saying, Mr. President, still unfortunately true: "When the white man grows thin, the black man starves."

Let us examine South African economic growth and unemployment as related to the efficacy of the further imposition of sanctions. Mr. President, South African economists estimate that South Africa's economy must grow a steady 4 percent a year in order to provide employment for new blacks entering the work force even under the system as it existed 5 years ago without sanctions and without the loosening of apartheid made easier by the improving economic conditions. Let us look at boycotts and their effectiveness. If boycotts of South African exports were imposed and became 20-percent effective, the following number of people would lose their jobs in South Africa: 90,000 whites, 343,000 blacks.

If we boycotted their exports to the point of 50-percent effectiveness, there would be a 1.1 million loss of jobs, with income falling by $1.5 billion a year, in direct effects without including multiplier effects.

It is interesting to note that at the outset of the international sanctions campaign South African unemployment was already high due to worldwide recession and depressed world prices for the commodities exported by South Africa. Since 1980, the average growth rate has been far less than 2 percent. The ban on new loans will assure that GNP growth will remain low. That ban is one of the previous sanctions ordered by the President, upon which S. 2701 expands.

In 1981, South African unemployment was 13,000. Today it is 80,000. That 80,000 does not reflect the number of unemployed blacks but is comprised of whites, coloreds, and Asians. It is unfortunate that unemployment statistics do not exist for blacks, but the projected losses I quoted above in black jobs are true, notwithstanding the unfortunate lack of those statistics regarding current black unemployment.

The effects of limited sanctions are already being felt. Further punitive sanctions will most assuredly bring hardship for those whom we wish to help the most. There is no way around that.

Let us take a look at certain commodity sectors in terms of the effect of sanctions. For example, the coal industry. The Chamber of Mines reports that under limited sanctions export sales have already fallen 17 percent. The employment in the coal sector is roughly 110,000 total, 95,000 of whom are black. Thirty-five percent of South African coal workers could lose their jobs under an import embargo, which means that when dependents are taken into account—an average of 5 per laborer—200,000 men, women, and children would be deprived of their means of living.

Let us go to steel. The Iron and Steel Corp. [ISCOR] has 58,000 employees. ISCOR exports account for 25,000 jobs, of which 13,500 are held by blacks. To give you an idea of the multiplier effect, each ISCOR ironsteel job generates an additional four jobs in transportation, harbors, and supplier industries. Thus, 100,000 jobs could be affected by an embargo, approximately 50,000 of these held by black South Africans. So the potential number of black employees losing jobs because of lost ISCOR exports is 63,500, not including dependents.

Let us move to textiles—140,000 people are employed in the industry: 40 percent are colored, 36 percent are black, 1 to 2 percent are white, the rest Asiatics. The industry has had regular wage increases, most of that going to blacks. Wage discrimination based on race was prohibited by the South African Government in 1981. I say again, wage discrimination was prohibited in 1981.

Lost jobs in the textile and apparel industry if a trade embargo were to be levied, would be as follows:

With a U.S. embargo on textiles and apparel, 9,700 employees would lose their jobs, 34,000 indirect job losses would also occur, 136,000 when dependents are included.

With a joint United States and European embargo on textiles and apparel: 48,500 employees would become unemployed, with an additional 169,800 indirect job losses; with dependents, a total of almost 700,000 human beings could be deprived of their means of well-being.

Those are some of the direct economic hardships that could be imposed, inevitably imposed, by sanctions.

Let us move now to the second part of the point—namely, that black South Africans oppose sanctions, particularly if it means economic hardship. I am going to report on all the polls at my disposal. I am going to refer to polls showing both ways.

Polling data generated each year since 1984 show considerable opposition to punitive economic sanctions and disinvestment, as a general statement.

In July and November 1984, in a poll by the Center for Applied Research, conducted under the direction of Dr. Lawrence Schlemmer, and questioning urban blacks alone: 74 percent opposed sanctions in July and 84 percent opposed them in November 1984.

A 1985 poll: six different polls were conducted among urban blacks by Human Sciences Research Council, the Sunday Star, Market and Opinion Research International—MORI. Only one poll, the MORI poll, showed significant support for disinvestment—77 percent. I cannot account for the difference in those polls.

In 1986, three polls were conducted—one by the Human Sciences Research Council, in March. Among urban blacks, 67.7 percent opposed international sanctions; 73.3 percent when it meant the loss of their jobs.

A poll conducted in March by the Institute for Black Research headed by Fatima Meer, a prominent pro-UDF activist showed 73 percent of urban blacks opposing sanctions.

A later poll by MORI, which had the anomalous results, showed this time, polling both rural and urban blacks, 32 percent opposed sanctions, 29 percent supported. The rest had not ever heard of sanctions or did not know what to think. Thus, 52 percent of those who know the issue or about the issue opposed sanctions.

Numerous uncontestedly reliable black South Africans, on behalf of their constituencies, have also spoken out against sanctions. Most well-known, perhaps, is Gatsha Buthelezi, leader of the almost 7 million Zulus.

The third point: Sanctions will hurt black South Africans politically and will, with high probability, leave them far worse off than they are now.

I ask Senators to listen to this point: Black South Africans as well as white ones know something that many in this body and many other Americans do not know and are not permitted to know by the way much of the media has handled this question—namely, that the South African business sector, unlike those in most of the world, is well to the left of the white political center, and most of those black and white South Africans know that the Government itself is now convinced, and has been for some time, that apartheid and the homeland system are mistakes, tragic mistakes.

Now, government, urged by the business sector, is moving to correct, at an increasing pace, those mistakes. I do not deny that many of those who are in opposition to me on this issue today and those like them may have helped develop that pace, and I applaud them for that. But we can cause a reversal of that pace, we can bring about a reversal of the pace toward improvement, and change it toward tragedy, toward great human loss, toward great loss in the interests of the United States.

We cannot deny something that is evident in some of the liberal media which they try to disguise. Throughout South Africa's black townships, the principal force and trend is terrorism. Township residents are being forced by terrorism and intimidation to choose between a horrible death on the one hand and, on the other hand, taking part in, or at least not opposing, violent revolution.

The principal opponents of these tactics are the African National Congress, South African Communist Party Alliance, and elements of the broad coalition organization known as the United Democratic Front.

I do not say that all or any of those organizations are for that. I am saying that the weight, on balance, of the African National Congress is, and that many in the United Democratic Front are also involved.

Mr. President, I do not want to overplay my involvement in this area, but I have been involved in it for the entire time I have been in the Senate; and I find candid Members saying that they do not know very much about it. I do not know everything about it. I do know the sum of that which I have learned through having to apply myself to it as chairman of the Subcommittee on Security and Terrorism. By duty, I have been forced to follow internal events in South Africa quite closely. My staff has made numerous trips to South Africa. We have been visited by parties from all sides on this issue.

We have watched necessarily—and I acknowledge this—the activities of the African National Congress, as a matter of security. I make note that many of those who advocate sanctions also believe that the African National Congress presents a real alternative to the present South African Government, and a concerted campaign is underway to broadcast this organization as the patient long-suffering national movement that it once was. Indeed, it once was....

Different Senators are saying different things now about this. I am not speaking from subjectiveness. I am speaking from what facts I have learned from studying this matter and from witnesses who have testified.

Unfortunately, although many South African blacks and whites who express support or sympathy for the ANC may share our vision of a peaceful transition to a government based on the consent of the governed, which protects the rights of all, evidence presented in 1982 before my subcommittee clearly established that the ANC leadership does not share that vision.

There was brave testimony, unforgettable testimony to this Senator from several witnesses, coupled with the exposition of numerous original ANC documents, which established irrefutably the degree to which the goals, strategies, and leadership of the South African Communist Party and ANC are integrated.

One of the most painful experiences of my life was the interview of one of our witnesses, Bartholomew Hlapane, who had held leadership positions concurrently in the ANC and the South African Communist Party. He told me that as a result of his testimony he knew that he would be assassinated. Indeed, on December 16, 1982, within weeks of the publication of our hearing report he was murdered because of his testimony, and the ANC publicly took credit for the assassination, referencing his testimony at the hearing. His murder also left his wife dead and one of his young daughters, Brenda, a paraplegic.

My staff and I have tried to acknowledge our debt to Mr. Hlapane for his courage and commitment to a better future for his people by looking out for his children. For example, two daughters, Charmaine and Audrey. They are now studying in Alabama at the University of Montevallo, thanks to the contributions of many generous people.

That man was not lying. That man knew he was giving his life for telling the truth. I do not see why this body does not respect that. If you do not believe it go and look at what he said; go look at what the other witnesses said.

If anything, the evidence that has become available since the 1982 hearings on ANC intentions and links to the Soviet Bloc and international terrorist groups further substantiates our conclusions. At its first party conference in many decades, the watershed Kabwe Conference of June 1985, the ANC acted to expand Communist influence on its national executive committee. They acted to expand that influence in 1985, not to decrease it as many Senators are saying. Roughly two-thirds of the committee are now SACP members or Communist advocates. The U.S. intelligence community across the board has provided the subcommittee with detailed classified information on irrefutable SACP influence in the ANC.

One of the witnesses was taken to Moscow, an attractive young woman. When she refused to engage in terrorist training, which they afforded her in response to her accepting an offer of a college education, they took her to the Soviet Union, not to some neighboring African state. After they took her to the U.S.S.R., kept her in a room with dead people night after night, they multiply raped her. She pretended to go along with them, then came back and escaped. She subsequently came to us and told us about her experiences in Moscow. There was no doubt in her mind who was running the show.

In the intervening years since our hearings, the ANC has also acted to solidify its ties to its foreign allies. Virtually all of its material support, estimated at $80 million, comes from the Soviet Union. Furthermore, it conducts a persistent anti-Western rhetorical campagin—I am referring to ANC—which includes generous expressions of solidarity with the Marxist-Leninist regimes in Vietnam, Nicaragua, Afhganistan, and others. Last week, a high-ranking representative of the Iranian Government met with Oliver Tambo in Lusaka, Zambia to strengthen relations between Iran and the ANC.

I think that Alfred Nzo, Secretary General of the ANC, explained the ANC's foreign alignment best in a contribution to the World Marxist Review in December 1984.

I am not saying that if it walks like a Communist, talks like a Communist, looks like a Communist, it is a Communist; I am quoting this man in the *World Marxist Review* in December 1984. He is the Secretary General of the African National Congress.

> ...the ANC invariably stresses that the socialist countries and all democratic, progressive forces which help the oppressed masses of South Africa in their struggle against the apartheid regime at home and against imperialist pressure from abroad are friends we can rely on. This struggle is part of the overall anti-imperialist struggle...The African National Congress is very active in the worldwide peace movement and in other move-

> ments which mobilize the forces of peace in different countries to rebuff imperialist forays....
>
> We express our solidarity with all those who uphold their legitimate rights and rebuff attempts on their countries' sovereignty and independence. We support the courageous Palestinian people who are repelling the imperialist and Zionist aggression and affirm that the objectives of the Palestine Liberation Organization and the African National Congress are similar. The ANC supports the peoples of Nicaragua, El Salvador, Chile and Lebanon in their struggle. We urge greater unity of the democratic and progressive forces fighting off the imperialist onslaught in all parts of the world.

What a benign, sweet, peace-loving organization with which to go along.

The statement gives only a hint of the ties that exist between the ANC and the PLO, a relationship that has existed since at least the early 70s. In 1981, ANC cadres received training from the PLO in Mozambique. In 1982, further training was conducted in Tyre, Lebanon, and as I understand it, the PLO offices in Zimbabwe, Mozambique, and Zambia serve as communication and supply links for the ANC.

It may interest my colleagues to know that the ongoing PLO/ANC alliance has finally become serious enough to draw the attention of the Anti-Defamation League of the B'nai B'rith. Its May 1986 *Bulletin*—that is not very long ago—carries a revealing article by Nathan Perlmutter and David Evanier.

I ask unanimous consent that it be printed in the RECORD and urge all of you to review it for additional detail on the issue of the ANC and its alliances....

There is further cause for us to reject the notion that the ANC provides a respectable solution to South Africa's internal problems, and further cause to concern ourselves with their heavy involvement with the debacle which we by sanctions would further. The African National Congress is openly committed to revolutionary armed struggle. I refer you to only one of many statements by the ANC leadership on the subject. On July 23, 1985, Oliver Tambo, the head of and a so-called moderate in the ANC, declared:

> Our own tasks are very clear: To bring about the kind of society that is visualized in the Freedom Charter we have to break down and destroy the old order.

I do not think that those objectives are the objectives of anyone in this body. I think we would rather accelerate the existing government toward improvement. I respect that motivation.

I only ask that caution be exercised with respect to the ANC and its connections with the problem.

The ANC is doing in South Africa what the Nicaraguan-backed guerrillas are doing in El Salvador.

Both want confrontation and violence. Both want political and economic chaos. Both want the respective governments to crack down, appear repressive, more repressive than they really are in South Africa, appear more repressive because for survival they are going to try to protect the blacks being killed by blacks.

They do not want peace. They do not want negotiations. They want control of South Africa for the reasons that are evident in the quotations I have given.

Sadly, the ANC works with "necklacing." In an ANC press release in Lusaka, July 1, 1965, the ANC urged:

> Let us turn every corner of our country into a battlefield...every patriot a combatant, every combatant a patriot.

ANC spokesman at California State University on October 10, 1985: Alosi Moloi stated:

> Among us we have people who have openly collaborated with the enemy. You have to eliminate one to save hundreds of others.

Tim Ngubane, an ANC man, said at the same meeting:

> We want to make the death of a collaborator so grotesque that people will never think of doing it.

Winnie Mandela, mentioned with near reverence many times in this body, wife of Nelson Mandela, according to the Washington Post of April 14, 1986, said:

> The power is in our hand—we have people's power...with our necklaces we shall liberate this country.

There are others who also encourage necklacing.

Before mentioning that, I will show you photographs of what necklacing is.

Here is the description from an article entitled "The Nacklace: How they Die," describing what death by necklace is like.

> The terrified victim is captured by his (her) executioners. Frequently, his hands are hacked off as a first deterrent to resistance. Barbed wire is otherwise used to tie the helples victim's wrists together.
>
> An automobile tire is placed over the shoulders and filled with petrol or diesel (the latter has been found to stick to the skin when it burns. It is therefore in greater demand). The fuel is ignited with a match.

And it so happens that I have seen this kind of thing in Vietnam.

> (Exhibiting boxes of matches is the way the comrades earn the respect and fear in the townships.)

In other words, everybody is so familiar with this, the intimidation of it is so great, all you have to do is wave a box of matches.

> The victim is usually forced to light his own necklace.
>
> The fuel ignites the tyre which rapidly attains a temperature of 400°C to 500°C.

Internally

As the tyre burns great clouds of black smoke spiral upwards. Various short-chain hydro-carbon type fumes are released which reach a temperature of 300°C. They are inhaled and destroy the lining of the throat and lungs.

Externally

The rubber melts and the molten rubber runs down neck and torso, burning as it goes, deeper and deeper into flesh and tissue. (The tyre cannot be removed by others e.g. family, at this stage, neither can the fire be doused with water). The victim is now a living corpse.

The victim may take up to twenty (20) minutes to die whilst he or she endures this agony, the Comrades stand about laughing and ridiculing him or her. Often members of the victims family are encouraged to attempt to save the victim. The Comrades know that this cannot be done. The molten rubber is similar to boiling tar and cannot be separated from the scorched flesh.

The elements of UDF who participate in that are among those members of the UDF who wish to polarize the issue at any cost, regardless of what developments take place in terms of improvement on the government's part.

UDF executive member, Mr. Curtis Nkondo, stated in Johannesburg on May 17—and this was reported in the CIA's Foreign Broadcast Information Service:

> Anybody who does not want to join the liberation struggle must join the police. There is no such thing as the politics of neutrality.

Another quote, more grim, by a *Newsweek* reporter, Richard Manning, reported on June 2 that a grim joke is making the rounds on the eastern cape. The joke is: "What does the UDF stand for? Answer: Uniroyal, Dunlop, and Firestone."

I remind my colleagues that the definition of a "collaborator" is not very definitive. Those whom the ANC consider to be legitimate targets for necklacing have included migrant miners, liquor store owners, a 62-year-old woman who sold funeral insurance in a funeral parlor, and many other innocent people who were in no way collaborators.

That kind of terrorism should be something we are focusing our attention on and trying to see what part it plays in the dynamism of South Africa.

In a classic pattern, outlined in Carlos Marighella's Minimanual for Urban Guerrilla Warfare, moderates are the targets of attack by the radical extreme.

To some people, like Claire Sterling, a female author, a self-acknowledged member of the Young Communist League while in college, a self-acknowledged liberal today, these tactics used by the ANC, used originally or classically in Uruguay, used by the guerrillas supported by the Sandinistas, used in Afghanistan, used in Vietnam, Laos, Cambodia, those are old stories with which she and men like Arnaud DeBorchgrave from his studies and experiences, are very familiar.

Men like Joel Lisker, my staff director is very familiar with it. They are an old theme with which the West Germans, the Italian Government and its judiciary are very familiar.

Why is not this body, to a man, so familiar? Why was it that when the CIA was briefing us years ago about Carlos possibly crossing a certain border, we had no Senators in the room who had ever heard of "Carlos the Jackal." No one knew who he was.

The same extreme elements regard punitive international sanctions as integral to their efforts to obtain revolutionary change. ANC President, Oliver Tambo, in his 1984 annual address, described sanctions as the "fourth pillar" of their struggle.

To the extent that the African National Congress, which is materially supported and ideologically aligned with the Soviet Union, and extreme elements of the UDF appear to have been successful in delivering on their agenda—imposition of international sanctions; that is one of their biggest aims—their position is strengthened vis-a-vis moderate blacks who are steady, but less high profile actors in the process of change.

Why not give them a chance?

Punitive sanctions that do not take into account and accurately assess other actors—like the ANC—can only contribute to greater political polarization in South Africa and be counterproductive to our objectives for peaceful change to a genuine democratic, fully representative government.

The worst case results of this cycle to which I referred would be a bloodbath in South Africa and the installation in that country of a regime that is much more highly repressive than the present government, built on the kind of terrorism that is now wracking the townships.

I have talked tonight only about the violence/sanctions cycle. I will later address the potential economic and strategic disasters that could occur unless we reasonably try to reach a perspective.

I invite with all of my heart, any Senator here to come to my office, or in any way inform me of anything to the contrary about what I have said, or anything about the way the Government can be improved. I think it is changing and moving more and more rapidly in the right direction.

I again commend the chairman of the Foreign Relations Committee for his effort in committee and his skillful and extremely generous conduct in floor management of the bill. I say that, too, to the ranking minority member because he always comports himself in that manner.

While I have serious doubts, I reserve my judgment on the bill because I do not know what further changes we are going to impose. I personally believe, without any insight from consultation, that the President himself might approve it if we amend it enough. Maybe we do not want that. But every President that I know of who is alive today thinks that we in the Senate and the Congress in general are taking too much away from the rights and prerogative of the President in the field of foreign policy.

From: *Congressional Record,* August 14, 1986 511705–09.

ISSUE 8

Is Comparable Worth a Necessary Remedy in Wage Discrimination?

All known human societies seem to have some division of labor by sex. Whether men or women do a particular job varies from society to society, but certain jobs are differentially set aside for one sex or the other. For example, tasks such as hunting appear to be nearly universally assigned to males. Traditionally, anthropologists have argued that this is rooted in the biological differences between the sexes. It is said that men's jobs in hunting and gathering societies are those requiring physical strength, speed, and the freedom to travel some distance from home. "Women's work," on the other hand, tends to be the jobs that can be carried out close to home due to the limitations of pregnancy and child rearing. The role of the hunter is felt by many to be the root cause of male dominance. The extent to which these generalizations are correct is open to debate.

The specific form of the division of labor of a particular society goes far beyond any biological differences. The historical development of the traditions and customs of a particular society depends on a variety of factors. Each society must be studied individually to determine its patterns of the division of labor between men and women. Even though some tasks are routinely performed by men and others by women, variation from society to society is the prevalent pattern.

In an industrial society, any biological factors underlying the sexual division of labor have been largely overcome by technology. Brute strength is rarely a requirement in contemporary technological occupations, and some women are stronger than some men.

Many of the traditional discriminatory labor practices in this country which operated to the disadvantage of women have officially been eliminated by federal and state laws. Laws that limited the hours women could work and the amount of weight a woman could lift on the job have been repealed. These laws were used to eliminate women from many industrial jobs. Not too long ago, the help wanted columns in the newspapers would have a section for male jobs and a section for female jobs.

Even though much of the occupational sex discrimination has been legally eliminated (we now have laws that require equal pay for equal work), data on comparative salaries indicate that such discrimination still exists. It had been a common practice for employers to pay men more than women for the same job. One college we are aware of had an unofficial policy of starting male student assistants at ten cents more an hour than female student assistants. The unspoken assumption was, of course, "The male is the breadwinner." Needless to say, that policy disappeared in the 1970s.

Income data have consistently found that women's income is about 60 percent of men's income. The percentage seems to hold across occupational categories from service workers to professionals. The difference between incomes is reduced when variables such as age are taken into account. Younger women come closer to parity with men of the same age. However, no matter what variables are controlled for, there is still a significant gap between men's and women's incomes. Many of the hiring and promotion procedures of employers are subjective, which probably operates against women. How many decisions and connections are made at all-male functions such as poker games? Are males more likely to take other males on as protégés? How many men think women are too emotional or suffer from "raging hormones"?

The present debate goes beyond equal pay for equal work and equality of opportunity. Comparable worth deals with the issue of whether jobs or occupations of equal value should receive equal pay. If two occupations require the same education, training, experience, and so forth, should equal pay be mandated by law? Should secretaries make the same salaries as electricians? Should librarians make the same as engineers? Has the prestige and income of traditional female occupations suffered because they are traditional female occupations? If they have suffered, what if anything is to be done? Can you make an accurate measurement of the value of different jobs and occupations? Would the abandonment of market forces as the primary determinant of wages create chaos? Do market forces actually determine wages? These and other questions are discussed in the following articles. The first article by Joy Ann Grune argues that comparable worth is a necessary remedy to a system of wage discrimination that operates to depress wages of traditional female occupations. The second article by June O'Neill argues that comparable worth is not in line with the traditional goals of the women's movement and would be disruptive to the economic system.

ISSUE 8 YES:

Pay Equity Is a Necessary Remedy for Wage Discrimination

Joy Ann Grune

INTRODUCTION

The entry of working women into the U.S. labor force is one of the most significant developments of the 20th century. Although most women work because they need to and many because they want to, the most powerful explanation for the extraordinary movement of women into the paid work force is the accelerated demand for their labor. The transformation of the U.S. economy, particularly since World War II, would not have been possible without women's response to the call for new workers, to fill new jobs, in growing industries. This is the terrain that gives birth to pay equity.

As a historical development, pay equity is a direct response to the societal importance—so often denied and ridiculed—of females and female-dominated jobs in today's economy. Women demand pay equity as they reject their trivialization as workers.

Culture, history, psychiatry, and social relations all have a role in wage discrimination, as they do in other legal rights issues. They contribute to the creation and maintenance of a gender-based division of labor in the market economy that is old, pronounced, and pays women less. But the focus of pay equity is on the translation of theory into practice, which occurs when an employer sets discriminatory wages for a job classification because of the sex, or race or ethnicity, of a predominant number of its occupants.

This paper defines pay equity as a matter of discrimination and shows why affirmative action is not a substitute. It examines five fallacies behind market-based arguments against pay equity and assesses the question of cost. Recent activities of Federal, State, and local governments are described; the Federal Government's lack of enforcement of the 1964 Civil Rights Act is reviewed; and recommendations are offered for effective government involvement.

PAY EQUITY IS A NECESSARY REMEDY FOR WAGE DISCRIMINATION

The principle of pay equity requires the elimination of discrimination in pay within a firm that has operated to depress the wages of entire job classifications because of the sex of the overwhelming majority of occupants. The goal of pay equity is accomplished by raising the wages of predominantly female jobs in a workplace to match the wages of similarly valued male jobs.

The challenge of pay equity is deliberate and focuses directly on the wage-setting process. It does not rely on indirect or laissez faire overtures such as affirmative action programs or the market, which have shown themselves historically to be inadequate to the task of significantly reducing overall wage bias.

Pay equity is an essential remedy for wage discrimination based on sex. It is uniquely capable of reaching deeply structured patterns of wage discrimination associated with job segregation.

The majority of pay equity initiatives have been efforts to reach sex-based discrimination. When patterns of job segregation and wage depression in a workplace are associated with race or ethnicity, the principle of pay equity also can be applied. In New York State, for example, the pay equity job evaluation study now taking place is studying race and sex. U.S. House Resolution 239 introduced by Congresswoman Olympia Snowe (R-Me.) in 1984 calls for a pilot pay equity job evaluation study of the Federal sector that is not restricted to sex.

The U.S. Supreme Court, in *Gunther* v. *County of Washington*, has decided that wage discrimination involving jobs that are comparable, though not equal, is illegal. Such violations of Title VII of the Civil Rights Act must be stopped if women, and the men who work with them in predominantly female jobs, are to be released from employment discrimination.

The persistence of the wage gap and job segregation; the findings of virtually every pay equity job evaluation study showing that predominantly female jobs are paid less than male jobs of comparable worth; favorable court decisions in *Gunther, Washington State,* and *IUE* v. *Washington;* and growing research and understanding of how the labor market operates—all indicate that wage discrimination is at work in creating consistently low pay for female-dominated jobs.

EQUAL PAY FOR EQUAL WORK AND THE ELIMINATION OF DISCRIMINATION IN HIRING AND PROMOTION ARE NOT SUBSTITUTES FOR PAY EQUITY

A comprehensive program to eliminate employment discrimination against women needs to include provisions for pay equity, equal pay for equal work, and the elimination of discrimination in hiring and promotion. These are complementary, but analytically distinct approaches to related, but different problems encountered in a workplace. All are required by law.

Equal Pay for Equal Work

With few exceptions, equal pay for equal work is accepted by the public as a fundamental right of working people. The Equal Pay Act, passed by the U.S. Congress in 1963, mandates equal pay for equal work performed by men and women.

In 1962, 1 year before the Equal Pay Act was passed, full-time, year-round working women earned 59.5 cents for each dollar earned by their male counterparts. Today, the figure is 61 cents. The inability of the act to significantly reduce the wage gap should not be misconstrued. For example, 6 years ago Daniel Glisberg, then Assistant Secretary of Labor, reported in a speech to the Coalition of Labor Union Women that the Equal Pay Act "has obtained $164 million for some 272,000 employees, nearly all women. These figures do not include the $150 million settlement obtained for 13,000 employees of AT&T. In 1978 alone, we were able to restore income or other compensation to more than 15,000 workers for a total of $8.7 million."

Enforcement of the Equal Pay Act has brought higher wages to many women. Stronger enforcement is still needed, particularly since greater numbers of women are slowly assuming jobs equal to men's.

Unfortunately, however, the vast number of employed women do not hold jobs equal to those held by men, and, therefore, the right to a nondiscriminatory wage afforded by the Equal Pay Act does not apply to their situation. In addition, the movement of women into nontraditional jobs over the last 20 years has been outpaced by the movement of women into the work force through low paying, mostly female jobs.

In 1982 over 50 percent of working women were found in 20 out of a total of 427 occupations. It is estimated that two-thirds of all women and men would have to change jobs to achieve equality of distribution by sex. The degree of occupational segregation by sex is as severe today as it was over 80 years ago.

Women of all colors are concentrated in low paying, overwhelmingly female jobs. Although the employment distributions of different ethnic and racial groups of women are converging, there are still differences. For example, in 1979, clerical work employed more than 35 percent of all working women, including 35.9 percent of white women, 29 percent of black women, 31.1 percent of Mexican women,

38.4 percent of Puerto Rican women, and 31.2 percent of Cuban women. Two out of 12 occupational groups—service and clerical work—employ about 60 percent of black women and 53 percent of white women.

Increasingly, women of color are moving into the same occupations as those in which White women work, so that:

- Clerical work now accounts for almost one-third of women workers in nearly every racial and ethnic group;
- Only Cuban, Chinese and Native American women have slightly higher percentages in operative, blue-collar work than in clerical;
- The jobs held by Black women have shifted significantly from blue-collar, operative work to white-collar work: clerical, professional, technical, managerial and sales;
- Mexican American and Puerto Rican women remain concentrated in operative occupations, although this occupational category is second for both of these populations to clerical work.

The facts indicate that the vast majority—perhaps 80 percent—of women work in predominantly female jobs. The wage discrimination they experience is more often and more directly in reference to predominantly male jobs that are comparable, not equal. Thus, the Equal Pay Act is limited in its ability to help them.

The Elimination of Discrimination in Hiring and Promotion

Women workers are moving into predominantly male, white-collar and blue-collar jobs. This movement has not seriously reduced the index of job segregation or the wage gap because simultaneously even more women have entered the work force through predominantly female jobs with low wages.

The entry of women into nontraditional jobs with nondiscriminatory wages is in large measure due to the Equal Pay Act, Civil Rights Act, and Executive Order 11246. If these laws had not been in place, it is likely that the degree of job segregation and the wage gap would have dramatically increased over the last 20 years because the entry of women into feminized jobs with low wages, particularly into the expanding clerical and service sectors, would have even more outpaced their movement into nontraditional work with higher wages.

The elimination of discriminatory obstacles that impede or prevent women from moving into jobs is required by law. It is one essential component of an antidiscrimination program that can allow women to operate as workers without being victimized by illegal acts. However, this approach is no substitute—legally or pragmatically—for requiring the elimination of sex-based wage discrimination.

First of all, the law is already clear in stating that wage discrimination is illegal and must be eliminated whether it occurs between jobs that are equal or between jobs that are comparable. The availability of an affirmative action program does not transform an illegal act of wage discrimination into a legal one. Similarly, a woman's decision to enter or stay in a job—regardless of her reasons for so deciding—does not give the employer license to discriminate. This is the case in equal pay for equal work situations and in situations with comparable jobs. Finally, employer efforts to stop discrimination against women who try to move into male-dominated jobs do not, under any circumstances, permit the employer to reduce wages for other jobs because they are held by women.

A nurse has the right to an opportunity to be a doctor, and a secretary has the right to an opportunity to be an executive or a management analyst. To tell a nurse that she must be a doctor to escape discrimination in employment is to blame the victim and to turn antidiscrimination laws inside out.

Along similar lines, it has been suggested that pursuing job integration through affirmative action can take the place of pay equity. It is argued that if typists, nurses, secretaries, and librarians, for example, were to leave their fields and find jobs in higher paying, traditionally male jobs, the wage gap would close. This approach cannot legally substitute for pay equity, for the reasons offered above. It is an important complement, but has difficulties.

First, as indicated earlier, it is estimated that two-thirds of men and women would have to change jobs for equality of occupational distribution to occur. Given these numbers, closing the wage gap through job integration and affirmative action would take a very long time, perhaps forever.

Second, this approach calls on women to forsake years or decades of experience and training. Some women may want to; many may not. But in any event, such an employment policy makes little sense because its success would depend on millions of skilled women deserting the service sector infrastructure of the economy.

Third, an employment policy whose goal is to place millions of women into industries and occupations that are male dominated presents the problem of training and attracting men to replace them. Finally, although the service sector has numerous predominantly female jobs and contains some of the fastest growing occupations, many traditionally male jobs, especially in basic industry, are suffering growing rates of unemployment. A wage gap reduction policy that tries to move growing numbers of women from high growth jobs to shrinking, predominantly male jobs is doomed to failure.

It is distinctly possible that the implementation of pay equity will do as much as or more than any other policy to promote job integration, affirmative action, and the elimination of discrimination in hiring and promotion:

- The empowerment of women, which is already a frequently visible accompaniment to pay equity, will result in more determined women seeking new types of work;
- There will be much less of an incentive to employers for maintaining sex-segregated jobs once pay equity is implemented;
- Affirmative action will be used by employers to integrate jobs so as to avoid financial and legal liability in pay equity cases; and
- Higher wages in predominantly female jobs will attract men.

THE FAILURE OF MARKET ARGUMENTS AGAINST PAY EQUITY

Great confusion is being created around pay equity and the market. It has been alleged that pay equity would destroy the market and is unnecessary and impossible because of the market. These arguments are not accurate and are based on five fallacies:

(a) The market is free and operates without interventions.
(b) The market will eliminate discrimination.
(c) Pay equity requires the setting of wages outside of a market economy and is an alternative to market-based wage determination.
(d) Employers currently respond directly and uniformly to market forces.
(e) Wages are currently set almost exclusively and directly on the basis of market wage rates.

The Market Is Free and Operates without Interventions

There are few political tendencies today which claim that the market is or should be completely free. For the sake of employers, children, and adult workers, government has long intervened in the economy with legislation, Executive orders, appropriations, tax codes, etc. These steps are taken because of the belief that some principles take precedence over the right of a market to be free. Child labor laws, collective bargaining laws, antidiscrimination laws, health and safety laws, environmental laws, tax breaks, and targeted subsidies to ailing companies are examples of the belief in action.

In addition to government, companies have also intervened in market behavior. In the employment area, for example, 9 to 5: National Association of Working Women has claimed that "large employers in major cities form consortia to discuss wage rates and benefits. Working Women believes that such groups have been influential in holding down clerical salaries over the years." Nine to 5 has specifically identified the Boston Survey Group, a group of large employers that has met for the purpose of setting clerical salaries.

The Market Will Eliminate Discrimination

The market has not eliminated discrimination, and there is nothing to indicate that it will. In fact, according to the National Academy of Sciences, "market wages incorporate the effects of many institutional factors, including discrimination."

When an employer sets wages directly on the basis of market rates for predominantly female jobs, it incorporates prior discrimination by other employers. Without efforts to remove bias from market rates, this type of reliance on the market becomes one of the most damaging transmitters of discrimination because it serves to carry discrimination from employer to employer to employer.

Pay Equity Requires the Setting of Wages outside of a Market Economy and Is an Alternative to Market-Based Wage Determination

Pay equity does not mean the destruction of an external, market-based, salary-setting scheme that will be replaced by a purely internal one. The goal of pay equity is to eliminate bias and discrimination in wage setting. This bias may operate through market rates, through the way the employer responds to or relies on the market, through biased job evaluation systems, or through purely subjective judgments made by employers. The objective of pay equity is not to overturn the market, but merely to eliminate bias, whatever its sources.

> The Comparable Worth strategy can be seen as an attempt to bring wages of female-dominated jobs up to the going market wage rates for similar type work that is not female-dominated. Wages for female-dominated jobs are seen to be artificially depressed by discrimination. In this view it is not Comparable Worth that interferes with a free market, but discrimination. Given that there is discrimination in the labor market, which depresses the wages of women's jobs, intervention is necessary to remove discrimination and its effects. It is therefore unnecessary to have an alternative to market wages; it is necessary only to adjust them. A variety of mechanisms, particularly job evaluation systems, exist that can be used to adjust wages to remove the effects of discrimination.

It would be virtually impossible for firms to establish wages with no reliance on the market, and pay equity activists have not asked employers to do so. They usually suggest that wages for predominantly male jobs be derived from prevailing market rates and be used as the baseline. Under this approach, wages for predominantly female jobs are raised to match those of similarly valued, predominantly male jobs. This, for example, was the remedy that Judge Jack Tanner ordered in Washington State.

For all of these reasons, it is incorrect to characterize pay equity as necessarily a full substitute for or alternative to market-based wages. Pay equity requires a wage structure that is not consistently marred or dented by wage depressions that are tied to gender or race. On top of such an equitable structure, it is possible to build in contingencies that permit an employer to respond legitimately and fairly to real shortages, to seniority requirements, to employment needs of a labor pool. But in its essence, the structure needs to be nondiscriminatory and, therefore, cannot be entirely market dependent.

Employers Respond Automatically and Uniformly to Market Forces

Pay equity advocates are beginning to believe that employers rely on and respond to market forces differently depending on the sex composition of the job for which wages are being set. In the area of supply and demand, an employer has choices in how to respond to a shortage of workers. The choices—relative to a shortage of nurses, for example—include temporarily absorbing the shortage, hiring temporary nurses, having the nurses who are employed work overtime, redesigning the workload, changing recruitment techniques, or possibly, raising wages. Pay equity advocates fear that the last choice—raising wages—is less likely to be used or will be used less quickly when the job is mostly female. They also fear that wages will be raised a smaller amount. The nurse shortage of several years ago was experienced by numerous metropolitan areas and led to a great variety of innovative recruitment techniques, including international forays to the Philippines and elsewhere. But wages did not increase as much or as quickly as might be expected.

The use of surveys to calculate prevailing wage rates is another example of how employers can incorporate bias into their reliance on the market. In West Virginia, for example, clerical workers are concerned that their large employer tends to survey lower paying firms in a smaller geographical area when the job in question is predominantly female or minority.

As pay equity activists begin to research seriously the wage-setting procedures in their places of employment, they are finding that employers have latitude in responding to and relying on the market and that it is too often exercised to the disadvantage of the predominantly female jobs.

Wages Are Set by Employers Exclusively and Directly on the Basis of Prevailing Wage Rates

Many employers use a combination of standards to determine wages. These include prevailing wage rates, job evaluation systems, and subjective judgments about the worth of a job. Some employers, such as Washington State, select a limited number of jobs whose wages are directly tied to the market. These are called benchmarks, and other jobs are then slotted into place. Slotting is sometimes accomplished formally through the use of a job evaluation system and sometimes informally through the personal judgments of those doing the slotting. The number of employers who tie every job classification directly to the market is probably a distinct minority.

It has been estimated that 60–65 percent of all public and private employers use job evaluation systems. They are standard management tools that permit the internal ranking of job classifications on the basis of worth for purposes of salary setting. They have been used by public and private employers to meet considerations of internal equity, to provide rationality and justification to the wage hierarchy, and to make it unnecessary to perform wage surveys for every job classification.

Some employers rely primarily on their own judgments concerning the value of a job. The judgments determine wages when there is no formal system, but sometimes the subjective judgment takes precedence over formal findings. In *IUE* v. *Westinghouse*, for example, the court ruled that Westinghouse had discriminated because it ignored the findings of its own point ratings and reduced wages for women's jobs, offering stereotypic judgments about women as justification.

THE COST OF IMPLEMENTING AND NOT IMPLEMENTING PAY EQUITY

There are no sound estimates of the overall implementation costs of pay equity in the United States. As individual employers begin to implement pay equity and to complete pay equity job evaluation studies, workplace by workplace costs and most estimates are becoming known.

In Minnesota, implementation will cost 0.3 percent of the total biennial budget. It costs 4 percent of the State's annual payroll budget, and the State determined it could afford this at 1 percent a year for each of 4 years. In spring 1983, $21.8 million was appropriated for the first 2 years.

In Washington State, the implementation ordered by Judge Tanner will cost approximately 1 percent of the State's budget. However, on top of this will be the backpay award ordered by the court of approximately $500 million.

The primary reason for the cost difference between the two States is that Minnesota voluntarily identified discrimination in its civil service system and voluntarily decided to eliminate it. Washington State also voluntarily identified discrimination in its civil service system. This was first done in 1974. Unfortunately, despite several followup studies with the same findings of discrimination, the State refused to implement pay equity. It risked a lawsuit, lost, and was ordered to raise wages and provide backpay.

Given that wage discrimination is illegal, the most fiscally responsible route for an employer to take is voluntary compliance. This avoids long, expensive court battles and backpay awards. It allows an employer to stay in more control of the process and more effectively plan for orderly implementation.

It should be noted that because so little is known about the cost of implementing pay equity, the National Committee on Pay Equity is surveying all employers who have begun implementation and all employers who have estimates of cost based on completed pay equity job evaluation studies.

In 1982 full-time, year-round working women were paid 61 cents relative to every dollar of their male counterparts. In 1980 the equivalent figures were 56 cents in the private sector, 62.8 cents in the Federal sector, and 71.5 cents in State and local government. In Table 1, these figures are broken down by race and ethnicity.

These statistics indicate that the greatest expense, on the average, will be in private firms, followed by the Federal Government and then by State and local governments. But cost will vary workplace by workplace. For example, according to the Communications Workers of America (CWA), AFL-CIO, women earned 78 cents for every man's dollar at AT&T in the late 1970s. A Midwestern State preparing for a possible job evaluation study found that full-time, year-round women in State employment earn approximately 85 cents for every man's dollar.

The elimination of wage discrimination against women and men who work in predominantly female jobs will cost money. The single most important step an employer can take to contain costs is to act quickly and voluntarily. But in any case,

TABLE 1 Mean Earnings of Year-Round, Full-Time Workers by Work Experience, Sex, and Race as a Percentage of the Earnings of Men of All Races, 1980

Mean earnings as a percentage of the earnings of all men

Work experience	All men	White men	Black men	Hispanic men	All women	White women	Black women	Hispanic women
Federal government	$24,050	103.1	80.8	90.7	62.8	63.1	62.2	N/A
State and local government	18,748	102.5	76.0	82.8	71.5	72.7	64.8	62.9
Private wage and salary	21,011	102.9	68.1	72.1	56.0	56.8	50.2	47.9

Source: *The Wage Gap: Myths and Facts,* National Committee on Pay Equity, 1983.

to paraphrase Winn Newman, the cost of correcting discrimination is no excuse or defense for breaking the law. Society makes regular judgments through the laws it makes about which corners may and may not be cut to save money. It has decided that money cannot be taken from the paychecks of women and used in other ways.

THE ROLE OF GOVERNMENT IN ELIMINATING WAGE DISCRIMINATION

Federal Government Activities

The Civil Rights Act forbids discrimination in compensation when the jobs in question are equal and when they are comparable. The law, which celebrates its 20th anniversary this year, is sufficient. No new Federal legislation of this sort is necessary.

Unfortunately, however, the Equal Employment Opportunity Commission (EEOC) is not adequately meeting its statutory obligation to enforce the law. Pay equity charges have been warehoused; no litigation is taking place in this area; and existing EEOC policy, first adopted in September 1981, which gives guidelines on how to investigate wage discrimination charges, is not being followed or enforced. The National Committee on Pay Equity has recommended that the EEOC take concrete steps in these directions.

About the time of the congressional oversight hearings on the EEOC and pay equity that were held by Congressman Barney Frank (D-Mass.) in 1984, EEOC Chair Clarence Thomas announced that he had established a task force in headquarters that would review the backlog of charges, search for a litigation vehicle, and develop policy. The review of charges, assuming it is thorough and accurate, is long overdue, as are efforts to litigate in this important area. The development of new policy may be unnecessary, given that Commission policy already exists, and could easily become another excuse for postponing antidiscrimination actions.

These failures on the part of the executive branch of the Federal Government have provoked Congress, private citizens, and private organizations to take initiatives. Members of Congress have held hearings on the EEOC's role, introduced a resolution criticizing Federal enforcement agencies, and introduced legislation to give specific direction to enforcement agencies. Of particular note are House and Senate resolutions that call for a pilot pay equity job evaluation study of the Federal Government.

Private individuals and organizations are lobbying the EEOC and Congress for more enforcement. They are also assuming the expense of filing their own pay equity charges and lawsuits. Discrimination charges have been filed against Illinois, Hawaii, Los Angeles, Chicago, Philadelphia, Fairfax County (Va.), St. Louis Post-Dispatch, and elsewhere. Lawsuits have been filed against Michigan Bell and Nassau County (N.Y.).

State and Local Government Activities

In large part because of the inaction of the Federal Government, the balance of pay equity activities shifted to State and local levels over the past 3 to 4 years. They have become the most productive areas. Well over 100 efforts have taken place in more than 30 States, with more now on the way. The overwhelming majority of these apply only to the employers of the government taking action. They have occurred through collective bargaining, executive order, legislative action, and personnel department action. State, county, municipal, and school board governments have:

- Held hearings and collected data on job segregation and the wage gap;
- Mandated and funded pay equity job evaluation studies;
- Amended civil service policies to require pay equity; and
- Enforced existing laws, such as equal and fair employment practice laws, to provide pay equity.

Pennsylvania is the only State seriously considering an amendment to State law specifically to forbid wage discrimination among comparable jobs in the private sector. This is still pending. Minnesota is the only State to pass legislation requiring that local governments move to pay equity. This passed in April 1984.

All of these victories have made pay equity activists determined to move more often and more quickly from pay equity policies and studies to implementation. Minnesota is the only State to adopt fully an implementation plan. New Mexico's legislation allocated $33 million to upgrade the 3,000 lowest paid jobs in the State government, 86 percent occupied by women, before the results of its job evaluation study. Connecticut public employee unions have negotiated small pay equity funds pending study results. Washington State has been ordered to implement pay equity by a judge. Months before the trial, and 9 years after the first study, the Washington Legislature allocated $1.5 million to begin upgrading.

There are additional partial and full implementations that have taken place at the municipal level.

What the Government Should Do

Many people may think that the most effective, fiscally sound, and least disruptive approach to eliminating discrimination is voluntary compliance. But if voluntary compliance is to work, the Federal Government must provide strict law enforcement.

A few public employers are now taking this route, but virtually no private employers appear to be. AT&T and CWA negotiated a joint labor-management committee that developed and field tested a job evaluation system in 1980–83. The 1983 contract calls for joint committees in all operating and other AT&T companies to develop systems. But no implementation of the plan or pay equity has yet occurred. Westinghouse, General Electric, and Charley Brothers have begun to implement pay equity because of lawsuits that they lost or that led to settlements. If private employers are engaging in voluntary compliance, they are keeping it a big secret. Employers have stated that voluntary compliance requires incentive and that the best incentive is strict enforcement of the law. Since this is not taking place, it should come as no surprise that there are so few private sector initiatives.

With the accumulation of preliminary victories in cities and States, activists will be turning to the EEOC directly and through their elected representatives for assistance, enforcement, and litigation. There are activists in every State, and their numbers, enthusiasm, and determination are growing. They see progress in virtually every tactical area, except the Federal Government's enforcement of laws already on the books. The legal victories, particularly in *Gunther* and *Washington State*, have given people confidence that although pay equity is a moral, social, political, and personal right, it is also a legal right.

The Federal Government's role does not require it to develop a master job evaluation plan for all workplaces. This will take place workplace by workplace as it does now. Of course, it does not require establishing wage boards to determine wages. But the role of the Federal Government does require an executive branch commitment to enforcing laws that Congress has passed and a previous President has signed into law.

CONCLUSION

Pay equity is one of the most fundamentally democratic women's issues to appear in the past 15 years. It will help the many, not the few, and the needy more than the privileged. It is also an issue at the intersection of economic and personal concerns; that is, it promises an end to unnecessarily low wages, but also expresses a new respect for much of the work that women do in this society.

The powerful sentiments that have carried pay equity this far will carry it further. But the elimination of this type of wage discrimination, which runs deep and deprives many, will be easier, faster, and less expensive if the Federal Government can be counted on as an ally in enforcing its own laws.

From: *Comparable Worth: Issue for the 80s:* A Consultation of the U.S. Commission on Civil Rights, Vol. 1, June 6–7, 1984.

ISSUE 8 NO:

An Argument against Comparable Worth

June O'Neill

The traditional goal of feminists has been equal opportunity for women—the opportunity for women to gain access to the schools, training, and jobs they choose to enter, on the same basis as men. This goal, however, basically accepts the rules of the game as they operate in a market economy. In fact the thrust has been to improve the way the market functions by removing discriminatory barriers that restrict the free supply of workers to jobs. By contrast, the more recent policy of "comparable worth" would dispense with the rules of the game. In place of the goal of equality of opportunity it would substitute a demand for equality of results, and it would do this essentially through regulation and legislation. It proposes, therefore, a radical departure from the economic system we now have, and so should be scrutinized with the greatest care.

The topics I will cover in this paper and the main points I will make are as follows:

1. The concept of comparable worth rests on a misunderstanding of the role of wages and prices in the economy.
2. The premises on which a comparable worth policy is based reflect misconception about the reasons why women and men are in different occupations and have different earnings. Both the occupational differences and the pay gap to a large extent are the result of differences in the roles of women and men in the family and the effects these role differences have on the accumulation of skills and other job choices that affect pay. Discrimination by employers may account for some of the occupational differences, but it does not, as comparable worth advocates claim, lower wages directly in women's occupations.

3. Comparable worth, if implemented, would lead to capricious wage differentials, resulting in unintended shortages and surpluses of workers in different occupations with accompanying unemployment. Moreover, it would encourage women to remain in traditional occupations.

4. Policies are available that can be better targeted than comparable worth on any existing discriminatory or other barriers. These policies include the equal employment and pay legislation now on the books.

THE CONCEPT OF COMPARABLE WORTH

By comparable worth I mean the view that employers should base compensation on the inherent value of a job rather than on strictly market considerations. It is not a new idea—since the time of St. Thomas Aquinas, the concept of the "just price," or payment for value, has had considerable appeal. Practical considerations, however, have won out over metaphysics. In a free market, wages and prices are not taken as judgments of the inherent value of the worker or the good itself, but reflect a balancing of what people are willing to pay for the services of these goods with how much it costs to supply them. Market prices are the efficient signals that balance supply and demand. Thus, in product markets we do not require that a pound of soybeans be more expensive than a pound of Belgian chocolates because it is more nutritious, or that the price of water be higher than that of diamonds because it is so much more important to our survival. If asked what the proper scale of prices should be for these products, most people—at least those who have taken Economics I—would give the sensible answer that there is no proper scale—it all depends on the tastes and needs of millions of consumers and the various conditions that determine the costs of production and the supplies of these products.

What is true of the product market is equally true of the labor market. There is simply no independent scientific way to determine what pay should be in a particular occupation without recourse to the market. Job skills have "costs of production" such as formal schooling and on-the-job training. Different jobs also have different amenities that may be more or less costly for the employer to provide—for example, part-time work, safe work, flexible hours, or a pleasant ambience. And individuals vary in their talents and tastes for acquiring skills and performing different tasks. The skills required change over time as the demand for products changes and as different techniques of production are introduced. And these changes may vary by geographic region. In a market system, these changing conditions are reflected in changing wage rates, which in turn provide workers with the incentive to acquire new skills or to migrate to different regions.

The wage pattern that is the net outcome of these forces need not conform to anyone's independent judgment based on preconceived notions of comparability or of relative desirability. The clergy, for example, earn about 30 percent less than brickmasons. Yet the clergy are largely college graduates; the brickmasons are not. Both occupations are more than 95 percent male—so one cannot point to sex discrimination. Possibly the reason for the wage disparity lies in unusual union power of construction workers and is an example of market imperfections. But other explanations are possible too. The real compensation to the clergy, for example, may include housing and spiritual satisfaction as fringe benefits. On the other hand, the high risk of unemployment and exposure to hazards of brickmasons may be reflected in additional monetary payments. If enough people require premiums to become brickmasons and are willing to settle for nonmonetary rewards to work as clergy, and if the buyers of homes are willing to pay the higher costs of brickmasons, while churchgoers are satisfied with the number and quality of clergy who apply, the market solution may well be satisfactory.

One can also think of examples of jobs that initially may seem quite comparable but that would not command the same wage, even in nondiscriminatory and competitive markets. The following example is based on a case that has been used before, but it illustrates the point so well it bears repeating. Consider two jobs—one a Spanish-English translator and the other a French-English translator. Most job evaluators would probably conclude that these jobs are highly comparable and should be paid the same. After all, the skills required, the mental demands, the working conditions, and responsibility would seem to be nearly identical. But "nearly" is not equal, and the difference in language may in fact give rise to a legitimate pay differential. The demand for the two languages may differ—for example, if trade with Spanish-speaking countries is greater. But the supply of Spanish-English translators may also be greater. And this would vary by geographic area. It would be difficult to predict which job will require the higher wage and by how much in order to balance supply and demand.

What the market does is to process the scarcity of talents, the talents of heterogeneous individuals and the demands of business and consumers in arriving at a wage. The net outcome would only coincidentally be the same as a comparable worth determination. There are simply too many factors interacting in highly complex ways for a study to find the market clearing wage.

WHY ABANDON THE MARKET?

The argument for abandoning market determination of wages and substituting "comparable worth," where wage decisions would be based on an independent assessment of the "value" of occupations, is based on the following premises: (1) the pay gap between women and men is due to discrimination and has failed to narrow over time; (2) this discrimination takes the form of occupational segregation, where women are relegated to low-paying jobs; and (3) pay in these female-dominated occupations is low simply because women hold them.

The Pay Gap

In 1983 the pay gap, viewed as the ratio of women's to men's hourly pay, was about 72 percent overall (Table 1).* Among younger groups the ratio is higher (and the pay gap smaller)—a ratio of 89 percent for 20–24-year-olds and 80 percent for the age 25–34 years old. Among groups age 35 and over the ratio is about 65 percent.

What accounts for the pay gap? Clearly, not all differentials reflect discrimination. Several minorities (Japanese and Jewish Americans, for example) have higher than average wages, and I do not believe anyone would ascribe these differentials to favoritism towards these groups and discrimination against others.

A growing body of research has attempted to account for the pay gap, and the researchers have come to different conclusions. These studies, however, use different data sources, refer to different populations and control for many, but not always the same set of variables. Even the gross wage gap—the hourly earnings differential before adjusting for diverse characteristics—varies from study to study, ranging from 45 to 7 percent depending on the type of population considered. Studies based on national samples covering the full age range tend to show a gross wage gap of 35 to 40 percent. Studies based on more homogeneous groups, such as holders of advanced degrees or those in specific professions, have found considerably smaller gross wage gaps.

After adjusting for various characteristics, the wage gap narrows. Generally, the most important variables contributing to the adjustment are those that measure the total number of years of work experience, the years of tenure on current job, and the pattern or continuity of previous work experience.

Traditional home responsibilities of married women have been an obstacle to their full commitment to a career. Although women are now combining work and marriage to a much greater extent than in the past, older women in the labor force today have typically spent many years out of the labor force raising their families. Data from the National Longitudinal Survey (NLS) indicate that in 1977 employed white women in their forties had worked only 61 percent of the years after leaving school, and employed black women had worked 68 percent of the years. By contrast, men are usually in the labor force or the military on a continuing basis after leaving school.

In a recent study I examined the contribution of lifetime work experience and other variables using the NLS data for men and woman aged 25 to 34. White women's hourly wage rate was found to be 66 percent of white men's—a wage gap of 34 percent. This wage gap narrowed to 12 percent after accounting for the effects of male-female differences in work experience, job tenure, and schooling, as well as differences in plant size and certain job characteristics, such as the years of

*The commonly cited pay gap—where women are said to earn 59 cents out of every dollar earned by men—is based on a comparison of the annual earnings of women and men who work year round and are primarily full time. In 1982 this ratio was 62 percent. This figure is lower than the figure of 72 percent cited above because the annual earnings measure is not adjusted for differences in hours worked during the year, and men are more likely than women to work overtime or on second jobs.

TABLE 1 Female-Male Ratios of Median Usual Weekly Earnings of Full-Time Wage and Salary Workers, by Age, 1971–1983

I. Unadjusted Ratios

Year Age	May 1971	May 1973	May 1974	May 1975	May 1976	May 1977	May 1978	2nd quarter 1979	Annual average 1979	 1982	 1983
Total, 16 years and over	.62	.62	.61	.62	.61	.61	.61	.62	.62	.65	.66
16–19	.89	.82	.82	.86	.86	.88	.86	.85	.87	.88	.94
20–24	.78	.77	.76	.76	.80	.78	.75	.75	.76	.83	.84
25–34	.65	.64	.65	.66	.67	.65	.66	.67	.66	.72	.73
35–44	.59	.54	.55	.57	.55	.56	.53	.58	.58	.60	.60
45–54	.57	.57	.57	.59	.57	.56	.54	.57	.56	.59	.58
55–64	.62	.63	.60	.63	.61	.59	.60	.60	.58	.60	.62

II. Adjusted for Male-Female Differences in Full-Time Hours[1]

Year Age	May 1971	May 1973	May 1974	May 1975	May 1976	May 1977	May 1978	2nd quarter 1979	Annual average 1979	 1982	 1983
Total, 16 years and over	.68	.68	.67	.68	.68	.67	.67	.68	.68	.71	.72
16–19	.94	.86	.87	.90	.90	.92	.91	.90	.92	.91	.96
20–24	.85	.83	.82	.82	.86	.84	.80	.81	.82	.88	.89
25–34	.73	.72	.72	.73	.74	.72	.73	.74	.73	.79	.80
35–44	.66	.61	.61	.63	.61	.62	.59	.64	.64	.66	.66
45–54	.62	.62	.62	.63	.62	.61	.59	.63	.61	.64	.63
55-64	.67	.69	.65	.67	.67	.65	.65	.66	.64	.65	.67

[1]Female-male earnings ratios were adjusted for differences in hours worked by multiplying by age-specific male-female ratios of average hours worked per week (for nonagricultural workers on full-time schedules).

Source: Earnings by age and sex are from unpublished tabulations from the Current Population Survey provided by the Bureau of Labor Statistics, U.S. Department of Labor. Hours data are from U.S. Bureau of Labor Statistics, Employment and Earnings series, January issues, annual averages.

training required to learn a skill, whether the occupation was hazardous, and whether the occupation had a high concentration of women.

The gross wage gap between black men and black women was 18 percent. The gross wage gap was smaller for blacks than for whites because job-related characteristics of black women and black men are closer than those of white women and white men. Black women have somewhat fewer years of work experience in their teens and early twenties than white women, which may be related to earlier childbearing. They are more likely to work continuously and full time later on, however, and thus accumulate more total work experience and longer tenure on their current jobs than white women. The adjustment for differences in the measured characteristics cited above narrowed the wage gap of black men and women to 9 percent.

Are the remaining, unaccounted-for differences a measure of discrimination in the labor market?

If all the productivity differences between women and men are not accurately identified and measured, labor market discrimination would be overestimated by the unexplained residual. Many variables were omitted from this analysis and from other studies because relevant data are not available. These include details on the quality and vocational orientation of education; on the extent of other work-related investments, such as job search; and on less tangible factors, such as motivation and effort. Differences in these factors could arise from the priority placed on earning an income versus fulfilling home responsibilities. If women, by tradition, assume the primary responsibility for homemaking and raising children, they may be reluctant to take jobs that demand an intense work commitment.

On the other hand, the unexplained residual may underestimate discrimination if some of the included variables, such as years of training to learn a job, or the sex typicality of occupations, partially reflect labor market discrimination. Some employers may deny women entry into lengthy training programs or be reluctant to hire them in traditionally male jobs. It is difficult with available data to distinguish this situation from one where women choose not to engage in training because of uncertainty about their long-run career plans or choose female occupations because they are more compatible with competing responsibilities at home.

Occupational Segregation

Although occupational segregation clearly exists, it is in large part the result of many of the same factors that determine earnings: years of schooling, on-the-job training, and other human capital investments, as well as tastes for particular job characteristics. In a recently completed study, I found that women's early expectations about their future life's work—that is, whether they planned to be a homemaker or planned to work outside the home—are strongly related to the occupations they ultimately pursue. Many women who initially planned to be homemakers, in fact, became labor force participants, but they were much more likely to pursue stereotyped female occupations than women who had formed their plans to work at younger ages. Early orientation influences early training and schooling decisions, and as a result women may be locked into or out of certain careers. Some women, however, by choice, maintain an ongoing dual career—combining work in the home with an outside job—and this leads to an accommodation in terms of the number of hours that women work and other conditions that influence occupational choice.

Women and men were also found to differ sharply in the environmental characteristics of their occupations. Women were less likely to be in jobs with a high incidence of outdoor work, noisy or hazardous work, or jobs requiring heavy lifting. These differences may reflect employer prejudice or the hostile attitudes of male coworkers, but they may also reflect cultural and physical differences.

In sum, a substantial amount of the differences in wages and in occupations by sex has been statistically linked to investments in work skills acquired in school or on the job. Varied interpretations of these results are possible, however. Thus, the precise amount that can be labeled as the result of choices made by women and their families rather than the result of discrimination by employers is not known.

The Trend in the Pay Gap

A major source of frustration to feminists and a puzzle to researchers has been the failure of the gap to narrow over the post-World War II period, despite large increases in women's labor force participation. In fact, the gap in 1982 is somewhat larger than it was in 1955.

The wage gap would not, however, narrow significantly over time unless the productivity or skill of women in the labor force increased relative to men's, or discrimination in the workplace diminished. Because the gross wage gap widened somewhat after 1955, either discrimination increased or women's skills decreased relative to men's. Findings from a recent study suggest that changes in skill, as measured by the changes in the education and work experience of men and women in the labor force, strongly contributed to an increase in the wage gap.

In 1952 women in the labor force had completed 1.6 more years of schooling than men. This difference narrowed sharply so that by 1979 it had disappeared. One reason for this is that the educational level of men advanced more rapidly than that of women during the 1950s. Aided by the GI bill educational benefits, more men attended college. Another reason is that the labor force participation of less educated women increased more rapidly than the participation of highly educated women. Thus, the female labor force became increasingly less selective over time in terms of schooling attainment.

The rise in the number of women in the labor force may also have had an effect on the lifetime work experience of the average working woman. A large number of less experienced women entering the labor force may have diluted the experience level of the working woman. Although the total number of years of work experience of women is not available for periods of time before the late 1960s, data on job tenure—years with current employer—show that in 1951 men's job tenure exceeded women's job tenure by 1.7 years. This difference widened to 2.7 years in 1962 and then slowly declined, reaching 1.9 years in 1978 and 1.5 years in 1981.

The decline in working women's educational level relative to men's alone would have caused the pay gap to widen by 7 percentage points. The initial widening in the job tenure differential contributed another 2 percentage points to the gap. Together the change in education and job tenure would have increased the wage gap by more than it actually increased. Possibly then, discrimination declined during this period even though the wage gap widened. Since the mid-1960s, educational and work experience differences have moved in different directions. Male educational attainment rose slightly more than that of working women, which alone would have widened the pay gap slightly. Difference in work experience declined overall. Recently (between 1979 and 1983), a narrowing has occurred in the wage gap, from 68 percent to 72 percent overall.

Evidence from the NLS and other sources suggests that the pay gap is likely to narrow perceptibly in the next decade. Not only are young women working more continuously, but they are also getting higher pay for each year of work experience than they were in the late 1960s. This could reflect a reduction in sex discrimination by employers or a greater willingness of women to invest in market skills, or both. Women's career expectations also seem to be rising. In response to an NLS question asked in 1973, 57 percent of women between 25 and 29 indicated their intention to hold jobs rather than be homemakers when they reach age 35. Among women reaching ages 25 to 29 in 1978, 77 percent expressed their intention to work.

Young women have also greatly increased their educational level relative to men. Female college enrollment increased significantly during the 1970s, while male enrollment fell between 1975 and 1980. Moreover, women have made impressive gains in professional degrees during the 1970s. Work roles and work expectations of women and men may well be merging. As these younger women become a larger component of the female labor force, it is anticipated that the overall wage gap will be reduced.

Are Women's Occupations Underpaid?

A major contention of comparable worth supporters is that pay in women's occupations is lower because employers systematically downgrade them. The argument differs from the idea that pay in women's occupations is depressed because of an oversupply to these occupations. An oversupply could arise either because large numbers of women entering the labor force choose these occupations (which is compatible with no discrimination) or because women are barred from some causing an oversupply in others (a discriminatory situation). Although comparable worth advocates have taken the view that overcrowding is caused by restrictive measures, they have lately come to believe that this explanation is not the whole cause of "low payment" in women's jobs. The argument is made that employers can pay less to women's jobs regardless of supply considerations, simply reflecting prejudice against such jobs because they are held by women.

The ability of firms to wield such power is highly questionable. If a firm underpaid workers in women's occupations, in the sense that their wages were held below their real contributions to the firm's receipts, other firms would have a strong incentive to hire workers in these occupations away, bidding up the wages in these occupations. Thus, competition would appear to be a force curtailing employer power. This process could only be thwarted by collusion, an unrealistic prospect considering the hundreds of thousands of firms.

Killingsworth has suggested that the market for nurses may be an example of collusion by a centralized hospital industry that has conspired to hold wages down. Without more careful analysis of the hospital industry, it is difficult to verify whether this is a valid hypothesis. Basic facts about wages and supply in nursing, however, suggest that collusion either does not exist or is ineffective. Despite a perennial "shortage" of nurses that seems to have existed as far back as one can go, the number of nurses has increased dramatically, both absolutely and as a percentage of the population. In 1960 there were 282 registered nurses per 100,000 population. In 1980 there were 506 nurses per 100,000. This rate of increase is even more rapid than the increase in doctors over the past decade, and the supply of doctors has been rapidly increasing. Why did the increase occur? Were women forced into nursing because they were barred from other occupations? That does not seem to be the case in recent times. What has happened is that nursing, along with other medical professions, has experienced a large increase in demand since the middle 1960s when medicare and medicaid were introduced, and private health insurance increased. As a result, the pay of nurses increased more rapidly than in other fields. Between 1960 and 1978 the salary of registered nurses increased by 250 percent, while the pay of all men rose by 206 percent and the pay of all women rose by 193 percent. During the 1970s the rate of pay increase for nurses slowed, which is not surprising considering the increase in supply. And entry of women into nursing school has recently slowed, suggesting a self-correcting mechanism is at work.

Another way to attempt to evaluate the contention that lower pay in female-dominated occupations reflects discrimination is through statistical analysis of the determinants of earnings in occupations. In a recent study, I asked the question—after accounting for measurable differences in skill, do these predominantly female occupations still pay less? In an analysis of data on more than 300 occupations, I found that after adjusting for schooling, training, part-time work, and environmental conditions (but not actual years of work experience or job tenure, which were not available), the proportion female in an occupation was associated with lower pay in that occupation for both women and for men. But the effect was not large. For each 10 percentage point increase in the percent female in an occupation, the wage in the occupation went down by 1.5 percent. Again, however, one is left with a question mark. Are there other characteristics of occupations that women, on the average, may value more highly than men because of home responsibilities or differences in tastes and for which women, more so than men, are willing to accept a lower wage in exchange? Characteristics that come to mind might be a long summer vacation, such as teaching provides, or a steady 9 to 5 job close to home that certain office or shop jobs may provide. The true effect of sex on occupational differences or wage rates is, therefore, another unresolved issue. There are many good reasons why women would be in lower paying occupations than men, even in the absence of sex discrimination on the part of employers. That does not rule out the existence of discrimination, but it weakens the case for seeking an alternative to the market determination of occupational wage rates.

COMPARABLE WORTH IN PRACTICE—THE WASHINGTON STATE EXAMPLE

What would happen if wages were set in accordance with comparable worth standards and independently of market forces? Any large-scale implementation of comparable worth would necessarily be based on job evaluations that assign points for various factors believed to be common to disparate jobs. For example, in the State of Washington, where a comparable worth study was commissioned, a job evaluation firm assisted a committee of 13 politically chosen individuals in rating the jobs used as benchmarks in setting pay in State employment. The committee's task was to assign points on the basis of knowledge and skills, mental demands, accountability, and working conditions. In the 1976 evaluation a registered nurse at level IV was assigned 573 points, the highest number of points of any job—280 points for knowledge and skills, 122 for mental demands, 160 for accountability, and 11 for working conditions. A computer systems analyst at the IV level received a total of only 426 points—212 points for knowledge and skills, 92 points for mental demands, 122 points for accountability, and no points for working conditions. In the market, however, computer systems analysts are among the highest paid workers. National data for 1981 show that they earn 56 percent more than registered nurses. The Washington job evaluation similarly differs radically from the market in its assessment of the value of occupations throughout the job schedule. A clerical supervisor is rated equal to a chemist in knowledge and skills and mental demands, but higher than the chemist in accountability, thereby receiving more total points. Yet the market rewards chemists 41 percent higher pay. The evaluation assigns an electrician the same points for knowledge and skills and mental demands as a level I secretary and 5 points less for accountability. Auto mechanics are assigned lower points than the lowest level homemaker or practical nurse for accountability as well as for working conditions. Truckdrivers are ranked at the bottom, assigned lower points on knowledge and skills, mental demands, and accountability than the lowest ranked telephone operator or retail clerk. The market, however, pays truckdrivers 30 percent more than telephone operators, and the differential is wider for retail clerks.

Should the market pay according to the comparable worth scale? Or is the comparable worth scale faulty? In Washington State, AFSCME, the American Federation of State, County, and Municipal Employees, brought suit against the

State on the grounds that failure to pay women according to the comparable worth scale constituted discrimination. Judge Jack E. Tanner agreed and ruled in favor of the union. The decision was based largely on the fact that the State had conducted the study. Whether or not the study was a reasonable standard for nondiscriminatory wage patterns was never an issue. The State, in fact, was disallowed from presenting a witness who would have critically evaluated the study.

What would happen if comparable worth were to be adopted as a pay-setting mechanism? Take the example of registered nurses and computer systems analysts. Nurses are 95 percent female; systems analysts are 25 percent female. If a private firm employing both occupations were required to adopt the rankings from the Washington State comparable worth study, it would likely have to make a significant pay adjustment. It could either lower the salary of systems analysts below that of nurses or raise the pay of nurses above systems analysts. If it lowered the pay of systems analysts, it would likely find it impossible to retain or recruit them. The more popular remedy would be to raise the pay of nurses. If the firm did so, it would also be compelled to raise its prices. Most likely, demand for the firm's product would fall, and the firm would of necessity be required to cut back production. It would seek ways of lowering costs—for example, by reducing the number of registered nurses it employed, trying to substitute less skilled practical nurses and orderlies where possible. Some women would benefit—those who keep their jobs at the higher pay. But other women would lose—those nurses who become unemployed, as well as other workers who are affected by the cutback.

Of course, if the employer is a State government, the scenario may be somewhat different. The public sector does not face the rigors of competition to the same extent as a private firm. I suspect this is one reason why public sector employees seem to be in the forefront of the comparable worth movement. The public sector could not force workers to work for them if the remedy was to lower the wage in high-paying male jobs. But that is not usually what employee groups request. It can, however, pay the bill for the higher pay required to upgrade wages in female-dominated occupations by raising taxes. But in the long run, the State may have financing problems, since taxpayers may not be willing to foot the bill, and the result would be similar to that in the private firm—unemployment of government workers, particularly women in predominantly female occupations, as government services are curtailed.

CONCLUDING REMARKS

Advocates of comparable worth see it as a way of raising women's economic status and, quite expectedly, tend to minimize costs. A typical comment is as follows (Center for Philosophy and Public Policy):

> Certainly, the costs incurred would vary widely depending on the scope of the approach chosen. But the economic costs of remedying overt discrimination should not prove staggering. Employers and business interests have a long history of protesting that fair

> treatment of workers will result in massive economic disruption. Similar claims were made preceding the abolishment of child labor and the establishment of the minimum wage, and none of the dire predictions came to pass.

Evidently the author is unaware of the numerous economic studies showing the disemployment effects of the minimum wage. However, what this statement fails to see is that comparable worth is in a bigger league than the child labor law or the minimum wage laws that have actually been implemented. It is far more radical. Instituting comparable worth by means of studies such as the one conducted in Washington State could be more like instituting a $15 an hour minimum wage or passing sweeping legislation like Prohibition. Moreover, the costs in terms of economic distortion would be much more profound than the dollars required to pay the bills. Curiously, this is recognized by one comparable worth proponent, who then suggests "that we give very serious consideration to the idea that firms that do raise pay for 'disadvantaged occupations' get special tax incentives for capital equipment that will raise the productivity of these workers. We can't expect firms to swallow these losses; that's crazy." Barrett is willing to go to these lengths because she thinks it might be a way to raise the incomes of poor women heading families on welfare. Long-term welfare recipients, however, are not the women holding the jobs covered by comparable worth schemes. The work participation of women in this situation is very low. Moreover, the lesson of studies of minimum wage effects has been that those who are most vulnerable to disemployment as a result of wage hikes that exceed national market rates are the disadvantaged—those with little education, poor training, and little work experience. Comparable worth would hurt, not help, these women. Subsidies to try to prevent these effects from occurring would be impractical to implement and prohibitively costly.

With all the difficulties that would ensue from implementing comparable worth, it is striking that it would not achieve many of the original goals of the women's movement such as the representation of women as electricians, physicists, managers, or plumbers. In fact, it would likely retard the substantial progress that has been made in the past decade. Younger women have dramatically shifted their school training and occupational choices. They have been undertaking additional training and schooling because the higher pay they can obtain from the investment makes it worthwhile. Raising the pay of clerical jobs, teaching, and nursing above the market rates would make it less rewarding to prepare for other occupations and simply lead to an oversupply to women's fields, making it still harder to find a stable solution to the problem of occupational segregation.

Another byproduct of comparable worth is that it diverts attention away from the real problems of discrimination that may arise. Such problems need not be confined to women in traditional jobs. Pay differences between men and women performing the same job in the same firm at the same level of seniority may no longer be an important source of discrimination. The form discrimination more likely takes is through behavior that denies women entry into on-the-job training or promotions on the same basis as men. The obvious solution is the direct one—namely, allowing or encouraging women whose rights are being denied to bring suit. Existing laws were intended to cover this very type of problem.

The pay-setting procedure in all levels of government employment is another area where remedies other than comparable worth would be more direct and effective. Governments usually do not have the flexibility to meet market demands. The need to adhere to rigid rules under considerable political pressure may result in paying wages that are too high in some occupations and too low in others. (By "too high" I mean that an ample supply of workers could be obtained at a lower wage.) This could occur if the private plants covered in a pay survey for a particular occupation are themselves paying above market—for example, as the result of a powerful union. Such a situation could lead to unnecessary pay differentials between certain occupations that are male dominated (which are more likely to be represented by such strong unions) and other male, mixed, and female occupations whose private sector wages are more competitive. Comparable worth is not the solution, however, since it does not address the problem. Pay-setting procedures can be improved by changing the nature of the pay surveys and by introducing market criteria—for example, by considering the length of the queue to enter different government jobs and the length of time vacancies stay open. Such changes may help women and also improve the efficiency of government.

Dramatic changes have occurred in women's college enrollment, in labor force participation, and in entrance into formerly male occupations, particularly in the professions. These changes are taking place because of fundamental changes in women's role in the economy and in the family—changes that themselves reflect a response to rising wage rates as well as changing social attitudes. Pay set according to comparable worth would distort wage signals, inducing inappropriate supply response and unemployment. If women have been discouraged by society or barred by employers from entering certain occupations, the appropriate response is to remove the barriers, not try to repeal supply and demand. Comparable worth is no shortcut to equality.

From: *Comparable Worth: Issue for the '80s:* A Consultation of the U.S. Commission on Civil Rights, Vol. 1, June 6–7, 1984.

ISSUE 9

Should We Prohibit Mandatory Retirement?

Retirement from the workforce is a relatively recent phenomenon in the United States. Until World War II, most people continued working until they became incapable of doing so. Social Security was instituted in 1935 in the United States and was patterned after the German system, established in 1889, which was the first modern national system of support for the elderly. The United States government, many private pension plans, and many private and public organizations adopted age 65 as the expected age of retirement for employees.*

In the 1960s, there was a general trend to eliminate discrimination in employment. The Civil Rights Act of 1964 attempted to prohibit employment practices that discriminated on the basis of race, sex, religion, or national origin. Although the act did not prohibit discrimination based on age, it did direct the Secretary of Labor to make a report to the Congress on age discrimination. That report documenting the existence of age discrimination became the basis for the Age Discrimination in Employment Act of 1967 (ADEA), which provided widespread protection for older employees. One of the provisions of the act eliminated mandatory retirement prior to age 65.

*For additional information, see *Congressional Digest,* March 1986.

The ADEA was amended in 1974 to include public employees. Major amendments were made in 1978 that raised the age at which organizations could require mandatory retirement to age 70. Exemptions were granted for certain executives and higher education was temporarily exempted. The ADEA and its subsequent amendments have primarily focused on attempts to restrict age discrimination in employment.

Social issues concerning older Americans will continue to arise in the coming decades. The demographic data indicate an aging of the population with a larger proportion of the population over age 65. During the 1920s, a time of relative prosperity, there was high fertility. Children born at that time are beginning to reach age 65 and will continue to do so well into the 1990s. The proportion of older Americans should then level off due to the low fertility during the Depression of the 1930s. The biggest jump will come when the baby boomers of the late 1940s and 1950s reach age 65 beginning around 2015.

If the above demographic data are combined with the trend of fewer older Americans participating in the labor force, it becomes clear that there will be some adjustments to be made in our system. How long can we sustain an increasing dependent population with a decreasing workforce? Will the young be willing to support a large nonworking elderly population?

There have already been modifications in the Social Security system. If a retired person's income is above a certain amount, Social Security benefits are partially taxed. Some are arguing that all Social Security payments should be taxed above certain income levels; others believe that Social Security payments should be eliminated for high-income people. Since many of these people will have paid tax dollars into Social Security for forty or more years, such proposals will arouse controversies.

Other people are concerned about the increased concentration of wealth in pension plans. Will the older population use its numbers to exercise political power? Will the country become more conservative and static? Will lines be drawn between the young and the old?

Our current issue involves mandatory retirement. Should people be required to retire at some arbitrary age? The federal government and many states have now eliminated mandatory retirement for most occupations. There are a number of pros and cons presented by those who favor or oppose mandatory retirement. Those who oppose mandatory retirement argue that older workers will be needed in the workforce of the future and that the arbitrary exclusion of older workers is a form of agism—discrimination on the basis of age. Those who favor mandatory retirement feel that allowing older workers to remain in the work force limits the opportunities of the young by inhibiting upward mobility, creates a variety of bureaucratic problems, and creates great stress for older workers who will have to be removed for "cause," such as incompetence.

These and other issues are taken up in the following debate. U.S. Representative Claude Pepper presents the case against mandatory retirement, and Robert Thompson of the U.S. Chamber of Commerce presents the opposing view.

ISSUE 9 YES:

Mandatory Retirement Should Be Prohibited

Claude Pepper

This bill is an important step toward ending the remaining vestiges of age discrimination facing our nation's workforce.

The bill you are considering, S. 2617, and its companion in the House (H.R. 6576) is landmark legislation that makes only a small change in the Age Discrimination in Employment Act and thereby extends fundamental job protections to the more than 800,000 workers age 70 and over and to approximately 7 million older Americans who are not now in the labor force but who are interested in and capable of making a contribution to this nation's productivity.

It was just four years ago that Congress enacted legislation that I introduced resulting in the complete elimination of mandatory retirement for nearly all Federal workers and an increase from 65 to 70 in the permissible mandatory retirement age for non-federal workers. Those were the 1978 Amendments to the Age Discrimination in Employment Act (ADEA).

The bill you are considering today would build upon those earlier amendments by extending the Act's coverage to most workers over 70. By so doing, it is estimated that 195,000 more older workers each year will remain in the labor force by the year 2000 than would do so under current law. This would be a substantial boost to Social Security and will help meet a growing demand for experienced labor.

The Prohibition of Mandatory Retirement and Employment Rights Act of 1982 is unlike much of the legislation before the Congress today because it is not designed just to meet the needs of a narrow constituency. Age discrimination touches the lives of every American. It is perhaps for this reason that this legislation has the nearly unanimous support of the American people. According to a 1981 nationwide Lou Harris survey commissioned by the National Council on the Aging, nine out of ten Americans *of all ages* believe no older person should be denied a job because of their age, as long as they are capable of performing that job. Thus, the failure to enact this legislation is not a mere disappointment to the several million older workers affected by it. It would be an irresponsible abrogration of our duty to serve the people of this country. This is compelling enough reason to act immediately on this legislation. But there are many more reasons why this bill should be enacted at once.

The increase in labor force participation by older workers brought about by enactment of this bill would come at a time when our nation begins to face critical labor shortages. These labor shortages, which will emerge in the next five years, stem from a dramatic decline in the birthrate and a subsequent reduction in the number of young age workers entering the labor force. The Bureau of Labor Statistics reports that the population aged 18 to 24, which during the decade 1970–80 grew by 22.5 percent, will decline by 15 percent during the decade 1980–90. Moreover, our nation's colleges and universities will fall far short in meeting industry's demand for skilled workers, such as engineers and computer technicians. The result of these shortages will be an increased demand for older workers.

Encouraging older persons to remain employed longer by, among other things, removing age barriers in the workforce, is critical to our economy and important for the future of Social Security and other retirement income systems. According to a Data Resources Inc. study presented to the Select Committee on Aging earlier this year, an increase in labor force rates of older men to 1970 levels would by the year 2005 add $10 billion annually to the Social Security trust funds. Moreover, this increase in older worker employment would increase the GNP by 4 percent, add $40 billion annually (in 1980 dollars) in new Federal, State and local tax revenues and provide an average annual increase of $1,050 in income to the elderly. Eliminating mandatory retirement would be a start toward increasing older workers employment levels and adding a needed stimulus to the economy.

As you consider this legislation you will hear numerous stories about its "catastrophic" impact. These "cries of wolf" were heard when the 1978 ADEA Amendments were under consideration. The difference is that today we have the benefit of extensive research to refute most of the myths and stereotypes that were prevalent in 1978. The Department of Labor has undertaken four years of study to determine the impact of eliminating mandatory retirement and the results cited in their interim report to Congress are crystal clear: abolishing mandatory retirement will have no significant negative effects on this nation's workforce.

Let's examine some of the myths you are likely to hear.

Eliminating mandatory retirement will disrupt corporate personnel systems. Many employers argued in 1978 that raising or eliminating the mandatory retirement age would force them to implement stricter performance evaluations that might work to the detriment of all older workers. The Labor Department study found that this did not occur. On the contrary, strict performance criteria existed alongside mandatory retirement rules rather than as a replacement for them. This finding may explain why 38 percent of the Fortune 500 companies have no mandatory retirement age and why 51 percent of employees recently surveyed said they favored the complete elimination of mandatory retirement.

Eliminating mandatory retirement will cause unemployment for younger workers, women and minorities. The Department of Labor, which has been studying the effects of the 1978 Amendments to the ADEA, has concluded that raising the mandatory retirement age to 70 has had no significant negative effect on youth, women, or minorities. According to the Labor Department report: "The estimated additional number of comparable age 65 workers are potential competition for less than one-quarter of one percent of all full-time workers ages 16–24; less than one-half of one percent of all full-time black workers ages 16–59; and around one-tenth of one percent of all full-time female workers ages 16–59."

Eliminating mandatory retirement would, in fact, increase the rights of minorities and women, since members of these groups also grow older. It would indeed be ironic if after years of struggling to gain their employment rights, minorities and women were to be denied these rights by the mere fact that they survive to old age.

Eliminating mandatory retirement would retard promotional opportunities for younger workers. Again, the findings in the Labor Department report refute this. According to a study cited by the Labor Department, a substantial increase of ten percent in labor force participation rates of men over 65, nearly twice the effect of abolishing mandatory retirement, would on average delay promotions at the highest ranks by one-half year, while at the lower ranks individual promotions would be retarded by five to ten weeks. These are insignificant effects, especially when weighed against the harmful consequences of forced retirement based on age.

Eliminating mandatory retirement will cause a decline in the nation's productivity. The overwhelming weight of scientific evidence refutes this myth. Older workers are more dependable, stay at their jobs longer and do as much work of similar or superior quality as younger workers. Employers understand this. Nine out of ten employers in a 1981 study stated that older workers perform as well on the job as younger workers and that older workers are more committed than younger workers.

With all of the benefits we can expect from enacting the Prohibition of Mandatory Retirement and Employment Rights Act of 1982, I still don't believe this bill goes far enough. Even with this legislation older workers will still face significant obstacles to equal employment opportunities.

One such obstacle is the policy of some employers to discontinue pension contributions for workers who are age 65 or older. A quirk in the legislative history of the 1978 ADEA Amendments allowed this loophole, and the result is that roughly one-half of all employers are taking advantage of it to freeze pension benefits at age 65 and discourage older workers from continued productive employment. The practice of freezing pension benefits at 65 is not done for cost reasons; a major new study by a prominent actuary firm that was released recently by our Aging Committee clearly demonstrates that there is no cost justification for freezing pensions at age 65. Apparently, this practice is followed either out of ignorance of the actuarial facts or, worse yet, because some employers wish to force older workers into retirement prematurely. In either case, the practice should be abolished.

A second loophole in the ADEA not addressed by this bill is the provision allowing forced retirement at age 65 for some high policymaking executives who would receive $27,000 or more in private pension benefits upon retirement. This exemption, which was included to allow employers to create turnover at the highest corporate levels, results in legalized discrimination against a selected group of employees and should be abolished. At the very least, the pension test of $27,000 should be indexed to the CPI or the wage base to ensure that this exemption is not applied too broadly.

These and other problems—such as the restrictive filing requirements required by the Act and the vague wording of the "bona fide occupational qualification" provision—must be addressed as soon as possible. But we cannot afford to hold back our efforts to uncap the ADEA. America awaits our action on this bill and we owe it to ourselves and our constituents to send a clear message to the nation that age discrimination in employment will no longer be tolerated at any age. Having done that, we can assess the validity of some of these other provisions that would further strengthen the Act.

I am willing to forego for the time being any amendments to strengthen the ADEA's protection of older workers beyond uncapping the ADEA, but only if the same promise is made by those who would weaken the Act. Here I speak of the suggestion by some business groups that the right of an aggrieved worker to have a trial by a jury of his peers should be taken away, allegedly because juries are "too sympathetic" to older workers. The jury trial provision for non-federal workers was firmly established in the ADEA in 1978 by Congress after it was earlier affirmed by the Supreme Court in *Lorillard* v. *Pons*. No conclusive evidence exists that juries are more sympathetic to older plaintiffs than are judges. If anything, juries lessen the bias in age discrimination cases because the decision is made by more than one juror, whereas a judge makes his determination alone. I believe very strongly, as I think most of our colleagues do, that the jury system in this country is fair and should be retained. It is abhorrent to think that the Congress would even consider taking away this right because some employers are worried about being sued.

I am equally opposed to the suggestion that liquidated damage awards be abolished. The ADEA allows such awards only when the employer is found to have willfully violated the Act. Under all other circumstances the plaintiff is allowed simple back pay. This is eminently fair. To remove this provision would be to eliminate an important deterrent to future discrimination.

It is encouraging to me that this Administration, despite its strong ties to business, is adamantly opposed to any change in the jury trials and liquidated damages provision at this time. The President sees these as obstacles to swift enactment of legislation to end mandatory retirement and is apparently unconvinced by the arguments that they should be altered in any way.

Last, I am strongly opposed to any special treatment for universities and colleges. In recent weeks I have heard that abolishing mandatory retirement will destroy the tenure system in higher education. I suppose the same arguments were made in support of slavery, that to abolish it would destroy the great plantations of the South. I say if the tenure system requires discrimination based on age then it should change to reflect the times. When faced with a choice between the rights of individuals and the needs of institutions our nation has nearly always opted to protect the rights of the individual. The Labor Department study offers no clear support for an exception for universities and colleges. Moreover, the Labor Department study found that "60 percent of all faculty respondents indicated that they 'favor' or 'strongly favor' complete elimination of mandatory retirement ages for faculty members."

After you have reviewed all the evidence I am confident you will agree that the best way to proceed is to enact the Prohibition of Mandatory Retirement and Employment Rights Act as soon as possible, with no amendments. The legislation would bring an end to one of the most wasteful forms of discrimination in our society and would, therefore, be good for the nation, for its older workers, and for all future generations of workers who have much to contribute well beyond their 70th birthday.

Reprinted with permission by Congressional Digest Corp., from "Should Congress Adopt Pending Measures to Prohibit Mandatory Retirement?" *Congressional Digest,* November 1982.

ISSUE 9 NO:

Mandatory Retirement Should Not Be Prohibited

Robert T. Thompson

We are here to express opposition to S. 2617—a bill that would lift the age 70 cap in the Age Discrimination in Employment Act of 1967 (ADEA).

The Chamber of Commerce of the United States is the largest federation of business and professional organizations in the world and is the principal spokesman for the American business community. The U.S. Chamber represents more than 255,000 members, of which more than 250,000 are business firms, more than 2,800 are State and local chambers of commerce, and more than 1,300 are trade and professional associations.

More than 85 percent of the Chamber's members are small business firms having fewer than 100 employees, yet virtually all of the nation's largest industrial and business concerns are also active members. We are particularly cognizant of the problems of smaller business, as well as issues facing the business community at large. A significant number of our members are covered by ADEA.

Besides representing a cross-section of the American business community in terms of number of employees, the U.S. Chamber also represents a wide management spectrum by type of business and location. Major classifications of American businesses—manufacturing, retailing, services, construction, wholesaling, and finance—all have more than 15,000 businesses represented as members of the U.S. Chamber. Yet no one group represents as much as 23 percent of the total Chamber membership. Further, the Chamber has substantial membership in all 50 states.

ADEA prohibits employers with 20 or more employees from refusing to hire, discharging, denying employment opportunities or promotions, or otherwise discriminating against employees aged 40 to 70. ADEA applies to employment practices including compensation, terms, conditions, or privileges of employment.

ADEA is a hybrid reflecting the influences of both Title VII of the 1964 Civil Rights Act (Title VII) and the Fair Labor Standards Act (FLSA). The objectives of ADEA, elimination of discrimination from the workplace, and the employment practices which are prohibited, parallel those of Title VII. However, the enforcement mechanism of ADEA is modeled after FLSA.

Congress passed the ADEA in 1967, and although tailored after Title VII, there was general concern that including age discrimination under Title VII would "overload" the Equal Employment Opportunity Commission (EEOC) since it was a relatively new agency. Enforcement authority was therefore given to the Secretary of Labor (DOL).

Coverage of ADEA applied to workers between the ages of 40 and 65. In 1978 Congress lifted the age cap from 65 to 70. It also overturned a Supreme Court decision which allowed companies to force retirement before expiration of the cap if done in compliance with a nondiscriminatory pension plan, and enacted a provision explicitly authorizing jury trials.

The 1978 Amendments also instructed DOL to complete a study on the effects of the 1978 Amendments and on the possible effects of lifting the age cap. In 1979, based on a reorganization plan issued by President Carter, enforcement of ADEA was shifted to the EEOC.

Although the law was enacted in 1967, it has been only within the last several years that it has received marked attention by both the plaintiff community concerned with enforcing its rights and with the business community in terms of its compliance burden.

During the past generation this country has undergone a retirement revolution. It used to be that many workers would labor at their jobs until ill health or perhaps death intervened. Today, it appears that workers are retiring earlier than before with an average retirement age of under 65 and perhaps as low as 62.

One of the most influential events in bringing about this change was passage of the Social Security Act. This Act provided a new source of retirement income, thereby easing the necessity to work for the bulk of the nation's elderly workforce. The Social Security System also established retirement as an expected occurrence, with retirement by age 65 being generally accepted as a "normal" retirement age.

Then, during World War II, wage and salary controls and a corporate excess profits tax made private pension benefits an advantageous alternative to restricted pay increases. This alternative pay or fringe benefit was kept and expanded by many companies so that a sizeable segment of the working population received social security plus private pension benefits. This combination made early retirement more attractive to many and economically possible to many more. More recently, self-employed pensions (Keogh plans) and Individual Retirement Accounts (IRA's) have further stimulated retirement savings during an individual's working lifetime.

In addition, the general health of the population has increased over the past generation permitting better health throughout a lifetime of work.

Many jobs have become less physically demanding and life spans have also increased. Thus, even though Americans are living longer, more workers are choosing to retire earlier. Today, only 47 percent of the male population aged 55 or older is in the labor force compared to 61 percent in 1960.

This trend is relevant when analyzing the reasons offered for lifting the age 70 cap in ADEA. Proponents suggest that lifting the cap would increase the nation's productivity, would allow for more labor to meet the nation's economic needs, would enhance the well being of older persons, and perhaps most significantly would reduce social security costs.

Most studies suggest that income and health are the two most important considerations for the elderly, and that they are the reasons why people retire early. Poor health promotes early retirement, while adequate income and good health also promote early retirement. Thus it appears the primary motivation for working beyond normal retirement age is financial necessity. Furthermore, a DOL study estimates that by 1990, only 195,000 male workers would be added to the workforce—almost half between the ages of 68 and 70—as a result of lifting the age 70 cap.

Based on current trends, policy makers must not deceive themselves or the public that lifting the age 70 cap would increase older workers' participation to the point of rectifying the social security system's financial crisis.

The business community has provided substantial assistance to its older workers and to its retired employees. Although a complete business survey is not available, a sufficient sampling can provide a good picture on business's contribution to meaningful retirement.

First and foremost are financial benefits. Approximately half of the workforce is covered by some type of employer's pension/welfare fund available upon retirement. Besides annuities, these benefits typically include medical benefits and group life insurance. In addition, a host of other benefits are provided by employers to older workers or retirees.

These include pre-retirement and post-retirement counseling; flexible work hours; gradual retirement; tuition aid plan assistance; retiree publications; group travel tours; employee discounts on company items and retirees clubs which provide a wide variety of recreational and cultural activities; and reunions such as clam bakes, dinners, luncheons, golf tournaments or similar affairs which allow the retirees an opportunity for renewing old acquaintances.

Many companies afford older workers an opportunity to work and apply their invaluable experience as consultants, or long range strategic planners, or on the boards and staffs for community, civic, or professional associations such as local chambers of commerce.

In general, business views older workers and retirees as an invaluable component of the company, the community, and the nation.

Despite all the horror stories by proponents of lifting the age 70 cap, most workers are not faced with an arbitrary removal from employment. As we showed earlier, the current trend with the workforce is to voluntarily retire earlier.

Mandatory retirement suffers from bad press or misunderstanding. Opposition to mandatory retirements seems to be greatest among those furthest from retirement. A recent survey found that while 75% of those under age 25 oppose mandatory retirement, only a bare majority of those 65 and older share this position.

A survey of readers in *Retirement Living* magazine showed that 55% of the respondents who were already retired said that a law permitting retirements at a fixed age would be "desirable for most people."

This essentially parallels the Chamber's position opposing the lifting of the age 70 cap. Namely, it is the wisest course for the nation to establish a reasonable retirement age while attempting to provide adequate retirement income for all workers at that particular age. A fixed retirement age would constantly remind business and workers of the inevitability of retirement and the advisability of planning for it.

Thus although the age 70 cap in ADEA does not mandate retirement, it seems to be a logical focal point for planning. It is already five years beyond age 65 when full Social Security benefits are payable.

It is also important to note that the final results on raising the limit from age 65 to 70 are not in yet. The disruptions caused by the 1978 Amendments to ADEA are just being worked out. Clearly, more study is needed and more analysis of the potential adverse effects should be provided before new legislation is enacted. And there are additional reasons for maintaining the age 70 cap:

Long term collective bargaining agreements would be upset and would have to be reopened and renegotiated to provide for the necessary adjustments if the age 70 cap is removed.

Sound employment practices would also be disrupted. It is not uncommon for management to retain for several years older workers who should or could be dismissed for cause. Without a set retirement date, management would have to alter its policies and begin performance evaluations and dismissals of some workers who would otherwise be retained to retirement. The shock of being dismissed for cause would be far worse than being retired according to a plan.

Lifting the age 70 cap would also remove flexibility from managing and would reduce job opportunities. Corporate management is viewed as being predominantly white and male. To the extent that restraints are put on retiring managers and supervisory personnel, opportunities for bringing in females and minorities would be restricted. This is particularly true today when many companies are being forced to cut back workforces.

Indeed, lifting the age 70 cap represents a broad leap into the unknown with little, if any, study of the implications to the economy, the impacts on older workers, and human resources planning for companies.

In addition to the policy considerations which argue against lifting ADEA's age 70 cap, the law has created practical problems in its implementation which need to be fully addressed before any changes are made.

Compliance with the requirements of ADEA has been difficult for business. For example, a major auto manufacturer recently had to undergo substantial reductions in its workforce (RIF) as a result of economic ill health. The company selected a certain number of operations for RIFs and decided that rather than just lay off longtime employees, it would provide them with an opportunity to retire and provide pension benefits.

A U.S. District court found that job elimination or RIFs are not a factor which renders an otherwise "illegal voluntary retirement" lawful. Thus, under this holding, the company is now faced with the option of laying off an employee and providing no benefits or laying off an employee, providing pension benefits and possibly being sued under ADEA. The ADEA, in this case, forces bad personnel practices.

In another case, an employer dismissed an employee within the protected age group and hired another employee, 10 years the senior of the dismissed employee. Yet this was insufficient proof by itself to rebut a case of age discrimination under ADEA.

Some of our members have told us that, because of the confines of ADEA, they are being forced to lay off minority and women employees. This weakens their overall effectiveness as affirmative action employers. These problems result when, faced with a reduction in force, employers cannot retire older workers with benefits, but must lay off those most recently hired. Employers in this situation face potential lawsuits under either Title VII or ADEA, with no clear guidance as to the legal course of action.

Business also faces uncertainty regarding ADEA compliance on the question of pension and benefit accruals beyond normal retirement age and the conflicting requirements of certain State laws which go beyond the Federal law.

Given the compliance problems employers have had with ADEA, we believe lifting the age 70 cap at this time would only result in more confusion and inequity.

The elimination of mandatory retirement is not as simple a matter as proponents would have Congress believe. It would result in fundamental changes in the employment practices of all covered employers regarding the hiring, routine evaluation, and promotion of employees and would reduce the number of hiring and promotional opportunities available in the private sector.

Of particular concern is the apparent unwillingness of the Administration and the legislation's proponents to confront the administrative problems that would result from the elimination of mandatory retirement. Employer experience with the Act since passage of the 1978 amendments demonstrates that ADEA in its present form is neither fair nor equitable. Its procedures place such a heavy burden of proof on employers that it is extremely difficult for them to rebut claims of age discrimination at the trial level.

Because the advantage is clearly with plaintiffs, most employers faced with an age claim are forced to try to buy their way out of the problem no matter how meritless the charge. The Act should be used to protect those who have been victimized by unlawful age discrimination; it should not be used as a device to shake down innocent employers.

There has been some discussion that Congress should refrain from considering the Act's administrative problems at the same time that it considers broadening its coverage. For Congress to act in such a manner, however, would only exacerbate the problems that already exist. Unless management's concerns are taken up when Congress addresses the mandatory retirement issue, they will not be taken up at all.

The economic condition of our nation's businesses make it abundantly clear that Congress at this time should approach cautiously any proposal to impose additional requirements and liabilities on employers, particularly if those requirements are incapable of being fairly administered.

We urge that Congress enact the reforms we recommend and that S. 2617 not be enacted.

ISSUE 10

Should Abortion Rights Be Restricted?

Attempts to control abortion through the legal system were not undertaken until the nineteenth century. The British Parliament passed a statute forbidding abortion in 1803, and the first abortion statute in the United States was passed in Connecticut in 1821. These laws differed from the old English common law, which did not condemn abortion before quickening. *Quickening* was the point in a pregnancy when the mother could feel the developing fetus move, usually around sixteen to eighteen weeks.*

The early laws passed by state legislatures in the 1800s resulted from physicians' concerns about the moral and ethical aspects of abortion, as well as the quickening doctrine. Other physicians, who were among the better trained, hoped the laws would drive untrained and careless practitioners out of business. Part of the motivation for these early laws was to regulate the medical profession and to improve professional standards. After 1840 the laws became increasingly restrictive and generally imposed criminal penalties on the abortionist and, to a lesser extent, on the woman. Most states eventually allowed some abortions to be performed under extraordinary circumstances. These were the laws that governed abortion until the 1960s and 1970s.

*For additional information, see Eva R. Rubin, *Abortion, Politics and the Courts*. Westport, Conn.: Greenwood Press, 1982.

These laws did not stop abortions. Unmarried women sought abortions to avoid the social stigma of having illegitimate children. Many married women sought abortions to control family size and spacing, for health reasons, for economic reasons, and for a multitude of other factors. The estimates of the number of illegal abortions per year range as high as one million in the 1960s. A variety of home remedies and illegal (frequently untrained) abortionists were available to meet the need. Newspaper stories of deaths from illegal abortions, some involving implements such as coat hangers, were not uncommon in the 1960s. Some women who could afford to do so sought out physicians who were willing to provide illegal abortions in the United States or went to medical clinics in Mexico or Europe.

By the 1960s, abortion laws in the United States were much stricter than in most non–Catholic countries. A number of incidents in the early 1960s provided an impetus to the growing sentiment to reform abortion laws. One of these was the infamous thalidomide incident. Thalidomide, a tranquilizer, produced horrible birth defects when taken by pregnant women. Few American women had taken the drug, but one of those who had, Sherri Finkline, attempted to get an abortion in the United States. Her court case and subsequent trip to Sweden for an abortion were widely publicized. In addition, a German measles epidemic in the early 1960s produced thousands of deformed babies.

The National Organization of Women (NOW), formed in 1966, and other feminist groups took on abortion as an issue and redefined it as an issue of the right of women to control their own bodies. They believed that the state should not be able to enforce compulsory pregnancy. A woman's ability to control her reproduction was considered to be a basic right.

During the 1960s and early 1970s, a variety of court cases tested various aspects of the abortion laws. The historic case that changed abortion law is *Roe* v. *Wade.* This decision was handed down by the U.S. Supreme Court on January 22, 1973. The Court held that the constitutional concept of liberty and the right to privacy protect a woman's right to choose to terminate a pregnancy, at least in the early weeks of pregnancy. After the first trimester of pregnancy, the state could regulate abortion and could forbid it after the second trimester. States were prohibited from unduly burdening the performance of first trimester abortions.

While the Court's decision was greeted with jubilation by the women's movement, others reacted in horror. A coalition of Catholics, conservatives, and religious fundamentalists formed a loose alignment now termed the pro-life movement. These groups tended to perceive abortion as a human rights issue and equated abortion with murder. They generally believe that life begins at conception and that the fetus has the same right to life as any other human being.

Since the *Roe* v. *Wade* decision, courts and legislatures have had to deal with a variety of related issues, such as teenage abortions and parental permission for such abortions; whether the husband must be involved in the abortion decision; and the use of public funds for abortions. A constitutional amendment to ban abortion has been proposed. Abortion clinics have been bombed. Politicians running for office have been targeted for defeat depending on their views on abortion. The democratic candidate for the Presidency in 1988, Michael Dukakis, took a position favoring legal abortions and as a result had a number of campaign meetings disrupted by pro-life activists.

In the articles that follow, Kenneth Kantzer and Paul Fromer argue that there is a growing consensus for abortion law reform, particularly restrictions for abortion on demand. Amanda Spake argues that public opinion is basically pro-abortion and that the danger of restricting abortion rights comes from conservative judges appointed by the Reagan administration.

ISSUE 10 YES:

Within Our Reach

Kenneth S. Kantzer and
Paul W. Fromer

An American consensus is shaping up on what to do about abortions. It is not what most evangelicals like. Rather, it poses a serious moral dilemma for them, and it calls for some hard decisions.

There is increasing evidence for this new consensus, which opposes abortion on demand, and especially all abortions of convenience. According to a current poll, its size has reached 58 percent. This is despite consistent support by public media of the prochoice movement's view (90 percent, according to a study by Samuel Rothman and Robert Lichter).

This new consensus is formed primarily of conservative Roman Catholics, conservative evangelicals, a sprinkling of Mormons, conservative Jews, and a growing body of ethically conservative blacks (generally evangelical, though not sailing under that banner). It also includes not a few liberals concerned over the growing erosion in Western culture of any commitment to the sanctity of life, and also some others not identified with any of these groups.

The presence of this broad consensus sets the stage for a dilemma among conservative evangelicals because most of them (66 percent, according to a Gallup poll taken in fall 1984) hold an absolutist or near absolutist opposition to abortion. (They oppose all abortions, or all except those where the mother's life is endangered, or, possibly, where rape or incest has occurred.) In this they have been able to count on traditional Roman Catholics and some others, but they have lacked the necessary support to secure a constitutional amendment for what they believe is right.

Their dilemma arises because, based on this broad national consensus, they could probably now get a stricter law than the one currently in force, but the new law would not be as strict as they believe to be morally justified. Can they honorably settle for less—on the ground that half a loaf is better than none?

The growing national consensus against abortion on demand rests in part on the broad heritage of Judeo-Christian values—still lively in Western culture and in America. The vast majority of Americans have always affirmed that their own personal and private conviction was opposed to abortion on demand, and a slight majority have gone on to state support for *laws* restricting it. Theodore Hesburgh, president of Notre Dame University, writes: "If, given a choice between the present law of abortion-on-demand, up to and including viability, or a more restrictive law,...the majority of Americans polled consistently have supported the more limited option." He acknowledges that "there is not a consensus in America for the absolute prohibition of abortion." But "there is and was a moral consensus...for a stricter abortion law. A remarkably well-kept secret is that a minority is currently imposing its belief on a demonstrable majority."

Before considering whether half a loaf is acceptable, we need to see the main factors leading to the rise of the prochoice movement in the sixties and seventies, and the subsequent resurgence of the prolife movement.

PROCHOICE UPSURGE

We have to admit that many more Americans today than, say, half a century ago or even 20 years ago, will defend the morality of abortion on demand (though this does not mean a majority, since the view started with little support). The movement away from the more traditional view first gained wide acceptance during the sixties.

In 1962 the American Law Institute published a study advocating a change in abortion laws to allow for abortions before viability in cases of rape, incest, the mother's health, or deformed and mentally retarded fetuses. ("Viability" occurs when the fetus can live outside the mother's body.) Five years later the American Medical Association endorsed these recommendations and reversed a medical history reaching back to Hippocrates. Planned Parenthood, NOW (National Organization for Women), and the ACLU joined the chorus of approval.

State legislation kept pace with this new attitude toward abortion. California, Colorado, and North Carolina repealed their strict laws in 1967, and state after state followed in quick succession. Finally, the *Roe* v. *Wade* Supreme Court decision of 1973 ruled unconstitutional most state laws that made abortions before viability a legal offense punishable in one way or another. This radical change in moral climate led many to conclude that, on moral grounds, Americans had generally come around to supporting abortion on demand.

Yet the result of this swift change in the law did not, in fact, mean this. Quite the contrary, most continued to affirm their own personal rejection of abortion except in extreme circumstances. But the will to support *laws* against abortion seemed to disappear.

At the same time, the church-state issue was heating up. Opposition to abortion is a private religious conviction, it was argued, which must not be written into a law that would violate the First Amendment with its guarantee of separation of church and state. Such a law would establish a religious viewpoint; further, it would deny the free exercise of religion to anyone who had no religious scruples against abortion, or whose religious convictions favored aborting children who would become a burden to society. Many Democrats in the election of 1984 objected strenuously to a plank in the Republican party platform demanding that appointed judges agree to the sanctity of human life. This, so they argued, was to make a religious viewpoint a requirement for office, and therefore violated our Constitution.

Further, many argued that it was unwise to pass such a law in present-day America because of the lack of a consensus supporting it. Unpopular laws cannot be enforced. In any case, it would affect only the poor and uneducated, and would inevitably, so it was said, lead to the scofflaw attitude of the latter days of Prohibition.

Gov. Mario Cuomo, in a speech at Notre Dame University, was typical of politicians taking this position. As a loyal Roman Catholic, he affirmed his own agreement with the traditional position of his church. But he said that as a responsible office holder representing the American people, he could not support laws the people did not want.

Finally, the most central argument supporting abortion on demand rested on the rights and freedom of women. No woman, it was felt, should be forced to go through an unwanted pregnancy. That would violate her inalienable right to privacy and her freedom as an independent citizen.

TURNING OF THE TIDE

Yet the traditional support even for laws against abortion was by no means completely eroded. In fact, the prolife forces, especially among evangelicals, began to gain momentum. In 1975, as a result of a meeting in the home of evangelist Billy Graham, the Christian Action Council was formed to combat the trend. Right-to-life organizations sprang up in almost every state. In seeking to bring America back to its moral heritage, Moral Majority made abortion a primary concern. Writers like Surgeon General C. Everett Koop (*The Right to Live: the Right to Die*) and the film by Dr. Koop and Francis Schaeffer, *Whatever Happened to the Human Race?*, aroused many lethargic evangelicals to active support of the prolife position.

Roman Catholic opposition to abortion was also stepped up. In a widely advertised position paper, the American bishops linked abortion on demand with nuclear war as a primary moral issue of our day.

Archbishop John O'Connor of New York has been especially outspoken for more stringent abortion laws; he has called Roman Catholics to act consistently with their faith. In what some felt was a direct attack on vice-presidential candidate Geraldine Ferraro, he pointedly expressed his disagreement with statements made by her and other Roman Catholics on the matter of abortion. He believed it was impossible to be a consistent Catholic and prochoice.

The influence of Roman Catholic leaders and the newly active evangelicals has significantly buttressed the prolife position. Their antiabortion stand is well thought out, and it obviously stems from the deep moral and religious conviction of people who care. No doubt the growing consensus occasionally received a temporary reversal from irresponsible extremists who bombed hospitals, or, drifting at the fringe of moral responsibility, seemed more concerned to gain headlines than to advance the prolife cause. Yet such setbacks were momentary, and the consensus is still growing.

STATISTICS OF MAYHEM

Undoubtedly, however, the greatest impact on the attitude of the American public did not come directly from these traditional sources. Rather, it arose from the growing awareness of what is really going on. From 8,000 legal abortions in the United States in 1966, the number grew to 400,000 in 1971 and has now soared to 1.6 million annually—about half as many abortions as live births. At least 14 major cities scattered across the United States are recording more abortions than live births, and the total number of abortions for the last decade has reached well over 15 million—two to three times the number of deaths in the ovens at Hitler's Auschwitz.

As the awesome statistics came bit by bit to public attention, many Americans, though not willing to identify themselves either as conservative Roman Catholics or evangelicals, became appalled. What originally they had seen as part of a broad movement toward freedom they now saw to have gotten completely out of hand.

What further disturbed those who were neither Roman Catholic nor evangelical concerned the increasingly trivial reasons for abortion. John Brown III, president of John Brown University, writes: "Abortions have become a matter of convenience, not of conscience. A pastor told me of a couple who chose to have an abortion because the unexpected pregnancy interferred with vacation plans." The life of an unborn child is all too often reckoned to have little intrinsic value, and to be disposable at the convenience of the mother. But the twisted morality that leads to such a conclusion has become revolting to many Americans.

ON TO INFANTICIDE?

The killing of unborn infants, moreover, is by no means the end of the matter. The logic that leads to abortion on demand also leads straight to infanticide. Peter Singer and Helga Kuhse, a medical team writing in the *New York Review of Books*, declared: "The Prolife groups were right about one thing: the location of the baby inside or outside the womb cannot make such a moral difference. We cannot coherently hold that it is all right to kill a fetus the week before birth, but as soon as the baby is born everything must be done to keep it alive." Mary Tedeschi, writing in *Commentary*, points out where this leads: "Thus, infanticide presents the champions of abortion on demand with an uncomfortable choice. They can either describe events that seem increasingly arbitrary—like 'viability' or birth—as the points at which a fetus or baby attains its rights, or they can allow, as the more outspoken 'ethicists' already have done, that infanticide, or at least certain instances of it, is as justifiable as abortion."

In this regard, Joseph Fletcher, the liberal who has long favored situation ethics, writes, "Why stop with the unborn? The only difference between the infant and the fetus is that the infant breathes with its lungs....If through ignorance or neglect or sheer chance...the damage has not been ended prenatally, why should it not be accordingly ended neo-natally?"

Probably the most famous American case of infanticide is "Baby Doe" of Bloomington, Indiana. He was born with Down's syndrome, and with a detached esophagus (the latter easily remedied by a simple operation). Lawyer Carl Horn III notes that though many parents petitioned to pay for the necessary medical care and to adopt him, the baby's parents and the courts rejected all offers. As a result, Baby Doe starved to death.

So the logic that leads to prenatal abortions leads also to freedom to kill newborn babies. It will, in fact, lead to the right to put to death any human being of whatever age if that person becomes a burden to society.

Further, science is more and more making nonsense of the *Roe* v. *Wade* guideline on abortion, which many accepted as the enlightened standard for the future. That decision was predicated on the right of the mother to choose to abort up to the time of viability—the sixth or seventh month of pregnancy. But as Sandra Day O'Connor in a dissenting opinion (*Akron* v. *Akron Center for Reproductive Health*) notes, "The *Roe* framework...is clearly on a collision course with itself." Medical progress is pushing farther and farther back into pregnancy the time at which the fetus is viable. Eighteen-week-old fetuses frequently live outside the womb today, and University of Tennessee researchers predict that in several years they will have perfected an artificial womb capable of sustaining a fetus only a few weeks old. Accordingly, the mother's freedom to choose whether to bring her child to birth or to kill it is shrinking. Her choice based on the *Roe* v. *Wade* principle could soon be practically eliminated.

POLITICS AND MORALITY

Finally, a conviction is growing on the part of many that it is, indeed, morally right and truly American to make certain moral demands on politicians. A separation between church and state is assuredly guaranteed by our Constitution. But for the good of the state as well as of religion, that separation must never become complete. "Thou shalt not murder" is a religious conviction of all Christians, but it is not wrong to impose it on society. It is the moral duty of conscientious religious citizens to seek to impose certain moral requirements on society—to advance not their own personal religious viewpoint, but the good of society as a whole.

During the last presidential election, Archbishop O'Connor argued for the right of citizens to question a candidate about his stand on abortion, and for the right of a candidate to state his opposition to abortion and his intent to work within the law to bring about a change in the law. There is nothing either un-American or unconstitutional about that. O'Connor asserted: "You have to *uphold* the law, the Constitutions says. It does not say that you must *agree* with the law, or that you cannot work to *change* the law." He called on Roman Catholics to ask candidates to state that they opposed abortion on demand and were committed to work to modify the permissive interpretations of the Supreme Court.

So the renewed opposition of conservatives and the growing reaction against the excesses of proabortionists have created a significant change of attitude toward abortion and the freedom-of-choice movement that grew so rapidly in the sixties and seventies. A sense of moral outrage is emerging. Things have gone too far too fast. Matters have gotten out of hand. Something must be done.

DENOMINATIONAL SECOND THOUGHTS

Consequently, many Protestant groups are taking another look. The Southern Baptist Convention had in 1974 supported the prochoice arguments. But in 1980 it reversed itself, and in June 1984 it passed a resolution opposing abortions even in cases of rape and incest.

In the late sixties and early seventies the United Presbyterian Church, the United Methodist Church, and the Protestant Episcopal Church all passed resolutions favoring a freer attitude toward abortions. But in 1983 the Presbyterian Church (USA) sent study materials to its member congregations urging a review of a statement that had earlier called abortions not only a right but sometimes an "act of faithfulness before God." In May 1984 the United Methodist Church voted to tighten its previous statement on abortion. This year the Episcopal Church faces a convention battle over abortion; leading the fight will be a new body calling itself the National Organization of Episcopalians for Life (NOEL). Last summer the African Methodist Episcopal Church reaffirmed its opposition to abortions except in cases of rape and incest; and in August 1984 the Lutheran World Federation passed a resolution deploring abortions of "pre-born children."

In May 1984 the Lutheran Church–Missouri Synod published an official report (*Abortion in Perspective*) calling Lutherans back to their biblical moorings against abortion, as reflected in writings of the early church fathers and in the Reformation heritage.

A QUESTION OF STRATEGY

This new stirring in the older mainline denominations indicates their growing realization that the Christian moral sense extending across the centuries may have been right after all. It may now be possible to reverse the position that has developed over the last two decades. A new consensus is forming. It is clearly against abortions for convenience, and all abortions on demand. There is even some evidence from polls, as President Hesburgh has noted, that the consensus might include laws against abortion except for rape, incest, and serious danger to the mother's life. (It is estimated that these exceptions account for only 1/2 of 1 percent of all abortions.)

But there is also abundant evidence that the American people are unprepared to approve any constitutional amendment or any law banning all abortions.

This poses a serious dilemma in strategy for all fundamentalists, conservative evangelicals, and traditional Roman Catholics—that is, for all antiabortion absolutists or near absolutists. Such conservatives agree that most—if not all—abortions are wrong. And so they fear, and rightly so, that any law insufficiently strict will be taken as approval of many morally offensive abortions. In fact, they suspect that such a law might preclude eventual passage of a more just law barring almost all abortions.

Yet Americans now clearly have it in their power to pass legislation outlawing the vast majority of abortions. Meanwhile, the deaths of over a million-and-a-half unborn children take place every year. In this case there appears literally to be a "moral majority" of antiabortionists. If they could agree on a course of action, much of this moral curse on our nation would be removed immediately.

Surely the path of moral and spiritual wisdom would dictate support for a second best. We would refuse to compromise moral conviction, however, because we would still hold our more stringent prolife views. But we would support a less-than-the-best law *for the present* since it is all that can now be passed. And we would pledge to work for a better law. Not only is this a legitimate area for immediate Christian action, but it would seem a moral imperative for evangelicals in view of the lives hanging in the balance. Accordingly, on more than one occasion the Reverend Jerry Falwell has publicly maintained his willingness to support any law that will reverse the abortion-on-demand, prochoice position now enforced by our courts. We applaud his strategy and warmly commend it to all evangelicals who are more interested in saving lives than in winning a point.

In summary, careful appraisal of the American scene makes evident that no absolutist law or constitutional amendment has the remotest chance of passing in the near future—certainly not in the next four years. But some sort of law that would at least eliminate one of the most frightening issues of our day in its most extreme form—abortion on demand—is within our reach.

ISSUE 10 NO:

The Propaganda War over Abortion

Amanda Spake

A few years ago, Olga Fairfax had what most right-to-life activists only dream of: an inside source in a hospital who revealed confidential patient information on who was scheduled for abortions and when. The hospital, Columbia Hospital for Women, in Washington, D.C., knew it had a problem when women patients reported calls and visits by Olga Fairfax only days or hours before their scheduled abortions. Olga's agenda was clear—to talk these women out of "killing their babies."

Calls came to Olga from an intermediary who received patient data from the hospital source. Then, Olga would call each patient in the early evening and introduce herself. "I told them I was not affiliated with the hospital and that I did crisis pregnancy counseling." Olga has a Ph.D. in counseling psychology from Valley Christian University. She has never practiced nor is she licensed as a therapist.

When she called, Olga asked the women if she could come to their homes and talk with them about their pregnancies. "Many would say, 'Oh, that'd be fine.' I'd only have thirty to forty minutes," Olga said, "because I was trying to see so many....I'd just show them my slide/tape show and give them the literature and then I'd say, 'I just want to listen to you. Tell me your story.' " Sometimes when Olga counsels, she uses a 12-week-old fetus, preserved and given to her by an obstetrician, which she's named "Baby Roe," after *Roe* v. *Wade,* the 1973 Supreme Court decision that struck down state restrictions on first-trimester abortion.

Of the 40 or so women Olga counseled, she says she persuaded 30 not to have their scheduled abortions but to carry their pregnancies to term. She doesn't know what happened to any of these 30 women—how they fared financially or emotionally—or their children. "I couldn't follow up," she apologizes.

I wondered how I would have felt if, 15 years ago, a night or two before my abortion, I had met Olga Fairfax and seen her presentation. Would I have canceled my abortion?

I don't know. I do know that a Second Great Abortion Debate is raging once again in our society, 13 years after the first one led to the legalization of abortion with the Supreme Court decision of 1973. The pro-life forces began organizing and gathering steam after *Roe* v. *Wade*, but the debate simmered on the back burner of public consciousness until the beginning of the Reagan Administration. Suddenly there was a pro-lifer in the White House. Despite Reagan, public opinion on abortion has not changed much since the First Abortion Debate in the 1960s and early 1970s moved the public to the pro-choice position it holds today.

Survey after survey, poll after poll consistently shows that a majority of Americans—from 55 to 70 percent depending on the phrasing of the questions—think that women in the first three months of pregnancy should be able to decide whether or not to have an abortion under some or all circumstances. The public has held this view for about 13 years. "One of the most remarkable aspects of the abortion controversy," says Cory Richards, Washington director for the Alan Guttmacher Institute, "is that it has not affected public opinion on abortion. The Supreme Court in 1973 was ratifying opinion on this issue, not leading it."

While public support for abortion has not changed, the rhetoric of the debate has. The war of words has become more emotionally charged primarily because the pro-lifers suddenly realized they were underdogs and they began fighting like underdogs—with a great deal of cunning. Pro-lifers, for example, have tried to cast doubt upon the need for legal abortion by saying there are "too many" abortions because women seek abortion "out of convenience."

Recently, they have argued, as does Ronald Reagan, that the fetus "feels pain" and insisted that eight- or 12-week-old fetuses are "babies." In this way, the pro-lifers have tried to make abortion a referendum on "the morality of killing." While there *are* moral questions surrounding abortion, it's important to remember that this society sanctions killing in a hundred ways—capital punishment, automobile fatalities, and reliance on armed military forces are only three. We even look the other way at "killing babies" when more than 10,000 children die yearly through unchecked poverty. These "moral questions," however, are not at issue for most pro-lifers.

In my view, the reasons they define "morality" so narrowly, the reason the medical debate over whether the fetus "feels" pain becomes so esoteric, the reason this Second Abortion Debate seems so emotionally wrenching is because by looking at only these issues, we are losing sight of what is at the core of the war. Abortion is not really about the unborn, it is about the born. Harsh words over strong feelings mark this abortion debate because at its center is the struggle over women's economic independence.

If women have access to abortion, they have control over when, how often, and in what context they become mothers. They can plan both their families and their careers and in so doing, compete independently in the same economic marketplace as men. If they have no access to abortion, women are economically dependent upon those who can compete freely for jobs...men. Those who would ban legal abortion seek to reinstitute a traditional family structure. But let's not kid ourselves. That was primarily an economic system, not an ethical one. Abortion is not so much a referendum on morality as it is a decision about economic opportunity.

Olga Fairfax opens the door for me with a warm greeting and a charismatic smile. She is tall, informal, lively, and I would guess about 45 years old, though she won't tell me her age. She has brown, curly hair, red nail polish, and she is dressed in a pastel blue pantsuit that reminds me of babies' pajamas. She lives in Wheaton, Maryland, and is not well-to-do. She told me she does not work for money, though she used to be a Methodist minister. Her husband supports her.

I am struck by her earrings. They are clear, glass, test-tube-looking things with something inside them that I can't quite see. They look like little amniotic sacs. She tells me later that her mother, who is not antiabortion, suggested she take out the little blue rocks inside the earrings and put in plastic fetuses. "At first I thought that's what was in them," I say.

As Olga sets up her slide show, a beautiful black baby whom she calls the "little fella" gurgles in a car seat she has propped against a chair. The "little fella" is about three months old and is the son of a young Nigerian woman who had originally planned to have an abortion. Olga is taking care of him full-time now, but the Nigerian woman will probably want him back after college.

The "little fella" has brought new insights into Olga's life. I respect her for admitting to me that "I see now that raising a child is a twenty-five-hour-a-day job. I can understand why women might consider terminating a pregnancy." Still, she obviously loves being a mother, and I ask her if she wants to keep the baby.

"I'd adopt him in a second if I could," she tells me sadly. I ask her if she has ever been pregnant.

"Once," she says.

"What happened?" I ask.

"I miscarried." Olga and her husband, Carl, have no children.

Fumbling with the projector, Olga tells me how she switched from being pro-abortion to antiabortion. "A very close friend of mine...she aborted and was immediately suicidal. That's when I began to change. She's sterile now, as are thirty percent of all women who abort, according to the World Health Organization."

The slide show begins. Pictures of tranquil scenes and children are mixed with photos of dismembered fetuses and stillborn, premature infants. The physical complications of abortion are reviewed, and the fact that "childbirth is much safer than abortion" is "documented." Psychological complications of abortion are enumerated: "depression, frigidity, anxiety, impotence for men, guilt, psychosis." The presentation argues against abortion in cases of rape and incest as well: "Ethel Waters was a product of rape." The 30-percent infertility rate after abortion comes up again. The show concludes with, "Abortion can leave you sterile or kill you."

"Pretty powerful," I tell Olga of the presentation. "That thirty-percent infertility figure..."

"WHO, the World Health Organization."

"And the 'childbirth is much safer than abortion.' The part about fifty abortion deaths to one death in childbirth. What's the source?"

"Centers for Disease Control. All of my statistics are documented."

Later, when I call Carol Hogue of the Centers for Disease Control, she tells me that recent U.S. studies indicate *no* increase in involuntary infertility after induced abortions in the United States, at least since 1973, nor does she know of any WHO studies that do. On the question of maternal deaths from childbirth and abortion, she says that the United States has about 350 to 400 maternal deaths each year, most related to childbirth. In 1981, there were eight deaths from induced abortion; one of those was from an illegal abortion.

Olga indicates that there will be a constitutional amendment banning abortion under any circumstances in the next few years, and I tell her, gently, that she is swimming against the tide. Most public opinion surveys show that about 55 to 60 percent of Americans do not favor such an amendment and it has almost no chance of being passed in Congress.

Olga argues that abortion at whatever time in pregnancy is immoral. "If the unborn baby is killed at six weeks, it's just as dead as if it were killed at six months." She is right. Few people dispute it. Public opinion polls also show a certain ambivalence about abortion and even those who are consistent supporters of legal abortion question its moral implications. For example, a September, 1981, Yankelovich, Skelly, and White survey of women showed that 67 percent believed in legal abortion; at the same time 56 percent said it was "morally wrong" even though 49 percent of this group still felt abortion should be legal.

What these statistics mean is that the right-to-life's "morality" argument doesn't go very far with most Americans and will not lead them to support a ban on abortions. Vague notions of what is or is not "morally wrong," while pervasive, are less important to them than the very tangible reality of being able to deal with an unintentional pregnancy. Legality and morality are separate issues in the public mind.

I don't know a single woman who has had an abortion who has not had to come to terms psychologically with the destruction of life involved. In my view, pro-choice women are better off to admit that the choice to have an abortion, like any other important life choice, has ethical significance. For centuries women have been coming to terms with the significance of abortions and are still having them.

Since the 1973 Supreme Court decision, women in this country have come to terms with an estimated 15 million legal abortions. At least 4 million women alive today came to terms with illegal abortions. Nearly 20 percent of all women between the ages of 18 and 44 have had an abortion, and about 25 percent of all pregnancies end in abortion.

If it seems as though "too many" women have chosen abortion recently, as the pro-lifers say, it is important to note that this demand for abortion has not changed appreciably since the 19th century. In 1871, an American Medical Association committee concluded that at least 20 percent of pregnancies were intentionally aborted (no doubt an underreported figure).

Coming to terms with abortion also does not seem to mean regretting it. One 1981 ABC News public opinion poll, reported by the Alan Guttmacher Institute, found that 79 percent of women surveyed said they were "better off today" because they'd had an abortion.

Of course there is a different moral question here and that is society's responsibility for children if abortion didn't exist. The Children's Defense Fund (CDF) reports that since 1980, the Reagan Administration has cut about $10 billion from the federal budget in survival programs affecting children and families. It also reports that in the fiscal 1986 budget, the Administration has proposed cutting another $1.9 billion in what are called entitlement programs: food stamps, child nutrition, Aid to Families with Dependent Children (AFDC), foster care, adoption assistance, and Medicaid. The Census Bureau estimates that about 13.3 million children now live in poverty, the highest child poverty rate in more than 18 years.

Lots of women understand that it is still too economically difficult for a young, unmarried, working mother to support herself and a child alone at the wages most women make. And that's exactly who gets 64 percent of all abortions—women between the ages of 15 and 24, while 81 percent of all women who have abortions are single. For many of these women, contraception has failed. Frances Kissling, executive director of Catholics for a Free Choice, put it well when she told me, "It's not the woman who's made the moral choice about abortion. Society has made the choice for her and then put the blame on women."

When I raise some of these issues with Olga Fairfax, I find she agrees with me that we can't, as she puts it, "get these babies born and drop 'em." I was disappointed, though, that on the question of social service cuts, even as bright a woman as Olga fell back on such standard lines as "there was a lot of fraud." She added that the Right-to-Life movement supports 3,000 outlets to distribute free food, clothes, baby accessories, and more to pregnant women.

I remain skeptical, however, that a small, private movement like the Right-to-Life can financially cover the cost of raising the 1.5 million or so children who would be born every year if abortion were outlawed. Based on the Urban Institute's estimate of an average $199,650 to raise a child to age 18, that's an additional $299.5 billion commitment somebody would have to make yearly, or a $5.4 trillion ongoing commitment each year by the time the first child reaches age 18 and her or his piece of the financial pie is given to another newborn.

It is after the tape recorder is off, and we are just talking that I think I see what Olga really believes will happen to women who are forced to carry unintentional pregnancies to term. She tells me about a young woman she knows.

This woman got pregnant at 15, decided to have the baby, and continued to live at home with her parents. She stopped going to high school and received home tutoring. She got a job in a department store and now, at 18, she has her high school diploma, continues to work at the department store, and, Olga says happily. "She's got a little diamond ring and she's going to be married."

There is another view of this familiar tradition. Consider the voice of the 28-year-old mother of three in Lillian Rubin's classic study of the working class, *Worlds of Pain* (Basic Books), who, in the 1960s, became pregnant, got married, never considered an abortion, and thinking back on it says: "I still remember how much I didn't want to get married. I wanted to get a job and have some things. I was afraid if I got married it would be the end of my chance for a better life. I wasn't wrong about that either."

When I was home at Christmas, I got in touch with Megan (not her real name), my best friend from high school, whom I had not seen in nearly 19 years. Megan and I grew up in Anaheim, California, a city rising from the southern California citrus groves. Megan's family and mine came early to Anaheim. The town was solidly "lower middle class," as Anaheimites described it, and still partly citrus groves; the air on a summer evening smelled of lemons.

Social roles for women in the lower middle class were just as restricted as in the blue-collar working class. Staying in Anaheim meant going to work at Kleenex or Sunkist or Ford semiconductors, preferably in an office and not on an assembly-line job. It meant marrying a man from Kleenex, going into debt to buy another of those "modestly priced" identical tract homes, staying home and taking care of the kids.

When Megan and I got together last Christmas, we tried to figure out how it was that we "got out" when so few other women we knew did. We talked of higher expectations and good grades, but lots of women in our high school class had expectations and grades.

There is another reason. When we each got pregnant accidentally, at 22, some combination of feminist expectation and class experience allowed Megan and me to fight off the enormous social pressure that said we "had to get married." We had abortions instead.

I tell my own personal abortion story because I want to set straight a dangerous and prevailing misconception, in particular among progressive men, that working-class women (or lower-middle-class women) do not use or support legal abortion. "You know, abortion is really a class issue," one progressive male friend said to me reproachfully. "Working-class women are not in favor of abortion." Although comments like this are more tactful than those articulated 13 years ago by people who were against legalizing abortion, their meaning is the same: "The only people who want abortions are those snotty, upper-class bitches who are taking our jobs."

Working-class women do support and use abortion. An Alan Guttmacher Institute analysis of poll results shows that the majority of women surveyed who have had abortions report family incomes in the $10,000 to $29,000 range, a solidly working-class or middle-class group. The second largest group are women with family incomes of $10,000 or less; this includes women who are working class or below. The third largest group are those with incomes of over $30,000. In another survey of women generally, 68 percent in the $10,000 to $29,000 family income group supported legal abortion while a slightly larger percentage, 73 percent, in the over $30,000 bracket also believed in legal abortion. The "upper-class bitches" are only slightly more favorable to abortion than are their working-class sisters.

How did this idea that working-class women do not use or support abortion get started? It seems to me it started when the media jumped on a very good book about abortion written by feminist sociologist Kristin Luker and then reinterpreted it. The book, *Abortion and the Politics of Motherhood* (University of California Press), studies the attitudes of more than 200 pro-choice and pro-life activists in California.

The question of working-class women's support for abortion surfaces when the media report Luker's profile of pro-choice and pro-life activists. Her average pro-choice activist was 44 years old, grew up in a large metropolitan area, and had a father who was a college graduate. She was married at 22, has one or two children, has some graduate or professional training beyond a college degree, is married to a professional, and is employed in a regular full-time job. Her family income is about $50,000 a year. She rarely attends church.

The average pro-life activist, in Luker's survey, was also 44 years old, grew up in a large metropolitan area and had a father who was a high school graduate. She was married at 17, has three or more children, completed some college and possibly obtained a college degree, is married to a small businessman or lower-level white-collar worker, and is not employed in the paid labor force. Her family income is about $30,000 a year. She attends church at least once a week.

What we see here are two slightly different profiles of fairly well-educated, middle- to upper-middle-class women. Both are profiles of women in a higher socioeconomic status than the majority of women who have abortions.

Newsweek's interpretation of Luker's work is typical both of how the media rewrote her thesis and of the general anti-choice bias evident in most media coverage of abortion this year. "For the pro-choice woman, abortion is perhaps as much an economic issue as a psychological and physical one, while for her pro-life counterpart it may embody some class-based resentment of higher-status women," the magazine reported in January, 1985. Even a newsletter read by New Agers called "New Options" said of Luker's book. "In the struggle over abortion you can see a struggle between two classes of women." Where?

Luker's book was only one casualty in the tidal wave of anti-choice media coverage. The pro-life forces mounted what seems to me to have been a very effective propaganda campaign beginning in early January and running right through the spring. Coverage of "The Silent Scream" was, as one reporter admitted to me, "too sympathetic" to the film, given the overwhelming amount of medical criticism of the film that surfaced after it was released. By that time, though, it had been carefully promoted and shown to millions of Americans on the major news shows.

Public opinion polls were reinterpreted by such influential news outlets as *Newsweek* (January, 1985) to show "Divisions and Growing Doubts" and *The Wall Street Journal* (April 15, 1985) to mean that "Antiabortionists Gain as the Furor Spreads and Uneasiness Grows." These are the same polls that show no significant change in public opinion on abortion over the last 13 years. Like the fact that most women, even working-class women, support abortion, consistent support for choice has not been newsworthy. Is it any wonder people are confused about the real issues in the Abortion Debate?

For several months the Maryland Right-to-Life Education Fund has been running an ad on suburban buses that shows a picture of an eight-week-old fetus and reads:

> If Wombs Had Windows...
> Your 8-week-old baby
> has done a lot of growing since conception!
> Every 8-week-old baby
>
> - Has a heartbeat
> - Has brain waves
> - Has fingerprints
> - Will grasp objects
> - Responds to touch
> - Swims in fluid
>
> Don't Drink; Don't Smoke.

My first response to this ad was to say to a friend: "I hope fetuses can swim in fluid because that's all they've got."

My second response was: "Fifty percent of all abortions are in the first eight weeks. The pro-choice side had better change tactics fast." I wondered if we were winning the arguments but losing the war.

To find out something about the war and the tactics, I went to see Nanette Falkenberg, executive director of the National Abortion Rights Action League (NARAL), one of the most politically sophisticated of the national pro-choice groups and also the one Dr. Bernard N. Nathanson of "The Silent Scream" fame had a role in founding.

Things have changed since Nathanson, of course. NARAL is now an organization with 150,000 national members, 33 state affiliates with a total of 100,000 members, and a $700,000 political action committee that supports pro-choice candidates to Congress and the state legislatures.

Nanette Falkenberg is 34 years old—bright, single, very attractive, and a political pro, the kind of woman who plays the Washington game well. She worked for the American Federation of State, County, and Municipal Employees (AFSCME) and was the associate director of political action for the union from 1979 until she went to NARAL in 1982.

She thinks the pro-choice side has forced the pro-lifers to switch tactics. The pro-lifers' shift away from electoral politics and to an emotional, guerrilla-style political movement is, in Nanette's mind, "the outcome of us really besting them on the political front." Does that mean pro-choice now has to become more like the pro-lifers?

"It's clear," she says, "that we have people's heads. Where the other side is creating some ambivalence is on the gut side, the morality side, the emotional side. Their strategy at this point is to play to the potential softness in the public opinion data."

For those of you who don't speak Washingtonese, "playing to the potential softness" means the pro-lifers are going after those people who tell pollsters they are pro-choice when in fact they are ambivalent about abortion. In general, those are people who have not had firsthand experience with abortion. They are people who are *uncommitted* on the issue and can be easily swayed; men and younger women who have always had access to safe and effective contraception are two obvious targets of the Right-to-Lifers.

Nanette believes this means pro-choice women will have to talk more about the positive outcomes of abortion. "People have to stop thinking about abortion as a necessary evil."

While the Hyde Amendment cut off federal funding for abortion, Washington, D.C., and 14 states, including California and New York, continue to fund abortion for poor women. It is not clear to most observers what pregnant women who are poor and cannot get a state-funded abortion do to get the money.

Despite the success of the Hyde Amendment, though, it is not the Congress or even the state legislatures that most pro-choice activists believe pose any great threat to legal abortion. It is the court system in general and, ultimately, the Supreme Court.

Three conservative members of the Senate Judiciary Committee in March sent Joseph Rodriguez, a Reagan nominee for a federal judgeship in New Jersey, an eight-page questionnaire that included seven questions about the legalization of abortion. Orrin Hatch (R-Utah) defended this unprecedented practice by saying that abortion "is a controlling question to some of our people."

To his credit, Rodriguez responded to the questionnaire by saying: "A district judge is bound by oath to respect the authority of the Supreme Court and its interpretation of the Constitution." In hearings on Rodriguez's nomination in April, Hatch again defended use of the questionnaire. But Senate Judiciary Committee chairman Strom Thurmond (R-S.C.) was against its use and instructed Hatch to bring his questions on judicial nominations before the full committee in open hearings.

Nanette Falkenberg is concerned about what this incident means for the entire federal court system, from the district courts all the way up to the Supreme Court. "I think they have a series of test cases at the lower level ready," Falkenberg says. "The Supreme Court *does* change its mind. We're one, maybe two, votes away on the Court now, and it's pretty clear that this Administration will get to appoint one or two justices."

The "red flag" Nanette says was Sandra Day O'Connor's dissent in the recent *Akron* case in June, 1983, which reaffirmed *Roe* v. *Wade*. Under *Roe*, a state can bar abortion in the third trimester when the fetus is "viable" outside the mother's womb. O'Connor's dissent set the Court up for overturning *Roe* when she wrote: "It is certainly reasonable to believe that fetal viability in the first trimester of pregnancy may be possible in the not-too-distant future."

While many doctors argue that fetal viability is extremely unlikely before 25 weeks, that is not the point. The composition of the Court *is*, and in that, time is not on our side. How long do we have? "I would say four years," Nanette says. "It's possible that in four years *Roe* will be substantially restricted."

As Nanette Falkenberg said this, the Supreme Court was deciding to take on yet another abortion case, this one an appeal over a Pennsylvania abortion control statute that places several obstacles in the path of women seeking abortions. It is unclear why the Court decided to hear this Pennsylvania case since it is so much like the Akron case. Some speculate that the Supreme Court's decision means that one or more Justices have already changed their position on legal abortion.

One of the more hopeful things one can say about the future of legal abortion is that we have had access to it for 13 years now. The momentum, contrary to Reagan's assertion to the pro-lifers this January, is on *our* side. Even if states are allowed by the Supreme Court to restrict abortion in the first trimester again, it will be exceedingly difficult to do so. Women are unlikely to willingly return to the cost, pain, suffering, and unnecessary deaths of illegal abortion, even if the Supreme Court believes we can be forced to do so. Trying, at this point, to reinstitute restrictive laws on abortion will prove far too unpopular for most state politicians. We have time to organize.

In the meantime, I think Nanette Falkenberg is on to something when she says, "We have to begin to talk about the positive outcomes of choice." As I am leaving her office, I ask her if she has ever had an abortion. "Yes," she says. "You're the second reporter who's asked me that in the last week. It's an example of how this issue is changing. We're talking about our abortions again. The only thing is, now I have to tell my mother."

Why is abortion such an emotionally charged issue?

OLGA FAIRFAX: "Abortion is about sex, religion, and politics, and that's about as explosive as you can get."

NANETTE FALKENBERG: "It speaks at its core to people's most basic sense of what the world is and what gives their lives value in the world."

KRISTIN LUKER: "This round of the abortion debate is so passionate and hard-fought because it is a referendum on the place and meaning of motherhood.... While on the surface it is the embryo's fate that seems to be at stake, the abortion debate is actually about the meanings of *women's* lives."

Reprinted with permission by Amanda Spake, an editor at *The Washington Post Magazine*. This piece was previously published in *Ms.* Magazine, July, 1985.

ISSUE 11

Is the Religious Right a Threat to Basic Freedoms?

The phrasing of the above question was changed a number of times and still seems inadequate. The questions that concern us on this issue deal with the nature of church–state relations in the United States. To what extent should religious beliefs be reflected in the legal and legislative functions of society? How much control should religious institutions have over individual behaviors? The current concern is with the new religious right organizations such as the Moral Majority.

The relationship between church and state in the United States has always been different from that in most other societies. The First Amendment of the Bill of Rights states, "Congress shall make no law regarding the establishment of religion, or prohibit the free exercise thereof...." All of the states also guarantee the separation of church and state in their constitutions. Although the Bill of Rights prohibited us from establishing a state church, the line dividing state and church was not made clear and has remained ambiguous.

Through much of our history, religious beliefs and dogma have been reflected in our laws. Many jurisdictions in the Protestant South have "blue laws" that restrict business activity on Sunday. Catholic areas in the Northeast have banned the sale of birth control devices. Governmental institutions have included dogma and prayer as part of their procedures. Church property has been exempted from taxes. Some of these interrelations between church and state have been restricted in recent years by the courts. School prayer has been banned from public schools. The religious right has, of course, been involved in attempts to restore school prayer. There has been a proposal for a constitutional amendment, backed by President Reagan, that would make school prayer constitutional.

During the 1960s, some elements of organized religion became more active in the civil rights movement and the campaign against the Vietnam War. Martin Luther King and other black ministers used their churches as rallying points in the civil rights era. Some white churches, such as the Unitarian and Episcopalian, were also active in this movement. Many of the activist clergymen from the more liberal denominations carried over their social concerns from civil rights to Vietnam War protests. Some members of the Catholic church, (e.g., the Berrigan brothers) were also involved. In general, the civil rights and peace activists tended to come from the liberal religious groups, although it is difficult to tell what proportion of Protestants and Catholics were liberal at that time. Most traditional Southern white churches, however, remained neutral or negative. Jerry Falwell's Baptist church opened an all-white school when Lynchburg, Virginia, was threatened with integration.

Since the early 1970s, the evangelical churches, such as the Southern Baptist and Assemblies of God, have been gaining in membership. At the same time, mainline churches, such as the Methodist and Presbyterian, have lost members. The evangelicals, particularly the fundamentalists, stress conservative doctrine and morality and a generally literal interpretation of the Bible. The increase in fundamentalist membership has coincided with an increased social activism on the part of fundamentalist churches. These groups are generally anti-abortion; anti-homosexual; pro-prayer in schools; anti-communist; pro-creationist; pro-censorship of books, television, and movies; and, oddly enough, pro-Israel. Many feel the pro-Israel sentiment is combined with a form of anti-Semitism revolving around questions of whether God hears the prayers of Jews and their ultimate fate if Jews do not accept Jesus as their savior.

The activism of the fundamentalists has taken a variety of forms. Pressure groups have formed to defeat liberal candidates. They have taken credit for the election and reelection of President Reagan, who shares many of their beliefs. They have used pressure and litigation to have creationism taught in public schools as an alternative to evolution. They have forced school districts to remove from their libraries what they consider to be subversive or "dirty" books, such as *Catcher in the Rye* and Shakespeare's works. As a result of their pressure, 7-11 stores no longer carry *Playboy* and *Penthouse* magazines. The Coalition for Better Television, made up of fundamentalists including Jerry Falwell, is given credit for eliminating "jiggle" or "T and A" shows such as "Three's Company."

In the articles that follow, Daniel Maguire, in a selection taken from his book *The New Subversives,* agrees that the new right is a dangerous social movement at odds with basic American values. The second article, by Jerry Falwell, spells out the objectives of the Moral Majority specifically and the new right in general.

ISSUE 11 YES:

Politics of the Absurd

Daniel C. Maguire

The New Right is not almighty. It seems necessary to say that. Born-again politics arrived on the political scene at a time of terrible dullness. They found the center stage empty and filled it with raucous hoopla and the magic of instant success. *Newsweek* announced: "They are winning." The first chapter of Richard Viguerie's book is entitled "Why the New Right is Winning." The Congress of the United States has reacted with numbness and passivity to the President who endorsed the New Right in his campaign—and who was endorsed by them. It would seem as if the die is cast. We can only watch the dawning of the New Right age.

The first temptation to be guarded against is *paranoia*. Paranoia is an old-time resident of American politics. It affects right, left, and center. It proceeds from an overreaction to what may be a genuine threat. Paranoia endows the threat with demonic powers, and thus makes us less able to counter the real danger. As a noted analyst of political paranoia put it almost twenty years ago, paranoia makes us think of the enemy as possessing "some especially effective source of power: he controls the press; he directs the public mind through 'managed news'; he has unlimited funds; he has a new secret for influencing the mind; he has a special technique for seduction; he is gaining a stranglehold on the educational system." Some reactors to the radical right see all of that in this new phenomenon. Therefore, before examining their actual power—and it is considerable—it is well to look soberly at their debits—and they are also considerable. First of all, the New Right is funny. Laughter redeems, and we shouldn't miss out on it. Secondly, the New Right is loaded with contradictions that need public attention. Finally, the New Right shows some early signs of coming apart at the seams.

OPERATION FIASCO

On a simple scale of ridiculousness the New Rightists rank high. They combine all the elements of exquisite farce. Sadly for those who value religious experience, much that is funny about them comes from the deviant "Christian" fundamentalism that thoroughly animates the movement. This kind of deviant fundamentalism has always had a flair for a kind of comedy of the absurd. Some thought this had died away after the Scopes trial of 1925. John Scopes, a biology teacher, was put on trial in Dayton, Tennessee for violating state law by teaching the theory of evolution. The trial became a test of fundamentalism in the face of modernity. It was an epic moment of theatric absurdity not easily recaptured. H.L. Mencken's account of that event half a century ago serves to highlight the absurd-comic possibilities of all deviant fundamentalism. He summed up the overall scene as "an obscenity of the very first calibre." His further descriptions fill that bill. "There was a friar wearing a sandwich sign announcing that he was the Bible champion of the world. There was a Seventh Day Adventist arguing that Clarence Darrow was the beast with the seven heads and ten horns described in Revelation XIII, and that the end of the world was at hand. There was an evangelist made up like Andy Gump, with the news that atheists in Cincinnati were preparing to descend upon Dayton, hang the eminent Judge Raulston, and burn the town. There was the ancient who maintained that no Catholic could be a Christian. There was the eloquent Dr. T.T. Martin of Blue Mountain, Mississippi, come to town with a truckload of torches and hymn-books to put Darwin in his place. There was a singing brother bellowing apocalyptic hymns....Dayton was having a roaring time." Then some years later, there was Carl McIntire who got fired up about the evils of communism and led the feisty project to send a million gas-filled balloons, each of them six feet in diameter, across the iron curtain carrying portions of the Bible. In his *Christian Crusade* magazine he blamed the civil rights movement on the communists and argued that the postal zip code system was a Soviet plot.

The spirit of those times is not dead. The House Judiciary Committee heard testimony recently on the subject of prayer in the public schools. Television evangelist James Robison spelled out for Congress the "plagues" that descended upon our nation after the banning of prayer in schools by the Supreme Court in 1962–1963. The Vietnam war accelerated; prominent leaders were assassinated; there followed "escalation of crime, disintegration of families, racial conflict, teen-age pregnancies and venereal disease." All of this from banning prayer in public schools. California evangelist Bill Bright, like Robison, also believed that the

Supreme Court's ban on school prayers could be blamed for "crime, racial conflict, drug abuse, political assassinations, the Vietnam war, sexual promiscuity and the demise of American family life." (One wonders what caused calamities when school prayer was still in.)

One might marvel at the liberality of a society that stages such comedy in a hearing room of the House of Representatives, but the humor should not be missed. It was not missed by University of Chicago professor Martin Marty. He wryly noted that after people started wearing yellow "smile buttons," the rate of venereal disease increased. He also pointed out that "the divorce rate rose shortly after the invention of the electronic church...when born-again celebrities started writing born-again autobiographies, teen-age pregnancies increased; and when fundamentalists started writing sex manuals, the Vietnam war accelerated...and executive crime increased right after America decided that God was *not* dead."

All of us, liberal or conservative, bring our absurdities with us when we enter the political arena. Absurdities do not disenfranchise us. But they should not be overlooked. It is the indispensable political function of the jester to find them out and expose them to the appropriate response. Laughter chastens politics and exorcizes society's devils.

There are other examples of the fun the radical religionists bring to us. They are not just gloom boomers bombarding us with their "hit lists" of objectionable politicians and their unctuous, tedious sermonizings. James Wright, executive director of the Maryland Moral Majority, starred in an Annapolis comedy. It seems that a certain bakery was purveying gingerbread men and women with large smiles and prominent sex organs. Sales were brisk, and probably became brisker when Wright sniffed out the cookies. He sent two youngsters in to purchase the gingerbread images, and then charged that the store had sold obscene material to minors. The case failed when the assistant state attorney found the action unsavory but not illegal. It did lead some to wonder whether attempts would soon follow to introduce the "Antipornographic Gingerbread Persons Act" into Maryland law.

The humor of the radical religious right rises to high places. According to a report in *The Wall Street Journal,* Interior Secretary James Watt was being quizzed by the House Interior Committee about whether he really favored preserving wilderness areas for the benefit of "future generations." Watt stunned his questioners by bringing in his millenarian fundamentalist faith as a basis of policy. He avowed, without a blink: "I do not know how many future generations we can count on before the Lord returns." Admittedly, as here, the comic often touches on the tragic. Mr. Watt's private faith that there is little need to fret over future generations, because Jesus will be along to take care of things, may be harmless as a private belief. It is comedy transmuted into tragedy when it provides the basis for cabinet-level policy.

Other such tragicomic voices are heard around us and should be highlighted. When the Reverend Greg Dixon, National Secretary of the Moral Majority, said that the Moral Majority is a philosophical movement designed to return a right-wing God to government, when Reverend Bailey Smith, President of the Southern Baptist

Convention, tells us that God Almighty does not hear the prayers of a Jew, when Dan Fore, former head of the Moral Majority in New York, lets us know that Jews have an almost supernatural power to make money, or that "Christians" can't be blamed for the Inquisition because it was done by "Catholics," when an "inerrant" Bible tells the same folks to get into politics today that it used to tell to stay out, or when they try to write it into law that a newly fertilized ovum is a citizen of the United States, we must laugh as an act of political sanity. And we have to hail the pundits and cartoonists who perform a civil service by bringing this twisted humor to the light of day.

All of this is cited here to stress the point that the right-wing juggernaut is missing some of its essential parts. It is too deep in ridiculousness to be almighty.

CONTRADICTIONS OF THE RIGHTEOUS RIGHT

In a democracy, all must be welcomed into the political process, but the intellectual baggage one brings to that process is open to inspection by everyone else. All have a right to know just how much mental disarray one is bringing into the world of power and politics. Political debate deserves intellectual rigor, since it is in this arena that decisions are made about who will eat and who will go hungry, about who will live and who will die. One's credentials must be up front and on call when entering politics to influence what goes on there.

There is much that is weak in the internal "logic" of the movement. Its discourse is riddled with conflicting positions. It speaks from one side of the mouth and then from the other. In short, it is not coherent.

Pseudoconservatism

Given the simplistic either/or mentality of the New Rightists, one is either "liberal" or "conservative." They are manifestly not "liberal." Therefore they conclude that they are "conservative." That is a key assumption of the New Right, and one of their biggest lies.

Even their rhetoric shows that their claim to conservative status is shaky. They talk of "taking control" of the conservative movement, implying that there is a conservatism other than theirs that needs controlling. They also bicker with other conservatives, and express fears that even the conservative President Reagan, who delights them in most things, may stray from their conservative orthodoxy. At times, they even come right out and blatantly show their counterconservative hand. New Right leader Paul Weyrich says: "We are radicals who want to change the existing power structure...the New Right does not want to conserve, we want to change—we *are* the forces of change."

The pseudoconservative phenomenon is not new. Pseudoconservatives have been described as persons who, "although they believe themselves to be conservatives and usually employ the rhetoric of conservatism, show signs of a serious and restless dissatisfaction with American life, traditions and institutions. They have little in common with the temperate and compromising spirit of true conservatism in the classical sense of the word.... Their political reactions express rather a profound if largely unconscious hatred of our society and its ways...." As another study put it: "The pseudo-conservative is a man who, in the name of upholding traditional American values and institutions and defending them against more or less fictitious dangers, consciously or unconsciously aims at their abolition."

From this distrust of our traditions and structures flows the "amend the Constitution" syndrome, so obvious in pseudoconservative moments of American history. In the early fifties, when a pseudoconservative mood was in high fever, one hundred amendments to the Constitution were introduced in the eighty-third Congress. It is interesting to note what these proposed amendments were up to: to limit nonmilitary expenditures, to repeal the income tax, to bar all federal expenditures for "the general welfare," to redefine treason, etc. As one observer put it: "The sum total of these amendments could easily serve to send the whole structure of American society crashing to the ground."

In our day, Congress has before it some thirty similarly subversive bills to limit sharply the power of the federal judiciary. These bills spring from the New Right's discontent with the decisions the Supreme Court has made over the last two decades in areas such as mandatory prayer in public schools, a woman's right to abortion, and busing to end segregated education. The radically subversive thrust of these amendments is signaled by U.S. Court of Appeals Judge Irving R. Kaufman. These bills, he says, threaten "not only a number of individual liberties, but also the very independence of the Federal courts, an independence that has safeguarded the rights of American citizens for nearly 200 years." Such radical tinkering with the system is not conservative. It represents an attempted subversion of the method of checks and balances that was so central to the vision of the founding fathers and to that of true conservatives. These radical rightists are not conservative. That is their first and most basic contradictory claim.

Religious Tests in Politics

There are a number of other contradictions in the New Right. They proclaim the doctrine of the separation of church and state, and yet they impose religious, "Bible-based" tests on political candidates. These religious tests or checklists show little concern for the major political issues of peace and social justice. They are, rather, little catechisms of deviant fundamentalist faith. It is their goal to elect candidates who measure up to their religious criteria and thus, by majority vote, make their fundamentalist faith the law of the land. This goes contrary to the core purpose of the nonestablishment of religion—which later came to be called the separation of church and state. The radical rightists accept the rhetoric of separation but are fully occupied in frustrating its purposes.

A twofold advantage was seen by the founding fathers of the United States in the nonestablishment of religion: government could not intrude on the privacy and integrity of religious bodies, and no religious persuasion could be imposed by law on citizens who enjoyed other beliefs.

It was the American ideal not to put government behind any sectarian religious views. Thomas Jefferson prized religious freedom. But he clearly differed from today's moral majoritarians on how freedom and religion should relate in the American plan. True religion, he said, should not be propagated by "temporal punishments" and "civil incapacitations," but "by its influence on reason alone." He warned against those governments where rulers and legislators "being themselves but fallible and uninspired men, have assumed dominion over the faith of others, setting up their own opinions and modes of thinking as the only true and infallible, and as such endeavoring to impose them on others...." Where persons can impose their private religious interpretations on others by force of law, said Jefferson, the result is "hypocrisy and meanness." Once again, Jefferson, sounding like he saw the Moral Majority and others emerging, wrote: "Our civil rights have no dependence on our religious opinions, any more than our opinions in physics or geometry; and therefore the proscribing of any citizen as unworthy of the public confidence by laying upon him an incapacity of being called to offices of trust or emolument, unless he profess or renounce this or that religious opinion, is depriving him injudiciously of those privileges and advantages to which, in common with his fellow-citizens, he has a natural right....It tends also to corrupt the principles of that very religion it is meant to encourage, by bribing with monopoly of worldly honours and emoluments, those who will externally profess and conform to it...." Jefferson adds that "though indeed these are criminals who do not withstand such temptation, yet neither are those innocent who lay the bait in their way."

This was the foundational dream of the United States. No particular religious views will be "established." Religions will make their appeals in freedom to the reasoned judgment of free persons. Ideals and principles bred of religious experience are free to compete for political expression, but no one bias shall work its way into law in such a way that legitimately debated differences are suppressed. Even the religious views of the majority will not become official. Majority rule with minority rights is the American ideal.

Ideals, of course, are not sweetly and easily realized. For a long period evangelical Protestantism did enjoy unofficial establishment status. Still, the ideal is clear and it is the soul of the separation doctrine.

The New Rightists oppose this American ideal. For all their talk about separation, they want establishment status for their religious views. Jerry Falwell, the founder of the Moral Majority, is not ambiguous on this point. This nation "was founded by godly men upon godly principles *to be a Christian nation.*" The unecumenical nature of his sentiments is not in doubt. "If a person is not a Christian, he is inherently a failure...." By "Christian" Pastor Falwell means his kind of "Christian." It does not include civil rights advocates, peace activists, environmentalists, feminists, supporters of civil rights for homosexuals or abortions for poor women, etc. It is Falwell's subcultural, right-wing Christianity that would be the mark of his "Christian" America. Religion's gentle appeal to reason, as championed by Jefferson, would be replaced by coercion, with "civil incapacitations" visited upon dissenters. The Falwellian hunger for majority status is a desire for tyranny of the majority through law. Hence the hit lists and the religious tests of political orthodoxy. The tactic is simple. If you can elect politicians on the basis of a bigoted religious test, you will get a bigoted religious government. Your bias will become unofficially, but effectively, established. The wall of separation will be ruptured. This is the second elementary self-contradiction and weakness in the program of the new religious-political right.

Civil Liberties and Government Intrusion

There are other contradictions in the position of the rightists. Their rhetoric drips with love of freedom and fear of government encroachment on that freedom. Stripped of its puff and fluff, their prescription is this: freedom (read anarchy) for the elite, and tyranny for women, the poor, libraries and educational institutions, and homosexual citizens.

The most extreme libertarian views are held by the New Right as far as business is concerned. Laissez faire freedom is a matter of biblical faith for them. They preach the divine right of free enterprise. With an appalling misunderstanding of biblical literature, Falwell proclaims: "The free enterprise system is clearly outlined in the Book of Proverbs in the Bible. Jesus Christ made it clear that the work ethic was a part of his plan for man." Nothing should impede the free march of business. All inhibiting regulations about worker safety, environmental protection, monopoly busting, affirmative action and, above all, labor unions, must be restrained or abolished in the name of the "conservative" God.

When we move from boardroom to womb, the contradiction emerges without subtlety. Government must be placed on the backs of the pregnant woman. Here there is no laissez faire or individual freedom. A woman who believes that for somber but moral reasons she must terminate a pregnancy must be prohibited by government from exercising her judgment—and this even though a number of religious and ethical authorities support her judgment. Homosexual citizens are to be blocked by law from pursuing certain careers or from seeking legal redress for discrimination. This would allow government to intrude into career choice and self-defense—areas of the most personal and sacred freedom. Libraries must not be free to supply books that offend the narrow canons of deviant fundamentalist faith. Censorship is the first passion of the fascist mind, and it is in full bloom in the New Right. The denial of government funds is the preferred weapon of the New Right to bludgeon institutions of learning and health care that do not hew to the right-wing checklist of virtues.

A student of civil liberty in the United States described the ideals of our country this way: "*The essence of civil liberty is the right to be wrong*. That is, the civil right to be wrong, not necessarily the moral right, or the intellectual right. Civil liberties deny *to the government* the authority to determine what is right or true in theology, economics, biology, diet, or political theory. Unless you believe in your opponent's *civil right* to be wrong, you cannot really believe in your *civil right* to be right, but only in your *power* to be right."

The New Right dissents from this ideal. For them, error has no rights. And "error" is disagreement with them on the things they take seriously. Business, of course, which God wishes to be untrammeled in its freedom, is free to be wrong. It is not to be inhibited if it strays. Educators, librarians, women, gay persons, and political officers who disagree with the radical right do not have a right to be wrong. For such as these, the New Right, not freedom, shall reign.

Pro-Israel/Anti-Semitic

Illogic arises again in the attitude of the New Right toward Jews. In what is a tour de force of absurdity, the New Right manages to be at once pro-Israel and anti-Semitic. The New Rightists come on like Israel's best friends. But friends like this Israel, and Jews everywhere, do not need. Israel is important to the religious rightists, but not for its own sake. Using the Bible as they do, as a kind of ouija board to predict the future, Israel is in a starring role. Through a fanciful reading of the Hebrew prophets, New Right seers like Hal Lindsey, in his best seller *The Late Great Planet Earth,* show the place of Israel in the rightist scheme of things. Lindsey gives us the most detailed version of the millenarian faith, which, in various forms, suffuses the religious soul of the right.

In the gospel according to Lindsey, the prophets saw the future and spelled it out with incredible exactitude. As we near the end of history, in this view, certain configurations of national power will appear as signals of the impending end and the coming of Jesus. The Common Market will be formed as a new Rome. Russia will rise militarily. The United States will become a Christian nation and the light of the world. But at center stage is Israel. "All of this would be around the most important sign of all—that is the Jew returning to the land of Israel after thousands of years of being dispersed. The Jew is the most important sign to this generation."

That is why large segments of the evangelical Christian world have been in such a tizzy since the establishment of Israel as a nation. They believe that the excitement of the "latter days" is upon us. The millennium is at hand.

Judaism, Israel, and Jews in general are of major importance—but only as signals of the Christian triumph that is to be. Israel is valued only as the staging ground for the return of Jesus, at which point, of course, the only good Jew will be a Christianized Jew. There is simply no respect in the radical right for the authenticity of Jewish religious experience. The Jews are either pawns in the revelation of millennial bliss expected for Christians, or they are grist for the mills of conversion. Jews as Jews are literally damnable. God would not even hear their prayers, as the Reverend Bailey Smith pointed out to us in a moment of candor concerning the right's assessment of Jews. Only prayers offered in the name of Jesus get through to God.

Falwell at first agreed with Smith on this, but then, after a hurried conference with Rabbi Marc Tannenbaum, Falwell (and apparently God) had a change of mind.

In a politic statement, Falwell restored Jewish access to God in prayer. Falwell's conversion here, however, could only be verbal. In the hard-nosed fundamentals of his creed, neither a Jew nor anyone else can bypass Jesus en route to God. Jews, after all, are not "born again," and in Falwellian theology, that leaves them religiously dead.

Prolife/Prodeath

The contradictions do not end. It is no simple matter to catalogue them all. The New Right is on the one hand prolife, and on the other hand, prodeath. They are prolife in a very limited sense and are prodeath in a potentially unlimited sense. "Prolife" is sloganese for being unqualifiedly antiabortion. The rightists do not just favor fetuses, however. They also sacralize life after birth—for upwardly mobile white people.

Black life is of concern to the "prolife" forces of the New Right only in its prenatal state, since that would come under the abortion ban that the New Right wants to put into law. After birth, the life of blacks seems to be of little importance. The self-designated "prolifers" of the New Right take no note of the fact that in the United States at this time a black woman is three times more likely than a white woman to die in childbirth and twice as likely to lose her infant in the first year of its life. If the black child survives, he or she is five times more likely to be murdered than a white child. None of this impresses the new "Christian" right. In their brand of mean-spirited individualism, "them that gets deserves." Thus, blacks, who are not getting, are getting what they deserve. If blacks would seek help for their lives, they will have to look outside the "prolife" lobby of the New Right. The poor in general should be similarly advised. Their plight is something to which members of the New Right seem blind. Phyllis Schlafly, for example, while championing family life and the need for women to stay at home, is apparently unaware that there are women too poor not to have to work.

The prodeath bias of the New Right shows up even more in their attitude toward "defense" than it does in their disdain of blacks and the poor. The New Right is more militant than the Joint Chiefs of Staff. They weep over America's military impotence. They are scarcely satisfied now with President Reagan's proposal to spend 1.5 trillion dollars over the next five years for weapons—which comes to 34 million dollars per hour. They are unimpressed with the fact that if you gave the annual defense budget for the year 1979 to Jesus Christ, he could have spent one hundred thousand dollars a day from the day he was born right up to today, and still have 750 years of spending left. These massive expenditures for war do not slake their military thirsts. The logic of their position seems to be that only an invulnerable first-strike capability would keep us safe.

As I shall explain further..., the rightists need a war, just as they needed the foundation of Israel. Nuclear war squares nicely with some of the scriptural language about the fiery tribulation that will inaugurate the "latter days"—the big chastening blast that will set the stage for Jesus's triumphant return. There is a dangerous *need* for nuclear war implicit in the deviant fundamentalism of the New Right. Just as the coming millennium dispenses Interior Secretary Watt from care for future generations, that same millennial hope induces a pious nonchalance in New Right believers. The coming inaugural war will do them no harm. True believers can view this impending judgment with a "not-to-worry" calm. Their faith is their thermonuclear insurance. They will be saved by a blessed "rapture," lifted up to meet Christ "in the air," while the good earth and the unbelievers are scorched in the final holocaust. Those of us who do not carry "rapture" insurance do well to signal the danger when folks like this move into power. Prolife is what the "prolifers" of the New Right are not.

Family vs. Patriarchy

The rightists are also champions of private morality and family life, and yet their heroes are often tarnished by the very standards of the right. The rightists oppose divorce and support permanent marriage. And yet in the 1980 elections the undivorced Jimmy Carter was cast as the villain, and the divorced Ronald Reagan as the saint. Richard Viguerie could even confide to Mr. Reagan: "Your personal example, along with Mrs. Reagan's, can help lead America to a rebirth of greatness." Given their chaste horror of divorce, one might legitimately query: "Which Mrs. Reagan?" Similar delicious ironies are found in the fact that the New Right ratings systems for rigorous churchmen like Representative Paul Simon and Father Robert Drinan gives them a 0 percent, while a Richard Kelly, of Abscam fame, got a 100 percent rating. Again one senses that their act is not quite together.

The New Right also postures as the last bastion of profamily idealism. They are not. ... the Family Protection Act, around which the New Right rallies, is a blueprint for fascist family life. The act is more a Patriarchy Protection Act. Women and children are shortchanged. The family is the place where men rule.

Falwell is quite candid about that. Men are the natural rulers. "Men are the key to a moral revolution in America," says Falwell. "Men have led women and children a long way; now it is time for an 'army' of spiritually concerned men to lead America in the right way." In the Falwellian home, "the father is responsible to exercise spiritual control and to be the head over his wife and children: '...Women are to be feminine and manifest the ornament of a meek and quiet spirit, which is in the sight of God a great prize' (Peter 3:4). In the Christian home, the woman is to be submissive; ' wives, submit yourselves unto your own husbands, as unto the Lord' (Ephesians 5:22)." Patriarchy could scarcely be made of sterner stuff, with women submitting to their husbands *as if the husband were God*—"as unto the Lord."

Children are to be no less submissive. They must be taught that the father is boss in the home, and they must follow their mothers' good example and obey. There is recognition that children might resist this, and so the Family Protection Act tightens up the concept of child abuse so that it permits corporal punishment, applied by a parent or an individual authorized by a parent. The Act also senses that wives might not be as submissive as God, Falwell, Senator Laxalt, and the other men of the New Right want, and so it would prohibit the federal government from giving funds or instituting programs to prevent and treat child and spouse abuse, beyond what the states are doing. Runaway shelters are not to offer contraceptive or abortion procedures, or even counseling, without prior parental approval. Parental authority in this view is paternal authority, and is decidedly muscular in tone. No wife or child could see this as "profamily." Again, the rhetoric and the reality are at odds.

Religious Contradictions

Religiously, too, the New Right is shot through with contradictions. On the one hand, they express an unqualified trust in God: "If God is on our side," Falwell incants, "no matter how militarily superior the Soviet Union is, they could never touch us. God would miraculously protect America." That pious confidence hardly squares with the martial lusts they manifest for more and more missiles and nuclear kill-power.

They claim to be pro-Pope and pro-Catholic, but they never quote the popes on issues of peace or justice, and often their rhetoric slips and they reveal themselves as the children of the anti-Romanist Protestants of the last century. They claim that theirs is the very essence of evangelical faith, yet most evangelicals disavow them. Even many self-styled "fundamentalists" view them with disapproval. They proclaim the Bible to be inerrant and accessible to anyone of good will, but they disagree on its meaning with most biblical students, Christian and Jewish.

In short, the New Rightists are eccentric and self-contradictory. Here are people who would die for the Panama Canal but would not stir for civil rights, who seem to fear orgasms more than slaughters, who wrap themselves with flag and Bible and contradict both. Paranoia in the face of them can be cured by a closer look.

ISSUE 11 NO:

Future-Word

Jerry Falwell

These are the greatest days of the twentieth century. We have the opportunity to formulate a new beginning for America in this decade. For the first time in my lifetime we have the opportunity to see spiritual revival and political renewal in the United States. We now have a platform to express the concerns of the majority of moral Americans who still love those things for which this country stands. We have the opportunity to rebuild America to the greatness it once had as a leader among leaders in the world.

The 1980s are certainly a decade of destiny for America. The rising tide of secularism threatens to obliterate the Judeo-Christian influence on American society. In the realm of religion, liberal clergy have seduced the average American away from the Bible and the kind of simple faith on which this country was built. We need to call America back to God, back to the Bible, and back to moral sanity.

Positive Christianity recognizes that reformation of the institutional structure of the Church is futile without the spiritual revitalization of people's lives. It is the people whose lives have been dynamically changed by their personal relationship to Christ who are the real strength of the Church. It is no "mere pietism" that will dynamically energize the evangelical church into social action. In our attempt to rally a diversity of morally conservative Americans together in Moral Majority, we were convinced that millions of people were fed up with the fruits of liberalism, both in politics and in religion. I am well aware that it is unpopular in some circles to equate the two. But I say that they must be viewed as cousins of the same family because both rest upon the same foundational presupposition of the inherent goodness of mankind. The ultimate product of theological Liberalism is a vague kind of religious humanism that is devoid of any true Gospel content.

In 1969 Dr. Harold O. J. Brown observed that there was still a "moral majority" left in America when he said: "The United States may have a great deal of Christianity deep down. There is evidence of this. There is much to indicate that something basic in America is still healthy, both in a spiritual and in a moral sense. But wherever it is and whatever it is doing, it is not setting the tone, it is not giving direction to mid-twentieth-century America. It is not immune to disease. There is plenty of reason to think that America has a large reservoir of Christian faith, sound morality, and of idealism. But there is also a great deal of reason to fear that this reservoir is in danger of being polluted."

Dr. Brown further observed that it was the influence of the liberal impulse in American theology that had produced a climate that spawned celebrated "theologians" who openly taught atheism and left the average person in search of God as a "prisoner of the total culture." During the sixties and seventies, people felt confused and began to turn away from the liberalized institutional church that was not meeting their real spiritual needs. As attendance drastically declined in the main-line denominations, it dramatically increased in conservative denominations. Liberalism is obviously losing its influence on America. The time has come for the Fundamentalists and Evangelicals to return our nation to its spiritual and moral roots.

MORAL ISSUES

Imperative of Morality

As a pastor, I kept waiting for someone to come to the forefront of the American religious scene to lead the way out of the wilderness. Like thousands of other preachers, I kept waiting, but no real leader appeared. Finally I realized that we had to act ourselves. Something had to be done now. The government was encroaching upon the sovereignty of both the Church and the family. The Supreme Court had legalized abortion on demand. The Equal Rights Amendment, with its vague language, threatened to do further damage to the traditional family, as did the rising sentiment toward so-called homosexual rights. Most Americans were shocked but kept hoping someone would do something about all this moral chaos.

ORGANIZING THE MORAL MAJORITY

Facing the desperate need in the impending crisis of the hour, several concerned pastors began to urge me to put together a political organization that could provide a vehicle to address these crucial issues. Men like James Kennedy (Fort Lauderdale, Florida), Charles Stanley (Atlanta, Georgia), Tim La Haye (San Diego, California), and Greg Dixon (Indianapolis, Indiana) began to share with me a common concern. They urged that we formulate a nonpartisan political organization to promote morality in public life and to combat legislation that favored the legalization of immorality. Together we formulated the Moral Majority, Inc. Today Moral Majority, Inc., is made up of millions of Americans, including 72,000 ministers, priests, and rabbis, who are deeply concerned about the moral decline of our nation, the traditional family, and the moral values on which our nation was built. We are Catholics, Jews, Protestants, Mormons, Fundamentalists—blacks and whites—farmers, housewives, businessmen, and businesswomen. We are Americans from all walks of life united by one central concern: to serve as a special-interest group providing a voice for a return to moral sanity in these United States of America. Moral Majority is a political organization and is not based on theological considerations. We are Americans who share similar moral convictions. We are opposed to abortion, pornography, the drug epidemic, the breakdown of the traditional family, the establishment of homosexuality as an accepted alternate life-style, and other moral cancers that are causing our society to rot from within. Moral Majority strongly supports a pluralistic America. While we believe that this nation was founded upon the Judeo-Christian ethic by men and women who were strongly influenced by biblical moral principles, we are committed to the separation of Church and State.

Here is how Moral Majority stands on today's vital issues:

1. *We believe in the separation of Church and State.* Moral Majority, Inc., is a political organization providing a platform for religious and nonreligious Americans who share moral values to address their concerns in these areas. Members of Moral Majority, Inc., have no common theological premise. We are Americans who are proud to be conservative in our approach to moral, social, and political concerns.
2. *We are pro-life.* We believe that life begins at fertilization. We strongly oppose the massive "biological holocaust" that is resulting in the abortion of one and a half million babies each year in America. We believe that unborn babies have the right to life as much as babies that have been born. We are providing a voice and a defense for the human and civil rights of millions of unborn babies.
3. *We are pro-traditional family.* We believe that the only acceptable family form begins with a legal marriage of a man and woman. We feel that homosexual marriages and common-law marriages should not be accepted as traditional families. We oppose legislation that favors these kinds of "diverse family form," thereby penalizing the traditional family. We do not oppose civil rights for homosexuals. We do oppose "special rights" for homosexuals who have chosen a perverted life-style rather than a traditional life-style.
4. *We oppose the illegal drug traffic in America.* The youth in America are presently in the midst of a drug epidemic. Through education, legislation, and other means we want to do our part to save our young people from death on the installment plan through illegal drug addiction.
5. *We oppose pornography.* While we do not advocate censorship, we do believe that education and legislation can help stem the tide of pornography and obscenity that is poisoning the American spirit today. Economic boycotts are a proper way in America's

free-enterprise system to help persuade the media to move back to a sensible and reasonable moral stand. We most certainly believe in the First Amendment for everyone. We are not willing to sit back, however, while many television programs create cesspools of obscenity and vulgarity in our nation's living rooms.

6. *We support the state of Israel and Jewish people everywhere.* It is impossible to separate the state of Israel from the Jewish family internationally. Many Moral Majority members, because of their theological convictions, are committed to the Jewish people. Others stand upon the human and civil rights of all persons as a premise for support of the state of Israel. Support of Israel is one of the essential commitments of Moral Majority. No anti-Semitic influence is allowed in Moral Majority, Inc.
7. *We believe that a strong national defense is the best deterrent to war.* We believe that liberty is the basic moral issue of all moral issues. The only way America can remain free is to remain strong. Therefore we support the efforts of our present administration to regain our position of military preparedness—with a sincere hope that we will never need to use any of our weapons against any people anywhere.
8. *We support equal rights for women.* We agree with President Reagan's commitment to help every governor and every state legislature to move quickly to ensure that during the 1980s every American woman will earn as much money and enjoy the same opportunities for advancement as her male counterpart in the same vocation.
9. *We believe ERA is the wrong vehicle to obtain equal rights for women.* We feel that the ambiguous and simplistic language of the Amendment could lead to court interpretations that might put women in combat, sanction homosexual marriages, and financially penalize widows and deserted wives.
10. *We encourage our Moral Majority state organizations to be autonomous and indigenous.* Moral Majority state organizations may, from time to time, hold positions that are not held by the Moral Majority, Inc., national organization.

FACING THE OPPOSITION

We have been labeled by our critics as arrogant, irresponsible, and simplistic. They accuse us of violating the separation of Church and state. However, the National Council of Churches (NCC) has been heavily involved in politics for years, and virtually no one has complained. Since many moral problems, such as abortion, require solutions that are both legal and political, it is necessary for religious leaders to speak on these matters in order to be heard.

WHAT MORAL MAJORITY IS NOT

1. *We are not a political party.* We are committed to work within the multiple-party system in this nation. We are not a political party and do not intend to become one.
2. *We do not endorse political candidates.* Moral Majority informs American citizens regarding the vital moral issues facing our nation. We have no "hit lists." While we fully support the constitutional rights of any special-interest group to target candidates with whom they disagree, Moral Majority, Inc., has chosen not to take this course. We are committed to principles and issues, not candidates and parties.

3. *We are not attempting to elect "born-again" candidates.* We are committed to pluralism. The membership of Moral Majority, Inc., is so totally pluralistic that the acceptability of any candidate could never be based upon one's religious affiliation. Our support of candidates is based upon two criteria: (a) the commitment of the candidate to the principles that we espouse; (b) the competency of the candidate to fill that office.
4. *Moral Majority, Inc., is not a religious organization attempting to control the government.* Moral Majority is a special-interest group of millions of Americans who share the same moral values. We simply desire to influence government—not control government. This, of course, is the right of every American, and Moral Majority, Inc., would vigorously oppose any Ayatollah type of person's rising to power in this country.
5. *We are not a censorship organization.* We believe in freedom of speech, freedom of the press, and freedom of religion. Therefore while we do not agree that the Equal Rights Amendment would ultimately benefit the cause of women in America, we do agree with the right of its supporters to boycott those states that have not ratified the amendment. Likewise, we feel that all Americans have the right to refuse to purchase products from manufacturers whose advertising dollars support publications and television programming that violate their own moral code.
6. *Moral Majority, Inc., is not an organization committed to depriving homosexuals of their civil rights as Americans.* While we believe that homosexuality is a moral perversion, we are committed to guaranteeing the civil rights of homosexuals. We do oppose the efforts of homosexuals to obtain special privileges as a bona fide minority. And we oppose any efforts by homosexuals to flaunt their perversion as an acceptable life-style. We view heterosexual promiscuity with the same distaste which we express toward homosexuality.
7. *We do not believe that individuals or organizations that disagree with Moral Majority, Inc., belong to an immoral minority.* However, we do feel that our position represents a consensus of the majority of Americans. This belief in no way reflects on the morality of those who disagree with us or who are not involved in our organizational structures. We are committed to the total freedom of all Americans regardless of race, creed, or color.

OUT OF THE PEW AND INTO THE PRECINCT

Many Christians are raising the question of whether or not they should be involved in politics at all. Some raise the question of the separation of Church and State; others feel that politics is the devil's arena and Christians should stay out; and others say politics requires compromising and Christians should not compromise. Many liberal church people are also claiming that Evangelicals are violating the separation of Church and State. Recently Richard Dingman said: "As one who has held local public office for 10 years and worked in congress for 11 years, it is my opinion that it is not only proper for Christians to become involved, but it is absolutely biblical and absolutely necessary."

The recent emergence of the Fundamentalists and Evangelicals into politics in no way violates the historical principles of this nation. The incorporation of Christian principles into both the structure and the basic documents of our nation is a matter of historical fact. The doctrine of the separation of Church and State simply means that the state shall not control religion and religion shall not control the state. It does not mean that the two may never work together.

HERE IS HOW MORAL MAJORITY, INC., IS CONTRIBUTING TO BRINGING AMERICA BACK TO MORAL SANITY

1. *By educating millions of Americans concerning the vital moral issues of our day.* This is accomplished through such avenues as our newspaper, called the *Moral Majority Report,* a radio commentary by the same name, seminars, and other training programs conducted daily throughout the nation.
2. *By mobilizing millions of previously "inactive" Americans.* We have registered millions of voters and reactivated more millions of frustrated citizens into a special-interest group who are effectively making themselves heard in the halls of Congress, in the White House, and in every state legislature.
3. *By lobbying intensively in Congress to defeat any legislation that would further erode our constitutionally guaranteed freedom* and by introducing and/or supporting legislation that promotes traditional family and moral values, followed by the passage of a Human Life Amendment, which is a top priority of the Moral Majority agenda. We support the return of voluntary prayer to public schools while opposing mandated or written prayers. We are concerned to promote acceptance and adoption of legislation that keeps America morally balanced.
4. *By informing all Americans about the voting records of their representatives so that every American, with full information available, can vote intelligently following his or her own convictions.* We are nonpartisan. We are not committed to politicians or political parties; we are committed to principles and issues that we believe are essential to America's survival at this crucial hour. It is our desire to represent these concerns to the American public and allow it to make its own decisions on these matters.
5. *By organizing and training millions of Americans who can become moral activists.* This heretofore silent majority in America can then help develop a responsive government which is truly "of the people, by the people, for the people" instead of "in spite of the people," which we have had for too many years now.
6. *By encouraging and promoting non-public schools in their attempt to excel in academics while simultaneously teaching traditional family and moral values.* There are thousands of non-public schools in America that accept no tax moneys. Some of these schools are Catholic, Fundamentalist, Jewish, Adventist, or of other faiths. Some are not religious. But Moral Majority, Inc., supports the right of these schools to teach young people not only how to make a living, but how to live.

Moral Majority, Inc., does not advocate the abolition of public schools. Public schools will always be needed in our pluralistic society. We are committed to helping public schools regain excellence. That is why we support the return of voluntary prayer to public schools and strongly oppose the teaching of the "religion" of secular humanism in the public classroom.

The First Amendment says: "Congress shall make no law respecting an establishment of religion, or prohibiting the free exercise therof." This does not rule out church influence in government. Presbyterian theologian John Gerstner has said: "Establishment of religion is not the same thing as no influence of religion. I think Moral Majority is right in stating that the church should seek to have influence in political matters."

California pastor Dr. Tim La Haye believes that the pulpit must be active in resisting encroaching federal bureaucracy that threatens both the Church and the traditional family. He has stated: "God founded the government to protect the home against external enemies. The prophet of God is derelict if he does not, in God's name, rebuke government when it fails to protect the family."

Catholic theologian and journalist Father Robert Burns, C.S.P., stated in the national Catholic weekly *The Wanderer:* "If our great nation collapses, it will not be because of the efforts of some foreign power, Soviet or otherwise, but rather for the same reason that ancient Rome collapsed because it was morally rotten to the core." He further comments: "The members of Moral Majority believe in fighting for the basic moral values on which this nation was built and upon which its strength rests. They are determined to prevent materialists, secular-humanists, and non-believers from destroying these values by replacing them with a valueless, amoral society."

Christians are now realizing that governmental actions directly affect their lives. They are questioning the government's right to carry out such programs. They are beginning to realize that the only way to change the actions of government is to change those elected to govern. We are now beginning to do just that. We must continue to exert a strong moral influence upon America if our children and grandchildren are to enjoy the same freedoms that we have known.

SANCTITY OF HUMAN LIFE

Life is a miracle. Only God Almighty can create life, and he said, "Thou shalt not kill." Nothing can change the fact that abortion is the murder of human life.

As I warned in my book *Listen, America!*, an article in the January 9, 1980, issue of the *Washington Post* stated the grave fact that in 1978 nearly 30 percent of all pregnancies were terminated by legal abortions. A family-planning study estimated that there were 1,374,000 legal abortions during that year. About one third of these were obtained by teenagers, and about three quarters were for unmarried women. In 1979 more than 1.5 million babies were aborted in America. Experts now estimate that between 8 million and 10 million babies have been murdered since January 22, 1973, when the Supreme Court, in a decision known as *Roe* v. *Wade*, granted women an absolute right to abortion on demand during the first two trimesters of pregnancy—that is, the first six months of pregnancy. No other major civilized nation in history has ever been willing to permit late abortion except for the gravest of medical reasons.

Human life is precious to God. Christ died upon the cross for every man and woman who has ever lived and who ever will live. In the past, America was known for its honoring and protecting the right of a person to live. No one disagrees that the state exists to protect the lives of its citizens. But we are in danger of losing our respect for the sanctity of human life. America has allowed more persons to be killed through abortion than have been eliminated in all our major wars. Only a perverted society would make laws protecting eagles' eggs and yet have no protection for precious unborn human life.

Equally ironic, there is a great debate going on today regarding capital punishment. In America we kill babies and protect criminals, even though the death penalty is definitely a deterrent to crime. The time has now come that we must speak up in defense of the sanctity and dignity of human life.

In reality, life began with God and, since Adam, has simply passed from one life cell to another. From the moment of fertilization any further formulation of the individual is merely a matter of time, growth, and maturation. This is a growth process that continues throughout our entire lives. At three weeks, just twenty-one days after conception, a tiny human being already has eyes, a spinal cord, a nervous system, lungs, and intestines. The heart, which has been beating since the eighteenth day, is pumping a blood supply totally separate from that of the mother. All this occurs before the mother may even be aware of the new life within her body. By the end of the seventh week we see a well-proportioned small-scale baby with fingers, knees, ankles, and toes. Brain waves have been recorded as early as forty-three days. By eleven weeks all organ systems are present and functioning in this new embryonic life.

Dr. Thomas L. Johnson, professor of biology and embryology at the University of Virginia, observes that "an individual organism (the zygote) cannot be a part of the mother...it has an entirely different set of chromosomes...it has a separate and unique life." In reply to the statement that life begins as the infant leaves the mother's womb, Dr. Johnson says that the moment of birth is not a moment of magic when a potential being is transformed into an actual being. The unborn child is merely moving from a required aquatic environment to a required gaseous environment so that it can develop into its next stage of life.

Recently Doug Badger, the legislative director of the Protestant pro-life organization the Christian Action Council, stated: "The conviction that each human life is sacred has its roots in the scriptures. There God is revealed as the living God who bestows life. In contrast to the Gentile nations who manufacture gods in their image, Yahweh fashions human beings in God's image (Genesis 1:26, 28). Each person thus is vested with an inviolable dignity on the basis of his or her creation. From this flows the Torah's sixth commandment (Exodus 20:13) which functions not only as a prohibition of murder, but as a positive injunction to respect human life. Thus when Jesus assumes the role of Moses and expounds the law in the Sermon on the Mount (Matthew 5:17–20) he reveals that the commandment in fact requires that we love our neighbors, not merely that we do them no physical harm (Matthew 5:21–26)."

One of the major arguments of the pro-abortionists is that the unborn child is a fetus, not a person. It should be noted that "fetus" is Latin for "unborn child." Unfortunately, the tendency today is to change traditional terminology and substitute words like "conceptus" for "child." No one wants to use the term "murder" for abortion, so we simply call it "termination of pregnancy." This technique is usually employed to defend the indefensible. It is much easier to refer to the elimination of "P.O.C.s" (products of conception) than to the slicing, poisoning, and flushing away of a million little boys and girls. In her clever parody on this issue, Juli Loesch points out: "Here's what Planned Parenthood said in 1963: 'an abortion kills the life of a baby after it has begun' (*Plan your children for health and happiness.* Planned Parenthood/World Population, 1963). Here's what Planned Parenthood says today: "The fetal tissue...the uterine contents...the products of conception...'What changed? The baby? Or Planned Parenthood?"

Theologian Francis A. Schaeffer and Dr. C. Everett Koop, Surgeon General of the United States, recently released a movie and book entitled *Whatever Happened to the Human Race?* These men raised this vital issue: "Once the uniqueness of people as created by God is removed and mankind is viewed as only one of the gene patterns which came forth on earth by chance—there is no reason not to treat people as things to be experimental on and to make over the whole of humanity according to the decisions of a relatively few individuals. If people are not unique, as made in the image of God, the barrier is gone. Since life is being destroyed before birth, why not tamper with it on the other end?" They further ask: "Will a society which has assumed the right to kill infants in the womb—because they are unwanted, imperfect, or merely inconvenient—have difficulty in assuming the right to kill other human beings, especially older adults who are judged unwanted, deemed imperfect physically or mentally, or considered a possible social nuisance?"

Dr. Mildred F. Jefferson is a surgeon on the staff of the Boston University Medical Center. She is a remarkable woman who serves in key roles on many medical boards and committees. She is a diplomate of the American Board of Surgery and has received numerous honors and awards for her work. As a guest on the February 10, 1980, "Old-Time Gospel Hour" television broadcast, she made these comments regarding abortion: "Many people try to hide behind the confusion of not knowing what happens before a baby is born. But we do not have to be confused. We in medicine and science have a different name for every stage of the development of the baby, but it does not matter at all whether you know those names or not. When a young woman has not had much opportunity to go to school and she becomes pregnant no one has to tell her that she is going to have a baby." She went on to say: "I became a doctor in the tradition that is represented in the Bible of looking upon medicine as a high calling. I will not stand aside and have this great profession of mine, of the doctor, give up the designation of healer to become that of the social executioner. The Supreme Court justices only had to hand down an order. Social workers only have to make arrangements, but it has been given to my profession to destroy the life of the innocent and the helpless."

The surgeon further stated: "Today it is the unborn child; tomorrow it is likely to be the elderly or those who are incurably ill. Who knows but that a little later it may be anyone who has political or moral views that do not fit into the distorted new order. To that question, 'Am I my brother's keeper?' I answer 'Yes.' It is everyone's responsibility to safeguard and preserve life. A child is a member of the human family and deserves care and concern.

"We are in a great war for the hearts and minds of our people, for the moral future of our country, and for the integrity of a nation. It is a war that we must win.

When we win, that victory will not be for ourselves but for God, for America, and for all mankind."

HUMANISM IN THE PUBLIC SCHOOLS

In his recent book *The Battle for the Mind,* Dr. Tim La Haye defines humanism as "man's attempt to solve his problems independently of God." Humanism has its origin in man's attempt to place human wisdom above divine revelation. La Haye traces its formulation back to the Greek thinkers' belief that "man is the measure of all things." He then identifies the five basic tenets of humanism as (1) atheism; (2) evolution; (3) amorality; (4) autonomy of man; (5) one-world socialism.

In a recent interview in *Moral Majority Report,* Mel Gabler of Longview, Texas, who, with his wife, Norma, heads a group called Educational Research Analysis, stated: "Most parents don't realize the viewpoint in their children's textbooks...the vast majority of the textbooks in use today are written from a humanistic viewpoint. It's totally woven into the textbooks at all levels. And sometimes, it's not even so evident in the pupil's book—you have to look at the teacher's book to see the additional material they are asked to present, and the questions and exercises they are to give the students."

Gabler also denounced the move away from teaching academic skills in the public schools. He has warned that even Christian schools often fail to fully examine the content and world view of the textbooks they adopt. He cited several areas in which he claims humanism manifests itself in the textbooks: situation ethics, self-centeredness, evolution, the neglect or negation of Christianity, sexual freedom, death education, and internationalism. In the area of morals, he notes that humanist textbooks belittle the concept of sexual virginity and sexual abstinence and teach the legitimacy of abortion, premarital sex, homosexuality, lesbianism, and incest.

Today, however, more and more parents are beginning to read their children's textbooks and to take more of an interest in what their children are being taught. The Gablers are living proof that ordinary parents, without a specialized education or a background of public involvement, can be a potent force in public education.

SEX EDUCATION IN THE PUBLIC SCHOOLS

In a head-on debate on NBC's "Today" show with Dr. Sol Gordon, Syracuse University professor and leading sex educator, I stated that I believe in teaching sex education in public schools as a biological science. My objection to the current public school sex education program as it is now being taught is that it is "academic pornography." The materials used include wholesale endorsements of masturbation, premarital sex, extramarital sex, and homosexuality. They even include allusions to the acceptability of sex with animals!

It is no secret that the increase of an emphasis on sex education has paralleled the rise in teenage pregnancies, which is at epidemic proportions in the United States, with nearly one million teenage girls becoming pregnant out of wedlock every year! In a carefully documented study, Claire Chambers traces the "SIECUS Circle" to the larger humanist interest in population control, genetic engineering, legalized abortion, pornography, and homosexuality. The Sex Information and Education Council of the United States (SIECUS) has conducted sex education training seminars and produced a series of ten study guides for use in public schools. Based totally on the philosophy of situation ethics, one study guide claims: "The newer relativistic position on sexual morality is a rational one, backed up by research...this is the approach that seems to offer the most hope for consensus under modern conditions."

In a new wave of acceptance of immorality, Professor Benjamin DeMott wrote in a recent issue of *Psychology Today* that the idea of incest (sex between nonmarried family members) being immoral is now being challenged in reports presented to the American Psychiatric Association claiming that "some incest experiences appear to be positive and even beneficial." The attempted "normalization" of incest on the American public is being further fostered by a rash of new books and movies.

In the newsletter *Impact 80,* published by the Institute for Family Research and Education, of which Sol Gordon is the director, Moral Majority is labeled as "perennially dubious and chilling." The newsletter includes a full-page advertisement urging people to join the "United to Save America" group in order to protect the nation from "the so-called Moral Majority and the Bible Bigots." The same issue urges support of Planned Parenthood, the National Abortion Rights Action League, the Religious Coalition for Abortion Rights, and the National Organization of Women.

We must work to make sex education what it claims to be and not allow this avalanche of pornography to go on masquerading as a form of education. It is nothing more than pornographic brainwashing.

PORNOGRAPHY

The pornographers have labeled Moral Majority the "Extreme Right" because we speak out against Extreme Wrong! Pornography is a $4-billion-a-year business. Much of this money is used to influence legislators, judges, and juries, as well as the American people. I have often wondered how the majority of the people in this country feel about pornographers and pornography. My recent escapade with *Penthouse* magazine has brought a response of millions of letters from concerned Americans who have come to our defense. It is, as I have stressed, past time that a strong stand is taken against pornography. Why is it that when national polls show that nearly 80 percent of Americans oppose pornography, no major strides are being taken to rid our country of this menace?

Pornography is not something that is nice to discuss. I was sickened when I read in the book entitled *How to Stop the Porno Plague* by Neil Gallagher his description of the Bicentennial (July 1976) issue of *Hustler* including "a full-page color cartoon, 'Chester the Molester,' showing a man seducing a doll-clutching, pig-tailed girl; a centerfold showing caricatures of Jerry Ford, Henry Kissinger, and Nelson Rockefeller involved in sexual acts with an animated Statue of Liberty; and caricatures of George Washington, Paul Revere, and Ben Franklin involved in a variety of sex acts with prostitutes."

Child pornography is escalating at a frightening rate in the United States of America. I read of one social club that has a slogan on its letterhead that reads: "Sex before eight or it's too late." There are even such things as child seducers' manuals. There are such things as playing cards that picture naked children in sexual acts with adults. Children are a heritage of the Lord, and to review the violent, filthy acts committed against them by evil men is enough to prove that there is indeed a devil! Child pornography is certainly one of the vilest forms of child abuse and must be stopped.

A Christian author and professor of pediatrics at the University of Southern California, Dr. James Dobson, has also lamented what he calls "chicken porn" (which depicts sex between young girls and adult men). He cited one study of eighty other civilizations that degenerated to the level of sexual child abuse, all of which collapsed.

The pornographic explosion distorts the biblical view of women, perverts American youth, and corrupts the moral fiber of society. Moral Americans must hold up a standard. Proliferation of pornography into our society is striking evidence of our decadence. The moral fiber of our nation is so deteriorated that we cannot possibly survive unless there is a complete and drastic turnabout soon. A permissive society that tolerates pornography has the same hedonistic attitude that destroyed ancient civilizations. Pornographers are idolaters who idolize money and will do anything for materialistic gain. They are men who have reprobate minds and who need divine deliverance.

Dr. Harold Voth, professor of psychiatry at the University of Kansas, spoke at a recent American Family Forum in Washington, D.C., stating that pornography results in "serious psychological disturbances" for millions of Americans. William Stanmeyer, professor at the Indiana University School of Law, stated to the same audience that criminal studies are now clearly contradicting ACLU claims that there is no link between pornography and crime.

Christian physician Dr. Gary Hall (a former Olympic gold medalist) recently stated: "Children and adolescents are very susceptible to pornography, when moral principles are not deeply established, and when peer pressure is as important as parental approval. If it is the 'in thing' to accept pornography, to go to 'adult' movies or to watch 'mature' TV shows, then that is what adolescents will do."

The most organized effort against the plague of pornography has been the work of Charles Keating's Citizens for Decency through Law (CDL) organization. Founded in 1957, CDL has recently taken aggressive action against so-called adult bookstores and movie theaters in Cincinnati, with the result of closing down every one of them in that area. Keating states that there are nearly three hundred smut magazines in the United States alone. He warns: "I frequently speak before Christian groups on the Christian's duty to fight pornography. I am happy to say that the mistaken notion that the Lord has no work for moral Americans to do in the public policy arena is fast dissipating. Still, some Christians are unfamiliar with politics, the law, and the whole field of policy-formation."

In light of the concern of decent Americans who are shocked at the impact of pornography in our society, it is distressing to read the comments of left-wing Evangelical Richard Quebedeaux when he states: "Pornography is not condoned, yet it does not warrant undue concern; there are worse evils to fight than pornography." What could be worse in Quebedeaux's scheme, since he "rejects legalism in sexual matters," regards oral sex as mere "petting," and views abortion as a "tragic choice"? I recall what the poet Dante wrote centuries ago: "The hottest places in hell are reserved for those who, in time of great moral crises, maintained their neutrality."

HOMOSEXUALITY

Less than a decade ago, the word "homosexual" was a word that was disdained by most Americans and represented the nadir of human indecency. It was utilized as a word of contempt. All of this has changed. What was once considered a deviant life-style is now considered by many Americans as an alternative life-style. There is even legislation pending that would legitimize homosexuals as "normal." Today thousands of men and women in America flaunt their sin openly. The entire homosexual movement is an indictment against America and is contributing to its ultimate downfall.

History confirms that when homosexuality reaches epidemic levels in society, that society is in serious crisis and on the verge of collapse. God considers the sin of homosexuality as abominable. He destroyed the cities of Sodom and Gomorrah because of their involvement in this sin. The Old Testament law is clear concerning this issue: "Thou shalt not lie with mankind, as with womankind: it is abomination" (Lev. 18:22). God still abhors the sin of homosexuality. In the New Testament, there are numerous references to it. In Romans 1:26–28, we read: "For this cause God gave them up unto vile affections: for even their women did change the natural use into that which is against nature: And likewise also the men, leaving the natural use of the woman, burned in their lust one toward another; men with men working that which is unseemly, and receiving in themselves that recompence of their error which was meet. And even as they did not like to retain God in their knowledge, God gave them over to a reprobate mind, to do those things which are not convenient." These people willingly rejected God's revealed truth. Consequently, God "gave them up to uncleanness through the lusts of their own hearts, to dishonour their own bodies between themselves" (Rom. 1:24).

A bill has been introduced in Congress which, if passed, would establish homosexuals in America as a bona fide minority like women, blacks, or Hispanics. This "Gay Rights" bill, H.R. 2074, would require every employer to employ a minority of homosexuals commensurate with the population in that area. Pastors, private school administrators, and employers would be adversely affected by this new bill. There are currently fifty-one cosponsors of this bill in the House of Representatives. This is a clear indication of the moral decay of our society. Americans began by accepting homosexuality as an alternate life-style, recognizing it as legitimate, and now they are attempting to legalize it.

The October 12, 1979, Washington *Post* contained an article: "50,000 Marchers Turn Out for Gay Rights Demonstration." It reported that "the turnout of an estimated 50,000 marchers here Sunday shows that gay rights are a 'matter of national concern,' says a congressman who wants to extend this Civil Rights Act to protect homosexuals. 'I think most Americans are ready for it,' Republican Ted Weiss, New York, said....Weiss' bill has spurred Rep. Larry McDonald, (D-Ga.,) to introduce a resolution...opposing any special legal status for homosexuals."

In light of our opposition to the sin of homosexuality, we must always make it clear that we love people and are genuinely interested in their personal needs. I believe that homosexuals require love and help. We must not allow homosexuality to be presented to our nation as an alternate or acceptable life-style. It will only serve as a corrupting influence upon our next generation and will bring down the wrath of God upon America. I love homosexuals as people for whom Christ died, but I must hate their sin. Jesus Christ offers forgiveness and deliverance from that sin and from all other sins.

ISSUE 12

Are Professors Too Liberal?

This issue strikes at the heart of a concept held dearly by most academics—academic freedom. The American Association of University Professors defines academic freedom in terms of full freedom in research and publication and full freedom in the classroom in discussing the subject, with some care related to discussing controversial issues unrelated to the subject. In the search for knowledge, all relevant facts must be accepted and considered. Honest debate and rational rebuttal must be a given. Since knowledge is tentative, we must be prepared to revise our theories and assumptions.

Academic freedom does not, however, give us the right to say or do anything in the classroom. We should not propagandize for a particular view but should make the attempt to present all sides of controversial ideas. Easier said than done! The state or institution may properly require a certain subject to be taught but should not require the specific materials and books to be used. Freedom to pursue any relevant topic or issue to its logical conclusion is a cherished value in academia. Liberals and conservatives in American education have experienced infringements of this freedom.

Those of us who were students in the 1950s and 1960s clearly remember the effects of McCarthyism. Joe McCarthy, a U.S. Senator from Wisconsin, was chairman of the Senate Un-American Activities Committee.

This committee accused many public figures of being communists or communist sympathizers. The allegations were frequently flimsy and unsubstantiated, but many careers were ruined. Hollywood's famous blacklist, which contained the names of writers, directors, actors, and so forth, was based on the McCarthy committee's hearings. People on the list were effectively eliminated from jobs in the movie industry during that time.

The hysteria created by the hearings led to problems in a variety of professions, including teaching. We recall a biology professor who very deliberately wrote evolution on one side of the blackboard and religion on the other, explaining that they had nothing to do with each other. Professors who discussed Marx were generally very careful to distance themselves from communism and were overly conscientious in pointing out criticisms and shortcomings of Marx's theories.

Student activism in the late 1960s and early 1970s put pressure on conservative faculty members. Campus audiences were not receptive to those who were in favor of the war in Vietnam. More recently, speakers advocating a position of genetic racial differences in intelligence have had difficulty presenting their positions.

The current issue revolves around the "liberal" bias of professors. Are professors too liberal? The answer depends in part on time, place, discipline, and definition. If you take a list of issues such as women's rights, affirmative action, abortion, and so forth, sociologists more than members of other disciplines probably wind up on the "liberal" side of the issue. The nature of our discipline with its historic focus on social problems lends itself to such a position on these issues. However, even in this "liberal" discipline there are conservatives. Our textbooks generally attempt to present competing arguments and competing theoretical positions.

The current controversy revolves around an organization that planned to become a watchdog over the liberal academic biases of university faculty members. Accuracy in Academia (AIA), a spinoff group of the equally conservative Accuracy in Media, attempted to set up a network of student informers in American universities to report on the liberal biases of professors. In the articles that follow, Malcolm Lawrence, the former president of AIA, provides examples of biased faculty as well as the rationale for the organization. Jon Wiener argues that AIA has been a flop. Its attempt at organizing a student network has failed, and the primary effect has been to mobilize the political center to defend the academic freedom of the New Left.

ISSUE 12 YES:

Accuracy in Academia: Is It a Threat to Academic Freedom?

Malcolm Lawrence

It is a pleasure for me to be here in Ames, Iowa, and I appreciate your kind invitation and splendid hospitality. The question before us is an interesting one, to wit: "Is Accuracy In Academia a Threat to Academic Freedom?" I could respond with one word and let it go at that, but instead shall give some justification for my answer which is, of course, no. Accuracy In Academia is not a threat to academic freedom or anything else on university campuses except inaccuracy and imbalance.

My purpose in being here today is to explain what Accuracy In Academia is, what it hopes to do, and how it will go about doing it. I am an administrator, charged by AIA's Board of Directors to launch an exciting new program.

Accuracy In Academia is a non-profit corporation established in 1985 in Washington, D.C. The first board meeting was held in April, at which time I was elected to the position of President. We began operations on August 1.

The statement of purpose of Accuracy In Academia reads as follows:

> "The Corporation is formed for the purpose of educating the public, the learned societies, professional educators, and academicians as to desirable standards of accuracy and truth in academic teaching and how to raise professional standards in academia with respect to objective truth and acceptable standards of balance and fairness. In furtherance of these objectives, the Corporation shall examine cases in which academic performance is alleged to fall short of these standards and it shall publicize its findings. The Corporation shall publish and distribute literature, provide speakers at seminars and other meetings and gatherings, conduct classes, cooperate with other like-

> minded societies and corporations and individuals, and employ such other means as are deemed feasible by the Board of Directors to communicate to the public its views on the standards of accuracy and truth in academia."

Accuracy In Academia is a spin-off of Accuracy in Media or AIM, an organization founded 16 years ago to monitor the news media—the newspapers, radio, and television. Over the years, AIM has done a creditable job of detecting inaccuracy and imbalance in the news and reporting such incidents faithfully to its membership, which numbers some 35,000.

It is the contention of AIM, through its own findings and the work of other surveyors, that there is a liberal bias among most individuals employed in analyzing and reporting news to the American public.

For example, four years ago Professors Robert Lichter and Stanley Rothman published an article revealing the overwhelmingly liberal views of what they called "the media elite." Lichter and Rothman had surveyed 240 journalists employed by the leading national newspapers, news magazines, wire services and TV networks. The results confirmed what many people suspected. Their views on various social, political and economic issues revealed that they were far more liberal than the general public.

Recently, the *Los Angeles Times* (see *Washington Inquirer* for September 6, 1985) published the results of a survey of 3,165 newspaper editors and reporters throughout the country which show that the gap between the views of the people and the journalists who purport to speak for them is not confined to the media elite. The *L.A. Times* at the same time surveyed 3,000 members of the public. The paper concluded that its survey had demonstrated that members of the press are predominantly liberal, in fact considerably more liberal than the general public. It found only a slight difference between the staffs of Lichter and Rothman's "elite" papers and those of all 621 papers surveyed. The responses given to selected issue questions revealed that 68 percent of all reporters were liberal, compared to 72 percent for those with the big papers.

Now, one of the reasons Accuracy In Academia was formed was to measure to what extent, if any, the liberal bias in the media originates in the classrooms of American universities and colleges. This in itself will be an interesting thing to research. However, the principal function of AIA will be to set up a broad-based network of students and other volunteers to report on university professors and instructors with a view to obtaining truth and balance whatever the persuasion—left, right or center.

We are interested in learning what students are being told in such subjects as history, political science, sociology, economics and international relations.

We are not targeting individual schools or professors. Instead, we are seeking the cooperation of students on college campuses beginning with the 1985–86 school year to identify courses they believe useful for reporting purposes. AIA does not train students. We do not pay students for information. All we ask is that they provide us with what they consider to be glaring examples of misinformation, disinformation, or lack of balance.

Also, we are looking to work with more mature persons, such as retired teachers, ex-foreign service officers and the like, who may wish to audit classes in the social sciences which I have cited. In some schools senior citizens may audit classes free of charge or at reduced rates.

AIA would also hope that Accuracy In Academia chapters can be formed on campuses where students and other members of the community wish to work together.

What happens when we receive information? If we consider it to be worthy of investigation, we shall research it and contact the professor involved to verify that he was the source of the information as reported. If, for example, the information was taken out of context or was mis-quoted, that would be the end of the matter. If, on the other hand, it turns out that the information was as reported and that the professor has provided inaccurate statements and proclaims he will stand by those statements, Accuracy In Academia may consider publishing an item in our newsletter or perhaps offer the story to the school newspaper or the local town press.

I want to stress that AIA recognizes the right of the professor to freedom of speech and the right to express his attitudes, beliefs and feelings. It is the information we seek, the indicators or data that support his conclusions. Also, we shall be most careful to weed out reports that relate not to facts, but to students' grievances, personality problems, and other non-academic matters.

Accuracy In Academia will serve as an outlet for students who fear that an open confrontation with a professor might result in a lower grade. From the student's point of view, grading is a powerful tool in the hands of a professor. Students invest thousands of dollars in their education and many would hesitate to provoke a professor. For these reasons as well as for our desire to protect the privacy of students on other grounds, AIA will not reveal names. Students who form or join local AIA chapters or who wish to reveal their names may do so, of course, on their own.

As for professors, we shall release their names only with their full knowledge. Obviously, we reserve the right to cite their names if the incidents being reported are already in the public domain. As a matter of course, students take notes in class and have the basic right to tell their friends, relatives, Accuracy In Academia, or anyone else about the product they are receiving in the classrooms. The professors work for the students, not the other way around. Thus the classroom is an open forum, not an inner sanctum. There is no lawyer/client or doctor/patient relationship between professor and student.

The classroom can be compared to a newspaper. The professor is the source of information or service for which the student pays. We see the student as a reporter who is free to complain on his own or through Accuracy In Academia in much the same fashion as one would write a letter to the editor. Incorrect or phony information in the classroom should be corrected just as a newspaper should be corrected when it provides misleading or inaccurate stories.

A good illustration of a phony newspaper story was the fictitious feature article in the *Washington Post* a few years back about "Jimmy," the reported child heroin addict, a story that won a Pulitzer prize for the journalist who wrote it and then ended her career in journalism when the falsification was discovered.

Michael Lindsay, Professor Emeritus of Far Eastern Studies, American University, Washington, D.C., in an essay entitled, "Journalists and Professors" (January 1982) states:

> "Completely fictitious stories are uncommon in academic writing but many professors have made false statements and distorted evidence to support some general thesis that was very far from the truth. There has been no similar public indignation against these professors. In fact, many of them have retained a reputation as distinguished scholars."

In addition to a regular newsletter, Accuracy In Academia will provide research reports, speakers and other services for students. Membership charges will be $25 for regular members and $5 for students, with special consideration for student reporters.

As I said, Accuracy In Academia began operations on August 1. What have been the results?

First a word about media interest. I have spent most of my waking hours during the past seven weeks talking to reporters, doing radio talk shows, and appearing on television. I have been on Cable Network TV twice, the MacNeil/Lehrer show, Latenight America, the Today show, and numerous regional TV news programs and feature spots. I have done National Public Radio twice, spoken on other broadcast outlets representing hundreds of stations throughout the country, and have been interviewed by scores of newspapers. And it is still going on. The mere creation of AIA has struck a truly responsive cord.

The reaction of college students has been a particularly upbeat phenomenon. Within the short span of seven weeks, we have received phone calls, letters and cards from hundreds of students who are registered in schools for the 1985/86 school year. We already have reporters in more than 80 colleges and universities in all geographic regions of the United States.

Students on a number of campuses are forming AIA chapters and some schools are seeking advice from us on achieving balance in university programs. For example, the George Mason University in Fairfax, Virginia, has asked us to recommend speakers for two panels at an upcoming conference on nuclear armaments.

Of course, Accuracy In Academia has come under criticism in some quarters. The principal sour notes have been sung by Ernst Benjamin, the General Secretary of the American Association of University Professors. On August 4, the *Washington Post* quoted Mr. Benjamin as follows:

> "They [AIA] seem to be trying to frighten faculty members into supporting their obviously right-wing point of view. It is not only frightening, it is reprehensible."

I can only classify Benjamin's remarks as premature, knee-jerk paranoia.

Mr. Benjamin subsequently appeared on two TV network programs with me—the MacNeil/Lehrer show and Latenight America—and failed on both occasions to explain just what a right-wing point of view is or how professors could be forced to support such views. On one of the shows, Benjamin said that AIA was not only right-wing, it was "radical right." He didn't comment about where the American Association of University Professors fits on the political scale.

Shortly thereafter, Benjamin issued an undated news release in the name of the AAUP claiming that Accuracy In Academia will inhibit academic freedom, discourage students from testing their ideas, and cause professors to hesitate presenting new or unpopular theories that would stimulate "robust intellectual discussion." The AAUP release also claimed that the quality of academic performance is controlled through peer evaluation by skilled professionals and that AIA's intentions were "arrogant" and "hollow."

On September 11, Accuracy In Academia issued the following response to the AAUP statement:

> "1. Accuracy In Academia was formed for the purpose of raising professional standards in academia with respect to objective truth and acceptable standards of balance and fairness. AIA will work to expand academic freedom by widening the debate and exposing students to a broader range of information.
>
> "2. Accuracy In Academia is committed to a staunch defense of academic freedom and the freedom of ideas. However, as pointed out by the Association of American Colleges in a February 1985 report entitled, *Integrity in the College Curriculum*, professors with their right of academic freedom have a responsibility to students 'not to use the classroom as a platform for propagandizing. Professional ethics demand that they be balanced and that they be fair.'
>
> "3. On the basis of numerous comments received to date from students, AIA is far from convinced that the quality and balance of academic performance are adequately judged and controlled through peer evaluation of the teaching profession as claimed by the American Association of University Professors. Nothing being planned by AIA runs counter to the statement of Professional Ethics developed by the AAUP."

Incidentally, the AAUP has only 60,000 members and, therefore, speaks for less than 10 percent of the 825,000 university professors in the United States. According to an article by Lawrence Cranberg, Ph.D., in *The University Bookman*, Winter 1981 edition, the AAUP lost half of its members during the 1970s. Cranberg points out that the spirit of AAUP has eroded. He says:

> "Increasingly, the issues which engage the energies of the Association are focused on security and the pocketbook, not on the classroom and campus. And where, once upon a time, the AAUP spearheaded battles for academic freedom, it now acts like a fighter swinging wildly at an adversary barely discerned."

There have been a few other imaginative but unwarranted attacks against Accuracy In Academia. On the editorial front, the *Philadelphia Inquirer* takes the cake. In a self-destructive tirade on August 9, the *Inquirer* called us book-burners and brownshirts in business suits. The editorial concluded with the following passage:

> "Still they march on, now beneath the banner of 'accuracy,' the torch of McCarthyism held high. They would stamp out free inquiry, muffle discordant voices, revive Red-baiting, restore the blacklist.
>
> "They would tie academic freedom to the stake. And, blissfully, they would strike the match of ignorance."

What a beautiful piece of fiction! If Archimedes were with us today, I'm sure he would shout "eureka!"

Adverse criticism notwithstanding, we in AIA are elated by the positive reactions we are hearing from students, professors and others. Let them speak for themselves.

A senior from the University of Wisconsin wrote:

> "I sincerely believe that an organization such as Accuracy In Academia is needed at the University of Wisconsin campus (Milwaukee).
>
> "Two semesters ago, I was enrolled in a Sociology course. My professor, of Marxist political beliefs, continually disinformed the class about the demise of Allende in Chile as well as Castro's great humanitarian attributes. I attempted to rebut the professor several times; however, I was cut off after little debate.
>
> "I can think of several professors who would be more than willing to help expose leftist professors. I would be willing to start an Accuracy In Academia chapter at the University of Wisconsin with your consent."

A student from Midwestern State University in Wichita Falls, Texas, wrote:

> "I have been wanting to form a group at our local university for some time to deal with the problem of disinformation being perpetrated in our departments of English, History, Political Science, and Journalism by our distinguished professors. I have been a victim (gradewise) for standing up for what I believe to be true, and for pointing out what I believe to be an inaccurate statement by my professors....It distresses me to see college students, especially freshmen and sophomores who are so impressionable that they believe the professor to be an authority on any matter that may come up in a classroom discussion. Many professors know this, and use the freshmen and sophomores to disseminate their views, both politically and philosophically.
>
> "I would like you to send me any and all information necessary to spearhead an organization on campus of students for Accuracy In Academia."

A recent graduate of Earlham College in Richmond, Indiana, wrote:

> "I recognize the serious need for such an organization as Accuracy In Academia, for I experienced directly for four years professors who were not interested in teaching, but in indoctrinating students with their leftist propaganda. I am more than willing to back this accusation up with proof such as class notes, reading lists, guest speakers, and course syllabi."

The writer indicated he was going to another school for a masters degree and provided the names of contacts still at Earlham college.

A student from California wrote:

"We are interested in starting a chapter of Accuracy In Academia on the San Jose State University campus. There are many professors at State who abuse their academic freedom by using their lecterns as pulpits to spread socialist and communist lies. I have enclosed an article that appeared in the Spartan Daily to illustrate the one-sided treatment of issues practised on the campus. Both professors are among the most well-known Marxists at San Jose State. Conservative or moderate professors were not even contacted."

A former student at a community college in Pennsylvania wrote to say that an art professor was using his classrooms to induct his students into Marxism by brainwashing. He wrote:

"In Art Appreciation he shows slides, using subliminals and subaudibles, and motion pictures slanted toward anti-American points of view.

"I was forced to sit through a film dealing with the aftermath of the bombing of Hiroshima. What does that have to do with my learning Art Appreciation, or my learning how to draw?...When I protested I was cut off from making my point or voicing any pro-American opinions."

A student from the California Institute of Technology wrote:

"I write in support of your proposed Accuracy In Academia organization. It is a sorely needed antidote to festering liberal bias in the educational world.

"It is for the teacher to teach his students how to walk, not in which direction. Objectivity in all things is the teacher's Holy Grail: something which one can never quite reach, but which one strives for regardless. The negligence of most teachers in this is of mammoth proportions and borders on criminal.

"Sign me up as an auditor."

A former student from Pennsylvania wrote:

"I saw and heard you on the Today Show this morning and was pleased to know of your Accuracy In Academia effort. As it happens, my bride and I returned to school in 1970 in our mid-forties and completed graduate programs in 1975. We were given both biased and downright false information. Our young fellow students ran scared of our professors, but expressed thanks to us when we would question or protest some outrageous/outlandish statement. Our memories of 10 to 15 years ago are that the faculty was made up of 80 percent less-than-truthful people....One weapon which faculty members used against questioning students was ridicule.

"I hardly can see any comparison with the methods of totalitarian governments—notwithstanding the remarks of Professor Zinn of Boston University. Honest teachers will welcome objective review."

A resident of Illinois wrote:

"Bravo Mr. Lawrence. I watched MacNeil/Lehrer Newshour this evening and was delighted with the arrival of AIA. It should be great fun, plenty of fireworks and liberal thunder.

"Please find my enclosed contribution. Once again, well done Mr. Lawrence and AIA.

"P.S. My younger brother, a recent University of Wisconsin graduate, tells me that our university and college campuses are rancid with 'leftists,' may we use the word communist?"

An Oak Harbor, Washington, viewer of the MacNeil/Lehrer show wrote to Jim Lehrer as follows:

"Tonight your Accuracy In Academia segment was the best TV I have viewed in years. I am writing while my satisfaction is hot. Ernst Benjamin (of the American Association of University Professors) sweated and bled most generously and beautifully. I still can't believe it. America does have a chance after all—not because of PBS, not because of American media, but only because of Accuracy in Media and now finally Accuracy In Academia. Prayer does work."

Jon Utley, the syndicated writer, said on Voice of America:

"In many of the so-called best universities, young students are fed a diet of distortion with their idealism abused and twisted into supporting third world Marxists, or the surrender of their country to Soviet nuclear blackmail. Lecturers known for opposing communism are shouted down and prevented from speaking to college audiences. It's time that pro-totalitarian professors were challenged and exposed."

Mr. Utley continued:

"A few months ago I participated in a discussion panel at the prestigious University of Vermont. A full professor of economics on the panel gave the students a totally Marxist interpretation of everything happening in Central America. In the audience nearly ten percent of the students had visited Nicaragua with leftist 'guided' tours to promote the Sandanistas. My lecture was the first time many had ever heard an exposé of what communist society was really like. In Washington a professor mouthing such a one-sided view of the world would be laughed out of town. But at the state university few of the students had the background to question and challenge his distortions and idealizing of communism.

"Accuracy In Academia proposes that students...be given the chance to learn other points of view, in short that universities live up to their obligation of promoting the search for truth, not serving sheltered professors with...their fantasies, frustrations, and falsehoods."

The Chairman of the College Republican National Committee wrote to all of the local club chairmen as follows:

"I hope you will take the time to read the enclosed information and consider getting involved with AIA. The need here is great—too many students are being penalized for believing and trusting in American traditions and solutions. I hope you will decide to assist future students by helping AIA unmask those infamous academicians who are poisoning the minds of America's college students.

"These professors can be brutal with students like us when it comes to grades, so be diligent but careful."

Charles Moser, Chairman of Slavic Languages at George Washington University in Washington, D.C., wrote to the school paper as follows:

"Accuracy In Academia has come into being because debate on many of the great public issues of our time is so much more one-sided and restricted within the academy than it is in society at large. AIA seeks to open up that debate, not foreclose it.

"A professor should be dedicated to the search for truth. If he knowingly disseminates falsehood or deliberately suppresses essential information, then he should be confronted and his falsehoods exposed. If he does such things unknowingly, then he should be pleased to have error brought to his attention.

"Too many members of the academy, like many journalists in the mass media, suffer from inflated notions of their own infallibility."

Dr. Michael Lindsay, Professor Emeritus of Far Eastern Studies, American University in Washington, D.C., wrote me to say:

"Accuracy In Academia should certainly expose instances of academic falsehood and failure of the academic community to criticize them, but it should also point out that the root of this breakdown in standards is the widespread belief in false philosophies.

"In the natural sciences it is still true that someone who makes false statements about his observations or experimental results destroys his reputation in the scientific community and often ends his career....

"However, in the social sciences, many professors have published demonstrably false statements but have been allowed to retain a reputation as respected scholars. If the academic community in the social sciences is not prepared to maintain academic standards by penalizing falsehood, it has no right to object if some outside organization does it for them."

In an essay I cited earlier entitled, "Journalists and Professors," Dr. Lindsay wrote:

"It is interesting to consider why those members of the academic community in the social sciences who do have high standards have done so little to discredit their colleagues who fail to observe them. Why do not social scientists act like natural scientists in rejecting as a reputable member of their own community anyone demonstrably guilty of falsification? One reason may be the widespread acceptance of the positivist philosophy, exemplified by behaviorism, which teaches that truth is a matter of opinion."

A business administration professor with the University of California wrote:

"Your Accuracy In Academia is just what I have been advocating for years.

"Everyone is entitled to an opinion, but no one is entitled to knowingly dispense incorrect information. I don't understand why our own people tear our country down. We can be self-critical of our country, but not self-destructive.

"Most faculty members know as little about business as they do about forecasting earthquakes. Too much theory, not facts. Lots of opinion, no facts.

"It is all so crazy for our society to be unfriendly to enterprise. Too often I find in my MBA classes that managers and educators do not speak the same language. Too many academicians live by the rule: To err is understandable—to admit it is unlikely."

A professor from the University of Colorado wrote:

"The University of Colorado is so fouled up politically because of so many self-acknowledged Marxists who use the classroom to attack the United States that it deserves your attention. I suggest that you or one of your colleagues come to Boulder for a few days to assess the situation. Then you can decide what to do."

A professor of history from California State University wrote:

"I gather from the Latenight America (TV show) that you are undertaking a survey of teaching with a leftist bias on American campuses. It is certainly a phenomenon that needs to be studied and brought to national attention. In our own social sciences area there are numerous colleagues who are self-professed Marxists and many others who are still in the closet. One of the misleading lines they propound is the moral equivalence of the U.S.S.R. and the U.S."

In this same vein, the *Washington Post* recently carried a column by John Marshall, an educator who reported that 51 out of 53 high school seniors in an Arlington, Virginia, school saw "no moral difference between the United States and the Soviet Union." This is, of course, a tragic indication of brainwashing going on in the schools before students even reach college.

The nation's top educator, Secretary of Education William J. Bennett, made that example of perceived moral equivalency a major part of his address on September 21 before the Eagle Forum Leadership Conference in Washington, D.C. The values to be taught, he said, are patriotism, self-discipline, thrift, honesty and respect for elders. He added, "To be specific, one should know...that there is a moral difference between the United States and the Soviet Union."

As most of you here certainly know, some obvious freedoms we enjoy that the people of the U.S.S.R. do not are freedom to vote for the candidate of your choice, freedom of speech, freedom of the press, freedom of religion, and freedom to travel.

While on the subject of William Bennett, in a July 29 *Washington Times* interview, he said one reason that education is proceeding slowly at colleges and universities is that the public is intimidated by the higher education community. He said he would like to encourage a "consumer awareness" about higher education. I don't think the Secretary of Education had Accuracy In Academia in mind when he made those remarks, but maybe we in AIA can fill part of the bill.

On August 11, Cable Network TV did a news feature on Accuracy In Academia. William Bennett was included among those interviewed. He said and I quote:

"Universities are governed by principles of academic freedom and free speech, and so it should remain. Nevertheless an evaluation or assessment of whether people are teaching or whether people are just opining—just giving their opinions—would be part of the assessment."

Prior to his September 21 address to Eagle Forum, I spoke with Secretary Bennett about his TV remarks concerning Accuracy In Academia. He suggested that I respond to critics of AIA by using the statement of Justice Brandeis that "Sunlight is the best disinfectant." I thanked Secretary Bennett for the quote and said I would.

We have heard from other interesting public officials. In mid-August I received a letter from Minnesota State Representative Paul Thiede (Teedee) who wrote:

> "Dear Mr. Lawrence:
> "In just the past couple of days I have heard of the establishment of your organization—Accuracy in Academia.
> "It was on the same day that I heard of your organization's coming together that I received the letter enclosed from a cohort of mine in the Minnesota Legislature, Representative K. J. McDonald.
> "It just seems to me as though you might be interested in the subject matter of Representative McDonald's letter to me and therefore I am enclosing it for your information.
> "I wish you well in your endeavors."

Well, the subject of Representative McDonald's letter was one which he thought should be of interest—as he put it—to "every red, white and blue blooded American patriot." It dealt with a week-long conference at the University of Minnesota sponsored by the Marxist Educational Press. As reported in *The Wanderer* for July 18, 1985, many of the members of the Marxist Educational Press are in the Communist Party.

Representative McDonald's memo to his colleagues read:

> "It's another example of the crazy, confused mixed up world we live in. On the one hand, we ask the American taxpayers to spend $300 plus billion per year for a military system to defend ourselves against a Marxist worldwide conspiracy...Then we also allow the same Marxist, cancerous malignancy to grow here at home at taxpayers' expense on our university campuses....
> "I am going to ask you to join me in writing the University of Minnesota president and to your own Board of Regent member strongly protesting their allowing our tax supported school to be used by this bunch of well-trained agents of the Soviet KGB and ask to have the Marxist professors who are responsible for it thrown off the campus and given a one-way ticket to Moscow."

My purpose in bringing this incident to your attention is to illustrate that people and their elected officials are concerned about this sort of thing. That Marxist conference, held the last week of August, led to an impressive demonstration by protestors that drew front-page and TV coverage in Minneapolis. Representative McDonald and others are considering legislation to cut state appropriations from the University of Minnesota. Incidentally, Accuracy In Academia had an auditor at the Marxist conference. The Marxist Educational Press is sponsoring future conferences at the University of South Florida in Orlando, October 18–20, and at the University of Washington in Seattle, April 11–13, 1986.

Representative McDonald's reference to trained KGB agents brings to mind a revelation by Alex Kaznecheev (Kaznechef), a Soviet KGB agent who defected in Burma in 1957. Kaznecheev reports that when he received intensive training in Marxism by the KGB, the students were told that the instruction was for the purpose of propagandizing, manipulating and controlling other people and that if the students showed any indication that they actually believed in Marxism, they would be kicked out of the program. The point of this, of course, is that KGB agents who believe in Marxism might try to apply their tricks of the trade in the U.S.S.R., which is a no-no for that totalitarian state.

In the coming months, I expect to hear many stories from college students about America-bashers. Benjamin Hart, a recent graduate of Dartmouth, points out in his book *Poisoned Ivy* (Stein and Day, 1984) that there is a certain kind of person found at American universities called a "universal skeptic," a kind of cosmic critic who is not interested in improving what he criticizes.

Hart tells us that serious criticism of communist regimes at universities is rare indeed but claims that we do hear unmitigated attacks on American anti-communists. We hear excuses for the Soviet Union all the time, says Hart, even for the butchery in Afghanistan. He writes:

> "Pol Pot exterminated one-fourth of Cambodia's population. Stalin murdered at least 30 million of his own people, Mao 60 million. Half the world is ruled by communism, which is aggressively expanding. But for some reason, it is Senator Jesse Helms who is the 'warmonger' for pointing out that it is the Soviet Union, not the United States, that routinely violates SALT."

A number of observers have told me that the phenomenon of America bashers is not necessarily a conspiracy. It is an intellectual game to make an impression on students. I am also told that some professors are naive and never really come down out of their ivory towers, that they hide safely behind their academic pursuits and barely worry about such worldly things as the Soviet's shooting down of a Korean airliner or the invasion of Afghanistan. Such things do occur, and most Americans worry about them.

Let me close by reiterating my response to the question: "Is Accuracy In Academia a Threat to Academic Freedom?" The answer is no. As I have indicated, we have received positive indicators and encouragement from hundreds of students and others who believe what we are doing is a good idea. Many tell us it is an idea that is long overdue. We in Accuracy In Academia look forward to increasing our network of reporters over the coming months and years and to providing a sound information service for the American public.

ISSUE 12 NO:

Reed Irvine Rides the Paper Tiger

Jon Wiener

After seven months of existence Accuracy in Academia, the organization seeking to root out the dissemination of "disinformation or misinformation" by radical professors, looks like a paper tiger. News stories last August reported that the organization had an annual budget of $160,000, plans for a staff of twenty-five and a network of freelance informers at 160 colleges and universities. Matthew Scully, associate editor of A.I.A.'s bimonthly newsletter, recently said: "Lots of things that were announced have never come to pass. The organization has switched gears. We're now a journalistic venture....If someone told me today they were setting up a nationwide network of classroom monitors, I'd say it was a ridiculous idea."

Recent A.I.A. newsletters bear out Scully's account. Virtually none of the stories come from student monitors' reports about professors' classroom statements; for the most part they are accounts that have appeared in print elsewhere. When you call A.I.A.'s number in Washington, the person who answers says you've reached the group's parent organization, Accuracy in Media. If A.I.A. has an annual budget of $160,000, why can't it afford its own telephone?

So far A.I.A.'s attacks on radical professors have, if anything, backfired. The organization's first newsletter reported on "an unidentified midwestern professor" whose lectures on Latin American history criticized U.S. policy in the region. "We didn't print her name," executive director Les Csorba explained, "because when we interviewed her she was cooperative; she agreed to distribute some material we offered documenting Sandinista atrocities." That sounds like a case of successful intimidation.

The professor in question, Mary Karasch of Oakland University in Rochester, Michigan, tells the story differently:

> When Reed Irvine [the head of Accuracy in Academia as well as Accuracy in Media] called me, I said I would distribute their material in the classroom. I do explore controversies, and I hadn't thought through A.I.A.'s offer. But they never sent their material. Then, last month, Les Csorba came to the campus to debate our dean and brought me a copy of the material they wanted me to hand out, along with a phone number in Washington to call to get copies for the one hundred students in my class. After reading the material, I concluded it was inappropriate for my students. My union, the American Association of University Professors, advised me that I should not change my syllabus on the basis of pressure from outside political groups.

The case received extensive coverage in the local media, most of it strongly supportive of professors' rights, Karasch told me. A few pro-A.I.A. letters to the editor were also printed. She said that the entire academic community at Oakland—the student council, the faculty and the administration—all opposed A.I.A. When a television station prepared a fifteen-minute special on the group, its reporters had trouble finding a student to defend the organization, although they eventually succeeded. "My colleagues who go back to the fifties say it's nothing like the McCarthy days," said Karasch. "In this area at least, the people have grown and changed."

The target of A.I.A.'s March newsletter, its third, was Linda Arnold, a historian at Virginia Polytechnic Institute and State University in Blacksburg, Virginia. Although A.I.A. focused on Arnold as a result of a student complaint, the newsletter did not attack anything she said in class. Instead it objected to what she told Irvine when he called to confront her about the text she was using in her introductory course, Howard Zinn's *The Twentieth Century*. The newsletter criticized the book for portraying "American heroes" such as Henry Ford and Douglas MacArthur as "villains."

Arnold recalls receiving a phone call from someone who said, "My name is Reed Irvine; I work with A.I.A. Do you have a few minutes to chat?" She wasn't sure who he was, and agreed to talk.

> We ended up arguing for an hour, mostly about Zinn's book. Three times he asked, "Don't you think the book should be burned?" I said I'm against book burning. He told me he would like to send somebody down to lecture, with a critique of Zinn; I said no. I told him if he was so interested in the subject he should teach his own course. He said I should be teaching about the entrepreneurial spirit, for instance the people who created McDonald's. I told him I'm more interested in the people who eat at McDonald's. He never asked permission to quote what I regarded as private comments.

A.I.A. urged its followers to complain to the school's president, William Lavery, that by assigning Zinn, Arnold was not presenting "the fundamental facts and interpretations of American history." Lavery told me his policy in such cases is "to let the faculty member know, ask for their response, then support their views and protect to the hilt their academic freedom." He also said he would let the faculty know they do not have to respond to inquiries like Irvine's. In any case, although associate editor Scully says the organization printed 10,000 copies of the newsletter, Lavery has received "only four or five letters complaining about Arnold." The small number of letters reveals a lot about A.I.A.'s weakness.

From the beginning, A.I.A. said that Howard Zinn, who teaches at Boston University, was one of the professors whose classroom it was interested in monitoring. But the A.I.A. report on Zinn is limited to a critique of his book; it contains nothing about his teaching or political activities.

The target of the second newsletter, published in January, was David Abraham, the Marxist historian who has been attacked by several members of the profession allegedly for the errors in his book *The Collapse of the Weimar Republic*. Most of the article about him consists of previously published quotations, some of them going back as far as 1983. It does not report any complaints by student informers, but it does include an interview with a professor—Yale University historian Henry Turner, who worked with A.I.A. in order to breathe new life into his three-year-old vendetta against Abraham [see Wiener, "Footnotes to History," *The Nation*, February 16, 1985, and "Letters," March 23, 1985]. In the interview Turner attacked those who criticized his conduct in the Abraham case; he also provided A.I.A. with material from his files. Turner thus became the first, and apparently the only, historian to go against the American Historical Association's resolution condemning A.I.A.'s activities as a "threat to academic freedom." (I attempted to reach Turner for a comment, but he did not return my calls.) Richard Kirkendall, head of the A.H.A. professional division, which is monitoring A.I.A.'s attacks on historians, commented, "I'm surprised that Turner would cooperate with a group like A.I.A. It contradicts his stated position on the careful use of sources. These people are careless in their handling of documents."

The report on Abraham contains a number of inaccuracies. The lead sentence states that Abraham is "a Princeton University professor"; since July he has been a visiting associate professor at the New School for Social Research. The report implies that Hanna Gray, president of the University of Chicago, is a "radical historian," although she's in the mainstream. Turner's ally, historian Gerald Feldman, of the University of California, Berkeley, is quoted as referring to German President Paul von Hindenberg as "Hinderberg." It seems Abraham is not the only one who makes mistakes.

Another A.I.A. target, historian Terry Anderson of Texas A & M University, is suing the organization. Anderson, who won the college's teaching award in 1984, was quoted in an A.I.A. story last November: "I do not believe in the institution of marriage....I'm an atheist....I am not patriotic toward Texas A &

M, the flag or America." Csorba and Scully wrote: "Lucifer himself could not have framed his credo any better. But such erudite comments make us wonder just what a man does revere who has no wife or party or country or God." The story is "totally inaccurate," says Anderson. "They never checked any of those quotes with me. They say I'm an atheist; in fact I'm a humanist. They say I'm not patriotic; in fact I'm a Vietnam vet." A.I.A. took the quotations from Texas A & M's *Battalion* and sent the story to "a couple of hundred campus newspapers across the country," Csorba says. "Ten or twelve reprinted it," he adds, including the University of Maryland's *Diamondback*, the *Arizona Daily Wildcat* and Hofstra University's *Chronicle*.

Anderson's suit for defamation and libel will be filed—probably this week—in Minnesota, since the University of Minnesota's *Daily* was one of the newspapers to publish A.I.A.'s story. Anderson's attorney, William Harper, explains, "Although Terry has tenure at Texas A & M, A.I.A.'s untrue depiction of him might affect his employability if he sought another job." Anderson is seeking exemplary and punitive damages. Csorba says: "Our story is accurate. The papers that published it are the ones to be sued, if anyone is."

Only one A.I.A. victim, its first, made the national news: political scientist Mark Reader, a 52-year-old tenured associate professor who has taught at Arizona State University for eighteen years. Reader was singled out not because of a report from a student but because Scully wrote attacks on Reader for a local newspaper in Arizona before Irvine hired him. Thus from the beginning, A.I.A.'s newsletters have been recycling old stories.

Reader is no Marxist; he describes himself as "a whole-Earth person who believes that we are at the end of the old ideologies of capitalism and Communism." In his view, "the need is now for a gentler, a more tolerant people than those who won for us against the ice, the tiger and the bear." It's hard to call that statement "inaccurate." Irvine charged him with teaching "fears of nuclear war, power and weapons." The president of Arizona State, J. Russell Nelson, said he "was not going to pay any attention" to A.I.A., and that was that.

The prototype for A.I.A. seems to have been Students for a Better America, a right-wing group at the University of California, Davis, headed by Les Csorba, which began a campaign against visiting history professor Saul Landau in January 1985. Asked whether he achieved his goals, Csorba commented: "I wanted to get the university to bring Jeane Kirkpatrick to speak; her anticommunist views would balance Landau's. I failed at that. But I did contribute to an awareness at Davis of what Landau had done."

The most ominous aspect of Csorba's campaign was his distribution of information on Landau's political activities going back twenty years. Landau suspected the material had come from his Federal Bureau of Investigation file, but Csorba insisted that it all came from published sources, including James Tyson's *Target America*, a column by Rowland Evans and Robert Novak and the *Congressional Record*. Much of this concerned Landau's alleged role in the Vencerenos Brigade, an organization of Americans helping with Cuba's sugar harvests since 1970, which Congressional investigators subsequently sought to link to "domestic terrorism." It's likely that the F.B.I. supplied material on Landau to Evans and Novak and to the House Un-American Activities Committee, but Csorba seems to have had no direct access to the F.B.I. files.

It's noteworthy that none of the three A.I.A. newsletters published thus far have reported on their targets' past political activities or statements. When Csorba was asked to explain this difference between his campaign against Landau and A.I.A.'s tactics, he said: "At Davis I was on my own. My role here is to publicize what's going on right now. We're not concerned about these people's histories; we want to promote balance in the classroom today."

Those who fear A.I.A. believe it may be following in the footsteps of *Red Channels*, the private anticommunist publication which printed information about left-wing memberships and activities of writers, actors and others during the 1950s and became a quasi-official enforcer of the Hollywood blacklist. A.I.A. initially had similar ambitions. Not long ago Csorba, sounding like a junior Joe McCarthy, boasted, "I have a list of over a thousand radical, commie professors I've compiled over the last three years." And Accuracy in Media, which started out as the letterhead and post office box of a right-wing crank, recently commanded an hour on PBS and space on the Op-Ed page of *The New York Times*.

Irvine sees the media and the universities as the two major bastions of liberal thought in America; he hoped the same strategy and tactics that had proved effective against one would also work against the other. But although professors are more likely to say outrageous things than newscasters, the networks are more vulnerable to pressure. No TV show has tenure, and most are sensitive to audience response in the form of declining ratings or cards and letters. Universities offer an amorphous target. Unlike TV shows, they are widely dispersed and do not enter people's living rooms. It is easier for Reed Irvine's constituents to get mad as hell at Dan Rather than at Howard Zinn. Finally, the pace of change and response at universities, unlike television stations, is very slow. For all these reasons, the tactics that won Irvine a respectful hearing from broadcasters have been firmly rejected by academics.

A.I.A. is hard-pressed to find any prominent academic supporters. Its literature gives the impression that Boston University president John Silber, notorious among university administrators for his dictatorial style and Reaganite political ambitions, has endorsed the organization. Silber denies it. Teachers should not expect to be immune from criticism, he says. "No professor, it seems to me, should be intimidated by Accuracy in Academia. If the presence of A.I.A. on campus restrains a professor from distorting the truth, then it will provide a benefit to those who care about the true purpose of a university. If, on the other hand, A.I.A. goes off on witch hunts against professors merely because they hold left-wing positions, it will quickly discredit itself."

Some of the strongest criticisms of A.I.A. have come from neoconservatives. Midge Decter, a member of the National Advisory Board of Accuracy in Media, called A.I.A. "wrong-headed and harmful" in a *New York Times* Op-Ed piece;

Harvard historian Richard Pipes, a Polish émigré and former National Security Council Soviet-affairs expert, condemned the group on the ground that "what goes on in the classroom is sacrosanct"; and Reagan's Secretary of Education, William Bennett, said A.I.A. was a bad idea that would only make martyrs of those it attacked.

It's not that the neocons disagree with A.I.A.'s diagnosis of academic life. Indeed, many of the people who denounced the New Left as anti-intellectual now argue that unrepentant New Leftists are taking over the intellectual life of the universities. They are concerned because the organization's main achievement to date consists of mobilizing the political center to defend the academic freedom of leftist professors from attacks by right-wing kooks. The American Association of University Professors and at least ten other official higher-education groups, including the American Historical Association, the Organization of American Historians and the American Council on Education, have said A.I.A. is "clearly inimical to the principle of free expression of views by all members of the academic community." Nothing could be more damaging to the neocons, who've spent "inaccuracy." Some targets of these threats have been the right that threatens the integrity of the university by injecting external political issues into academia.

A.I.A. has apparently intimidated a few academics, as have right-wing students acting on their own, ostentatiously monitoring classes and threatening to turn in their professors. But Reed Irvine in effect admitted that the quality of student reports has been low when he told a television interviewer that "students say a lot of things" and that their claims require verification. It may be that many self-selected informers are retaliating for bad grades rather than exposing "inaccuracy." Some targets of these threats have been shaken; others now begin their courses denying bias and affirming their patriotism. But the record of the past six months should reassure them. Midge Decter put it pretty well: "Bias is something that anyone with opinions can be accused of. How can a person without opinions be qualified to teach?"

As *The Nation* went to press, I learned that Matthew Scully has left A.I.A., reducing the organization to a single staff member, Les Csorba. Asked to explain Scully's departure, Csorba told me: "We were very happy with his work. There were no differences between us." Scully agreed.

ISSUE 13

Should Congress Limit the Power of Political Action Committees?

Political action committees (PACs) are campaign committees organized by groups of people to raise money for political purposes. The earliest PACs were formed by labor unions and generally supported candidates who were sympathetic to labor-related issues. The contributions made by these labor PACs partially offset the contributions to candidates made by corporations and wealthy individuals.

The growth of PACs is largely attributed to the 1974 amendments to the federal election laws. The amendments attempted to restrict the influence of wealthy individuals and "private" contributions of corporations and unions. Like many social reforms, there were latent or unintended consequences of the changes. PACs were intended to provide a well-regulated and open avenue for campaign contributions. Rather than solving the problem of campaign financing, many think they have become the problem.

In the 1982 congressional elections, labor unions contributed $20 million to campaigns through 350 separate PACs, 1,497 corporate PACs contributed another $30 million. Trade associations such as the National Associations of Realtors and the Associated Milk Producers give millions during an election year. The American Medical Association gave approximately $2,400,000 to congressional candidates in 1982.

The cost of running for public office has skyrocketed as PACs have proliferated. The average cost of a winning U.S. Senate campaign in 1976 was $600,000. By 1984 it was up to $2,900,000. Some people argue that the increased dependency of candidates on PACs for campaign funds has made them particularly vulnerable to special-interest pressure. Others argue that the $5,000 limit on PAC contributions limit their effectiveness at influencing Congress. Some disagree, as Congressman Thomas Downey of New York put it: "You can't buy a congressman for $5,000. But you can buy his vote. It's done on a regular basis" (*Time,* October 25, 1982).

There are numerous examples of direct correlations between PAC contributions and voting by individual members of Congress. According to *Time* magazine (October 25, 1982), Phil Gramm of Texas in 1982 received the highest total of PAC contributions of any member of the House of Representatives—$226,941—$85,000 from oil interests alone and "The Texan was rewarded for looking after oil interests..." Are votes for legislation advocated by special interest PACs a direct influence of PAC money, or are legislators simply voting the interests of their state's important industries? Are recipients of PAC money being rewarded for votes they would have made in any case, or are they swayed by PAC contributions?

Some PACs are clearly ideological in nature. The National Conservative PAC (NCPAC) mounted a severe negative campaign against liberal candidates in 1980. NCPAC took credit for the defeat of four liberal senators in that election. NCPAC rarely gives money directly to candidates and can therefore spend as much money as it wishes as long as its activities are not authorized by the candidate. The power of NCPAC has waned and has even been used as a weapon against candidates that NCPAC supported.

An additional criticism of PACs is that their money tends to go to the incumbent. Since they are pragmatic, many place their money with the favorite or hedge their bets by giving money to both candidates. Ideological positions of the PACs and the candidate also obviously affect contributions. Corporate PACs generally favor Republicans, while labor PACs favor Democrats.

Proponents of PACs argue that they have actually increased political participation and that the abuses cited existed prior to PACs. For example, incumbents have always received the bulk of political contributions. Another argument is that the number and variety of PACs provide a pluralism that did not exist in prior elections. The fact that many PACs represent small narrow interests is regarded as an asset in that minority interests now have a voice. Additionally, many PACs offset each other. PACs representing labor and conservation counteract those representing big business.

The current bill under debate would generally limit the amount a House candidate could receive from PACs to $100,000 and for a Senate candidate, an amount varying with the population of the state. It also lowers the current PAC contribution to a candidate from $5,000 to $3,000 while increasing the limit that an individual can contribute from $1,000 to $1,500, thus limiting the activities of PACs not directly associated with a candidate. The debate that follows is taken from the discussion of the bill on the floor of the Senate.

ISSUE 13 YES:

Congress Should Limit the Power of Political Action Committees

David L. Boren

I can think of no more important subject to the members of this body and indeed for consideration by the national agenda than the need to reform the way in which campaigns are financed in this country. We send observers to other countries where we have strong interests and alliances to make sure that the election process in those countries is carried out in a fair and impartial basis.

I have had the privilege at the request of the President, for example, to go to El Salvador to watch the election process there, to observe it, and report back to our colleagues on the fairness of that process. Recently I had an opportunity to be a part of the process of observing the elections in the Philippines.

It is appropriate that we show this kind of concern for elections in other countries. It is appropriate that we try to make certain that the people in other parts of the world have an opportunity to express themselves in fair and open elections.

But how much more important is it that we turn our attention to the integrity of the election process here in our own country.

What is going on and what has gone on in this country over the past decade threatens the very integrity of that process.

We are engaged in a struggle to determine whether or not we shall keep government of the people, for the people, and by the people or whether we shall have that government replaced by a government of the special interests, for the special interests, and by the special interests.

I do not think that any of our colleagues would say that what has happened in the financing of elections in the United States over the past several years has been good for the country or good for the political process.

We do not have a fair impartial election process. The whole cornerstone of this democracy is endangered.

And it is time for all of us to turn our attention to what we know is a mounting problem.

First, we are faced with a tidal wave of money pouring into the election process and influencing the election process. We run the risks that instead of elections being decided by the people themselves at the local level on the basis of the integrity and the policy positions taken by candidates, that elections more and more will be decided on the basis of which candidate has the funds to buy the access time necessary to get his or her message across to the people.

We must not allow the highest policymaking positions of this government which should belong to the people themselves to be placed on the auction block and determined primarily by the impact of money available for the campaigns instead of the merits of the candidates and the issues of the election process.

What has happened? The facts are all too clear for all of us to see. In 1976 the average winning candidate for the U.S. Senate spent $600,000 on his or her campaign. In 1976, $600,000.

In 1984 in the last elections the average winning candidate for the U.S. Senate, the average, spent $2.9 million.

So in just 8 short years the cost of running a successful campaign to be elected to the U.S. Senate has gone from $600,000 to $2.9 million, in some cases well over $10 million in some individual elections.

Where is it going to end? Can anyone in this body say that this tidal wave of money pouring into congressional campaigns has been good for the country? Can anyone say that it has enhanced the ability of the average citizen at the local level to have an impact on the campaigns where the campaigns are supposed to be decided? Can anyone say that it has helped the Senate of the United States as a deliberative body? Has it helped us that campaigns now cost an average of $2.9 million, requiring the time and attention of the Members of the Senate constantly to the money-raising process instead of being able to spend their time on the pressing issues of the day that determine the well-being of the next generation of Americans?

It is a shame and a disgrace that we have allowed this situation to go on so long. How much longer will we let it happen? How long will we wait? How long will we close our eyes to this growing avalanche of money that threatens the integrity of the political process? Will we wait until the average Senate campaign costs $5 million or $20 million or $50 million?

It is obvious the problem is not taking care of itself. It is obvious that this spiral is not slowing down. Like the arms race, it is increasing every single day that we wait to act.

There will always be another election. We are always within 2 years of an election. And if we continue to wait until after the election after that, we will never come to grips with this problem until it is too late, until it will already have destroyed the confidence of the people themselves in the integrity of the political process.

Already millions of Americans do not even go to the polls and vote. And I am convinced that part of the reason is that they are not convinced that their own individual votes, their own individual ideas, any longer have any impact and influence on the government, where money is having an undue influence in the outcome of campaigns.

It is not only the amount of money that should concern all of us that is going into campaigns, it is also where that money is coming from. The money is no longer coming from small, individual donations from citizens at the grassroots in the way in which the political process ought to work in this government of the people and for the people and by the people. That is where the money should be coming from to finance campaigns; from that average citizen back home in the State or district that the Congressman or Senator is sworn to represent in the national interests.

What has happened? Over the past decade, the proportion of funds coming for campaigns from that individual contributor back home at the grassroots has been cut in half. Where, then, is all this money coming from, as the cost of campaigns has been skyrocketing?

It is coming from special interest groups, largely headquartered in the Nation's Capital. During that same period of time in which the costs of campaigns have been going out of sight, the amount of money given by political action committees, PAC's, special interest groups, has increased in just one decade—in 1974, from $12 million being given to congressional candidates and in 1984 that figure was $104 million.

Can anyone be naive enough to believe that you can pump in $104 million of special interest money into the political process and not have that money spent in campaigns? Is there anyone naive enough to believe that there is not an indirect relationship between the skyrocketing costs of campaigns and the tens of millions of new money being pumped into campaign financing by special interest groups?

And what about the people back home? What is happening to the grassroots control of the election process itself?

In 1982, 98 Members were elected to Congress, the House and Senate, by receiving more than 50 percent of all of their campaign contributions from political action committees instead of from the people back home. That was in 1982. In 1984, just 2 years later, 163 Members elected to the House and Senate, virtually one-third of the membership of the Congress of the United States, had more than 50 percent of their campaign contributions come not from the people back home, not from the individuals at the grassroots, but from political action committees largely controlled here in Washington, D.C.

What is going to happen to the concept of grassroots democracy if we allow this trend to continue?

The tidal wave of money is a concern. It is a concern of what it is doing to this process, where that money is coming from, from special interest groups instead of people back home. That is a concern about the process; what it is doing in terms of foreclosing opportunity for new people to enter this process.

It is not surprising that it has been difficult to get the Congress of the United States to put this matter on the agenda; not surprising at all. It was reported just this week that those who will be voting on this particular proposal have received $87 million in political contributions since those committees began to be active in 1972. It is an incumbent protection plan, the current system. Eighty percent of all the money contributed by political action committees—80 percent of it—goes to incumbents rather than to challengers.

And so that new person back home that wants to have an opportunity to bring his thoughts, his creative ideas, into the political process is discouraged from running for office. They might be able to raise money back home at the grassroots. They might be able to have support of the people. But what happens when they are overwhelmed with the out-of-State PAC contributions, the millions of dollars, 80 percent of which go to incumbents? It is distorting the political process because it is also discouraging others, new people, from becoming involved in the political process.

In addition, the current system is fragmenting this country and fragmenting this Congress at a time in which we need to be building a consensus to deal with problems like the budget deficit and the trade deficit and when we need to be bringing people together to sacrifice as Americans, not as members of special interest fragmented groups, but as Americans, as one community to form a consensus to do something about the pressing problems of this country.

Can we be surprised, I would ask my colleagues, when we have difficulty forming a consensus to act in the national interest in this Congress, when our reelection campaigns are more and more and more being financed by the special interests instead of by all of the people?

People have asked me: "Senator, you take contributions from people back in your home State." I am proud of the fact that over 90 percent of my contributors come from my home State. That is where they should come from.

They say: "But how is it different? Obviously, every single individual that gives to you has to earn a living in some way."

In my State, some are in the oil business—fewer than used to be as we all know with the current economic conditions—some are in agriculture, they are farmers and ranchers; they are in small businesses; some are in real estate, and other occupations.

They say:

"How is it different? You get a contribution from a farmer or from an oil man or from a realtor or from a union member, how is that different from receiving money from the PAC of the oil company or the political action committee of the agriculture group? How is it different?"

It is essentially different because of this: That individual citizen can look at my whole record and the whole record of all of my colleagues in the Senate. They can say: "You know, I am a farmer, but that Senator may only vote only half the time on issues that affect farmers, and I like what he or she does on national defense," or "I like the fact that they are honest and they bring an overall independence, which is protective to government."

They can view the whole record, in other words, of the Member of the Senate.

Is that true of a political action committee? No. The political action committee has to take those two or three votes in a year's time, those two or three votes on that special economic issue, and see how the Senator voted on them, and then decide, "We will support candidates that have a 75 percent rating or more on that little issue of the special interest groups."

In other words, it becomes a mechanism for encouraging single-issue and single-interest politics in this country, further fragmenting us, further causing us to think of ourselves in our own self-centered identities with our own economic self-interests instead of thinking of ourselves as Americans seeking a consensus as to what is right in the national interest.

So we badly need to change this system—this system is causing the money to flow in without limit, this system that is causing the people at the grassroots to have less and less say in electing their own officials to the public office, the system that is discouraging new people with new ideas from entering the political process, and this system that has continued to fragment us at a time in which we need to build a national consensus.

I know there are those who raise the phony argument that it is a fine thing that people are contributing to PAC's now, and that in fact, it is causing more people to be involved in the political process.

If you really care about something you are not going to delegate out your participation in the process to someone else. We would not delegate out our right to vote to some committee just because we have to, to realtors, bankers, oil men, or union members. We would not let some boss, or some small committee cast our vote for us in the election.

We should not let them cast our dollars in elections, either, in a way that will have the kind of impact on the ultimate result.

So we have before us a proposal that has won bipartisan support, wide support from a whole cross-section of the Members of the U.S. Senate, who are concerned about what is happening to this country, who are concerned about what is happening to this institution as Members more and more must devote their time to raising money for campaigns instead of solving the real problems of the country.

I will just take one moment for a brief description of the provisions of this bill. It limits the amount that a House candidate can accept from a political action committee to $100,000, $125,000 if there is a runoff and $150,000 if there are three contested elections. It limits what Senate candidates can receive to $35,000, and under a congressional district in the State, with an overall cap of any State of a maximum of $750,000. It reduces the amount that PAC's can give to candidates or that candidates can receive from $5,000 to $3,000. It also closes the loophole under which now PAC's can bundle together contributions. Once they have given their $5,000 they can give under law, they can go out, solicit so-called individual contributions which they raise, bundle up and pass on to the candidate so that the PAC gets the credit for the contribution, and in this manner they get around the limits.

Once they have given the $5,000 they can go out and in one case it is estimated they raised $125,000 from individuals. They then took that $125,000, and in the name of the PAC gave it to a candidate for the Congress of the United States.

So the bundling which is going on because of misconstruction of the law by the Federal Election Commission must be stopped. Otherwise even the current PAC limits are totally meaningless.

It also provides that PAC's, so-called independent PAC's, when they make broadcasts on advertising they must carry disclaimers to show that these ads are not being carried on the air subject to any campaign spending limits.

It also tightens up the definition of what is an independent expenditure. We all know that there are independent groups—groups claiming they are independent. They go out, do the dirty work for a candidate, make the savage, negative attacks on candidates, and then claim that they are totally independent of the other candidate in the race. We know very often that is only a veil, only a cloak for collusion between the so-called independent groups and the candidates.

So we provide, if they have the same media consultant, if they have been consulting with one another, sharing advice, that they can no longer pretend to be independent committees.

We also provide that if a candidate is attacked, if a candidate is attacked by these so-called independent groups on stations that have voluntarily accepted advertising, they must make free, equal time available to respond to the candidate who has been the subject of the attack by those who have bought the time.

So, we have an opportunity. We can stand aside as we have been doing before and say let us wait until after the next election before we do anything about it. Let us wait until the problem is more serious. Let us wait until instead of having one-third of all the Members of Congress receive half or more of all their campaign contributions from PAC's and interest groups in Washington instead of the people back home, let us wait until the whole Congress is in that situation and let us wait until they have 90 percent of their money. We are always within 2 years of an election.

For the sake of this country, for the sake of the integrity of the political process, for the sake of the confidence of the American citizens in their own government, for the sake of restoring their belief that their own vote back at the local level expressing their own views and opinions about the election process can make a difference, it is time for us to act. It is time for us to stop waiting until after the next election, to root out a cancer, a malignancy that is eating at the heart of the political process and the democratic process itself.

Our bill would close a loophole that increasingly is used by PAC's and other political committees to evade the current limits on campaign contributions. Under this loophole, PAC's and other political committees are raising contributions made out to a particular candidate instead of to the PAC or political committee and then turning over these checks or otherwise channeling them to that candidate without counting the contributions against the PAC's or political committee's contribution limits. This practice, known as "bundling," is a direct evasion of the existing statutory contribution limits.

In 1974, Congress enacted a series of limits of campaign contributions to congressional candidates designed to protect the integrity of the political process by preventing corruption or the appearance of corruption. In the case of what have come to be known as PAC's, for example, the law says that no individual PAC can give a candidate more than $5,000 for an election.

Thus, if a PAC raises individual contributions and uses those funds to make a contribution to a congressional candidate in the PAC's own name the PAC is limited to giving $5,000. Unfortunately, in an interpretation that makes no sense at all the Federal Election Commission has said that if the PAC instead raises or gathers together individual contributions in the name of a particular candidate and turns them over or channels them to the candidate, then the PAC can provide unlimited amounts to that candidate.

This incorrect interpretation of the law by the FEC has seriously undermined the contribution limits in the Federal Election Campaign Act. It has allowed a PAC to do indirectly what it cannot do directly and by doing so to get the kind of political credit and influence from providing large sums of money to a candidate that the $5,000 contribution limit is intended to prevent.

Not surprisingly, an increasing number of PAC's are taking advantage of the bundling loophole.

Our amendment would overturn the Federal Election Commission's incorrect interpretation of the law legislatively, rather than waiting for the courts or the Federal Election Commission to make the correction. The provision in our bill requires that any PAC or other political committee that raises or otherwise gathers contributions made out to a particular candidate and then turns over or channels or otherwise directs the contributions to the candidate has to count those contributions against its statutory contribution limits.

Similarly, if a PAC did not directly turn over the checks to a candidate but arranged for the checks to be received by the candidate in a manner that made clear to the candidate that the PAC was responsible for arranging for the contributions, this too would be treated as a contribution by the PAC subject to the $5,000 limit.

This provision has a very simple purpose. It restores the integrity of the existing contribution limits in the Federal Election Campaign Act by preventing PAC's and other political committees from using "bundling" practices to circumvent these limits in a manner that was never intended to be allowed by Congress.

The Boren-Goldwater PAC limit amendment includes a response time provision designed to address the problem faced by candidates who are the targets of independent broadcast advertisements. The provision does not limit such independent expenditures but rather awards free and equal air time to reply. Response time is a constitutionally sound way of restoring some measure of accountability to independent spending activities in a way that provides more opportunities for speech that informs the public of all sides of a political debate.

Under our response time proposal, radio and television stations would be required to provide free and equal response time to Federal candidates in cases where a broadcaster sells time to any person other than a candidate to broadcast material which either endorses or opposes a candidate. The provision would apply only if the broadcaster originally chose to sell the time—a decision which under existing law remains solely up to the broadcaster. If the broadcaster advertisement endorses a candidate, other legally qualified candidates for the same office would be entitled at no cost to an equal amount of broadcast time. If the advertisement opposes a candidate, that candidate would be entitled at no cost to an equal amount of broadcast time.

Congress has long recognized that an essential ingredient of our democratic system of government is a well-informed, voting citizenry. And citizens increasingly are turning to the airways for news and information.

The critical role of Federal elections requires that candidates for Federal office have the opportunity to fairly put their case to the American public. The response time provision fills in a gap—a gap that allows independent advertisements to undermine this opportunity. Promoting public access to a full and fair dialog between candidates—thus enhancing the prospects for good government—can only benefit the American public.

The phenomenon I have just described has become widespread in the past decade and threatens the integrity of the congressional decisionmaking process and our representative system of government. There is a growing awareness, both in Congress and in the general public, that PAC contributions can make a difference in the legislative process. PAC dollars often are given by special interests to increase their access to and influence on Members of Congress. PAC contributions, in other words, are generally made with a legislative purpose.

Members of Congress also are recognizing the dangers caused by the role PAC's are playing in financing congressional elections.

The need for limits on aggregate PAC contributions to congressional candidates is urgent. Without these limits, we are allowing our current system of limits on campaign contributions to be eroded. Without aggregate PAC limits, we are permitting special interests increasingly to dominate our legislative and electoral processes. In short, unless we enact the limits proposed in this legislation, we are standing by while the individual voter becomes, effectively, a second-class participant in representative democracy.

ISSUE 13 NO:

Congress Should Not Limit the Power of Political Action Committees

Dave Durenberger

The current system of financing elections, with its increased numbers of PAC's and growing reliance on PAC contributions, did not simply spring from the woodwork of American politics. It did not, in effect, happen because of the nature of politics in this country. It arose directly out of the 1974 amendments to the Federal Election Campaign Act and the Supreme Court's 1976 decision in Buckley against Valeo. These were supposed to be the reforms to end all reforms. Instead, they encouraged a seven-fold increase in the number of PAC's, opened the flood gates to unlimited campaign spending by independently wealthy candidates and so-called independent groups, and sharply reduced political party contributions to congressional campaigns. Some "reform"!

Can it happen again? You bet it can. And it will happen if the Boren amendment is adopted.

Effective campaign finance reform can only be accomplished by examining the whole system in a comprehensive manner, by looking at all sources of contributions. If we do, one fact immediately stands out. Rather than limiting PAC's, the most important need in campaign finance is to focus on strengthening political parties—especially at the State and local level.

We are considering an amendment that would significantly restructure Federal laws governing campaign finance practices for Federal elections. I hope that whatever the outcome of the vote, we will broaden our efforts to reform the campaign finance laws, and I will continue to play a role in that process.

As described by its chief sponsor, my distinguished colleague from Oklahoma, the amendment before us is supposed to enhance public confidence in congressional elections by restricting the role of narrow special interests and by increasing the role of individual contributors in electoral campaigns.

These are worthy goals which I know are shared by all the Members of this body and by our constituents back home. As is so often the case, the controversy centers not on the goals of this legislation but on the most effective means of obtaining these ends. If we have learned one thing during the past 15 years of continuous changes in our campaign finance laws, it is simply this: Beware of quick fixes. Beware of unintended consequences.

My reelection campaign in 1982 goes down in political history as a monument to the biggest loophole in our campaign finance laws. This loophole is only exacerbated by the Boren amendment. This travesty of equal representation in the election process was created by the Supreme Court and has nothing to do with PAC's or lobbies. This gaping loophole in our laws permits wealthy candidates to spend unlimited amounts of their own funds on their campaigns.

And there are other problems which require citizen concern.

It is outcomes like these which underscore the need for truly comprehensive reform—not the ad hoc approach represented by the legislation before us.

As far as PAC's go, there is one new and growing kind of PAC that raises disturbing questions about electoral accountability—the so-called candidate PAC's that funnel funds from one candidate's coffers to another.

Reforms that focus first and foremost on limiting the role of PAC's in our electoral system are doomed to failure. They will fail because they deal with a symptom, and not the cause, of what ails our political process. The growth of PAC's is only a reflection of a fundamental change from corporate to entreprenurial politics. Capping PAC contributions without dealing with the broader implications of this transformation will only drive PAC dollars to other, less accountable uses like independent expenditures, while doing nothing to strengthen our institutional decision making.

We used to run for office as members of a collective entity called political parties. The parties guided voters' decisions and provided most of the resources candidates required to run for office. They supplied the volunteers and the bumper stickers, they contacted the voters, nominated the candidates, and defined the issues.

But the parties have lost their dominant position in the electoral process. All of us—voters, candidates, and policy makers—are worse off for it. As candidates, all of us here now run as independent entrepreneurs. We're individually responsible for buying time on television, sending out letters by the million, hiring our own campaign staffs and consultants, coordinating our own volunteers and, above all, finding the money to pay for it all.

Combined with the skyrocketing costs of new technologies like television and direct mail, this new process has sent campaign costs through the roof. Spending on congressional campaigns rose fourfold between 1974 and 1984, rising from $72 million to $295 million in just 10 years.

And where are the parties in all of this? In 1984 Senate races, direct party contributions to Senate candidates comprised only 1 percent of total campaign contributions—1 percent. That's compared with 6 percent in 1974 and over 10 percent in 1972. Although campaign costs more than doubled during this period, the average size of party contributions to candidates actually declined by 40 percent—not counting inflation.

So the problem is much larger than PAC's and will not be solved by clamping down on PAC contributions. The Boren approach ignores the positive role that PAC's can play as one part of a balanced approach to campaign funding; it gives an unfair advantage to wealthy candidates; and it ignores the most effective means of reducing PAC influence—by strengthening our parties.

Although they are hardly perfect, in some ways PAC's have gotten a bum rap. In fact, they are the product of earlier reforms, and a real improvement over earlier fundraising practices. I have called PAC's the "united way of political giving" and I meant it. Consider the situation before 1974. At that time, campaign finance all too often was the province of a few big corporations and wealthy fatcats, who found ways to give nearly unlimited amounts of campaign funds with little or no disclosure.

In contrast, PAC's allow average citizens and small contributors to pool their resources and get involved in the political process. In fact, PAC's can act as a sort of half-way house to parties as a means of getting citizens involved in the process of self-government. People who donate to PAC's are more active, knowledgeable, and interested in the political process than the average citizen. And it's all done in the open, above board, with full disclosure.

So why do we hear more and more about the growing influence of PAC's in our elections? Because if you look at total campaign contributions, at all the money in politics, PAC's are up; parties and individual contributions are down. In the Republican-controlled Senate, PAC's now provide about 18 percent of all campaign funds, up from 11 percent 12 years ago. In the Democratic-controlled House, PAC's now provide 31 percent of all campaign dollars, up from 17 percent in 1974.

Those are the totals. But PAC's are not a single entity. They are a mirror of American society and getting more divided all the time. We've all heard the numbers on the growth of PAC's. Their numbers have increased from 608—12 years ago—to over 3,500 today. What does that mean? For any given PAC, that doesn't mean it is getting stronger. On the contrary, it means that each PAC's contributions are becoming less and less significant. And it means that on any given issue, we are more and more likely to find competing PAC's on every side.

The only problem with PAC's is that they accurately reflect the pluralism of our democracy. Most PAC's, it is true, represent narrow single interests in our society. There is nothing wrong with that. Such social and economic interests have a right to such representation in our political process if they choose to exercise it.

Each of us was elected to represent the interests of our State and our constituents. If you are like me, your PAC contributions mirror the social and economic makeup of your State. In my case that means agriculture, food processing, health care, transportation, and insurance.

Such representation is important, but it is not our only responsibility. As U.S. Senators, we also have a responsibility to represent the broader public interest as we understand it. That is where the problem may arise with PAC's, if we permit it to occur. For however worthy any single cause may be, this Nation cannot afford a political process that separates complex problems into tiny fragments, blindly hoping that the cumulative outcome will somehow total the general public interest. If we are to deal responsibly with the difficult issues that confront the Congress, we must assure that the electoral process enables us to place the collective interests of society above the growing multitude of special interest claimants.

That brings us back to the political parties. Because the problem of representing the broader public interest can not be solved by limiting PAC's. It can only be solved in a positive way by enhancing the role of parties.

This approach is nothing new. Our electoral system historically relied on the parties to perform this important representative function of combining disparate interests into broad coalitions, each representing a distinct public philosophy about the proper role of government in society. Our political parties have never been rigid and disciplined collections of single-minded ideologues—they allowed ample room for expressing individual interests and opinions.

But the parties were by far the most important organizations in our electoral system, providing a framework of shared ideals within which different points of view could be debated. And because our parties were decentralized, they provided avenues for representing regional and local values within the Federal Government as well as other social and economic concerns.

In recent years, the broadly based system of representation provided by the parties has been eroded. Though still important, the parties' role in government and elections has been diminished by the rise of new forms of campaign finance, heightened reliance on narrow single issue organizations, and new modes of political communication which flood your mail box and mine with carefully crafted appeals.

The upshot of this new system—including PAC single issue groups, and grassroots mail campaigns—has been to encourage citizens and Congress alike to deal with complex issues on a parochial, ad hoc basis. They encourage us to look at every problem in simple terms of "what's in it for me, right here, right now?" They make it easy to avoid, if only temporarily, the tough but unavoidable decisions we all must make to reconcile our competing goals with the resources available, and to consider how our individual interests fit within a framework of the broader interest of society at large.

In such decisions, the parties play an irreplaceable role. They begin the process of building coalitions, of identifying areas of consensus, of focusing attention on priorities. Far from limiting the role of parties in our electoral process, as we have done in recent years, we should be raising and removing limitations on party contributions in campaigns.

If our goal is to limit the influence of PAC's and improve our legislative process, this is clearly the way to proceed. If parties are allowed to contribute more, candidates would rely less on PAC's. This would not only limit PAC influence, it would enable the parties once again to command serious attention from both voters and candidates.

Despite what we often hear, this is not a matter of partisan advantage or debate. Although many Democrats believe they have some catching up to do in terms of fundraising, leaders of both parties are in agreement on the basic goal of easing limitations on effective party competition.

Raising the limits on party contributions and expenditures would mark a beginning toward strengthening the parties. Such an approach does most to enhance the role of the national party committees, since this is where most of both parties' resources are concentrated. But there is also a need to strengthen parties at the grassroots. It is at the State and local levels that the decline of party influence has been the sharpest. And it is there that the foundations for stronger parties must be built.

Is there a role for Congress to play in revitalizing parties at the grassroots level? I believe there is. As a first step, we can end the discrimination against State and local parties under Federal law. Current Federal campaign finance laws subject State and local parties to stricter spending and contribution limits than the national committees. Therefore, at the appropriate time, I would urge consideration of an amendment that would equalize the treatment of all party committees and enhance the role of grassroots parties in four specific ways:

First, we should raise the maximum limit on individual contributions to State and local parties from $5,000 to $20,000 per year, the level permitted national party committees;

Second, we should increase State party contributions to senatorial candidates to $17,500 per election, again equaling the national committees' limit;

Third, we should ease restrictions on local party contributions to congressional candidates by assuming their independence from State party committees, unless proved otherwise; and

Fourth, we should place congressional elections on the same footing as presidential elections by permitting unlimited expenditures for voter registration, phone banks, get-out-the-vote drives and similar party building efforts at the local level.

Rebuilding our parties at the grassroots is the most important reform we can undertake. But there are other problems that need to be addressed as well.

One new kind of PAC that may indeed be in need of immediate reform is the candidate PAC. Such PAC's are growing rapidly in number, and they raise unique questions of accountability.

I believe there are two aspects of candidate PAC's which give cause for concern. First, they weaken public accountability. Citizens give contributions to a particular candidate with the expectation that those funds will be used on behalf of that candidate. What is more, for those who are concerned about the origins of campaign contributions, when campaign contributions are funneled through a candidate PAC or campaign committee, their origins are nearly impossible to trace.

A second issue that deserves immediate attention is independent expenditures. This is one of the most egregious loopholes in our campaign finance laws, thanks to the Supreme Court's decision in Buckley versus Valeo.

As the law now stands, there are no limits on independent expenditures by PAC's or single wealthy individuals, so long as the independent spender does not communicate with or coordinate his activities with any candidates in an election. The effects of this provision, though unintended, can be substantial.

The most significant impact has been negative advertising. Of the $5.3 million spent independently by PAC's in 1981–82, $4.5 million was spent to oppose rather than in support of candidates. The point is not that independent expenditures are inherently negative. I was cochair of Americans for Change, which spent millions on behalf of Ronald Reagan's candidacy in 1980; we were not interested in negative advertising. Rather, my point is that this is a serious loophole in our present laws which is aggravated by the Boren amendment. Rest assured, once we cap PAC contributions to candidates, those funds will not simply dry up. They will find another outlet, and negative independent expenditures are likely to be it.

The third aspect of our present campaign finance laws that needs immediate reforming is unlimited campaign spending by wealthy candidates. This is another loophole opened up by the Supreme Court's Buckley decision.

Unless the complex system of campaign finance is approached as a whole, we are bound to aggravate existing inequities and create new ones, thus perpetuating the cycle of "reforming the reforms."

ISSUE 14

Should We Enact Immigration Reform Laws?

For most of the history of the United States, illegal immigration has not been considered to be a problem. The expanding frontier, industrial growth, and the need for cheap labor kept our borders open with few restrictions. The first serious attempt by the federal government to limit immigration was aimed at Asians. Many Chinese had migrated into the United States and were welcomed as cheap farm and railroad labor. When the railroads were completed and more whites moved west, hostility toward the Chinese increased. As a result, a series of Chinese Exclusion Acts was passed beginning in the 1880s. Growing prejudice against the Japanese resulted in the "Gentleman's Agreement" in 1907, with Japan agreeing to limit emigrants and the United States agreeing to limit discrimination against the Japanese.

Later, laws were created restricting the immigration of people with dangerous contagious diseases. The hostility was in part a reflection of old religious prejudices complicated by language and cultural differences. The new immigrants were predominately Jewish and Catholic. Anti-Semitism and hostility toward Catholics were a significant factor in the development of these laws.

Until the latter part of the nineteenth century, immigrants were primarily from Northwestern Europe. As the pattern changed and immigrants increasingly came from Southern and Eastern Europe, pressure grew to limit these "new immigrants." In 1917 a literacy requirement was passed at least in part as a reflection of the growing hostility to the new immigrants.

A further attempt to limit the imigration of Southern and Eastern Europeans was the National Origins System legislated in the 1920s. These laws went through a number of variations but were finally based on the national origins of the 1920 U.S. population. The number of immigrants from each country was determined and that country was allowed an immigration quota based on its proportion in the U.S. population. The Anglicizing of names and other record-keeping problems undoubtedly produced inaccurate country-of-origin designations. As a result, the countries in Northern and Western Europe were allowed the vast majority of immigrants. Immigration from Eastern and Southern Europe was dramatically reduced. Only a small proportion of the people on the waiting lists in Italy, Greece, and Poland were allowed to immigrate.

The McCarran-Walter Act of 1952 retained the system of national origins but added a system of preferences based on occupational skills. The 1965 Immigration Act eliminated much of ethnic and racial discrimination included in prior law but retained the limit on absolute numbers. The 1965 law placed a limit of 120,000 immigrants from the western hemisphere and 170,000 from the rest of the world. Preferences for relatives of U.S. citizens and members of certain occupations were modified and retained in the law. Exceptions were also made for refugee groups such as the Cubans and Vietnamese and for political refugees.

Since World War II American immigration policy has increasingly focused on gate-keeping. The number of professionals as a percentage of legal immigrants has increased, particularly from developing countries. This has created what some observers call a "brain drain." Countries in dire need of professionals lose them to the United States through immigration. The vast majority of the worlds' unskilled people have little hope of legal migration to the United States.

The estimates of the number of illegal immigrants into the country each year vary from 500,000 to 4,000,000. Mexico is probably the primary source of the illegal immigrants, although many come from other Latin American countries. Both Mexico and these countries are in a period of rapid population and labor-force growth. The fertility rates are about three times higher in Mexico than in the United States. Mexico is currently struggling with very high debt and unemployment. Jobs in the United States, even those paying minimum wages, pay considerably better than jobs in Mexico. There is, then, a considerable push-pull element in Mexican immigration into the U.S.*

The following articles are taken from a U.S. Senate debate on immigration law reform. The primary issues involve penalties for employers who hire illegal immigrants and the granting of amnesty for illegal aliens who

*For additional information, see "Pending Immigration Legislation." *Congressional Digest*, March 1986.

have resided in the United States for a period of time. In the articles that follow, Senators Mark Hatfield and Dale Bumpers argue for the enactment of immigration reform. Senators Jeff Bingaman and John Kerry argue against the legislation.

The Immigration Reform and Control Act of 1986 went into effect on June 1, 1987. The principal features of the law include: making it a federal crime to hire illegal aliens; creating an amnesty program granting legal status to aliens in the United States since January 1, 1982; providing legal status to foreign farm workers who worked in agriculture at least ninety days between May 1985 and May 1986; and imposing penalties on employers who discriminate against workers on the basis of national origin or citizenship. The last feature is an attempt to protect the rights of foreign-born Americans. Keep the features of the final bill in mind as you read the following articles.

ISSUE 14 YES:

We Should Enact Immigration Reform

Mark O. Hatfield

The Senate once again is faced with final passage of legislation to restructure our Nation's laws with respect to illegal immigration. I support S. 1200. Crafting immigration reform legislation which responds to the unique conditions of our day takes tremendous wisdom and requires a great deal of time.

As we are all aware, our Nation's present immigration laws have proven woefully inadequate in controlling the flow of persons entering the country illegally. For years it has been clear that immigration reform is necessary. Unfortunately, because of highly emotional and diverse views on the myriad of issues relating to immigration reform, Congress has been unable to reach agreement.

This paralysis is regrettable. Our Nation admits more legal immigrants and refugees than any other nation. However, unless Congress takes swift action to control the flow of illegal immigrants, the increased competition for jobs and the growing number of illegal workers, will likely spawn an outcry for the complete closure of our borders from the American people.

There are four basic components which form the foundation of this legislation's efforts to halt the flow of illegal immigrants. In my judgment, each plays an essential part in responding to the difficult challenge of immigration reform.

First, S. 1200 states that it is the sense of the Congress that the Immigration and Naturalization Service (INS) should increase its border patrol and other inspection and enforcement activities. Accordingly, the bill establishes the authority to increase funding for the INS by approximately $300 million in 1987 and 1988. The bill also increases penalties for bringing an alien into the United States, for the use and manufacture of counterfeit or altered entry documents and for the use and manufacture of false identification.

Second, the bill institutes employer sanctions for those employers who knowingly hire unauthorized aliens. Under current law it is not unlawful for an employer to hire an illegal alien. This fact, coupled with the fact that our nation is the most prosperous and promising country in the world, creates a powerful magnet which draws poor, and often desperate individuals to cross our borders illegally in search of a means to support themselves and their families. These aliens are often subject to inhumane and oppressive treatment by unscrupulous employers who know full well that the worker will not report to law enforcement authorities any violations for fear of being deported.

Employer sanctions would place a civil fine of up to $2,000 per alien on an employer of four or more persons, who knowingly hires an illegal alien. A second offense would bring a fine of up to $5,000 per illegal alien, and upon conviction of a third violation the fine could be as high as $10,000 per illegal alien. Additionally, the third offense would establish a pattern or practice of violations. Once a pattern or practice of violations has been established, any additional offense would bring a criminal penalty of up to $3,000 per alien, and imprisonment of up to 6 months.

The employer sanctions, however, would not go into full effect until one year after enactment of the bill. The first 6 months would be an "education period." Should an employer be found in violation during the second 6 months, he or she only would receive a warning, unless a warning had already been given earlier in the period.

With the imposition of penalties on employers, the availability of American jobs to illegal workers will drop significantly. Additionally, without the employment incentive, the numbers of persons seeking to immigrate illegally also will be reduced.

The third foundational component is closely related to employer sanctions. It provides a voluntary employer verification system. This system will establish an affirmative defense for an employer found to have employed an illegal worker after enactment of S. 1200. This is intended to protect employers who, after making a good faith effort to abide by the law, are found to have inadvertently hired illegal workers.

Under the system an employer must keep records on all newly hired employees which verifies that he or she had checked specified documents, such as a U.S. passport, certificate of U.S. citizenship, driver's license, or Social Security card, to determine the prospective employee's identity and work authorization status. If an employer chooses not to keep the verification records and is found to have employed an illegal alien, he or she is presumed to have knowingly hired the alien and must rebut the presumption with "clear and convincing evidence."

Finally, S. 1200 institutes a legalization program for certain illegal aliens already in the country. It does not grant legal status to all illegal aliens. Such an act would be far too burdensome to State and local governments and would send a dangerous signal to those considering entering this country illegally. Also, the legalization program does not make all forms of public assistance available to these newly legalized persons. S. 1200 does grant temporary legal status, not citizenship, to aliens who can prove they have resided continuously in the country since January 1, 1980.

There are an estimated 6 million undocumented aliens in our country. It is both impractical and unwise to attempt to round up these aliens and throw them out of the country. In parts of the United States such an attempt by the Federal Government would precipitate a near civil war, and would subject legal residents of foreign appearance to gross invasions of privacy.

Studies have shown that between 64 to 75 percent of all undocumented aliens pay Federal income taxes, and as many as 88 percent pay Social Security taxes. Eight years ago, a report by the Federal Government stated that undocumented aliens pay almost $6 billion a year in Federal, State, and local taxes. By setting the cutoff date at January 1, 1980, those aliens legalized will have been the ones who are holding jobs and producing identifiable benefits for their communities.

As I stated before, S. 1200 is not a perfect piece of legislation. There are aspects of the bill with which I am not completely comfortable. One specific concern, which I raised earlier in the debate, relates to our almost unconscious drift toward the establishment of a national ID card. I strenuously oppose creation of such a card and I believe that the vast majority of the American people do also. Such an ID card would be a gross invasion of privacy and a violation of the liberties secured to all citizens by the Constitution. Regardless of how legitimate the immediate need may be, such as immigration law enforcement, a national ID card, in the long run, could be used for appalling purposes.

During consideration of a similar immigration reform measure 2 years ago, I offered an amendment which granted Congress a legislative veto power over any Presidential proposal to implement a national ID card. This year, S. 1200 includes provisions which insures that Congress will have a role in any Presidential efforts to establish a national ID card. It also will enable the Congress to express disapproval for any minor change in an existing identification document.

Even though S. 1200 contained the above provisions, I still sought, and received, assurances from Senator Simpson, the chairman of the Subcommittee on Immigration and Refugee Policy, that it was neither the intention of Congress to establish a new national ID card nor to expand the use of the Social Security card for such purposes.

Let me address one final concern. I realize many Senators expressed reservations about the adoption of an amendment, offered by Senator Wilson, establishing a more realistic foreign worker program for perishable agriculture. Because of the highly vulnerable nature of perishable crops, growers needed an alternative to the present H-2 Program. Unfortunately, the expanded H-2 Program in S. 1200 does not provide the flexibility necessary to respond to the rapidly changing labor needs of perishable growers.

Consequently, I supported Senator Wilson's amendment. The amendment was not what its opponents claimed. It would not have taken jobs away from American workers. Foreign workers would be given visas only if it was determined by the Attorney General, after consultation with the Secretary of Labor and Agriculture, that there was not a sufficient number of qualified domestic workers available. Further, the amendment required that the foreign workers be paid sufficient wages so as to not depress domestic rates. It obligated employers to provide housing, workman's compensation and afforded certain labor law protections to guest workers. Finally, Senator Wilson's amendment included certain provisions to insure that the foreign workers involved in the guest worker program return to their countries when their visas expire.

Again, let me make it clear, I support S. 1200. I believe it represents a reasonable and effective response to bringing about the necessary reform of our nation's outdated illegal immigration policy. Through increased enforcement activities, the removal of employment incentives and a limited legalization program, our nation will be better equipped to stem the flow of illegal immigrants across our borders and to respond to the problems and abuses which accompany the presence of a significant illegal population.

Reprinted with permission by Congressional Digest Corp., from "Should Congress Enact Senate-Passed Immigration Reform Legislation." *Congressional Digest*. Washington, D.C. March 1986.

Dale L. Bumpers

I rise today to voice my support for the Immigration Reform and Control Act of 1985, which is presently pending before the Senate. The enactment of this very important legislation has been long overdue. I have supported similar measures in the 97th and 98th Congresses and I continue to believe that this legislation is in the national interest of the United States.

No other country in the world accepts or resettles the numbers of immigrants that the United States accepts. We can be proud of this heritage and of our commitment to the principles that are so eloquently enunciated in the words etched in stone on one of this country's most beautiful monuments—the Statue of Liberty. Those words describe the open arms of this country that still extend to the "huddled masses" yearning to breathe the free air of democracy. Reform of our immigration laws does not mean that the United States will isolate itself from the world. It simply means that this government has a responsibility to allow immigration to occur in an orderly and lawful fashion with a sense of fairness and reasonableness.

For years, we have known that immigration into this country has been out of control and no action has been taken to reform our badly outdated immigration laws. I am hopeful that the House will now proceed with, and pass, a comprehensive immigration measure during this 99th Congress. We all recognize that the first duty of a sovereign nation is to control and protect its borders and it is time that we meet that responsibility.

Immigration into this country—legal and illegal—now exceeds over 750,000 per year and accounts for 30 to 50 percent of our annual population growth. No one disputes that immigrants have been the building blocks of this country. The problem arises when immigration is in violation of the law and when we have no programs to assimilate new immigrants. Net illegal immigration is estimated at 500,000 per year, or over two-thirds of all immigration. Should illegal immigration continue unabated, by the year 2025, some 100 million of the estimated 300 million people in the United States will be post-1980 immigrants.

We need to get control of this influx for many reasons. Most importantly, we need to know how our country is changing. The Select Commission on Immigration has estimated the number of illegal immigrants in this country to be between 3.5 to 6 million. This figure represents data that was compiled 7 years ago. Surely, there are many more illegal immigrants in this country today than in 1978. In a recent expose on immigration into the United States, *Time* magazine reported that there may be as many as 12 million illegal immigrants in the United States.

The point is that we don't know. Not only are we not aware of the number of illegal immigrants, we do not know how many of these immigrants have displaced American workers. Nor do we know how much the U.S. Government spends in health care, education, and other social services for illegal immigrants. While many have argued that lack of data is a reason to postpone immigration reform, I contend it is the very reason why we must proceed with this legislation. It is essential in the responsible management of our economy and of fiscal policy that we know the full extent of illegal immigration.

There have been many concerns that we not enact a bill designed to control the influx of illegal immigrants that may be discriminatory or a bill that is inconsistent with our longstanding tradition of providing refuge for the downtrodden. I share these concerns, yet I am pleased that over the many years that immigration reform has been considered and the many hours of hearings and testimony on these questions, a bill has been put together that addresses these concerns. I congratulate my colleagues who have worked so many hours on a bill that will be fair, yet effective.

Again, I urge the Senate to adopt this legislation so that we may deal effectively with a problem that grows increasingly harder to solve every year. The United States accepts and is honored by the fact that freedom and democracy are attractive to people throughout the world. Yet, with that, we must also accept our last responsibility to the citizens of this country, to the thousands of legal immigrants, and to the untold millions of illegal immigrants, to forge a fair and effective policy to stem the rising tide of illegal immigration and equalize the opportunity this bountiful land provides for all.

ISSUE 14 NO:

We Should Not Enact Immigration Reform

Jeff Bingaman

I commend the Senator from Wyoming for his diligence and leadership in attempting to craft a workable solution to the serious immigration problem that exists in this country. But I feel, after careful consideration, that the bill still does not meet the fundamental tests of fairness and effectiveness, and I must reluctantly oppose it in its current form.

The seriousness of the immigration problem is not disputed. The committee report accompanying S. 1200 states that:

"No other country in the world attracts potential migrants as strongly as the United States of America. No other country approaches the United States in the number of legal immigrants accepted or refugees permanently resettled. The committee believes that most Americans are proud of both the reputation and the history of this country as a land of opportunity and refuge. We believe that this reputation and this history have generally had a positive effect on America.

"However, current U.S. immigration policy is no longer adequate to deal with modern conditions, including the growing immigration pressure on the United States. Immigration to the United States is 'out of control' and it is perceived that way at all levels of Government and by the American people—indeed by people all over the world."

I agree with the statement of the committee—that immigration is out of control—and I, too, believe reform is imperative. However, I am very concerned with the approach taken in S. 1200 for several different reasons.

Therefore, I have cosponsored and supported those amendments that I feel would make the immigration bill a more equitable measure. Minority Americans, farmers, business owners and employers all have a stake in this legislation and I have tried to balance their concerns. Some important additions have been made to S. 1200. In particular, an amendment I cosponsored would require the General Accounting Office to study the implementation of the employer sanctions to determine if a pattern of discrimination has resulted against prospective employees. Additionally, I am pleased the Senate passed an amendment I cosponsored to protect farmers against unreasonable and warrantless searches.

However, even in light of these improvements, I am dismayed that the Senate failed to approve an amendment which would have provided an administrative procedure for redress of employment discrimination as a result of employer sanctions.

Of great concern to me, in particular, are the revisions in S. 1200 that rely on employer sanctions as a means of enforcing the law. This is of critical concern to New Mexico, where 36.6 percent of the residents are of Hispanic origin. They are loyal U.S. citizens who share the ethnicity of many present undocumented workers.

While there is serious concern about the impact of increased illegal immigration into this country, I believe it would be tragic to create a system which aggravates discrimination problems and which submits American citizens and legal immigrants to indignities and suspicion because of their surnames or the color of their skin.

The reason for employer sanctions is to remove the economic incentive for illegal aliens to come to the United States for jobs. Sanctions exist today in Canada and a number of European countries. However, a General Accounting Office study of these programs reveals that they have not achieved their goal of reducing knowing employment of illegal aliens and I believe we must proceed carefully on this issue.

Also of concern to me is the new "triggering" mechanism in S. 1200 to start legalization. This is certainly a step backward, for legalization will not occur immediately but must be delayed for as long as 3 years. My concern is that this will lead to "witch hunts" for illegal aliens that may occur during the interim—after enactment and before legalization period.

As a Senator from a State that shares a long border with Mexico, I feel that I have a good understanding of the problems that have resulted and will result if we continue to ignore the immigration problem.

The present bill does not adequately take into account some of the unique conditions that exist along the United States–Mexican border, the effect of our long term relations with Mexico or the impact on the economy of the Southwest.

The border region between the United States and Mexico is unlike any other international boundary. There is a unique cultural and economic interdependence between the communities on both sides of the border. This interdependence, which benefits both Mexicans and Americans, requires the smooth flow of goods and people between the border cities. Of course this flow must be regulated according to the laws of both countries, but I am concerned that no serious analysis has been undertaken to assess the effect of this legislation on these border communities.

Another concern is how the economy of Mexico is likely to respond if this bill becomes law. We cannot ignore what happens to Mexico, as economic and political turbulence there will directly affect the United States. Thus, if an unintended result of this legislation was to push Mexico even further into economic crisis, the pressure on our southern border will become even greater than it is now.

We have also not adequately examined how this bill will affect our own economy, particularly in the Southwest. In some cities, like Los Angeles, there would be no apparel industry if it were not for workers from Mexico. In Houston almost one-third of all construction workers are undocumented—doing jobs that many Americans refuse to do. I am not suggesting that we rely on illegal workers to underpin our economy, but rather that we need to examine the true role these workers play in our economy, and to make sure that this legislation does not harm us in the long run. That is why I opposed establishing a new temporary worker program. I believe S. 1200 does provide some flexibility to address the needs of the perishable crop industry and that further attention is needed to better assist this unique industry.

In the long term we must maintain better control of the border. I am seriously considering a plan to develop a border management agency that will help combat illegal activities along the border. Presently, law enforcement along the border is handled by at least three different Federal agencies: the Customs Bureau, the Immigration and Naturalization Service, and the Drug Enforcement Administration. The border agency would combine many of these functions now performed by these separate agencies, thereby strengthening law enforcement along the border. The border management agency would also address the many other problems, such as water and boundary disputes, air and water quality, and health and sanitation.

I know the solution to our immediate immigration problem is a complex one, and although I cannot support the bill before us today I believe that we must not turn our backs on the problem. We must all search for the correct combination that balances the civil liberties of individuals and the interests of all Americans, while still taking into consideration the very real problems of the neighbor on our southern border.

Reprinted with permission by Congressional Digest Corp., from "Should Congress Enact Senate-Passed Immigration Reform Legislation." *Congressional Digest*. Washington, D.C. March 1986.

John F. Kerry

I applaud the efforts of the Senator from Wyoming to achieve a comprehensive bill for reform of our immigration laws. I realize how difficult it is to put together a package which attempts to satisfy many different interest groups, and at the same time addresses the very real problems posed by a massive influx of immigrants into our society. I admire the dedication and persistence of my colleague from Wyoming, and I appreciate his efforts in this task.

However, having said that, I must add that I have serious reservations about this legislation in its current form. I am very mindful of the need for reform of our immigration laws, and I had very much hoped that a bill would emerge from our deliberations here which I could support without reservation. Regrettably, because of certain amendments which have been added to this legislation, particularly with regard to allowing a massive influx of "guest workers" which would create a reprise of the failed Bracero program of an earlier era, I can no longer support this legislation in its current form.

I am also concerned that this bill, in its current form, perpetuates an injustice to aliens currently residing in this country who are eligible for legalization by saying to them, in effect, that you can live here and become eligible for legal status in 3 years, but you can't be legally hired in the meantime. This is an unfair result which we cannot in good conscience permit.

Many undocumented aliens have been in this country for a number of years, and have families and children here. Many of them have come from countries where they suffered from political persecution, death squads, repression, and guerrilla warfare. In many cases, it would be impossible for these people to return to their homes. In addition, these are people who have come to this country seeking a better life, and have settled here and developed roots here. They have become productive members of our economy and our society, even without the benefit of U.S. citizenship. Surely we have not forgotten that we are, in the words of John F. Kennedy, "a nation of immigrants." It is therefore appropriate that we recognize the suffering that these people have endured, and the contributions that they have made, by legalizing their status in this country, and allowing them to enjoy the full benefits of U.S. citizenship. For this reason, I have supported the amendment of my distinguished colleague from Massachusetts, Senator Kennedy, which would advance the cutoff date for legalization to January 1, 1981, and would eliminate the requirement for a legalization commission to study this problem.

I am deeply concerned that this legislation may become a vehicle for discriminatory actions against Hispanic Americans and other minority groups. For this reason, I have strongly supported efforts to strengthen the bill in this regard.

In addition, I have been pleased to cosponsor an amendment which would ensure that visitors to this country are not denied nonimmigrant visas because of their political beliefs. Under current law, a visitor to this country may be denied a temporary visa for any one of 33 reasons contained in the McCarran-Walters Act. This act is an outgrowth of the McCarthy era in our country. It is a national embarrassment. The fundamental difference between our system and that of other repressive regimes is that we enjoy freedom of thought and freedom of speech. Our society has benefited immeasurably from the free flow of ideas and information. We should be setting an example to the rest of the world of what a free society is. By removing the present ideological restrictions on visitors to this country, we send a message to the world about the kind of society we are. I might add that this amendment would continue to exclude those who would engage in terrorism, espionage, sabotage, criminal activity, or would be a threat to our national security. But at the same time it would say that no one will be excluded on the basis of his or her lawful political beliefs, activities, or associations. An open society makes us stronger, not weaker.

I supported efforts to prevent discrimination on the basis of alienage. All of these amendments strengthen this legislation, and make it more fair and equitable. I deeply regret that the Senate has chosen to pass an amendment expanding the "guest worker" provisions of this legislation.

This amendment allows expansion of the foreign guest worker program to unpredictable levels. Many Americans recall the Bracero Program which existed in this country from 1946 to 1964. It permitted nearly 500,000 Mexican nationals into this country to work in agriculture, and led to widespread abuse by employers. The current amendment would expand the current guest worker program to nearly the scope of the Bracero Program, and would repeat the mistakes of that program.

With the changes I have outlined, I would feel free to give my wholehearted support to this legislation. Without them, I fear that we would do more harm than good. I support the effort to reform our immigration laws. But let us be sure that we do so in a manner that does justice to our Constitution, our American values, and our tradition as a nation of immigrants.

History has shown that, once an immigration law is enacted, Congress does not act again for many years. It is therefore imperative, when we are considering the subject of reform of our immigration laws, that we be sure to pass the very best bill we can, in order to correct the injustices that have been done in the past, and to ensure that they are not perpetuated into the future. I am very hopeful that many of the problems with this bill can be resolved in conference, and that a bill will then emerge which I can support wholeheartedly. But for now, I must reluctantly cast my vote against this legislation.

ISSUE 15

Is the Women's Movement Over?

Inequality between the sexes existed before the 1960s and may have always existed. From what is known of preliterate societies, men seem to have been generally dominant. Many anthropologists argue that the superior strength of the male and the reproductive function of the female are responsible for this traditional male dominance. Most societies have been patriarchal, with power residing in the male head-of-the-household.

The view of women during the early Christian era was based on the Hebrew tradition which considered women to be a necessary evil subject to the authority of men. There was even debate over whether or not women had souls. It was Paul who said in I Corinthians: "For the man is not of the woman, but the woman is of the man. Neither was the man created for the woman; but the woman for the man." Women were considered to be inferior to men and as Christianity spread, so did this conception of women.

In Colonial America, wives had little legal status apart from their husbands. Women had fewer property and other legal rights than did men. Abigail Adams beseeched her husband John to limit the power of husbands over wives in the new American government.

Most historians place the beginnings of the women's movement in the first half of the nineteenth century. The anti-slavery movement seems to have been the catalyst for the early feminists. At the World's Anti-Slavery Convention in England in 1840, two delegates from the United States were not seated because they were women. Eight years later, the first women's rights meeting in the United States was held in Seneca Falls, N.Y. Prominent women such as Susan B. Anthony, Julia Howe, and Lucy Stone attended and worked from that time until the Civil War to eliminate slavery.*

After the Civil War was over and black males had been given the vote, these women focused more directly on women's issues. After years of effort, only four states, Wyoming, Colorado, Idaho, and Utah, had given the vote to women. Congress finally approved the Nineteenth Amendment to the Constitution, giving women the right to vote, in 1919.

There was hope, and fear in some quarters, that women would vote as a bloc. It soon became apparent that there was little difference between the voting behavior of men and women. They both tended to vote along class lines.

Between 1920 and 1963 there appears to have been a lull in the women's movement. The Great Depression of the 1930s made opportunities scarce for everyone. The prevailing sentiment seems to have been that if there was a job available, it should go to a man. World War II produced a permanent change in U.S. society. With millions of men going into the military during the early 1940s, the United States turned to the most logical pool of available labor: women. Millions of women got better jobs at better pay with better conditions than ever before.

After the war, there was a new conflict for American society. Many women who had gone into the labor force were unwilling to return to the traditional roles of wife and mother. During the "baby boom" years, stretching from the late 1940s to the early 1960s, the number of women in the labor force continued to increase. Working mothers became a fixture of the American scene.

The publication of Betty Friedan's *The Feminine Mystique* in 1963 is considered by many to represent the revival of the women's movement. Her book was an attack on the notion that women could only be happy in the traditional roles of wife and mother. In 1966 Friedan, along with other prominent women, formed the National Organization for Women (NOW). Many NOW members are middle-class professional women who push for structured changes in the legal, economic, and political spheres. There are now a number of other feminist organizations—some pushing for radical changes and some focusing on interpersonal relationships.

Many things have been accomplished by the women's movement. Most feminists would argue, however, that the job is not complete. Women still experience discrimination in a variety of areas. When the Equal Rights Amendment (ERA) was not ratified, some of the spark seemed to have left the movement. Phyllis Schlafly played a significant role in the demise of the ERA. Coming out of a conservative background, she argued that the

*For additional background, see Lucile Duberman, *Gender and Sex in Society*. Praeger, 1975.

American family would be seriously disrupted and that relations between the sexes would be changed to the woman's disadvantage if the amendment were passed. In the articles that follow, Schlafly presents her opinion that the women's movement is over, and Friedan discusses how to get the movement moving again.

ISSUE 15 YES:

The Two-Class American Society

Phyllis Schlafly

Is the traditional family an anachronism in the 1980s? That seems to be the assumption of television and radio talk shows, lecture platforms, lifestyle sections of metropolitan newspapers, magazines, the theater and movies, public opinion surveys, and all the channels that report socio-cultural trends. This dreary message is beamed at the public, overtly and subliminally, in a thousand ways every week.

The economic side of this message is that all wives will soon be out of the home and in the paid labor force, and that this trend is not only an economic "necessity" but a social good. We are told incessantly that a single-earner couple cannot support a family, that mothers "have to work" in order to support their families, and that the wife in the home is as extinct as the dodo bird.

What is presumptuously called "the women's movement" has supposedly "liberated" women from the menial drudgery of housework and given women new opportunities for careers in the paid labor force, especially in nontraditional (formerly all-male) occupations (from astronaut to coal miner).

The social side of this message is that "sexual liberation" has permanently changed moral attitudes, made any sexual activity socially acceptable, and redefined the "family" to include any group of persons living together even if not related by blood, marriage or adoption. "Alternate lifestyles" are now supposedly acceptable, including serial marriage (frequent changing of partners through multiple divorces), cohabitation without marriage, and homosexual and lesbian couples.

Premarital sex among teenagers is asserted to be a permanent fact of life. We are not supposed to be judgmental about this but instead make it free from guilt and pregnancy by contraceptives and abortion clinics without parental knowledge or consent. Some people even propose that high school clinics aid and abet promiscuity by handing out free contraceptives.

Everybody, we are told, will probably be divorced at some time in their life. "Single parenthood" is the modern-style family. Divorce-on-demand must be made available to any spouse without the consent of the other. Abortion-on-demand should be available to any woman without the consent of the other spouse (or the parent of the minor).

Taxpayers are supposed to pay the horrendous financial costs of all these policies, including child-care for mothers who prefer to be in the paid labor force, separate housing and generous money payments to teenagers who have illegitimate babies, tax-paid abortions, and a variety of costly benefits to divorced wives whose husbands have been allowed to evade their support obligations.

We have the freedom to choose our own values and goals. But the frequency and intensity (often combined with ridicule and sarcasm) with which media spokespersons try to thrust these anti-family attitudes down our throats indicates their emotional demand for social acceptance of these changes in values. They seem determined to make those who live by traditional moral standards the ones who are out of step with the times.

These anti-family attitudes have established themselves as dominant in the fantasy world of communications, but they have not succeeded in the real world. Despite persistent hammering through news and entertainment, the majority of Americans have rejected the whole line. In this other unreported portion of our society, people believe in the work ethic, and they resent paying high taxes for handouts.

In this other unreported section of our society, people consider marriage a lifetime commitment, in sickness and in health, for richer and for poorer. They look upon marriage as the beginning of a new family in which children will bear their father's name and are entitled to faithful nurturing by a full-time mother. A recent survey shows that, among couples who marry in church and continue to attend church regularly, the divorce rate is only one in 50.

America has become a two-class society. The class division has nothing whatsoever to do with level of income or education or job status or talent or sex or race or color or advantage/disadvantage of birth. It has everything to do with whether or not you have a commitment (1) to moral values (i.e., respect for God, church/synagogue, and the Ten Commandments), (2) to family values (i.e., marital fidelity, mothercare of children, and parental rights in education, (3) to the work ethic (i.e., hard work, thrift, savings, and the right to enjoy the fruits of one's labor and improve one's economic lot in life).

The Americans who share these traditional commitments have almost no voice in the channels of communication today. But these Americans exist, and the more the media claim they are obsolete, the more the media lose credibility.

FASHIONS IN MORALS

One day I asked my children, "Why is it that none of the six of you is a smoker? Is it because your dad and mother don't smoke? Or is it because you were dissuaded by our repeated sermons on the health risks of smoking?" "Neither," one of my children replied. "It's because it isn't 'cool' to smoke any more. Maybe it was 'in' to smoke when you were young, but it just isn't fashionable any more."

The *Wall Street Journal* discovered this phenomenon in a page-one news story. Smoking is not only becoming socially non-acceptable; non-smoking is becoming more identified with career success at the high-income business and professional levels. The *Journal* even quoted a professor at the University of California at San Diego who predicts that cigarette smoking will continue to decline and will "disappear in the next 20 to 25 years." It will become, he says, "like cigar smoking—unusual."

The decline is particularly marked among teenagers. That's also particularly significant because those who don't begin smoking before age 21 seldom start at all. What is so fascinating about this topic is the cause of the decline. It appears to be much more a matter of fad and fashion than of logic, health, morals, or money.

If anyone had predicted 25 years ago that the percentage of smokers would voluntarily and massively decline, despite high-powered advertising and teenage peer pressure, the prophet probably would have been laughed at. Common wisdom tells us that we can't stop teenagers from experimenting; and that's when their addiction starts.

The profiteers of promiscuity have a much larger advertising budget and more effective advertising techniques than the tobacco companies. The powerful forces making money out of the playboy lifestyle include the commercial industries selling abortion, contraceptives, divorce, pornography, and entertainment.

Some of these profiteers of promiscuity sell their wares through the powerful medium of television (now banned to tobacco companies). The big majority of dramatizations about sex on primetime television involve sex outside of marriage.

Some of these profiteers of promiscuity even advertise their wares in the public schools. Most so-called sexuality education classes are really sales meetings for contraceptives and abortion services, and the "teen clinics" that some people are now trying to put into the public schools would be exactly that.

For the last 15 years, the promiscuity propaganda has been falsely telling young women that they are just the same as men, just as sexually driven, and have just as much right as men to be promiscuous and independent of family and children. The trouble is that sex is not equal as between men and women.

The playboy lifestyle is the real exploitation of women. The pregnancy is borne by the woman, not the man. The contraceptives with their side effects and the abortion with its trauma are thrust upon the woman, not the man. The out-of-wedlock births usually mean permanent poverty for the mothers. Venereal diseases are more hurtful to the woman than the man and can be deadly to her future babies.

Easy divorce, heralded in the early 1970s as legislation to liberate women, has caused economic devastation to women. The divorced woman's financial status is usually cut in half while her ex-husband's lot is significantly improved.

Can we hope that teenage promiscuity, like smoking, might go out of style and that virginity until marriage might again become fashionable? Brooke Shields' new message to teenage girls is to remind them of their right to say "no," and, "if the situation gets out of control, leave. You'll probably gain his respect." Even Dan Rather on the CBS Evening News has proclaimed that weddings, complete with white bridal gown, are back again, even for women marrying for the first time in their thirties.

BLURRING GENDER IDENTITY

A recent article by a left-handed writer summarized very well the centuries-old unreasonable and unfeeling discrimination which society has imposed on left-handed persons. He told how growing up in the New York public schools in the 1930s and 1940s meant repeated whacks from teachers who tried to force him to write with his right hand.

This writer reminded us that anti–left-handed bias is enshrined even in the language of Western civilization. The Latin for left hand, "sinister," translates into evil in English. The French for left hand, "gauche," means crude or awkward in English.

When the mistaken belief that enlightened education should endeavor to correct left-handedness was finally relegated to the junk heap of quack psychology, a remarkable fact occurred in U.S. statistical annals. Between 1932 and 1970, the recorded percentage of left-handed people rose from 2% to 10% of our population. Since it is incredible that the percentage actually increased so dramatically, the statistics could reflect a new willingness of southpaws to admit they are different, or the anonymous bureaucrats' willingness to admit that left-handedness is just as normal as right-handedness, or both.

Modern scientific, medical, and psychological opinion now teaches that it is wrong—physically and psychologically—for teachers to try to force left-handers to be right-handers. I wonder if, a few decades hence, writers will comment as condescendingly on the peculiar pedagogical passion of the 1970s and 1980s to force boys to abandon their boyishness and girls to abandon their girlishness.

Those who have not kept up with trends in the classroom would be surprised to learn how pervasive is this passion. The feminist women's movement, operating like a censorship gestapo, has combed the primary-grade readers, all school textbooks, and career-guidance materials in order to eradicate the natural gender traits of youngsters and to produce a gender-neutral society.

In the late 1970s, the major textbook publishers, such as Macmillan and McGraw Hill, published "guidelines for the elimination of sexism," which listed the words, illustrations, and concepts that would henceforth be censored out of all textbooks. This impudent intolerance galloped unchecked through school materials, so now the feminists have presumed to rewrite children's stories in order to teach that women are strong and men are bad.

Once upon a time, children read a charming allegory about "The Little Steam Engine That Could." It told how the little engine, with a lot of effort and another engine's help, climbed a mountain. The currently-used edition published by Scholastic, Inc., identifies itself on the title page as "The Complete, Original Edition retold by Wally Piper." What does "retold" mean? It means that the good, kind, hard-working engines in the story are identified as female, while the bad, arrogant, selfish engines are identified as male.

Despite all the attempts to blur gender identity by, for example, showing pictures of girls playing with snakes and boys using hair spray, and even to pervert the English language by forcing schoolchildren to use such pronouns as he/she or s/he, there is no evidence that human nature is changing. The attempt to change it confuses the youth and frustrates the adults.

A case in point is a hilarious article in the *Washington Post* called "Boys Just Want to Have Guns." The *Post's* staff writer admitted that her three-year-old son, and the sons of all her pacifist-feminist-yuppie friends, despite their parents' persistent efforts (bringing them up sex-neutral, with no toy guns, and no TV except "Sesame Street"), nevertheless are naturally, irrepressibly male: boyish, aggressive, and fascinated by guns.

In addition, she moaned, the daughters of "what used to be the Berkeley left," given trucks and airplanes, still go for dolls and dress up with jewelry. "The boys slug each other and the girls paint their fingernails. Where are they getting this stuff?", she asks.

It's not just little girls and little boys who rebel at the blurring of gender identity. The magazine *Working Woman* featured an article called "Does the New Woman Really Want the New Man?" The consensus in this feminist magazine was a frustrated No. The author complained that, while the New Man is no longer possessive, he's also no longer committed. So, warns the author, the New Woman won't find "the classic knight on the white charger" and may have to settle for a man who just benefits from her energy and follows where she leads. But, the author ruefully concludes, "her heaviest liability is a likelihood of winding up alone."

BETTY FRIEDAN AND THE FEMINIST MYSTIQUE

The *New York Times Magazine*, which three years ago gave us an article called "Voices from the Post-Feminist Generation," put another nail in the coffin of feminism by publishing Betty Friedan's article called "How to Get the Women's Movement Moving Again." That title and the accompanying artwork clearly convey the message that the women's liberation movement is stopped dead in its tracks.

Friedan has discovered that young women believe that "women's rights are not chic in America any more" and that feminism has become "a dirty word." She admits that "the movement is in trouble," that it has been wasting its energy in "a bitter, vengeful internal power struggle," and that feminist nostalgia harks back to "old rhetoric, old ideas, old modes of action."

Friedan made her fame and fortune by interviewing suburban housewives, diagnosing their difficulties as a "problem that had no name," and reciting their litany of tiresome complaints in her 1964 best-seller called *The Feminine Mystique*. She is the founder of the movement of women who believe that they are an oppressed minority.

Friedan's article is a direct appeal to the nonradical feminists to regroup and take up the fight for "second-stage feminism." Her betes noires in this battle are the Reagan Administration and "the paralysis that fundamentalist backlash has imposed on all our movements," on liberalism and humanism as well as feminism.

It's clear that Friedan has learned a lot that her radical feminist sisters have yet to learn. Since she is the godmother of the 21-year-old women's liberation movement, her admissions in this article are significant.

Friedan's recent interviewees, she says, are women "trying to 'have it all,' having second thoughts about her professional career, desperately trying to have a baby before it is too late, with or without husband, and maybe secretly blaming the movement for getting her into this mess."

She urges women to "confront the illusion of equality in divorce," citing the new book by Lenore Weitzman called *The Divorce Revolution: The Unexpected Social and Economic Consequences for Women and Children in America*. This book details how, after all states adopted easy, no-fault divorce laws, divorced women and their children suffered an immediate 73% drop in their standard of living, while their ex-husbands enjoyed a 42% rise in theirs.

Weitzman shows how the "equal" division of the marital property was grievously hurtful to wives because it denied the wife a share in the growth of the husband's earning power which she had helped to create, and also because it usually meant the forced sale of the house (which formerly was awarded to the wife and children).

The truth of the matter is that the economic consequences of the no-fault divorce laws were not unexpected; they were predicted by those who then opposed easy divorce laws. Millions of women have been economically devastated by the change in divorce laws—one of the few legislative "successes" of which the feminist movement can boast.

Friedan freely admits that "feminists originally supported" no-fault divorce laws. Now she calls for "urgent grassroots political support" to get rid of them.

After admitting they were wrong about divorce laws, Friedan calls on women to "affirm the differences between men and women." Would you believe! She brashly admits a fundamental error of her movement: that "first-stage feminism denied real differences between women and men except for the sexual organs themselves."

Now she says what must be to unenlightened first-stage feminists the ultimate heresy: "Bring in the men. It's passe, surely, for feminists now to see men only as the enemy."

Finally, Friedan admonishes feminists to "move beyond single-issue thinking" because she does not think that "women's rights are the most urgent business for American women. The important thing is somehow getting together with men."

Perhaps Friedan's *Times* article will develop into another best-selling book under a new title, "The Feminist Mystique." It certainly is an interesting study in psychology to catalogue the changing attitudes of feminists as the biological clock ticks on.

However, an even better title when Friedan writes about "beyond the second stage" would be "The Feminist Mistake."

MS. MAGAZINE DISCOVERS HUMAN NATURE

I must confess that I never would have read the magazine if Eastern Airlines hadn't provided free copies as I boarded the shuttle at LaGuardia Airport. But as I thumbed the pages of Gloria Steinem's *Ms. Magazine,* waiting for my plane to take off, I was fascinated at the change that has come about in this magazine since I last read it.

Fourteen years ago, the magazine featured pre-marriage contracts obliging husbands to do half the dishes and the diapers, and housewives' declarations of independence from essential housework. Today, there aren't any husbands or babies to complain about.

The first article that caught my eye was entitled "Learning to Flirt at 37." It was the confession of a mature feminist with a good job and an apartment of her own, who grew up in the sixties believing that flirting was "Victorian in the midst of the sexual revolution." After all those years of buying her own flowers, opening her own doors, and cooking dinner for herself after going to the movies alone, she actually answered an ad in the local newspaper headlined "Learn to Flirt."

She called the number listed, and the flirting teacher convinced her that even a feminist can flirt, if she uses time-tested arts. The teacher taught this feminist such simple techniques as *do* cross, uncross, and recross your legs, but *don't* cross your arms, and *do* imitate the seductive glances on soap operas, but *don't* initiate conversations on toxic waste removal. Next there was a tear-jerker article by a female author commiserating with a friend who was still mourning a break-up with her live-in boyfriend a year after it happened. As he told her when he casually signed off a two-year relationship, he "wasn't looking, it just happened; so don't take it personally."

The author then interviewed 87 victims of break-ups of live-in lovers. She found that the average duration of these extra-marital relationships was two years. The typical break-up occurs when the man wants out; but instead of saying so, he makes signals that the thrill is gone and leaves it to the women to define the relationship as ended.

I turned to an article called "Star Wars" but, alas, it wasn't about Reagan's SDI. It was about how men feel threatened when women's careers move faster and higher than their own. The illustration showed the man with a vacuum sweeper while the woman goes out with her briefcase; the unhappy look on the man's face is a sure sign that he won't be sticking around that household very long.

Another article confessed that the main topic on the conversation agenda of brainy, successful women is "the man shortage." The author acknowledged painfully that, "after 15-plus years of consciousness-raising and general feminist hell-raising, most middle-class women who are single and heterosexual still confine their search for mates to men who are well upscale of them in income and status."

Feminists since the 1970s have been trying to force us into a gender-neutral society and bring about sex-role reversals. Their ideology is based on the notion that gender differences are caused by stereotyped education and an oppressive male-dominated society.

So it was fascinating to read the article called "Designer Genes" which admits that men and women are naturally, biologically different. It proposes that "a committee of reputable biologists" engage in "genetic manipulation" to change human nature so that men and women will have an equal motivation, desire, and enjoyment of the sex act.

There are still, as in its early years, ads in *Ms. Magazine* for sexual aids mailed in plain wrappers and for lesbian contacts, but, mirabile dictu, there are bigger ads for diamond engagement rings, make-up, and sheer panty hose, plus a large color ad for a $195 doll called Scarlett O'Hara. It looks like "voices from the post-feminist generation," proclaimed three years ago by the *New York Times Magazine*, have even invaded *Ms. Magazine*.

Reprinted with permission by Phyllis Schlafly, from *The Phyllis Schlafly Report*, Vol. 19, No. 8, Section 1, March 1986.

ISSUE 15 NO:

How to Get the Women's Movement Moving Again

Betty Friedan

This is addressed to any woman who has ever said "we" about the women's movement, including those who say, "I'm not a feminist, but..." And it's addressed to quite a few men.

It's a personal message, not at all objective, and it's in response to those who think our modern women's movement is over—either because it is defeated and a failure, or because it has triumphed, its work done, its mission accomplished. After all, any daughter can now dream of being an astronaut, after Sally Ride, or running for President, after Geraldine Ferraro.

I do not think that the job of the modern women's movement is done. And I do not believe the movement has failed. For one thing, those of us who started the modern women's movement, or came into it after marriage and children or from jobs as "invisible women" in the office, still carry the glow of "it changed my whole life," an aliveness, the satisfaction of finding our own voice and power, and the skills we didn't have a chance to develop before.

I do believe, though, that the movement is in trouble. I was too passionately involved in its conception, its birth, its growing pains, its youthful flowering, to acquiesce quietly to its going gently so soon into the night. But, like a lot of other mothers, I have been denying the symptoms of what I now feel forced to confront as a profound paralysis of the women's movement in America. And this, in turn, has forced me to think about how we can get the women's movement moving again—a new round of consciousness-raising, for instance, or utilizing the networks of professional women, or ceasing the obsession with the matter of pornography.

I see as symptoms of the paralysis the impotence in the face of fundamentalist backlash; the wasting of energy in internal power struggles when no real issues are at stake; the nostalgic harking back to old rhetoric, old ideas, old modes of action instead of confronting new threats and new problems with new thinking; the failure to mobilize the young generation who take for granted the rights we won and who do not defend those rights as they are being taken away in front of our eyes, and the preoccupation with pornography and other sexual diversions that do not affect most women's lives. I sense an unwillingness to deal with the complex realities of female survival in male-modeled careers, with the new illusions of having it all in marriage and equality in divorce, and with the basic causes of the grim feminization of poverty. The potential of women's political power is slipping away between the poles of self-serving feminist illusion and male and female opportunism. The promise of that empowerment of women that enabled so many of us to change our own lives is being betrayed by our failure to mobilize the next generation to move beyond us.

Evidence of the movement's paralysis has been impinging on my own life in many ways:

- Over the last few years, I've noticed how the machinery for enforcing the laws against sex discrimination in employment and education has been gradually dismantled by the Reagan Administration, and how the laws' scope has been narrowed by the courts, with little public outcry. Professional lobbyists for women's organizations objected, of course, but there have been no mass protests from the women in the jobs and professions that those laws opened to them. In the early days of the National Organization for Women, nearly 20 years ago, we demanded and won an executive order banning Government contracts to companies or institutions guilty of sex discrimination; it was the first major weapon women could use to demand jobs. Some officials in the Administration are proposing the order's elimination. The Reagan Administration is also urging the courts to undo recent movement victories regarding equal pay for work of comparable value.
- The crusade against women's right to choice in the matter of childbirth and abortion, preached from the pulpits of fundamentalist churches and by the Catholic hierarchy, first achieved a ban on Federal aid to poor women seeking abortion, then the elimination of United States Government aid to third-world family-planning programs that counsel abortion. The Attorney General announced this summer he would seek to reverse the historic Supreme Court decision, Roe v. Wade, which 12 years ago decreed that the right of a woman to decide according to her own conscience when and whether and how many times to bear a child was as basic a right as any the Constitution originally spelled out for men.

At a recent meeting to mobilize women in mass communications to help save that right, I was amazed to hear a one-time radical feminist suggest that abortion should not be defended in terms of a woman's right. "Women's rights are not chic in America anymore," she argued.

- The main interest of many feminist groups in various states in recent years seems to be outlawing pornography. Laws prohibiting pornography as a form of sex discrimination and violation of civil rights have been proposed in Minnesota, Indiana, California and New York. A former NOW leader who practices law in upstate New York was startled, when she dropped in on a feminist fund-raiser, to be asked to support a nationwide ban on sexually explicit materials. When she warned, "A law like that would be far more dangerous to women than the most obscene pornography," she was greeted with incomprehension and hostility.

• At a black-tie banquet at the Plaza Hotel in New York in September, I proudly watched a sparkling parade of champion women athletes as they entertained the corporate donors who sponsor their games and scholarships through the 11-year-old Women's Sports Foundation. The women champions in basketball, judo, gymnastics, tennis, skiing, swimming, boxing, running and sports-car and dogsled racing paraded down the runway in sequined miniskirts and satin jumpsuits, clasping their hands over their heads in the victory gesture. They gave credit to parents and teachers, but not one mentioned the recent Supreme Court decision regarding Grove City College in Pennsylvania. That decision threatens to remove school athletic programs from the protection of the law banning sex discrimination in Federally assisted education—which is what provided crucial athletic training to these new female champions in the first place.

• At another reception, of one of the many new networks of women corporate executives, a woman in her late 30's, holding a job a woman had never been given before in a large insurance company, told me: "If my slot became open today, they wouldn't give it to a woman. Not because I haven't done a good job—I keep getting raises. But they've stopped talking about getting more women on the board—or in the company. The word has gone out from the White House: They don't have to worry anymore about women and blacks. It's over."

• At a media women's reception for Christine Craft, the last movement heroine to take a case to court against that particular mix of sex and age discrimination that threatens to impose a premature ceiling on the first generation of female broadcasters, women now hitting their 40's, many younger women competing for anchor jobs did not show up to support her.

• At one company, executives who faced class-action suits a decade ago now boast that their best new employees are the women. They were shocked when one of their star superwomen, on a rung very near the top, became pregnant with her second child and announced she was quitting. The boss even offered her an extended maternity leave, which is not required by law or union contract, but she quit anyway. "You may never have another chance like this," her colleagues, male and female, protested. "I'll never have these years with my children again," she answered. Most of them did not understand. They figured that whatever guilt or pressure she suffered trying to juggle baby and demanding job was her peculiar "personal problem."

• Another longtime feminist mother, with three "yuppie" daughters—banker, lawyer, talent agent—says, regretfully, "They're not feminists...they take all that for granted." She goes on to tell me that "Janey's problem is her love life and her job, and Ann's is her kids and her job, and Phyllis thinks maybe she should go back and get an M.B.A. With all that and exercise class, they don't have time for the meetings we used to go to. Why do they have to be feminists when they never had to suffer like we did?"

But the center for displaced housewives where this mother works—in a not-too-secure administrative job—may close down soon because of a cutoff in Government funds for job training. Seeking a part-time typist at $6,000 a year, the center was amazed to get more than 100 answers to a single ad, including women with degrees and years of job experience. Among the applicants was a long-divorced woman of retirement age who had served as a role model for feminist independence, enjoying brief celebrity for the self-help book she had written about her first brave years alone. Now she is applying for "any kind of job, typing, sales"—and has begun studying the ads for "household help." She is, to put it bluntly, desperate.

• I have breakfast with two of my younger colleagues in the movement, the best and brightest, the kind that should be moving now into national leadership. One tells me she is leaving for a new job in foreign affairs. She has developed her women's rights office into such fine professional shape that "any good pro can run it now." She needs a new purpose, room to grow. The other, barely 30, has the professional skills, honed during 10 years of service to the women's movement, but is not interested in the movement job. "What's the use of all this professionalism if the grass-roots movement isn't there?" she shrugs. "What's wrong with it?"

I ask. "There's a yearning for the same old music, the same old marches, by the ones who still meet in the church basements," she says. "But they are the desperate ones, the lonely ones and the pros like myself who still make some kind of living off the movement. Let's face it, the yuppies—I hate that word—who are in the halfway decent jobs that the movement opened to women don't relate to the old rhetoric. The new professional networks, which supposedly help them get ahead, don't even pretend to be feminist anymore."

Thinking of my own daughter-the-doctor and my daughter-in-law the editor-mother, I realize how much more complex, confident, vital and pressured their lives are than ours were. Their problems, putting it all together, keep them too busy to go to meetings. But are their problems as serious as those of the desperate housewives and the invisible women in the offices 20 years ago? Or as serious as those of the women struggling alone for economic and emotional survival today? Do women who are moving ahead in their own lives have less in common with the desperate ones? Do they even want to deny the very possibility of that desperation? (We were all pretty desperate then.)

This last year, books, articles and notices of television programs have been piling up on my desk about these new problems of "the postfeminist generation." "Smart Women, Foolish Choices," for instance, and "Lesser Lives." This growing chorus expresses a personal disillusionment with male-defined careers, a faintheartedness about "having it all," a rebellion against superwoman standards, a sense of malaise or guilt or regret about prices paid in marriage or with children—and a recurring theme of "not wanting to be like a man."

- For most of this year, NOW has been locked in a bitter, vengeful internal power struggle. Eleanor Smeal, for whom the limit of a four-year presidency of NOW had been waived for the duration of the equal rights amendment battle, came out of retirement to run against her successor, Judy Goldsmith, in midterm. She blamed her for NOW's depleted treasury and loss of members, and demanded a return to street demonstrations for E.R.A. and free choice in abortion. Many older feminists, who thought both had been good leaders for their time, deplored the waste of energy in such a clash, as powerful enemies were closing in. Futile nostalgia for the radical marching tunes of another day will not enlist a new generation, in different circumstances, to save the rights now being taken away. But the weakening of the organization and the longing for the old sense of empowerment are real enough—and not likely to be solved by recriminations that, unfortunately, continue to divide NOW since Eleanor Smeal's return to power.

Aware of these symptoms, and yet denying my own sense that the American women's movement was over, not ready to admit defeat but wanting to move on to other things myself, I went to Kenya last summer out of a sheer sense of historic duty to see the thing through to its end. Most card-carrying American feminists were not even bothering with the meeting in Nairobi. NOW had scheduled its own convention in New Orleans at the same time as the United Nations World Conference of Women.

Ten years earlier, when the modern women's movement was spreading from America to the world, I had joined women wanting to organize in their countries in appealing to the U.N. to call a world assembly of women. At the first two world women's meetings, in Mexico in 1975 and Copenhagen in 1980, I had seen the beginnings of international networking among women broken up by organized disrupters led by armed gunmen shouting slogans against "imperialism" and "Zionism." I had been appalled at the way the official male delegates from Arab countries and other third-world and Communist nations that control the U.N. showed contempt for women's rights; using those conferences mainly to launch a new doctrine of religious and ethnic hate, equating Zionism and racism. And I had been repelled by the way the delegates from Western countries, mostly male officials or their wives and female flunkies, let them thereby rob those conferences of the moral and political weight they might have given to the advance of women worldwide. This year, the United States delegation had instructions from President Reagan to walk out if the question of Zionism was included in the conclusions reached at Nairobi.

To my amazement, the women's movement emerged in Nairobi with sufficient strength worldwide to impose its own agenda of women's concerns over the male political agenda that had divided it before. Despite, or because of, the backlash and other problems they face at home, nearly 17,000 women from 159 nations assembled, some 14,000 having paid their own way or been sent by volunteer, church or women's groups to the unofficial forum that is part of every such U.N. conference. Some traveled by plane three and four days, or by bus from African villages.

There was a bypassing, or bridging, of the old, abstract ideological conflicts that had seemed to divide women before—a moving beyond the old rhetoric of career versus family, equality versus development, feminism versus socialism, religion versus feminism, or feminism as an imperialist capitalist arrogance irrelevant to poor third-world women. What took the place of all this was a discussion of concrete strategies for women to acquire more control of their lives. Third-world revolutionaries, Arab and Israeli women, as well as Japanese, Greeks and Latins, gathered under a baobab tree where, every day at noon, like some African tribal elder, I led a discussion on "Future Directions of Feminism."

We shared common concerns about how to move ahead and earn a living in man's world—as women, even in African villages, now have to do—without losing, even using, one's best values and strengths as women. We talked about how to keep forging ahead as women when other questions—like the Israeli-Arab conflict or the superpowers' nuclear-arms race—are preoccupying our nations and using up their resources. We shared ideas on how to keep advancing, even underground, when fundamentalist groups try to take away a woman's right to control her own body or to move independently in the world, as they are doing in Egypt and the United States and have done in Iran.

When the black-veiled Iranian women, in their chadors and with their armed male guards, occupied my tree one day, we moved to another, and when they occupied both trees, we carried on our dialogue in the sun. "That's the way women have to move now everywhere in the world," I said. "We go forward, we get pushed back, we regroup. It's not a win-lose battle, to be finished in any year." "And we don't waste energy on nonessentials," said an African teacher.

At the official U.N. conference in Nairobi, American women delegates, mainly Republicans led by Maureen Reagan, the President's daughter, were working the hall for consensus on forward-looking strategies on equality that included things American feminists hardly dare dream of in Reagan's Washington—parental leave, child care, family planning and an economic value for women's work in home and field counted in a nation's G.N.P. as well as equal pay for work of comparable value. Many of the other delegations from European, Latin American, African and Asian nations were now led by or included women who had been fighting for women's rights at home. Ninety percent of the world's governments have set up national bodies for the advancement of women, most of them in this last decade, while ours in the United States have been dismantled.

At Nairobi, when Arab and Communist delegations engaged, as usual, in "anti-Zionist" and "anti-imperialist" rhetoric, these strong women delegates, especially the Africans, kept warning that the women of the world would condemn those who blocked consensus on equality. And they forced the male diplomats to negotiate round the clock until they deleted that anti-Zionist expression of hate that has been ritual at every U.N. conference since 1975. To the amazement of experts, a program involving forward-looking strategies to advance women to equality was adopted by consensus of the nations of the world, calling on the U.N. to implement them and to report back to another world assembly of women before the year 2000.

I and other Americans—as many black as white among the 2,000 of us at Nairobi—went home strengthened, resolved not to accept backward-nation status for American women. For though we had gone to Nairobi subdued by our own setbacks and sophisticated enough not to offer Western feminism as the answer to the problems of women of the third world, it was truly humiliating to discover that we are no longer the cutting edge of modern feminism or world progress toward equality. Even Kenya has an equal rights clause in its Constitution!

How can we let the women's movement die out here in America when what we began is taking hold now all over the world? I would like to suggest 10 things that might be done to break the blocks that seem to have stymied the women's movement in America:

1. Begin a new round of consciousness-raising for the new generation. These women, each thinking she is alone with her personal guilt and pressures, trying to "have it all," having second thoughts about her professional career, desperately trying to have a baby before it is too late, with or without husband, and maybe secretly blaming the movement for getting her into this mess, are almost as isolated, and as powerless in their isolation, as those suburban housewives afflicted by "the problem that had no name" whom I interviewed for "The Feminine Mystique" over 20 years ago. Those women put a name to their problem; they got together with other women in the new feminist groups and began to work for political solutions and began to change their lives.

That has to happen again to free a new generation of women from its new double burden of guilt and isolation. The guilts of less-than-perfect motherhood and less-than-perfect professional career performance are real because it's not possible to "have it all" when jobs are still structured for men whose wives take care of the details of life, and homes are still structured for women whose only responsibility is running their families. I warned five years ago that if the women's movement didn't move into a second stage and take on the problems of restructuring work and home, a new generation would be vulnerable to backlash. But the movement has not moved into that needed second stage, so the women struggling with these new problems view them as purely personal, not political, and no longer look to the movement for solutions.

Putting new names to their problems, they might stop feeling guilty for not being able to conduct their professional lives just like men, might give each other support in new patterns of professional advance and parenting, might together demand new political solutions of parental leave and child care from company or profession or community, or even, once again, from government. They might, then, find new energy to save the rights they now take for granted or even secretly resent, because they are so hard to live with.

2. Mobilize the new professional networks and the old established volunteer organizations to save women's rights. We can't fight fundamentalist backlash with backward-looking feminist fundamentalism. Second-stage feminism is itself pluralistic and has to use new pluralist strengths and strategies. The women who have been 30 and 40 percent of the graduating class from law school or business school and 47 percent of the journalism school classes, the ones who've taken women's studies, the women who grew up playing Little League baseball and cheered on those new champion women athletes, the new professional networks of women in every field, every woman who has been looking to those networks only to get ahead in her own field, must now use her professional skills to save the laws and executive orders against sex discrimination in education and employment. They must restore the enforcement machinery and the class-action suits that opened up all these opportunities to her in the first place.

The volunteer organizations, it became clear in Nairobi, have been given new goals and gumption and professional expertise by the women's movement. Let NOW heal its internal wounds and join with these other groups, as it did in the E.R.A. struggle, to face the current emergency, rather than indulge in wishful thinking about refighting the E.R.A. battle.

3. Get off the pornography kick and face the real obscenity of poverty. No matter how repulsive we may find pornography, laws banning books or movies for sexually explicit content could be far more dangerous to women. The pornography issue is dividing the women's movement and giving the impression on college campuses that to be a feminist is to be against sex. More important, it is diverting energies that need to be spent saving the basic rights now being destroyed.

Karen DeCrow, who once was elected president of NOW on the slogan "Out of the mainstream, into the revolution," wrote a recent article entitled "Strange Bedfellows" for Penthouse. She pointed out that the new feminist-supported proposals to make pornography an illegal violation of the civil rights of women have an unlooked-for effect. They aid the far right agenda that would also ban the teaching of evolution in schools, prohibit a woman's right to choose abortion, cut Government funding for textbooks that portray women in nontraditional roles, and repeal Federal statutes against spouse and child abuse.

What is behind some women's obsession with pornography? Women's sexuality has been distorted and suppressed in almost every society, we learned at Nairobi, and that suppression has gone hand in hand with a general attempt to deny women freedom to control their own lives, to move and earn independently in society. Pornography, and also the crusade to suppress pornography, reduce women to a single dimension, defining them as only passive sex objects, not people who can run their own lives.

But I think the secret this obsession with pornography may mask for women alone, for aging women, and for women still more economically dependent on men than they would like, is fear of poverty, which is the ultimate obscenity for Americans. I sat at a dinner table recently with several women, who I know are struggling personally with these problems, and could not believe their venom against the young rock star Madonna. I suggested that teen-agers identified with her gutsiness, strength and independence as well as with her not-at-all-passive sexuality, which to me was not a retreat from women's liberation, but a celebration of it. Whoever said that feminism shouldn't be sexy!

They were women in their 40's, 50's and 60's, and they virtually spat in disgust. Perhaps an unspoken reason so many women are protesting sexually explicit materials is that their own sexuality is denied by society. But I suspect that as long as sex is distorted by women's economic dependence, or fear of it, it can't be truly, freely enjoyed. The obscenity that not even many feminists want to confront in personal terms is the sheer degradation of being poor in opulent, upwardly mobile America. Of course, the women's movement in America, like all such revolutions everywhere, has been mainly a middle-class movement, but the shameful secret it has never really dealt with is the fact that more and more middle-class women are sinking into poverty.

America's first movement for women's rights died out after winning the vote, four generations ago, because women didn't tackle the hard political tasks of restructuring home and work so that women who married and had children could also earn and have their own voice in the decision-making mainstream of society. Instead, those women retreated behind a cultural curtain of female "purity," focusing their energies on issues like prohibition, much like the pornographic obsession of some feminists today.

4. Confront the illusion of equality in divorce. Economists and feminists have been talking a lot lately about "the feminization of poverty" in theoretical terms, but the American women's movement has not developed concrete strategies that get at its root cause. It's not just a question of women earning less than men—though as long as women do not get equal pay for work of comparable value, or earn Social Security or pensions for taking care of children and home, they are both economically dependent on marriage and motherhood and pay a big economic price for it. And this is as true for divorced aging yuppies as for welfare mothers.

A startling new book by the sociologist Lenore J. Weitzman, "The Divorce Revolution: The Unexpected Social and Economic Consequences for Women and Children in America," reveals that in the 1970's, when 48 states adopted "no-fault" divorce laws treating men and women "equally" in divorce settlements—laws feminists originally supported—divorced women and their children suffered an immediate 73 percent drop in their standard of living, while their ex-husbands enjoyed a 42 percent rise in theirs.

In dividing "marital property," Lenore Weitzman reports, judges have systematically overlooked the major assets of many marriages—the husband's career assets that the wife helped make possible, his professional education that she may have helped support, the career on which he was able to concentrate because she ran the home, and his salary, pension, health insurance and earning power that resulted. They have also ignored the wife's years of unpaid housework and child care (not totally insured by Social Security in the event of divorce) and her drastically diminished job prospects after divorce. And, for most, the "equal" division of property means the forced sale of the family home—which used to be awarded to the wife and children. Child support, which has often been inadequate, unpaid and uncollectable, usually ends when the child is 18, just as college expenses begin. Thus the vicious cycle whereby an ever-increasing majority of the truly poor in America are families headed by women.

A new generation of feminist lawyers and judges has now drafted, and must get urgent grass-roots political support for, the kind of law needed, a law that treats marriage as a true economic partnership—and includes fairer standards of property division, maintenance and child support. It should be a law that does not penalize women who have chosen family over, or even together with, professional career.

5. Return the issue of abortion to the matter of women's own responsible choice. I think feminists have been so traumatized by the fundamentalist crusade against abortion and all the talk of fetuses and when life begins that they are in danger of forgetting the values that made abortion a feminist issue in the first place. Underneath the hysteria, poll after poll shows that the great majority of women in this nation, and most men, still want to decide when and whether to have a child in accordance with their own conscience. This includes women of faith, including the majority of Catholic women. Attacks on the Pope and picketing the churches, as some desperate or deranged male and female abortion champions have lately proposed, would play right into the hands of our "right to life" enemies, who love to paint feminists as satanic opponents of God and family. We must not surrender family values and religious principles to the far right. Let the new women theologians and feminist women of faith in every church take on the fundamentalist preachers.

I think women who are young, and those not so young, today must be able to choose when to have a child, given the necessities of their jobs. They will indeed join their mothers, who remember the humiliations and dangers of back-street butcher abortions, in a march of millions to save the right of legal abortion. I certainly support a march for women's choice of birth control and legal abortion. NOW has called for one in the spring of 1986.

6. Affirm the differences between men and women. New feminist thinking is required if American women are to continue advancing in man's world, as they must, to earn their way, and yet "not become like men." This fear is heard with more and more frequency today from young women, including many who have succeeded, and some who have failed or opted out of male-defined careers. More books like Carol Gilligan's "In a Different Voice" and consciousness-raising sessions are needed. First-stage feminism denied real differences between women and men except for the sexual organs themselves. Some feminists still do not understand that true equality is not possible unless those differences between men and women are affirmed and until values based on female sensitivities to life begin to be voiced in every discipline and profession, from architecture to economics, where, until recently, all concepts and standards were defined by men. This is not a matter of abstract theory alone but involves the restructuring of hours of work and patterns of professional training so that they take into account the fact that women are the people who give birth to children. It must lead to concrete changes in medical practice, church worship, the writing of history, standards of ethics, even the design of homes and appliances.

7. Breakthrough for older women. The women's movement has never put serious energy into the job that must be done to get women adequately covered by Social Security and pensions, especially those women now reaching 65 who spent many years as housewives and are ending up alone. The need for more independent and shared housing for older women now living alone in suburban houses they can't afford to sell, or lonely furnished rooms—and the need for services and jobs or volunteer options that will enable them to keep on living independent, productive lives—has never been a part of the women's movement agenda. But that first generation of feminist mothers, women now in their 60's, is a powerful political resource for the movement as these women retire from late or early professional or volunteer careers. Women in their 50's and 60's are shown by the polls to be more firmly committed than their daughters to the feminist goals of equality. Let the women's movement lead the rest of society in breaking the spell of the youth cult and drawing on the still enormous energies and the wisdom that may come to some of us in age.

8. Bring in the men. It's passé, surely, for feminists now to see men only as the enemy, or to contemplate separatist models for emotional or economic survival. Feminist theorists like Barbara Ehrenreich cite dismal evidence of the "new men" opting out of family responsibilities altogether. But in my own life I seem to see more and more young men, and older ones—even former male chauvinist pigs—admitting their vulnerability and learning to express their tenderness, sharing the care of the kids, even though most of them may never share it equally with their wives.

And as men let down their masks of machismo, and admit their dependence on the women in their lives, women may admit a new need to depend on men, without fear of sinking back into the old abject subservience. After all, even women who insist they are not, and never will be, feminists have learned to defend themselves against real male brutality. Look at Charlotte Donahue Fedders, the wife of that Security and Exchange commissioner, who testified in divorce court about his repeated abuse—his repeated beatings caused black eyes and a broken eardrum. At one time, a woman in her situation would have kept that shame a secret. The Reagan Administration had to ask him to resign, because wife-beating is no longer politically acceptable, even in conservative America in 1985.

I don't think women can, or should try to, take the responsibility for liberating men from the remnants of machismo. But there has to be a new way of asking what do men really want; to echo Freud, a new kind of dialogue that breaks through or gets behind both our masks. Women cannot restructure jobs or homes just by talking to themselves.

9. Continue to fight for real political power. Although feminists do not now, and never really did, support a woman just because she is a woman, there is no substitute for having women in political offices that matter. But more women are discovering that they have to fight, as men do, in primaries where victory is not certain, and not just wait for an "open seat." After the E.R.A.'s defeat, feminists and their supporters raised money nationally to run women candidates in virtually every district in Illinois, Florida and North Carolina where legislators voted against the amendment. And in that single election they increased sizably women's representation in those state legislatures.

10. Move beyond single-issue thinking. Even today, I do not think women's rights are the most urgent business for American women. The important thing is somehow getting together with men who also put the values of life first to break through the paralysis that fundamentalist backlash has imposed on all our movements. It is not only feminism that is becoming a dirty word in America, but also liberalism, humanism, pluralism, environmentalism and civil liberties. The very freedom of political dissent that enabled the women's movement to start here has been made to seem unsafe for today's young men as well as young women. I think the yuppies are afraid to be political.

Women may have to think beyond "women's issues" to join their energies with men to redeem our democratic tradition and turn our nation's power to the interests of life instead of the nuclear arms race that is paralyzing it. I've never, for instance, seen the need for a separate women's peace movement. I'm not really sure that women, by nature, are more peace-loving than men. They were simply not brought up to express aggression the way men do (they took it out covertly, on themselves and on their men and children, psychologists would say). But the human race may not survive much longer unless women move beyond the nurture of their own babies and careers to political decisions of war and peace, and unless men who share the nurture of their children take responsibility for ending the arms race before it destroys all life. In that sense, I think the women's movement is only a particular moment in human evolution, and once its job is really done, then it can and should be allowed to fade away, honorably discharged.

ISSUE 16

Is the World Headed for Disaster?

In 1798, Thomas Malthus published one of the most pessimistic statements ever made about the future of humankind. He argued in *An Essay on the Principle of Population* that if the population continued to increase without restraints, available resources would not be sufficient. If food resources increase, population will increase and outgrow available resources. If population growth is not restricted, the Malthusian positive checks of war, famine, and disease will control population size. Malthus proposed moral restraints, such as sexual abstinence before marriage and the postponement of marriage, to control population growth. Artificial birth control was repugnant to Malthus and was not considered as an alternative. The logical conclusions from the Malthusian assumptions were that if population growth remained unchecked, misery, hunger, and poverty were permanent conditions of the human race.

Malthus's dire predictions did not come to pass in Europe and, to a lesser extent, North America. The rapid drop in birth rates that occurred with the industrial revolution and the increases in crop yields from agricultural improvements helped Europe and North America avoid the "Malthusian Trap." Although population growth has slowed in industrial societies, the underdeveloped countries are still undergoing rapid population growth. Even the most conservative estimates see world population pressures continuing through the next century.

Population growth produces pressure on other world resources. Ecology, the branch of biology that concerns itself with the relationship between organisms and their environments, has taught us to think of the world as an eco-system. An *eco-system* is a self-sustaining environment. This notion of the eco-system has given us the concept of the "Spaceship Earth," a life-sustaining environment in the void of space. One of the obvious concerns is the possible destruction of critical parts of the eco-system. One example is the possibility of a "greenhouse effect." Scientists have been debating for years the effects of increased carbon dioxide in our atmosphere. The increase in carbon dioxide comes from our burning of solid wastes and fuels and from the destruction of forests and vegetation that convert carbon dioxide back to oxygen. Carbon dioxide is permeable to radiation in the form of light but not in the form of heat. Proponents of the greenhouse effect thus argue that the sun's rays pass through the carbon dioxide creating heat and that the heat is then trapped in the earth's atmosphere, operating in much the same way as an ordinary greenhouse. Raising the temperature of the earth a few degrees could cause the polar ice caps to start melting, thereby raising the water levels of the oceans. This could put large parts of the world's coast under water.

The greenhouse effect is still unproven. Some argue that the material pollutants we have put into the atmosphere have countered the effect by blocking out sunlight. In any case, many scientists and scholars are concerned about the inadvertent effect of tampering with the environment. The effects of acid rain, DDT, and mercury have already been demonstrated.

The Club of Rome, a private group, commissioned a study by a research team from the Massachusetts Institute of Technology. The study was published in 1972 with the title, *The Limits to Growth.* The research team created a computerized model of the world's eco-system, tracing the effects that population increases, food production, industrial output, pollution, and depletion of natural resources would have on each other. The model first assumed that current trends would continue unchanged. If so, the model predicted a shortage of natural resources causing an industrial collapse. The model then assumed a new source of abundant natural resources was discovered. The resulting industrial pollution created agricultural and environmental collapse. The study concluded that a state of global equilibrium in population growth and industrialization was the only solution.

The Limits to Growth study has been widely criticized. It was argued that the study dealt with a fixed, limited mathematical system. No matter how elaborate the set of variables used, it is possible, even probable, that significant omissions will occur. Other critics have argued that the inflexibility of the model does not allow for human ingenuity in developing new scientific breakthroughs and social solutions to problems. The history of humanity is the resolution of problems, and the resolution is often a new step in progress.

In the following articles, two perspectives are presented concerning the future. The *Global 2000 Report to the President* presents a generally negative picture. The world will be more crowded, more polluted, less stable, and generally an unpleasant place unless we alter present trends. Julian Simon counters the above, arguing that in the long-range view of things, population growth is good, natural resources are becoming less scarce, and pollution as measured by life expectancy and general cleanliness has lessened.

ISSUE 16 YES:

Global 2000: Major Findings and Conclusions

Council on Environmental Quality

If present trends continue, the world in 2000 will be more crowded, more polluted, less stable ecologically, and more vulnerable to disruption than the world we live in now. Serious stresses involving population, resources, and environment are clearly visible ahead. Despite greater material output, the world's people will be poorer in many ways than they are today.

For hundreds of millions of the desperately poor, the outlook for food and other necessities of life will be no better. For many it will be worse. Barring revolutionary advances in technology, life for most people on earth will be more precarious in 2000 than it is now—unless the nations of the world act decisively to alter current trends.

This, in essence, is the picture emerging from the U.S. Government's projections of probable changes in world population, resources, and environment by the end of the century, as presented in the Global 2000 Study. They do not predict what will occur. Rather, they depict conditions that are likely to develop if there are no changes in public policies, institutions, or rates of technological advance, and if there are no wars or other major disruptions. A keener awareness of the nature of the current trends, however, may induce changes that will alter these trends and the projected outcome.

PRINCIPAL FINDINGS

Rapid growth in world population will hardly have altered by 2000. The world's population will grow from 4 billion in 1975 to 6.35 billion in 2000, an increase of more than 50 percent. The rate of growth will slow only marginally, from 1.8 percent a year to 1.7 percent. In terms of sheer numbers, population will be growing faster in 2000 than it is today, with 100 million people added each year compared with 75 million in 1975. Ninety percent of this growth will occur in the poorest countries.

While the economies of the less developed countries (LDCs) are expected to grow at faster rates than those of the industrialized nations, the gross national product per capita in most LDCs remains low. The average gross national product per capita is projected to rise substantially in some LDCs (especially in Latin America), but in the great populous nations of South Asia it remains below $200 a year (in 1975 dollars). The large existing gap between the rich and poor nations widens.

World food production is projected to increase 90 percent over the 30 years from 1970 to 2000. This translates into a global per capita increase of less than 15 percent over the same period. The bulk of that increase goes to countries that already have relatively high per capita food consumption. Meanwhile per capita consumption in South Asia, the Middle East, and the LDCs of Africa will scarcely improve or will actually decline below present inadequate levels. At the same time, real prices for food are expected to double.

Arable land will increase only 4 percent by 2000, so that most of the increased output of food will have to come from higher yields. Most of the elements that now contribute to higher yields—fertilizer, pesticides, power for irrigation, and fuel for machinery—depend heavily on oil and gas.

During the 1990s world oil production will approach geological estimates of maximum production capacity, even with rapidly increasing petroleum prices. The Study projects that the richer industrialized nations will be able to command enough oil and other commercial energy supplies to meet rising demands through 1990. With the expected price increases, many less developed countries will have increasing difficulties meeting energy needs. For the one-quarter of humankind that depends primarily on wood for fuel, the outlook is bleak. Needs for fuelwood will exceed available supplies by about 25 percent before the turn of the century.

While the world's finite fuel resources—coal, oil, gas, oil shale, tar sands, and uranium—are theoretically sufficient for centuries, they are not evenly distributed; they pose difficult economic and environmental problems; and they vary greatly in their amenability to exploitation and use.

Nonfuel mineral resources generally appear sufficient to meet projected demands through 2000, but further discoveries and investments will be needed to maintain reserves. In addition, production costs will increase with energy prices and may make some nonfuel mineral resources uneconomic. The quarter of the world's population that inhabits industrial countries will continue to absorb three-fourths of the world's mineral production.

Regional water shortages will become more severe. In the 1970–2000 period population growth alone will cause requirements for water to double in nearly half the world. Still greater increases would be needed to improve standards of living.

In many LDCs, water supplies will become increasingly erratic by 2000 as a result of extensive deforestation. Development of new water supplies will become more costly virtually everywhere.

Significant losses of world forests will continue over the next 20 years as demand for forest products and fuelwood increases. Growing stocks of commercial-size timber are projected to decline 50 percent per capita. The world's forests are now disappearing at the rate of 18–20 million hectares a year (an area half the size of California), with most of the loss occurring in the humid tropical forests of Africa, Asia, and South America. The projections indicate that by 2000 some 40 percent of the remaining forest cover in LDCs will be gone.

Serious deterioration of agricultural soils will occur worldwide, due to erosion, loss of organic matter, desertification, salinization, alkalinization, and waterlogging. Already, an area of cropland and grassland approximately the size of Maine is becoming barren wasteland each year, and the spread of desert-like conditions is likely to accelerate.

Atmospheric concentrations of carbon dioxide and ozone-depleting chemicals are expected to increase at rates that could alter the world's climate and upper atmosphere significantly by 2050. Acid rain from increased combustion of fossil fuels (especially coal) threatens damage to lakes, soils, and crops. Radioactive and other hazardous materials present health and safety problems in increasing numbers of countries.

Extinctions of plant and animal species will increase dramatically. Hundreds of thousands of species—perhaps as many as 20 percent of all species on earth—will be irretrievably lost as their habitats vanish, especially in tropical forests.

The future depicted by the U.S. Government projections, briefly outlined above, may actually understate the impending problems. The methods available for carrying out the Study led to certain gaps and inconsistencies that tend to impart an optimistic bias. For example, most of the individual projections for the various sectors studied—food, minerals, energy, and so on—assume that sufficient capital, energy, water, and land will be available in each of these sectors to meet their needs, regardless of the competing needs of the other sectors. More consistent, better-integrated projections would produce a still more emphatic picture of intensifying stresses, as the world enters the twenty-first century.

CONCLUSIONS

At present and projected growth rates, the world's population would reach 10 billion by 2030 and would approach 30 billion by the end of the twenty-first century. These levels correspond closely to estimates by the U.S. National Academy of Sciences of the maximum carrying capacity of the entire earth. Already the populations in sub-Saharan Africa and in the Himalayan hills of Asia have exceeded the carrying capacity of the immediate area, triggering an erosion of the land's capacity to support life. The resulting poverty and ill health have further complicated efforts to reduce fertility. Unless this circle of interlinked problems is broken soon, population growth in such areas will unfortunately be slowed for reasons other than declining birth rates. Hunger and disease will claim more babies and young children, and more of those surviving will be mentally and physically handicapped by childhood malnutrition.

Indeed, the problems of preserving the carrying capacity of the earth and sustaining the possibility of a decent life for the human beings that inhabit it are enormous and close upon us. Yet there is reason for hope. It must be emphasized that the Global 2000 Study's projections are based on the assumption that national policies regarding population stabilization, resource conservation, and environmental protection will remain essentially unchanged through the end of the century. But in fact, policies are beginning to change. In some areas, forests are being replanted after cutting. Some nations are taking steps to reduce soil losses and desertification. Interest in energy conservation is growing, and large sums are being invested in exploring alternatives to petroleum dependence. The need for family planning is slowly becoming better understood. Water supplies are being improved and waste treatment systems built. High-yield seeds are widely available and seed banks are being expanded. Some wildlands with their genetic resources are being protected. Natural predators and selective pesticides are being substituted for persistent and destructive pesticides.

Encouraging as these developments are, they are far from adequate to meet the global challenges projected in this Study. Vigorous, determined new initiatives are needed if worsening poverty and human suffering, environmental degradation, and international tension and conflicts are to be prevented. There are no quick fixes. The only solutions to the problems of population, resources, and environment are complex and long-term. These problems are inextricably linked to some of the most perplexing and persistent problems in the world—poverty, injustice, and social conflict. New and imaginative ideas—and a willingness to act on them—are essential.

The needed changes go far beyond the capability and responsibility of this or any other single nation. An era of unprecedented cooperation and commitment is essential. Yet there are opportunities—and a strong rationale—for the United States to provide leadership among nations. A high priority for this Nation must be a thorough assessment of its foreign and domestic policies relating to population, resources, and environment. The United States, possessing the world's largest economy, can expect its policies to have a significant influence on global trends. An equally important priority for the United States is to cooperate generously and justly with other nations—particularly in the areas of trade, investment, and assistance—in seeking solutions to the many problems that extend beyond our national boundaries. There are many unfulfilled opportunities to cooperate with other nations in efforts to relieve poverty and hunger, stabilize population, and enhance economic and environmental productivity. Further cooperation among nations is also needed to strengthen international mechanisms for protecting and utilizing the "global commons"—the oceans and atmosphere.

To meet the challenges described in this Study, the United States must improve its ability to identify emerging problems and assess alternative responses. In using and evaluating the Government's present capability for long-term global analysis, the Study found serious inconsistencies in the methods and assumptions employed by the various agencies in making their projections. The Study itself made a start toward resolving these inadequacies. It represents the Government's first attempt to produce an interrelated set of population, resource, and environmental projections, and it has brought forth the most consistent set of global projections yet achieved by U.S. agencies. Nevertheless, the projections still contain serious gaps and contradictions that must be corrected if the Government's analytic capability is to be improved. It must be acknowledged that at present the Federal agencies are not always capable of providing projections of the quality needed for long-term policy decisions.

While limited resources may be a contributing factor in some instances, the primary problem is lack of coordination. The U.S. Government needs a mechanism for continuous review of the assumptions and methods the Federal agencies use in their projection models and for assurance that the agencies' models are sound, consistent, and well documented. The improved analyses that could result would provide not only a clearer sense of emerging problems and opportunities, but also a better means for evaluating alternative responses, and a better basis for decisions of worldwide significance that the President, the Congress, and the Federal Government as a whole must make.

With its limitations and rough approximations, the Global 2000 Study may be seen as no more than a reconnaissance of the future; nonetheless its conclusions are reinforced by similar findings of other recent global studies that were examined in the course of the Global 2000 Study. All these studies are in general agreement on the nature of the problems and on the threats they pose to the future welfare of humankind. The available evidence leaves no doubt that the world—including this Nation—faces enormous, urgent, and complex problems in the decades immediately ahead. Prompt and vigorous changes in public policy around the world are needed to avoid or minimize these problems before they become unmanageable. Long lead times are required for effective action. If decisions are delayed until the problems become worse, options for effective action will be severely reduced.

THE GLOBAL 2000 STUDY COMPARED WITH OTHER GLOBAL STUDIES

In the course of the Global 2000 Study, the Government's several models (here referred to collectively as the "Government's global model") and their projections were compared with those of five other global studies. The purpose was not only to compare the results of different projections, but also to see whether and how different assumptions and model structures may have led to different projections and findings.

The Global 2000 Study's principal findings are generally consistent with those of the five other global studies despite considerable differences in models and assumptions. On the whole, the other studies and their models lack the richness of detail that the Government's global model provides for the various individual sectors—food and agriculture, forests, water, energy, and so on. However, the linkages among the sectors in the other models are much more complete. Many apparent inconsistencies and contradictions in the Global 2000 projections are due to the weakness of the linkages among sectors of the Government's global model.

Another important difference is that the Government's projections stop at the year 2000 or before, while the other global studies project well into the twenty-first century. The most dramatic developments projected in the other studies—serious resource scarcities, population declines due to rising death rates, severe environmental deterioration—generally occur in the first half of the twenty-first century and thus cannot be compared with the Government's projections. Up to the turn of the century, all of the analyses, including the Government's, indicate more or less similar trends: continued economic growth in most areas, continued population growth everywhere, reduced energy growth, an increasingly tight and expensive food situation, increasing water problems, and growing environmental stress.

The most optimistic of the five models is the Latin American World Model. Instead of projecting future conditions on the basis of present policies and trends, this model asks: "How can global resources best be used to meet basic human needs for all people?" The model allocates labor and capital to maximize life expectancy. It assumes that personal consumption is sacrificed to maintain very high investment rates (25 percent of GNP per year), and it posits an egalitarian, nonexploitative, wisely managed world society that avoids pollution, soil depletion, and other forms of environmental degradation. Under these assumptions it finds that in little more than one generation basic human needs could be adequately satisfied in Latin America and in Africa. Thereafter, GNP would grow steadily and population growth would begin to stabilize.

But in Asia, even assuming these near-utopian social conditions and high rates of investment, the system collapses. The model projects an Asian food crisis beginning by 2010, as land runs out; food production cannot rise fast enough to keep up with population growth, and a vicious circle begins that leads to starvation and economic collapse by midcentury. The modelers suggest that an Asian food crisis could be avoided by such means as food imports from other areas with more cropland, better crop yields, and effective family planning policies. Nonetheless, it is striking that this model, which was designed to show that the fundamental constraints on human welfare were social, not physical, does project catastrophic food shortages in Asia due to land scarcity.

The World 2 and World 3 models, which were the basis of the 1972 Club of Rome report *The Limits to Growth,* give much attention to environmental factors—the only models in the group of five to do so. The World models, like the Global 2000 Study, considered trends in population, resources, and environment. However, these models are highly aggregated, looking at the world as a whole and omitting regional differences. In the cases that assume a continuation of present policies, the World 2 and 3 models project large global increases in food and income per capita until 2020, at which time either food scarcity or resource depletion would cause a downturn. The two models do suggest that major changes of policy can significantly alter these trends.

The World Integrated Model, a later effort sponsored by the Club of Rome, is much more detailed than the World 2 and 3 models in its treatment of regional differences, trade, economics, and shifts from one energy source to another, but it is less inclusive in its treatment of the environment. This complex model has been run under many different assumptions of conditions and policies. Almost invariably the runs project a long-term trend of steeply rising food prices. Under a wide range of policies and conditions the runs indicate massive famine in Asia and, to a lesser degree, in non-OPEC Africa, before the turn of the century.

The United Nations World Model found that to meet U.N. target rates for economic growth, developing countries would have to make great sacrifices in personal consumption, saving and investing at unprecedented rates. Personal consumption would not exceed 63 percent of income in any developing region, and none would have a level of private investment of less than 20 percent. To meet food requirements, global agricultural production would have to rise fourfold by 2000, with greater increases required in many places (500 percent, for example, in low-income Asia and Latin America).

The Model of International Relations in Agriculture (MOIRA) confines itself to agriculture; it takes into account the effects of agriculture policies but not those of environmental degradation. Its results are more optimistic than the Global 2000 projections: world food production more than doubles from 1975 to 2000, and per capita consumption rises 36 percent. Even so, because of unequal distribution, the number of people subsisting on two-thirds or less of the biological protein requirement rises from 350 million in 1975 to 740 million in 2000.

The Global 2000 Study conducted an experiment with two of the more integrated nongovernment models to answer the question: "How would projections from the Government's global model be different if the model were more integrated and included more linkages and feedback?" The linkages in the two nongovernment models were severed so that they bore some resemblance to the unconnected and inconsistent structure of the Government's global model. Chosen for the experiment were the World 3 model and the World Integrated Model.

In both models, severing the linkages led to distinctly more favorable outcomes. On the basis of results with World 3, the Global 2000 Study concluded that a more integrated Government model would project that:

- Increasing competition among agriculture, industry, and energy development for capital would lead to even higher resource cost inflation and significant decreases in real GNP growth (this assumes no major technological advances).

- The rising food prices and regional declines in food consumption per capita that are presently projected would be intensified by competition for capital and by degradation of the land.
- Slower GNP and agricultural growth would lead to higher death rates from widespread hunger—or from outright starvation—and to higher birth rates, with greater numbers of people trapped in absolute poverty.
- A decisive global downturn in incomes and food per capita would probably not take place until a decade or two after 2000 (this assumes no political disruptions).

When links in the World Integrated Model (WIM) were cut, outcomes again were more favorable. The results of the unlinked version were comparable to the Global 2000 quantitative projections for global GNP, population, grain production, fertilizer use, and energy use. But in the original integrated version of WIM, gross world product was 21 percent lower than in the unlinked version—$11.7 trillion instead of $14.8 trillion in 2000. In the linked version, world agricultural production rose 85 percent instead of 107 percent; grain available for human consumption rose less than 85 percent because some of the grain was fed to animals for increased meat production. Population rose only to 5.9 billion rather than 6.2 billion, in part because of widespread starvation (158 million deaths cumulatively by 2000) and in part because of lower birth rates in the industrialized countries. The effects of severing the linkages are much less in lightly populated regions with a wealth of natural resources, such as North America, than in regions under stress, where great numbers of people are living at the margin of existence. In North America, the difference in GNP per capita was about 5 percent; in South Asia, about 30 percent.

The inescapable conclusion is that the omission of linkages imparts an optimistic bias to the Global 2000 Study's (and the U.S. Government's) quantitative projections. This appears to be particularly true of the GNP projections. The experiments with the World Integrated Model suggest that the Study's figure for gross world product in 2000 may be 15–20 percent too high.

From: Council on Environmental Quality, *Global 2000 Report to the President,* Vol. 1, 1982.

ISSUE 16 NO:

What Are the *Real* Population and Resource Problems?

Julian J. Simon

Is there a natural-resource problem now? Certainly there is—just as there has always been. The problem is that natural resources are scarce, in the sense that it costs us labor and capital to get them, though we would prefer to get them for free.

Are we now "entering an age of scarcity"? You can see anything you like in a crystal ball. But almost without exception, the best data—the long-run economic indicators—suggest precisely the opposite. The relevant measures of scarcity—the costs of natural resources in human labor, and their prices relative to wages and to other goods—all suggest that natural resources have been becoming *less* scarce over the long run, right up to the present.

How about pollution? Is this not a problem? Of course pollution is a problem—people have always had to dispose of their waste products so as to enjoy a pleasant and healthy living space. But on the average we now live in a less dirty and more healthy environment than in earlier centuries.

About population now: Is there a population "problem"? Again, of course there is a population problem, just as there has always been. When a couple is about to have a baby, they must prepare a place for the child to sleep safely. Then, after the birth of the child, the parents must feed, clothe, guard, and teach it. All of this requires effort and resources, and not from the parents alone. When a baby is born or a migrant arrives, a community must increase its municipal services—schooling, fire and police protection, and garbage collection. None of these are free.

Beyond any doubt, an additional child is a burden on people other than its parents—and in some ways even on them—for the first fifteen or twenty-five years of its life. Brothers and sisters must do with less of everything except companionship. Taxpayers must cough up additional funds for schooling and other public services. Neighbors have more noise. During these early years the child produces nothing, and the income of the family and the community is spread around more thinly than if the baby were not born. And when the child grows up and first goes to work, jobs are squeezed a bit, and the output and pay per working person go down. All this clearly is an economic loss for other people.

Almost equally beyond any doubt, however, an additional person is also a boon. The child or immigrant will pay taxes later on, contribute energy and resources to the community, produce goods and services for the consumption of others, and make efforts to beautify and purify the environment. Perhaps most significant of all for the more-developed countries is the contribution that the average person makes to increasing the efficiency of production through new ideas and improved methods.

The real population problem, then, is *not* that there are too many people or that too many babies are being born. It is that others must support each additional person before that person contributes in turn to the well-being of others.

Which is more weighty, the burden or the boon? That depends on the economic conditions, about which we shall speak at some length. But also, to a startling degree, the decision about whether the overall effect of a child or migrant is positive or negative depends on the values of whoever is making the judgment—your preference to spend a dollar now rather than to wait for a dollar-plus-something in twenty or thirty years, your preferences for having more or fewer wild animals alive as opposed to more or fewer human beings alive, and so on. Population growth is a problem, but not *just* a problem; it is a boon, but not just a boon. So your values are all-important in judging the net effect of population growth, and whether there is "overpopulation" or "underpopulation."

An additional child is, from the economic point of view, like a laying chicken, a cacao tree, a new factory, or a new house. A baby is a durable good in which someone must invest heavily long before the grown adult begins to provide returns on the investment. But whereas "Travel now, pay later" is inherently attractive because the pleasure is immediate and the piper will wait, "Pay now, benefit from the child later" is inherently problematic because the sacrifice comes first.

You might respond that additional children will *never* yield net benefits, because they will use up irreplaceable resources. Much of this book is devoted to showing that additional persons do, in fact, produce more than they consume, and that natural resources are not an exception. But let us agree that there is still a population problem, just as there is a problem with all good investments. Long before there are benefits, we must tie up capital that could otherwise be used for immediate consumption.

Please notice that I have restricted the discussion to the *economic* aspect of investing in children—that is, to a child's effect on the material standard of living.

If we also consider the non-economic aspects of children—what they mean to parents and to others who enjoy a flourishing of humanity—then the case for adding children to our world becomes even stronger. And if we also keep in mind that most of the costs of children are borne by their parents rather than by the community, whereas the community gets the lion's share of the benefits later on, especially in developed countries, the essential differences between children and other investments tend to strengthen rather than weaken the case for having more children.

Food. Contrary to popular impression, the per capita food situation has been improving for the three decades since World War II, the only decades for which we have acceptable data. We also know that famine has progressively diminished for at least the past century. And there is strong reason to believe that human nutrition will continue to improve into the indefinite future, even with continued population growth.

Land. Agricultural land is not a fixed resource, as Malthus and many since Malthus have thought. Rather, the amount of agricultural land has been, and still is, increasing substantially, and it is likely to continue to increase where needed. Paradoxically, in the countries that are best supplied with food, such as the U.S., the quantity of land under cultivation has been decreasing because it is more economical to raise larger yields on less land than to increase the total amount of farmland. For this reason, among others, land for recreation and for wildlife has been increasing rapidly in the U.S. All this may be hard to believe, but solid data substantiate these statements beyond a doubt.

Natural resources. Hold your hat—our supplies of natural resources are not finite in any economic sense. Nor does past experience give reason to expect natural resources to become more scarce. Rather, if the past is any guide, natural resources will progressively become less scarce, and less costly, and will constitute a smaller proportion of our expenses in future years. And population growth is likely to have a long-run *beneficial* impact on the natural-resource situation.

Energy. Grab your hat again—the long-run future of our energy supply is at least as bright as that of other natural resources, though political maneuvering can temporarily boost prices from time to time. Finiteness is no problem here either. And the long-run impact of additional people is likely to speed the development of a cheap energy supply that is almost inexhaustible.

Pollution. This set of issues is as complicated as you wish to make it. But even many ecologists, as well as the bulk of economists, agree that population growth is not the villain in the creation and reduction of pollution. And the key trend is that life expectancy, which is the best overall index of the pollution level, has improved markedly as the world's population has grown.

Pathological effects of population density. This putative drawback of population growth is sheer myth. Its apparent source is faulty biological and psychological analogies with animal populations.

The standard of living. In the short run, additional children imply additional costs, though the costs to persons other than the children's parents are relatively small. In the longer run, however, per capita income is likely to be higher with a growing population than with a stationary one, both in more-developed and less-developed countries. Whether you wish to pay the present costs for the future benefits depends on how you weigh the future relative to the present; this is a value judgment.

Immigration. Immigration usually has a positive effect on most citizens. The few persons whom the immigrants might displace from their jobs may be hurt, of course, but many of them only temporarily. On balance, immigrants contribute more to the economy than they take, in the U.S. and most other places.

Human fertility. The contention that poor and uneducated people breed like animals is demonstrably wrong, even for the poorest and most "primitive" societies. Well-off people who believe that the poor do not weigh the consequences of having more children are simply arrogant or ignorant, or both.

Future population growth. Population forecasts are publicized with confidence and fanfare, but the record of even the official forecasts made by U.S. government agencies and by the UN is little (if any) better than that of the most naive predictions. For example, experts in the 1930s foresaw the U.S. population as declining, perhaps to as little as 100 million people, long before the turn of the century. And official UN forecasts made in 1970 for the year 2000, a mere thirty years in advance, were five years later revised downward by almost 2 billion people, from 7.5 billion to 5.6 billion. Nor is the record better with more modern statistical methods. Perhaps most astonishing is a forecast made by the recent President's Commission on Population Growth and the American Future. In 1972 the commission published its prediction that "there will be no year in the next two decades in which the absolute number of births will be less than in 1970." But in the year *before* this prediction was made—1971—the number of births had *already* fallen lower than in 1970. The science of demographic forecasting clearly has not yet reached perfection.

World population policy. Tens of millions of U.S. taxpayers' money is being used to tell the governments and people of other countries that they ought to take strong measures to control their fertility. The head of the Population Branch of the U.S. State Department Agency for International Development (AID)—the single most important U.S. population official for many years—has publicly said that the U.S. should act to reduce fertility worldwide for its own economic self-interest. But no solid economic data or analyses underlie this assertion. Furthermore, might not such acts be an unwarranted interference in the internal affairs of other countries?

Domestic population activities. Other millions of U.S. taxpayers' funds go to private organizations making up the population lobby, whose directors believe that, for environmental and related reasons, fewer Americans should be born. These funds are used to propagandize the rest of us that we should believe—and act—in ways consistent with the views of such organizations as the Population Crisis Committee, the Population Reference Bureau, the Worldwatch Institute, the Environmental Fund, and the Association for Voluntary Sterilization.

Still more tens of millions of U.S. taxpayers' funds are being spent to reduce the fertility of the poor in the U.S. The explicit justification for this policy (given by the head of Planned Parenthood's Alan Guttmacher Institute) is that it will keep additional poor people off the welfare rolls. Even were this to be proven—and as far as I know it has not been proven—is this in the spirit or tradition of America? Furthermore, there is statistical proof that the public birth-control clinics, which were first opened in large numbers in the southern states, were positioned to reduce fertility among blacks.

Involuntary sterilization. Tax moneys are being used to involuntarily sterilize poor people (often black) without medical justification. As a result of the eugenics movement, which has been intertwined with the population-control movement for decades, there are now laws in thirty states providing for the involuntary sterilization of the mentally defective, and many thousands have been so sterilized. And these laws have led to perfectly normal women being sterilized, without their knowledge, after being told that their operations were other sorts of minor surgery...

ABOUT THIS AUTHOR AND HIS VALUES

This book originated in my interest in the economics of population. In order to show that population growth is not a straightforward evil, I had to show that more people need not cause scarcities or environmental decay in the long run. That's how this book came to be written.

Ironically, when I began to work on population studies, I assumed that the accepted view was sound. I aimed to help the world contain its "exploding" population, which I believed to be one of the two main threats to mankind (war being the other). But my reading and research led me into confusion. Though the standard economic theory of population (which has hardly changed since Malthus) asserts that a higher population growth implies a lower standard of living, the available empirical data do not support that theory. My technical book, which is the predecessor of this volume, is an attempt to reconcile that contradiction. It leads to a theory that suggests population growth has positive economic effects in the long run, though there are costs in the short run.

When I began my population studies, I was in the midst of a depression of unusual duration (whose origins had nothing to do with population growth or the world's predicament). As I studied the economics of population and worked my way to the views I now hold—that population growth, along with the lengthening of human life, is a moral and material triumph—my outlook for myself, for my family, and for the future of humanity became increasingly more optimistic. Eventually I was able to pull myself out of my depression. This is only part of the story, but there is at least some connection between the two sets of mental events—my population studies and my increasing optimism.

One spring day about 1969 I visited the AID office in Washington to discuss a project intended to lower fertility in less-developed countries. I arrived early for my appointment, so I strolled outside in the warm sunshine. Below the building's plaza I noticed a sign that said "Iwo Jima Highway." I remembered reading about a eulogy delivered by a Jewish chaplain over the dead on the battlefield at Iwo Jima, saying something like, "How many who would have been a Mozart or a Michelangelo or an Einstein have we buried here?" And then I thought, Have I gone crazy? What business do I have trying to help arrange it that fewer human beings will be born, each one of whom might be a Mozart or a Michelangelo or an Einstein—or simply a joy to his or her family and community, and a person who will enjoy life?

I still believe that helping people fulfill their desires for the number of children they want is a wonderful service. But to persuade them or coerce them to have fewer children than they would individually like to have—that is something entirely different.

The longer I read the literature about population, the more baffled and distressed I become that one idea is omitted: Enabling a potential human being to come into life and to enjoy life is a good thing, just as enabling a living person's life not to be ended is a good thing. Of course a death is not the same as an averted life, in part because others feel differently about the two. Yet I find no logic implicit in the thinking of those who are horrified at the starvation of a comparatively few people in a faraway country (and apparently more horrified than at the deaths by political murder in that same faraway country, or at the deaths by accidents in their own country) but who are positively gleeful with the thought that 1 million or 10 million times that many lives will never be lived that might be lived.

Economics alone cannot explain this attitude, for though the economic consequences of death differ from those of non-life, they are not so different as to explain this difference in attitude. So what is it? Why does Kingsley Davis (one of the world's great demographers) respond to the U.S. population growth during the 1960s with, "I have never been able to get anyone to tell me why we needed those 23 million." And Paul Ehrlich: "I can't think of any reason for having more than one hundred fifty million people [in the U.S.], and no one has ever raised one to me."

I can suggest to Davis and Ehrlich more than one reason for having more children and taking in more immigrants. Least interesting is that the larger population will probably mean a higher standard of living for our grandchildren and great-grandchildren. A more interesting reason is that we need another person for exactly the same reason we need Davis and Ehrlich. That is, just as the Davises and Ehrlichs of this world are of value to the rest of us, so will the average additional person be of value.

The most interesting reason for having additional people, however, is this: If the Davises and Ehrlichs say that their lives are of value to themselves, and if the rest of us honor that claim and say that our lives are of value to us, then in the same manner the lives of additional people are of value to those people themselves. Why should we not honor their claims, too?

If Davis or Ehrlich were to ask those 23 million additional Americans born between 1960 and 1970 whether it was a good thing that they were born, many of them would be able to think of a good reason or two. Some of them might also be so unkind as to add, "Yes, it's true that you gentlemen do not *personally* need any of us for your own welfare. But then, do you think that *we* have greater need of *you?*"

What is most astonishing is that these simple ideas, which would immediately spring to the minds of many who cannot read or write, have never even come into the heads of famous scientists such as Davis and Ehrlich—by their own admission.

The same absence of this basic respect for human life is at the bottom of Ehrlich's well-known restatement of Pascal's wager. "If I'm right, we will save the world [by curbing population growth]. If I'm wrong, people will still be better fed, better housed, and happier, thanks to our efforts. [He probably *is* wrong.] Will anything be lost if it turns out later that we can support a much larger population than seems possible today?"

Please note how different is Pascal's wager: Live as if there is God, because even if there is no God you have lost nothing. Pascal's wager applies entirely to one person. No one else loses if he is wrong. But Ehrlich bets what he thinks will be the economic gains that we and our descendants might enjoy against the unborn's very lives. Would he make the same sort of wager if his *own* life rather than others' lives were the stake?

A last, very personal word: I may come through the print to you as feisty or even tough, and able to take care of myself in this argument. But I am not very feisty in person. I have been trying—mostly unsuccessfully—to get a hearing for these ideas since 1969, and though times have changed somewhat, the difficulties of espousing this unpopular point of view do get to me; until recently they were near the point of shutting me up and shutting me down. If there weren't a handful of editors like Sandy Thatcher of Princeton University Press, you wouldn't hear from me at all. Some others hold a point of view similar to mine. But there are far too few of us to provide mutual support and comfort. So this is a plea for love, printer's ink, and research grants for our side. All contributions gratefully accepted.

Now let's see if my facts and arguments persuade you of the claims I have made....

CONCLUSION

In the short run, all resources are limited—natural resources such as the pulpwood that went into making this book, created resources such as the number of pages Princeton University Press can allow me, and human resources such as the attention you will devote to what I say. In the short run, a greater use of any resource means pressure on supplies and a higher price in the market, or even rationing. Also in the short run there will always be shortage crises because of weather, war, politics, and population movements. The results that an individual notices are sudden jumps in taxes, inconveniences and disruption, and increases in pollution.

The longer run, however, is a different story. The standard of living has risen along with the size of the world's population since the beginning of recorded time. And with increases in income and population have come less severe shortages, lower costs, and an increased availability of resources, including a cleaner environment and greater access to natural recreation areas. And there is no convincing economic reason why these trends toward a better life, and toward lower prices for raw materials (including food and energy), should not continue indefinitely.

Contrary to common rhetoric, there are no meaningful limits to the continuation of this process. There is no physical or economic reason why human resourcefulness and enterprise cannot forever continue to respond to impending shortages and existing problems with new expedients that, after an adjustment period, leave us better off than before the problem arose. Adding more people will cause us more such problems, but at the same time there will be more people to solve these problems and leave us with the bonus of lower costs and less scarcity in the long run. The bonus applies to such desirable resources as better health, more wilderness, cheaper energy, and a cleaner environment.

This process runs directly against Malthusian reasoning and against the apparent common sense of the matter, which can be summed up as follows: The supply of any resource is fixed, and greater use means less to go around. The resolution of this paradox is not simple. Fuller understanding begins with the idea that the relevant measure of scarcity is the cost or price of a resource, not any physical measure of its calculated reserves. And the appropriate way for us to think about extracting resources is not in physical units, pounds of copper or acres of farmland, but rather in the services we get from these resources—the electrical transmission capacity of copper, or the food values and gastronomic enjoyment the farmland provides. Following on this is the fact that economic history has not gone as Malthusian reasoning suggests. The prices of all goods, and of the services they provide, have fallen in the long run, by all reasonable measures. And this irrefutable fact must be taken into account as a fundamental datum that can reasonably be projected into the future, rather than as a fortuitous chain of circumstances that cannot continue.

Resources in their raw form are useful and valuable only when found, understood, gathered together, and harnessed for human needs. The basic ingredient in the process, along with the raw elements, is human knowledge. And we develop knowledge about how to use raw elements for our benefit only in response to our needs. This includes knowledge for finding new sources of raw materials such as copper, for growing new resources such as timber, for creating new quantities of capital such as farmland, and for finding new and better ways to satisfy old needs, such as successively using iron or aluminum or plastic in place of clay or copper. Such knowledge has a special property: It yields benefits to people other than the ones who develop it, apply it, and try to capture its benefits for themselves. Taken in the large, an increased need for resources usually leaves us with a permanently greater capacity to get them because we gain knowledge in the process. And there is no meaningful physical limit—even the commonly mentioned weight of the earth—to our capacity to keep growing forever.

Perhaps the most general matter at issue here is what Gerald Holton calls a "thema." The thema underlying the thinking of most writers who have a point of view different from mine is the concept of fixity or finiteness of resources in the relevant system of discourse. This is found in Malthus, of course. But the idea probably has always been a staple of human thinking because so much of our situation must sensibly be regarded as fixed in the short run—the bottles of beer in the refrigerator, our paycheck, the amount of energy parents have to play basketball with their kids. But the thema underlying my thinking about resources (and the thinking of a minority of others) is that the relevant system of discourse has a long enough horizon that it makes sense to treat the system as not fixed, rather than finite in any operational sense. We see the resource system as being as unlimited as the number of thoughts a person might have, or the number of variations that might ultimately be produced by biological evolution. That is, a key difference between the thinking of those who worry about impending doom, and those who see the prospects of a better life for more people in the future, apparently is whether one thinks in closed-system or open-system terms. For example, those who worry that the second law of thermodynamics dooms us to eventual decline necessarily see our world as a closed system with respect to energy and entropy; those who view the relevant universe as unbounded view the second law of thermodynamics as irrelevant to this discussion. I am among those who view the relevant part of the physical and social universe as open for most purposes. Which thema is better for thinking about resources and population is not subject to scientific test. Yet it profoundly affects our thinking. I believe that here lies the root of the key difference in thinking about population and resources.

Why do so many people think in closed-system terms? There are a variety of reasons. (1) Malthusian fixed-resources reasoning is simple and fits the isolated facts of our everyday lives, whereas the expansion of resources is complex and indirect and includes all creative human activity—it cannot be likened to our own larders or wallets. (2) There are always immediate negative effects from an increased pressure on resources, whereas the benefits only come later. It is natural to pay more attention to the present and the near future compared with the more distant future. (3) There are often special-interest groups that alert us to impending shortages of particular resources such as timber or clean air. But no one has the same stake in trying to convince us that the long-run prospects for a resource are better than we think. (4) It is easier to get people's attention (and television time and printer's ink) with frightening forecasts than with soothing forecasts. (5) Organizations that form in response to temporary or non-existent dangers, and develop the capacity to raise funds from public-spirited citizens and governments that are aroused to fight the danger, do not always disband when the danger evaporates or the problem is solved. (6) Ambition and the urge for profit are powerful elements in our successful struggle to satisfy our needs. These motives, and the markets in which they work, often are not pretty, and many people would prefer not to depend on a social system that employs these forces to make us better off. (7) Associating oneself with environmental causes is one of the quickest and easiest ways to get a wide reputation for high-minded concern; it requires no deep thinking and steps on almost no one's toes.

The apparently obvious way to deal with resource problems—have the government control the amounts and prices of what consumers consume and suppliers supply—is inevitably counter-productive in the long run because the controls and the price fixing prevent us from making the cost-efficient adjustments that we would make in response to the increased short-run costs, adjustments that eventually would more than alleviate the problem. Sometimes governments must play a crucial role to avoid short-run disruptions and disaster, and to ensure that no group consumes public goods without paying the real social cost. But the appropriate times for governments to play such roles are far fewer than the times they are called upon to do so by those inclined to turn to authority to tell others what to do, rather than allow each of us to respond with self-interest and imagination.

I do not say that all is well. Children are hungry and sick; people live out lives of physical and intellectual poverty, and lack of opportunity; war or some new pollution may do us all in. What I *am* saying is that for most of the relevant economic matters I have checked the *trends* are positive rather than negative. And I doubt that it does the troubled people of the world any good to say that things are getting worse though they are really getting better. And false prophecies of doom can damage us in many ways.

Is a rosy future guaranteed? Of course not. There always will be temporary shortages and resource problems where there are strife, political blundering, and natural calamities—that is, where there are people. But the natural world allows, and the developed world promotes through the marketplace, responses to human needs and shortages in such manner that one backward step leads to 1,000 steps forward, or thereabouts. That's enough to keep us headed in a life-sustaining direction. The main fuel to speed our progress is our stock of knowledge, and the brake is our lack of imagination. The ultimate resource is people—skilled, spirited and hopeful people who will exert their wills and imaginations for their own benefit, and so, inevitably, for the benefit of us all.